Glorious catastrophe

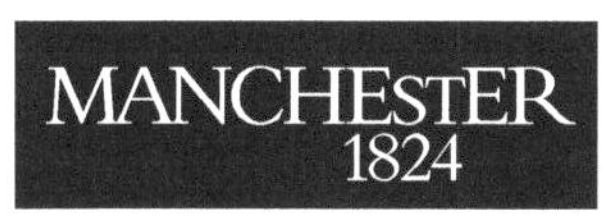

Manchester University Press

rethinking
art's histories

SERIES EDITORS
Amelia G. Jones, Marsha Meskimmon

Rethinking Art's Histories aims to open out art history from its most basic structures by foregrounding work that challenges the conventional periodisation and geographical subfields of traditional art history, and addressing a wide range of visual cultural forms from the early modern period to the present.

These books will acknowledge the impact of recent scholarship on our understanding of the complex temporalities and cartographies that have emerged through centuries of world-wide trade, political colonisation and the diasporic movement of people and ideas across national and continental borders.

Glorious catastrophe

Jack Smith, performance and visual culture

Dominic Johnson

Manchester University Press

Manchester and New York

distributed in the United States exclusively by Palgrave Macmillan

The right of Dominic Johnson to be identified as the author of this work has been asserted by him in accordance with the Copyright, Designs and Patents Act 1988.

Published by Manchester University Press
Oxford Road, Manchester M13 9NR, UK
and Room 400, 175 Fifth Avenue, New York, NY 10010, USA
www.manchesteruniversitypress.co.uk

Distributed in the United States exclusively by
Palgrave Macmillan, 175 Fifth Avenue,
New York, NY 10010, USA

Distributed in Canada exclusively by
UBC Press, University of British Columbia, 2029 West Mall,
Vancouver, BC, Canada V6T 1Z2

British Library Cataloguing-in-Publication Data is available

Library of Congress Cataloging-in-Publication Data is available

ISBN 978 0 7190 9147 6 paperback

First published by Manchester University Press in hardback 2012

This paperback edition first published 2013

The publisher has no responsibility for the persistence or accuracy of URLs for any external or third-party internet websites referred to in this book, and does not guarantee that any content on such websites is, or will remain, accurate or appropriate.

Printed by Lightning Source

Contents

List of figures

Acknowledgements

'Making art was never supposed to be easy,' Jack Smith tells us. Neither is researching Jack Smith, nor writing about him. Indeed, his difficulty has been an enduring pleasure in the years I have spent as a 'keeper of the flame' since this project's inception in 2003. Much of the current book took shape under Mignon Nixon's astute guidance at the Courtauld Institute of Art, University of London. I am deeply grateful for her careful attention to the development of my thought, in those tentative first years, and since. Amelia Jones and Marsha Meskimmon were generous and conscientious editors. I thank them and the production team at Manchester University Press for their support.

I have had the privilege of spending time with some of Smith's friends and peers over the years, and many of them granted me interviews in person, or engaged me in conversations in New York, London and Berlin. Penny Arcade was especially generous with her time and energies, opening her studio to me for six weeks in the Spring of 2005. During this time I rummaged through box after box of Smith's personal papers, part of a vast array of artefacts that she and Jim Hoberman had the inestimable foresight to rescue from oblivion in the days after Smith's death in September 1989. Without their establishment of the Plaster Foundation (which cared for the estate of Jack Smith), this book certainly would have not been possible. Penny Arcade has endured my attention many times since, and I am grateful for her unflagging commitment to Smith's legacy, and her support for my research, which included introductions to Smith's friends. One of the latter, John Vaccaro gave me plenty of information about Smith in an interview I conducted with him in 2005. In Berlin and New York, Uzi Parnes and Ela Troyano were generous interlocutors, and shared their memories of the last decade of Smith's life, when they were his closest friends. Mario Montez was wonderfully kind in Berlin in March 2009, suffering my questions about his work with Smith in the 1960s. During the same week, I was privileged to have a chance to meet and talk to Ronald Tavel about his recollections, days before his death en route to his home in Thailand. I have benefitted from Jonas Mekas and Jerry Tartaglia's extensive knowledge about Smith's films, and am grateful for their responses to my research. In

New York in 2009, Bruce Benderson shared anecdotes about Jean-Pierre Aumont, the widower of Maria Montez. Moreover, e-mail correspondence with Benderson caused panicked revisions to my manuscript rather late in the day. I solemnly regret not taking the opportunity to interview Yvonne de Carlo before her death in January 2007. Many thanks to Slava Mogutin and Brian Kenny for being exotic hosts during several research visits to New York.

At Gladstone Gallery, New York, Miciah Hussey and Ann Restak were generous and supportive, and gave me full access to the Estate of Jack Smith, which Ann Restak has carefully and conscientiously catalogued. Since their departure from the gallery, Sascha Crasnow has been exceedingly helpful with my requests for research assistance.

I am fortunate to work with supportive colleagues in the Department of Drama at Queen Mary, University of London. My thinking around performance and cultural politics has benefitted vastly from conversations with colleagues and graduate students in the department. I was granted research leave in 2009 to complete the manuscript draft. Maria Delgado, Jen Harvie, Nick Ridout, Catherine Silverstone and Lois Weaver have been especially supportive colleagues, and continue to mentor me in my work between performance and visual culture. I have learnt lots about the cultural politics of theatre and performance while working on the editorial team at *Contemporary Theatre Review*, and I thank Maria Delgado, Aoife Monks and the late David Bradby for their encouragement of my scholarship.

Drafts of various chapters have been developed at research seminars and conferences at various institutions, including: Brown University; National Review of Live Art, Glasgow; Courtauld Institute of Art; the Queer Discipline series at King's College, London; Queen Mary, University of London; University of Manchester; and at *Live Film! Jack Smith! Five Flaming Days in a Rented World*, a two-part event at Kino Arsenal Institute for Film and Video Art and Hebbel am Ufer, Berlin in March and October 2009. Organised by Marc Siegel, Susanne Sachsse and Stephanie Schulte Strathaus, this latter event was a particularly rich resource for my research.

Chapter 5 was published in an earlier form as 'The wound kept open: Jack Smith, queer performance and cultural failure', *Women and Performance*, Vol. 16, No. 4 (March 2007); chapter 7 was published in an earlier form as 'Jack Smith's rehearsals for the destruction of Atlantis: "Exotic" ritual and apocalyptic tone', *Contemporary Theatre Review*, Vol. 19, No. 2 (April 2009). Thanks to the publishers for permission to reproduce revised versions of these chapters.

Throughout the years of this book's gestation, a number of friends and colleagues have inspired my writing and challenged my thinking. I particularly thank Ron Athey, Gavin Butt, Jennifer Doyle, Adrian Heathfield, Amelia Jones, José Esteban Muñoz, Tavia Nyong'o and Alan Read, who have all responded to my work on Jack Smith in various states of progress.

Finally, I owe an exotic cocktail of love and thanks to Leo Hedman.

Introduction:
Jack Smith's glorious catastrophes

Jack and I think alike. I do glorious catastrophes, so does Jack. (John Vaccaro)[1]

Jack Smith reclines resplendent in his plaster-strewn Atlantis, listening for the death rattle of an encircled tradition. Tilting his weary head, he sees enchantment in a luminous land. The art and culture of the twentieth century is marked by two contrasting understandings of the burdens of modernity: on the one hand, trust in the rational transcendence furnished by the political and social transformations of the eighteenth century; and on the other, a vertiginous attitude that revels in the debris of a permanent break with traditional certainties. Jack Smith confirms and extends the latter. He sees a glimmer of hope in the faded legacies of billboard deities, but understands that the possibility for meaning is predicated upon accumulated catastrophes, represented in the logics of fragmentation, vulgarity, excess and waste.

Smith was a central figure in the birth of the New American Cinema, and a founder of what came to be known as performance art. Moreover, he was an innovative photographer, a prolific writer, designer and draughtsman, a rogue interior decorator and a vociferous critic of the art establishment. Inspired by the 1960s subcultures of gay New York, experimental performance and underground film, his was a total vision populated by flaming creatures and pasty novelties. In his bejewelled retreat to the horrors of Orchid Lagoon, he spurned fame for the enigmatic pleasures of infamy, and kept himself elaborately busy in the company of imagined lobsters, penguins, clowns and cobra women. In his performances and polemics he longed for lost and imagined utopias, including the esoteric myth of Atlantis, and the gaudy, 'gilded' visual worlds of 1940s Hollywood. Smith relied upon the committed work of continual self-reinvention, and presented calculated performances of self, for audiences who were by turns bemused and transfixed by his variant imagination. Smith's exercises in violated, transfigured identity were initially attempted through appearances in other artists' works in the late 1950s and, soon after, his own explorations into filmmaking. This project of imaginative self-actualisation, or creative autopoiesis, found its most effective manifestations in his epic live

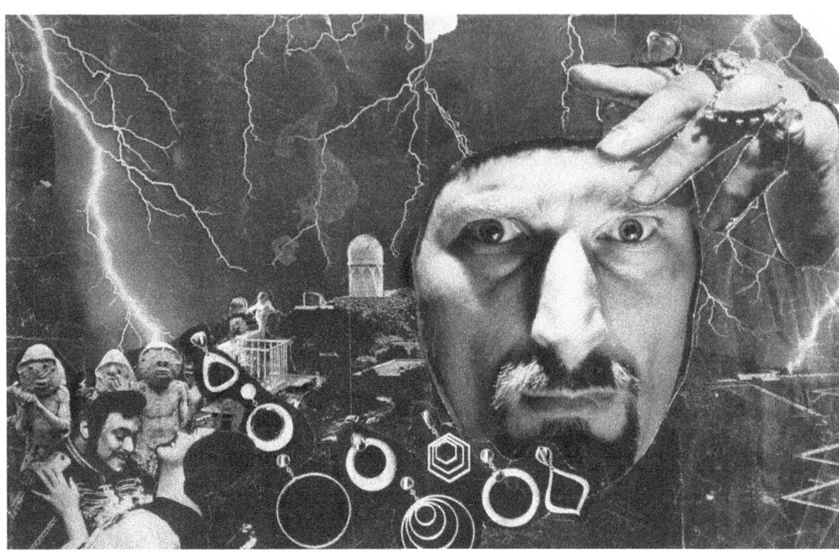

I.1   Jack Smith, *Untitled* (c. 1978).

performances. These were arduous revelries in the ceremonial splendours of failure, degradation and humiliation, and Smith presented them in makeshift spaces, including his own adapted lofts, from the mid-1960s until shortly before his death from AIDS-related pneumonia in 1989.

Over the course of three decades, Smith created a vivid, eccentric and wholly captivating persona, and documented his gruelling battle with a complex, obsessive vision of the world. His delirious world fiction crystallised around a horror at contemporary American consumer culture. This was typified by his profound disgust at the principle of rent, or 'landlordism', which he understood as the morally bankrupt compromise of 'paying sacrifices to the gods for protection to be left alone to do whatever it is you want to do'.[2] I explore many facets of Smith's glittering logic, which extends from his political and social grievances, to his idiosyncratic perspectives on aesthetics, and the problems entailed in a life lived towards art.

Through his fantastical assaults on received wisdoms, Smith enables a political account of cultural marginalisation, its troubles and its effects. His emphasis on failure, excess and collapse conspire to muddy any attempt to neatly historicise his activities. He commands a new historiography of performance and visual culture: specifically, one that is sympathetic to his obstinate refusal to fit the existing historical, theoretical and formal accounts that seek to make sense of twentieth-century experimental culture. Smith's practice encompassed both a camp affection for the refuse of contemporary culture, as well as a painful engagement with those experiences, objects, desires and practices that daily life commits beyond its borders. As Ken Jacobs noted, Smith's attraction to failure was conditioned by his 'horror of life, a deep disgust with existence. Jack indulged in it spitefully, he would plunge himself into the garbage of life [with] a hilarious and horrifying willingness to "revel in the dumps"'.[3] Smith's artistic practice sits in a continuum with the excesses of his personal life – his class anxieties, his bohemian impoverishment, his 'flaming' queerness, his rage, and his near-maniacal propensity towards paranoia. As such, the fruits of Smith's 'moldy' labours exceed traditional understandings of art's work. Smith demands that another cultural history be written, in counterpoint to the dominant stories that condition our understanding of the 1960s and its aftermaths. If, at the time of his death in 1989, Smith may have seemed out of touch with the developments of academic postmodernism as a dominant logic, he nevertheless has furnished a host of practical and theoretical possibilities for new critical accounts of the work of art and the labour of artists.

As the historical materialist E. P. Thompson wrote in 1963, history is usually written from the perspective of current preoccupations, which narrate only those achievements that are deemed representative of future developments. Retrospective evaluation tends to prohibit the fuller accounts that can be given of a period and diminish the actual plurality of past events. In orthodox histories of moments, figures, practices or events, he writes, only 'the successful (in

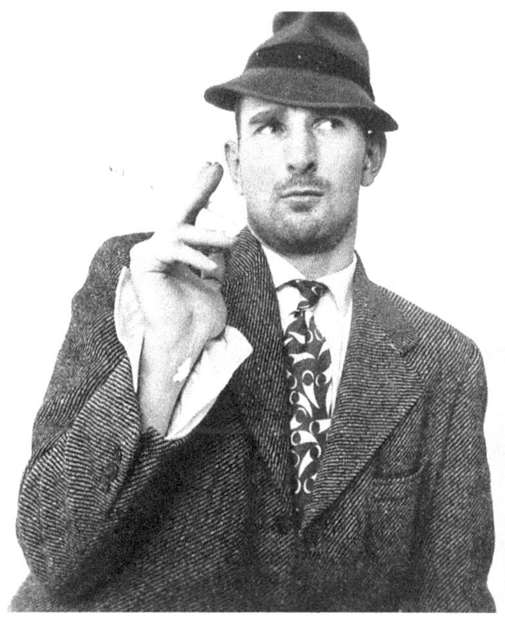

Jack Smith, *Untitled* (c. 1965).   **I.2**

the sense of those whose aspirations anticipated subsequent evolution) are remembered. The blind alleys, the lost causes, and the losers themselves are forgotten'.[4] In a frequently cited passage, Thompson argues for another kind of history that would seek to address the 'casualties of history', by privileging the 'obsolete' or 'utopian' practices that have otherwise been ignored. Smith is, I argue, implicitly afforded the status of a 'lost cause' in histories of performance and visual culture. This statement does not reflect a value judgment, but is rather an assertion that cultural history as conventionally formulated often fails to address the fact that the aspirations and achievements of specific artists are valid and interesting on their own terms – not least for the ways in which they demand that history must be constantly unfixed, so that the story of a period can be refigured and retold. As Walter Benjamin writes, 'In every era the attempt must be made anew to wrest tradition away from a conformism that is about to overpower it'. In this sense, the story of Jack Smith enables a revaluation of the recent history of performance and visual culture, seizing hold of (in Benjamin's words) 'a memory as it flashes up at a moment of danger'.[5] Through his perverse valorisation of trash, excess and failure, and his absolute refusal to support establishment arts and culture, Smith elaborated a theory of glorious catastrophe as the driving force of a life of renegade artistic production. As a volatile model for the production of art, Smith's attraction to crisis set aside the grand mythopoetics of Christian martyrdom, and urged the elaboration of an alternative mythology, namely an investment in an obstinate politics of marginality. In his difference, Smith refused the empty promises of artistic success by privileging underdog stamina and anarchic refusal. In his embrace of crisis, he also avoided the trend for existentialist heroics as performed by the leading male artists of the 1950s. Instead, Smith pursued the unabashed perversity that arises from a lifelong commitment to little triumphs of disaster. Or in the words of Derek Jarman (a near contemporary of Smith's, and a comparable polymath), 'We are all failures and we know it. It's that knowledge that keeps us trying.'[6]

Smith's biography is littered with evocative calamities. These begin with the details of his unassuming start in life. Born in 1932, in Columbus, Ohio, Smith spent his childhood there, moving at the age of seven to Corpus Christi in coastal South Texas, 200 kilometres from the Mexican border. He was raised in abject poverty, which deepened after the death of his father in a fishing accident. When his mother remarried, the family moved to Galveston, a depressed port town 150 kilometres up the coast of Texas that still struggled from the effects of a devastating hurricane in 1900. In 1945, his mother's third marriage drew the family to the Midwestern shores of Lake Michigan, settling in Kenosha, Wisconsin, a small industrial city dominated by automobile production plants. After fleeing the dreary series of rural trailer-homes for the fabled glamour of Hollywood, at the age of nineteen, Smith claimed

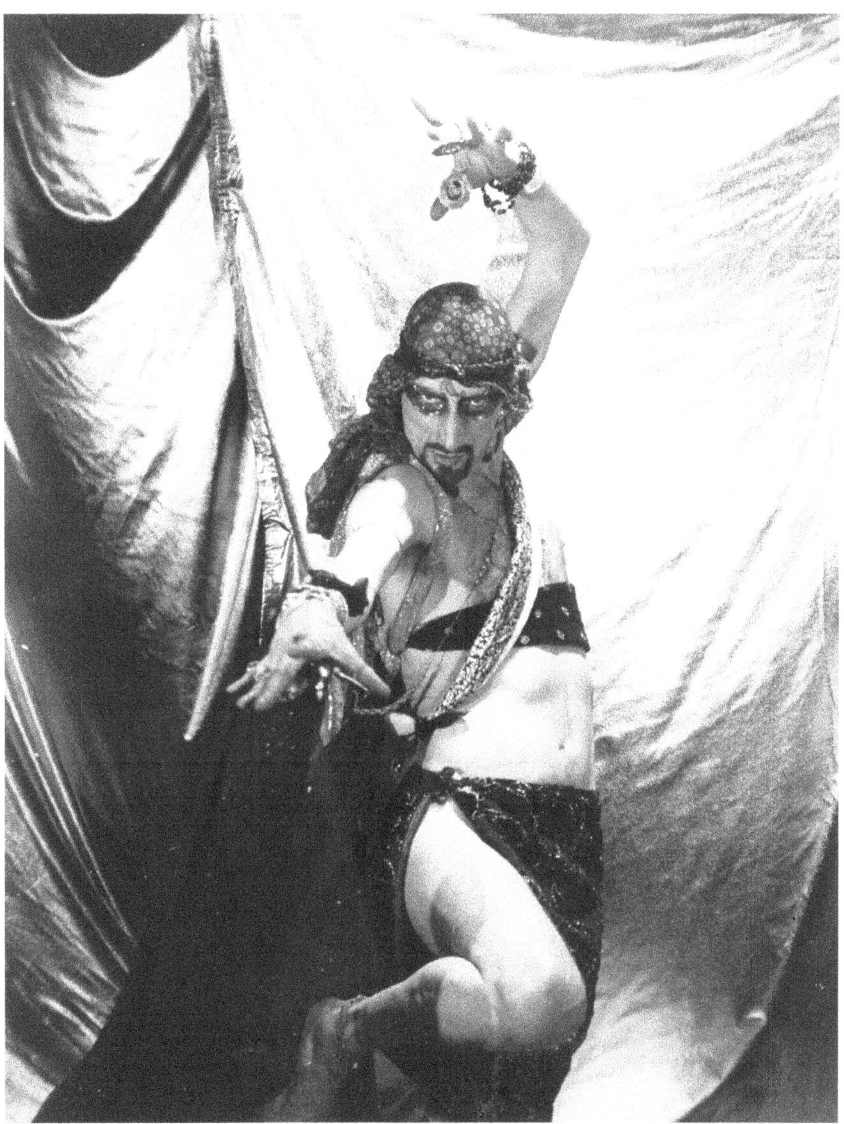

Jack Smith, *Untitled* (c. 1982). l.3

to have studied method acting with Lee Strasberg, and modern dance with Ruth St Denis, in Los Angeles in 1952. Arriving in New York the following year, he began his career as a commercial photographer, and soon made his underground debut as a performer in films by Ken Jacobs – the earliest being *Saturday Afternoon Blood Sacrifice* and *Little Cobra Dance* (both 1956). In the former, dressed in rudimentary drag, Smith leads children through the streets of Manhattan's Lower East Side, culminating in the mock 'sacrifice' after which the film was titled. Police officers break up the procession. In *Little Cobra Dance*, Smith twirls down metal stairs, in an apparent homage to St Denis, who pioneered 'oriental' dance after seeing an image of the Egyptian goddess Isis on a cigarette packet. Losing his makeshift headdress in the process of his voluptuous paean, Smith continues to dance across battered tenement roofs.

Smith went on to star in many of Jacobs' underground films, including his meanderings through a graveyard as the Vampire Fairy in *Death of P'Town* (1961), and the longer projects *Little Stabs at Happiness* (1958–63), *Star Spangled to Death* (1958–2003) and *Blonde Cobra* (1959–63). Parker Tyler described Smith's performance in the latter as 'camp-queen madness: hysterical exhibitionism, falsetto raving, infantile sadism', culminating in 'a drag act presented as a clown act' that the critic deemed to be the apotheosis of the infantilism of underground film in the 1960s.[7] Tyler gestures to Smith's mythic capacity for unsettling his audiences, in film as well as in live performances. Visionary, lunatic and clown, Smith's influence as an artist would be bolstered by appearances in works by many other key figures of the period. These included performances in plays by John Vaccaro, Charles Ludlam and Robert Wilson, designs for posters and costumes for productions by Ronald Tavel,

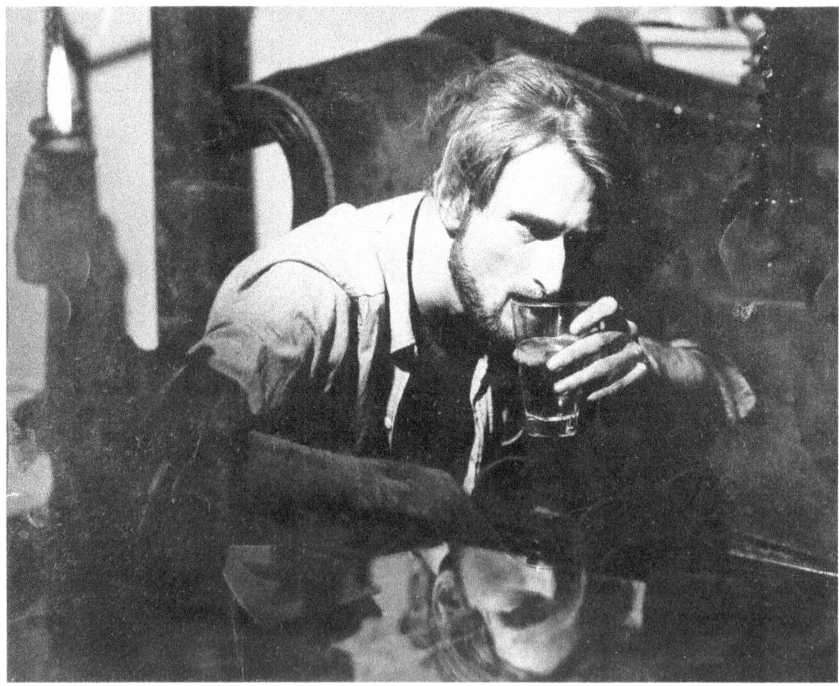

1.4   Jack Smith, *Untitled (Jack Smith in Dov Lederberg's 'Eargogh')*, (1964–65).

and his status as a 'superstar' in the underground films of Andy Warhol and others. Indeed, Smith's filmography as a performer is monumental, challenged only by the other key underground movie actor of the 1960s, Taylor Mead, Smith's co-star in Ron Rice's *The Queen of Sheba Meets the Atom Man* (1963). Across three decades, Smith would also appear in experimental films by Ira Cohen, Piero Heliczer, Dov Lederberg (see figure I.4), Gregory Markopoulos, José Rodríguez-Soltero, Ari Roussimoff, Ela Troyano, Bill Vehr, Avery Willard and many others. However, as a filmmaker in his own right, and then as a live performer, Smith would exceed the offbeat gravitas of his involvements in the work of other artists.

In 1959, Smith borrowed Jacobs' 16 mm camera and made his first film, *Scotch Tape*, a three-minute reverie of bodies frolicking in the rubble of destroyed housing in Manhattan. From this first self-directed project, transformation

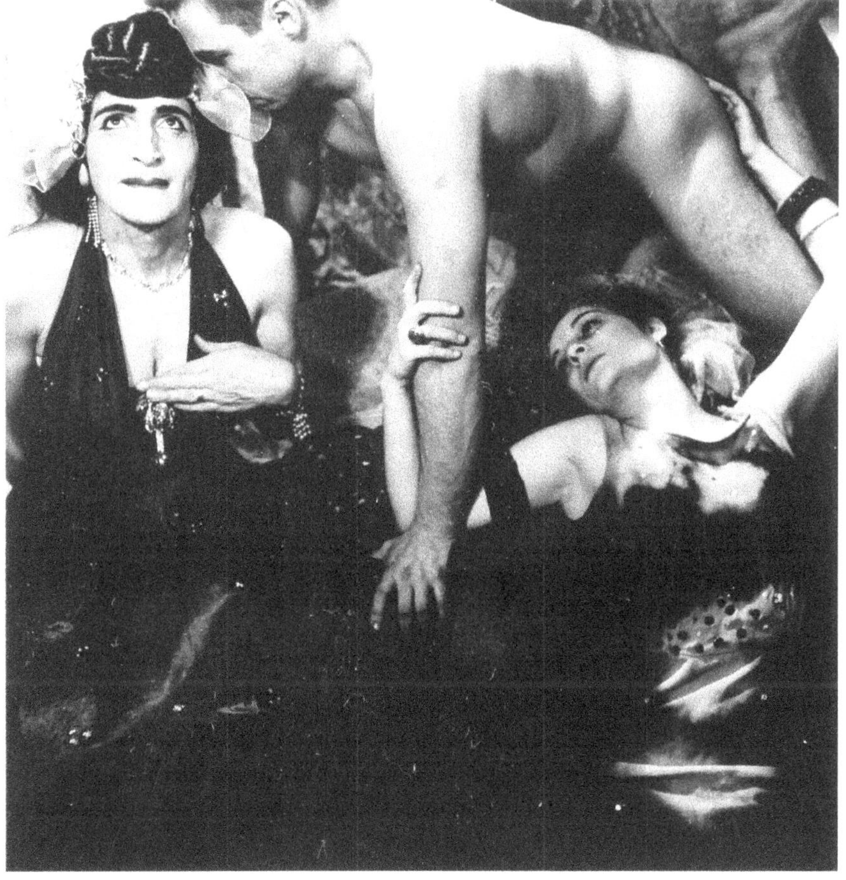

Jack Smith, *Untitled* (c. 1958–62).   I.5

and the overcoming of adversity emerge as key themes in Smith's work. In *Scotch Tape*, a lazily visible piece of adhesive tape stuck in the camera gate is transformed into a defining innovation – a static point of solitary continuity in contrast to the roving bodies and the tangle of building materials pictured in the film. After this early experiment, Smith would consistently turn failure into creative potential, carrying out 'little triumphs of disaster', and constructive violations of good technique.[8] *Scotch Tape* marked his first venture into filmmaking, and set a tentative precedent for his more ambitious descents into the moldy, the outlandish and the retrograde. Indeed, he would soon set a new artistic standard for the collision between glamour, disaster and sexual excess.

Smith achieved subcultural notoriety in 1963 as a result of the outrage caused by his film *Flaming Creatures* (1962–63), which David Ehrenstein has called 'the most important avant-garde film ever made in America'.[9] Filmed on the roof of the Windsor Theatre over eight consecutive weekends, *Flaming Creatures* presents a gang of performers who fondle, seduce and assault each other in tableaux vivants and jostling dances. Inspired by the ornate composition of bodies in his early photographic works (see figure I.5), the vignettes in the film are by turns languidly seductive and elegantly depraved. Smith's ramshackle cast included artists of his circle, a heady mix of local personalities, beatniks, layabouts and queens, and a cluster of strangers plucked from the street. After its controversial reception, and subsequent banning, those in the experimental scene on the Lower East Side viewed Smith with a mixture of awe and trepidation. His notoriety was lent legitimacy by New York's intelligentsia, most prominently Susan Sontag, and by Jonas Mekas's persistent championing in the pages of his journal *Film Culture*.

Suddenly notorious for his oppositional art practice, yet forever struggling to keep himself afloat financially (and, perhaps, emotionally), Smith actively politicised his own marginal position. Of his own formal and political achievements, he writes, 'They aren't noticed because everybody's minds are busily occupied by discussing how unrespectable I am, and other tempestuous brassiere curiosities like me. Well, it isn't my flimsy costume, only, that gives me a chill at the underground night of the film vaults of artcrust.'[10] To endure Smith's aggression is to attend to his protestations, however arcane, wide of the mark, or hysterical they appear. This critical orientation performs instances when the body returns with a vengeance, in the spaces where it has, as yet, only tentatively breached the skin of discourse. This enables me to pursue Smith's works – especially his practices between performance and visual culture – guided by his own politicised responses to what he understood as a perpetual state of exploitation, misrepresentation and abuse. Revisionist historiography may work to multiply the ruses that Smith introduced, disrupting or displacing the social and cultural discourses that govern his reception.

Counterhistories of performance and visual culture

Shortly before commencing *Flaming Creatures*, Smith gave his first public performance. In collaboration with Ken Jacobs, *The Human Wreckage Review* (1961) was presented in Provincetown, Massachusetts, at the Seahorse Inn, a bar owned by the abstract painter Peter Busa, for whom Jacobs was working during the summer. After deciding they wanted to 'put on a show for the drunks', Jacobs read stories, Florence Karpf (Flo Jacobs) danced, and Smith 'cavorted in a diaphanous gown'. The show and its title came from the fact that Smith and Jacobs 'were feeling like human garbage', a sensibility Jacobs roots in their contemporary enthusiasm for the writings of Beat authors, such as William S. Burroughs, Allen Ginsberg and Herbert Huncke.[11] Police shut down *The Human Wreckage Review* after several performances, for blasphemous portrayals of the Pope.[12]

If Smith's early innovations were developed primarily in film, after 1965 he capitalised on the tentative challenges posed by *The Human Wreckage Review*, and translated his budding catalogue of anxieties into a highly personalised, unprecedented performance practice. He presented largely unadvertised performances, at midnight, in his architecturally revamped lofts at 36 Greene Street, 18 Mercer Street, 89 Grand Street, and finally at 21 First Avenue. His

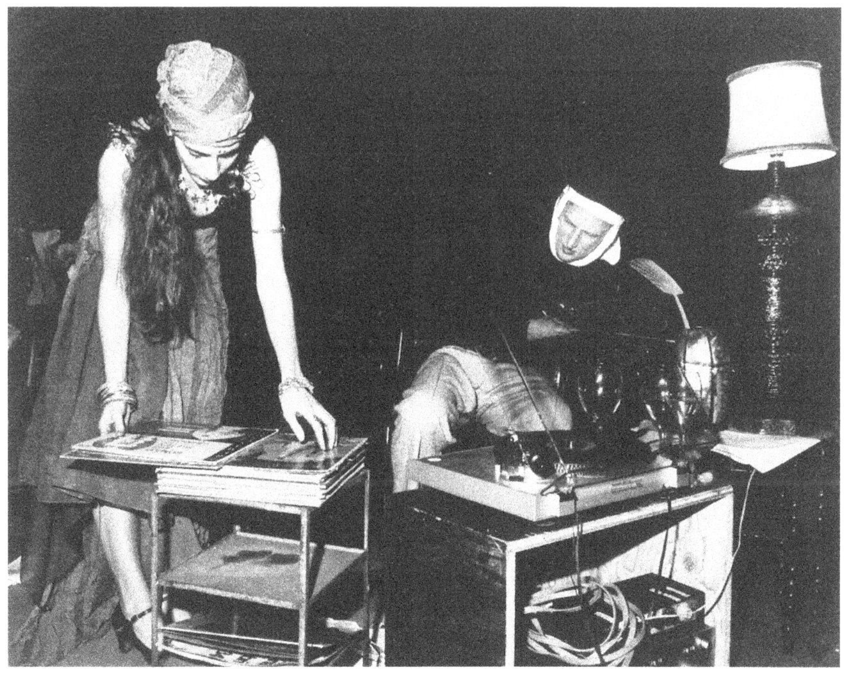

Jack Smith, *Jack Smith in 'Death of a Penguin'* (c. 1985). **I.6**

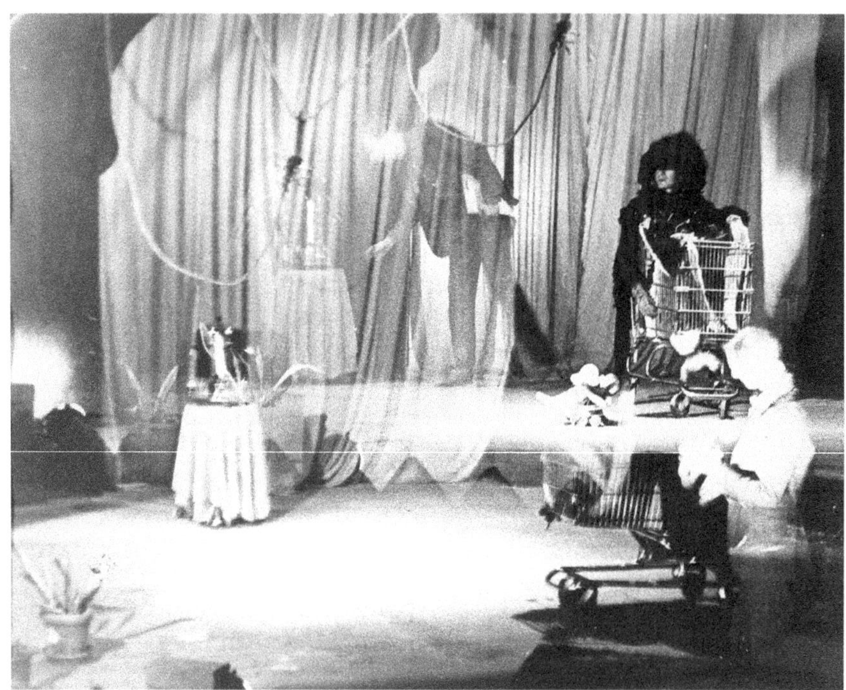

1.7   Jack Smith, *Jack Smith in 'Secret of Rented Island'* (1977).

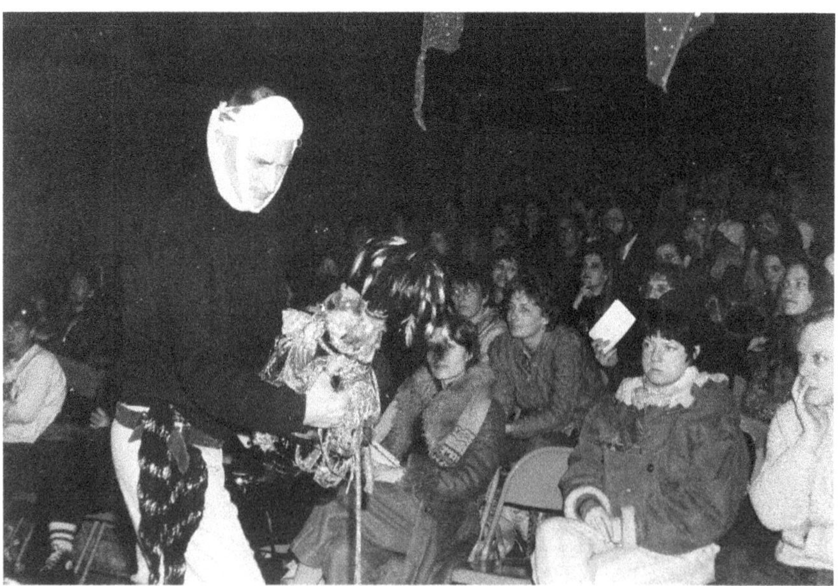

1.8   Jack Smith, *Untitled (Jack Smith in 'Death of a Penguin')* (c. 1985).

Lower East Side apartments were transformed into magnificent hovels and decked out with lights and rudimentary junkshop seating arrangements, providing a landscape of quirky decrepitude for his live performances. His solo and collaborative epics would be interminably slow, drawn out to four, six, eight hours and repeatedly interrupted by 'the ever present disruption of Jack himself, protesting against the horror and failure of [his own] event'.[13]

Alongside his durational loft performances, Smith was also a devotee of performing for camera. Throughout his working life he would engage friends and acolytes to document his performances in both private and public spaces, as shown in a striking image from an intervention in a petrol station. With his face painted silver and adorned in robes of clashing designs, he strikes a pose with a petrol pump handle; the image was used in his performance of *Gas Stations of the Cross Religious Spectacle* (1971), as publicity or as an accompanying slide.

Smith is an artist whose radical heterogeneity, eccentricity, and tendency towards failure make him a difficult figure to represent in dominant accounts of performance and visual culture. Exceeding easy categorisation, Smith is notable for his irregularities of style and a seemingly perverse celebration of failure in his work. He refuses the dominant intellectual and scholarly pursuits of the 1960s in favour of inhospitable interests. Gesturing to the resistant logic of his own artistic practice, Smith writes, 'I don't put pictures on a wall. When I finish with a wall it repels paintings … the interior design of my apartment is art itself. It doesn't want pictures. It repels any crust that you could put on it.'[14] This irreverence was premised on his adoration of the unfashionable refuse of recent popular culture, primarily the films of Maria Montez, a short-lived Universal Pictures film siren from the Dominican Republic. This parade of vapid ventures from the 1940s traded on the actress' smouldering beauty, and questionable representations of the 'Orient', thus indulging the fantasies of their original wartime audiences. Later admirers, such as Smith and his friends, were deeply invested in these movies, yet tempered their pleasure with the benefits of hindsight and the fertile possibilities that camp irony bestowed on their entertainment. In 1962, Smith wrote of his idol, Montez, 'Juvenile does not equal shameful and trash is the material of creators. It exists whether one approves or not … There is a (unsophisticated, certainly) validity there – also theatrical drama (the best kind) – also interesting symbolism, delirious hokey, glamour – unattainable (because once possessed) and juvenile at its most passionate.'[15] In his films and performances, Smith would revel in the 'unsophisticated', the 'juvenile', and the peculiar profundity of 'trash'.

In many ways Smith refused to assimilate to the tendencies and fashions of the 1960s. If his contemporaries listened to Jefferson Airplane, Captain Beefheart and the Grateful Dead, he preferred the exotic whimsy of Carmen Miranda, Yma Sumac or Xavier Cugat, indulging the dubious thrill of the

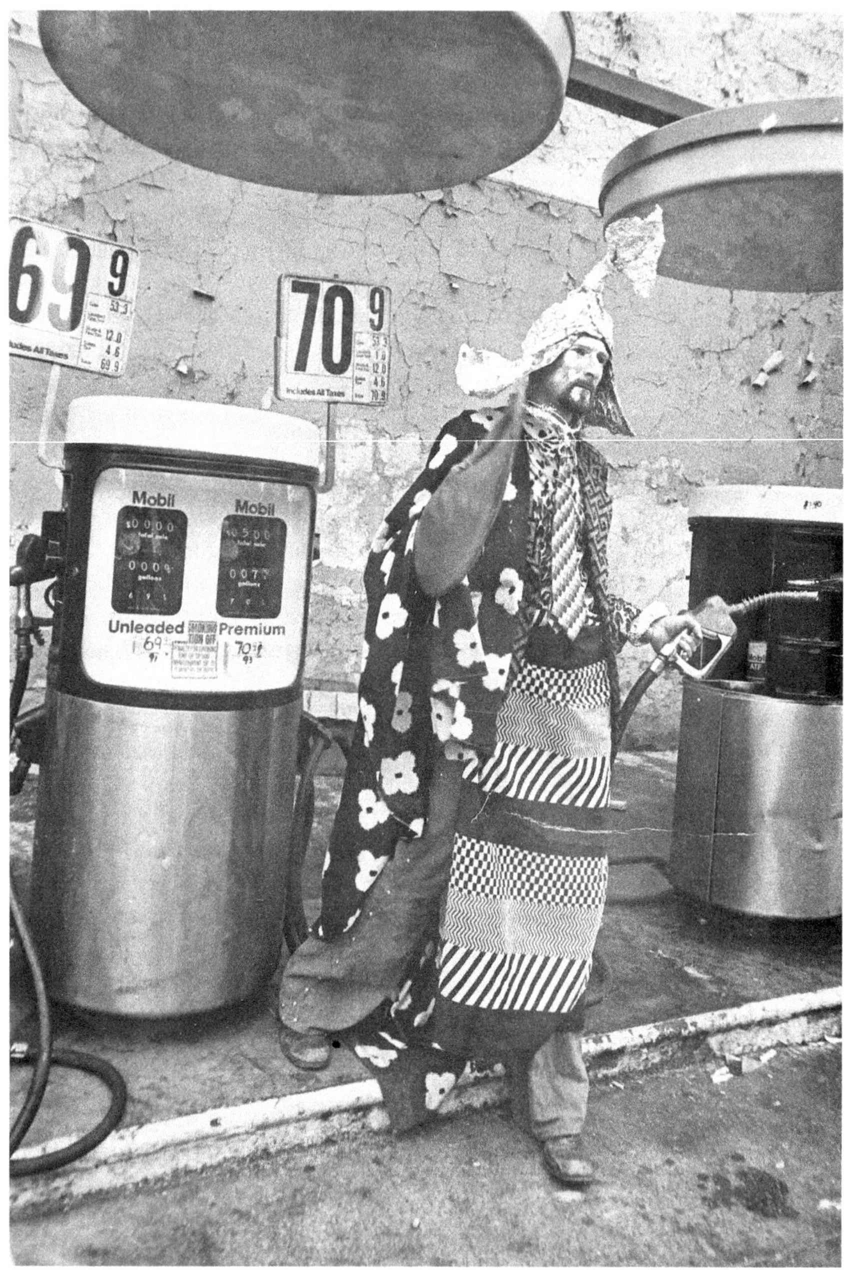

I.9   Jack Smith, *Jack Smith in 'Gas Stations of the Cross'* (1971).

passé long before this was culturally recognisable as knowing affectation. If his friends demonstrated their Beatnik erudition by attending screenings of the work of Jean-Luc Godard and François Truffaut, Smith passed them up for reruns of tired and tawdry vehicles for Judy Canova and Dorothy Lamour. But it was towards the faded grandeur of Maria Montez that Smith committed himself to performing his most profound deference. His unlikely pleasures were unfathomable in the days before the mainstreaming of kitsch tastes and retro chic, yet his beatification of trash provided the opportunity for an elaboration of alternative creative values. However, these indulgences also made it uncomfortably easy for him to find himself 'not being wanted', undermined as 'a drag on the industry' – much like the fate of his fateful, sequinned icon, Maria Montez.[16]

Bearing in mind the fervour of his curious pleasures, and the potency with which they shine through in his art works, it may well be counterintuitive to expect Smith to figure unproblematically in histories of postwar art. Not simply a maker of challenging work, Smith was also a notoriously difficult personality, as attested to in countless memories of his impediments to the efforts of critics and historians; in one such anecdote, the film writer Sheldon Renan remembered in 1968 that Smith 'agreed to an interview but replied to all my questions with his whole face pressed tightly against a pillow', which perhaps influenced Renan's description of Smith as definitively 'beyond categories' in his book *The Underground Film* of the same year.[17] (He does appear under a category later in the book, namely 'Madness'.)

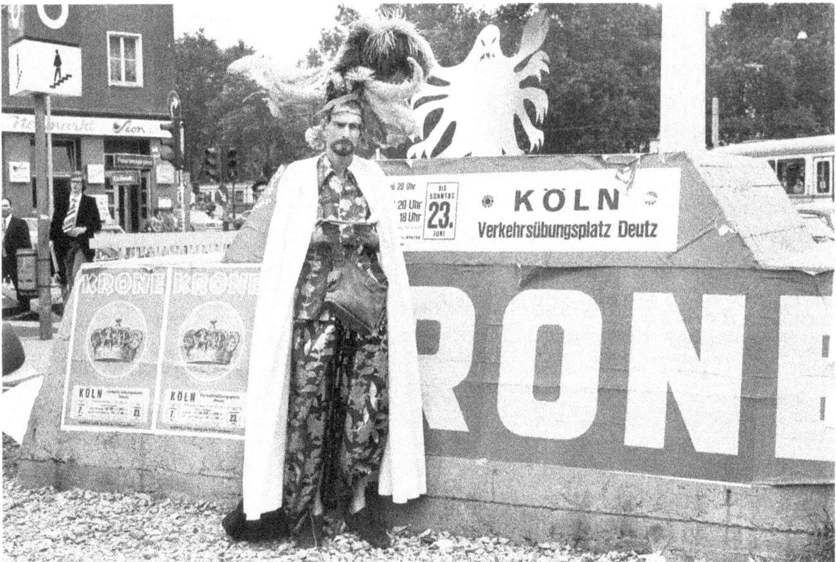

Gwenn Thomas, *Jack Smith in Cologne* (1974).   **I.10**

Whether specific artists have been overlooked – the result of apparently benign 'methodological' restrictions – or expressly elided from dominant histories, Linda Nochlin has demonstrated that there is much cultural, social and political mileage to be gained from outlining the shape of historical absences. In 1971, Nochlin was the first to expose the unstated domination of white male (implicitly heterosexual) subjectivity over the production and dissemination of art's histories. Nochlin demonstrated that the placement of women within (or outside) the canon had been punitively designated as a 'minor' question, a 'laughably provincial sub-issue grafted onto a serious, established discipline'.[18] Smith enables a critique of subsequent processes of marginalisation, as exemptions often confirmed according to the dubious logic of universal standards of value. For defenders of the canon, desires and interests are sublimated as quality, and coded, in turn, as objective. The philosopher Hannah Arendt notes the sublimated circularity of the canon, which obscures the privileges that bolster the deployment of cultural authority: 'Insofar as the past has been transmitted as tradition, it possesses authority; insofar as authority presents itself historically, it becomes tradition.'[19] The process of legitimisation is therefore tautological and self-serving. This conservative effect works to condition, limit and police the conferral of historical value upon objects surveyed by the discourse on art.

Glorious Catastrophe zones in on the borders between the mainstream and its outsides, veering suggestively outwards to marginal, minor, peripheral, emergent or oppositional spaces of culture. As should become clear, I do not seek to recuperate Smith into a reconstructed canon. Instead, I consider and in some ways privilege the off-kilter placement of Smith between (and to some extent outside) the distinct and often incompatible histories of performance and visual culture. Smith is apposite in this respect, as he both predates and endures the acknowledgement of performance art as a valid artistic category for formal, institutional, and academic consideration, from the late 1960s onwards. Smith is ideal for a 'minor' history of performance and visual culture, if we take minor in its musical sense, to suggest a style or idiolect emphasising a textural difference to – an affective and mobile modification of – the constants assumed by authoritative modes of reading. As it were, Smith interrupts those histories written in a major key.

The fall from grace

Smith exerted a profound influence over artists on the Lower East Side in the 1960s, and briefly became a household name on account of the obscenity scandal that enveloped *Flaming Creatures*. By the end of the decade, however, he had slipped into obscurity. The art of the late 1960s had given rise to a radical revaluation of art, but Smith's artistic practice has been afforded an ambivalent status in its dominant narratives, partly because of his itinerant movement across aesthetic forms, as well as by the inaccessibility of his posthumous archive.[20] His slide into invisibility was in – in no small part, at least – exacerbated by his contempt for the formal boundaries laid down by scholarly disciplines and the curatorial strategies of institutions of art.

The proliferation of new forms – including pop, minimalism, postminimalism, performance art, conceptual art and land art – contributed to a break from the modernist emphasis on pictorial essence, towards a 'post-medium condition' in and beyond gallery-sponsored art and culture. For Rosalind Krauss, the traditional aesthetic forms became obsolete, preventing unitary identifications of the 'physical support' of specific works.[21] Nevertheless, the problem of medium specificity – and the larger question of what now might count as art in the expanded field of cultural production – was not set totally aside in the wake of new forms, as older assumptions, values and prejudices inevitably persisted. Krauss notes as much when she continues that despite an expanded field of 'technical supports' in contemporary art – she cites examples as diverse as installation, television, animation and computer software – artists encounter an 'obligation to wrest from that support a new set of aesthetic conventions to which their works can then reflexively gesture, should they want to join those works to the canon of modernism', as a means of securing a position in key histories of art and culture.[22]

Smith's practice therefore troubles the attempt to record his place in the historical developments of performance and visual culture after 1960. This sense of trouble is heightened by his predilection towards new and ungainly aesthetic forms, from lengthy theatrical performances that eschewed dramatic fiction, to intermedial forms that blurred the boundaries between film and performance towards expanded cinema. The latter – which Smith referred to as 'live film' – involved 'experimenting with [playing] various records as the film is projected and making other small corrections'. In his live film performances, Smith would present rushes from *Normal Love* (1963–64), as well as a volley of slides and music, with 'the rest of the program … filled in from a huge mass of color film that will someday be two full length films', though which was never formally assembled.[23] Only a handful of films by Smith exist in a finite, properly 'finished' form – *Scotch Tape* (1959), *Overstimulated* (1959), *Flaming Creatures* (1962) and *No President* (1967). Further films are extant, including *Reefers of Technicolor Island* (1967), *I Was A Male Yvonne de Carlo* (1967), *Song For Rent* (1969) and *Hot Air Specialists* (1983), but the finality of the form in which they are screened is sometimes contested.

His performances were similarly diffuse and expansive. It is difficult to discuss specific performances by Smith, as the content and titles were used more or less interchangeably over the decades, and no full-length documents were made on film or video. His works had titles that signalled the 'delirious hokey' they celebrated, such as *Wait for Me at the Bottom of the Pool* (1968), *Brassieres of Atlantis* (1969), *Technicolor Sunset Easter Pageant* (1970), *Withdrawal from Orchid Lagoon* (1970), *Sacred Landlordism of Lucky Paradise* (1973), or *The Secret of Rented Island* (1976). These performances were scripted to varying degrees, but inadequately advertised, documented, or reviewed. When he did publicise his performances, he placed adverts in unlikely places – the religious classifieds of freebie bulletins, for example – and provided abstruse content, to deliberately limit his target market and preserve his cryptic marginality. In terms of strategies for documentation, shorter reels of video and film footage were made of some performances, as were audio recordings; scattered photographs are extant; and some preliminary sketches or scripts survive in his estate. However, he clearly has a curious relationship to archiving his practice. Disrupting the normative desire to promote his career, or to make the past last, his non-durable works of art defy the promise of immortality afforded to individuals proved worthy of 'making history'. Smith's movement between performance and underground film – two pursuits that are archetypically marginal to art history – exacerbated his position as a supplement to the authoritative histories of art since mid-century.

David Ehrenstein suggests that by the 1980s Smith had slipped from critical and academic horizons, despite his assertion that '[t]he American avant-garde *is* Jack Smith', his output having 'for three decades, produced less a "body of work" of comfortable definable contours than a radical aesthetic of perpetual fluidity and incalculable influence'.[24] By enduring a near-suicidal dispersal of artistic subjectivity – through a manifest tendency towards disaster, and a predilection for inhibiting his own success – Smith enacted his own disappearance from view, despite maintaining a striking productivity across three decades of artistic labour. 'By going against the avant-garde establishment grain,' Ehrenstein writes, 'he has risked rendering himself a cultural non-person – a fact underscored by a review of Carel Rowe's book [in 1982] which came to the conclusion from the evidence offered that Smith had *died*'.[25] Ehrenstein's statement is perhaps as much a critique of academic practice and cultural journalism in crisis, as it is a comment on the deathlike quality attained by – or conferred upon – artists who enact their own disappearance from history.

In histories of art, mostly those focusing on underground film, Smith is remembered for *Flaming Creatures* and the official conferral of obscenity in the early 1960s. This early work's notoriety has obscured the importance of his innovations in other media during the subsequent thirty-five years over which he was active. As a result, Smith is profoundly marginal in dominant narratives of art history, despite the longevity of his practice and the scope of his broad and persistent influence over peers and future generations of artists. However, I do not maintain that Smith has been actively excluded from historical narration, as this would afford a malign agency to history and historians. Rather, he has necessarily failed to register. As John Guillory argues, correlations between progressive social politics and critiques of canonicity rely on an assumed homology between two materially distinct political tendencies: processes of social exclusion and the refusal of cultural capital. Guillory notes that this conflation obscures the ways individuals and social groups experience marginalisation. Criticism also tends to vacillate between 'separatist' productions of alternative canons, and an 'integrationist' attempt to recuperate missing objects into the authoritative series.[26] Similarly, after Henry Louis Gates, Jr, I am wary of representing dominant culture as 'a marionette theatre of the political' in which cultural critique becomes a wishful corrective to systemic social inequalities, as though the insertion of new figures into art history might alleviate the deep inequities that persist among constituencies of differing needs and aspirations.[27] Instead, I look to Smith to ask a series of questions about the construction and maintenance of art-historical and other cultural narratives.

Although Smith came of age as an artist in the 1960s, and much of my analysis represents him as an artist of the decade, it is worth briefly putting this assumption under scrutiny. After all, what does it mean for an artist to be 'of' a decade? 'The sixties' as a historical construction has been the subject of much debate, not least because critics are undecided about when the decade began and ended. While decades often do seem to represent distinct paradigms in politics, art and other discourses, these shifts can hardly be expected to commence or be commuted with punctuality. The 1960s as a political phenomenon in the US may have started with the assassination of John F. Kennedy in 1963, and ended as early as 1967, with the race riots that occurred during the Summer of Love, or 1969, with the arrest of Charles Manson and the concomitant collapse of the hippie dream. In one of the most recent accounts of the decade, Jenny Diski writes that 'the sixties' began halfway through the decade, with the emergence of a fully industrialised popular culture, and ended as late as 1974, with the resignation of President Richard Nixon, and the rise of conservative politics in the UK.[28] Art, politics, or the vagaries of a life can rarely be expected to fall into line with the birth of a new decade. To constrain an artist to a particular decade entails a series of limitations, denials and caricatures. To restrict Smith by affording him a place in the 1960s forces a set of relations to an arbitrarily defined historical moment. It also forgets the relevance of his practice and the development of his ideas across a further sequence of (arbitrarily delimited) historical periods, namely the 1970s and the 1980s.

It is worth being sensitive to the problems that emerge from an attempt to historicise a decade. As Alice Echols has argued, the 1960s demands revisionist histories that emphasise multiple sites of radicalism and political contestation, to oppose the narrative containment and 'textual subordination' of achievements by women, queers, people of colour, and others who are routinely marginalised in accounts of the decade.[29] What does Smith's disappearance from the archive say about how the dominant stories of the 1960s are constructed, sustained, and disseminated? If the problem of cultural capital is one of distribution, and not one of representation (a problem of access to culture, not of ideological content of works), how does reading Smith's legacies offer new possibilities for reviving a sense of critical diversity in histories of performance and visual culture in the 1960s?

Canonicity and failure

In the first academic commentary on Smith's performance work to be published in the United States, in *The Drama Review* in 1979, J. Hoberman writes, 'The Plaster Foundation was both Smith's home and his theatre, and the spectator often had the feeling that what one saw enacted there was no more or less than Smith's daily existence, framed by an audience's presence.'[30] As such, Smith's performances gloried in framing the mundane under the guise of glamorous spectacle, yet simultaneously worked to hollow out the theatrical, parading its evacuated remnants before his audience. In responding to Smith's unique career, a tension emerges between, on the one hand, conceding to the fantasy of historical intelligibility by recuperating difficult practices, and, on the other, committing the fruits of such labours to the nowhere of marginality, sanctioning the historical oversights that suit the assumptions of a conservative politics of value. Breaking with this tension, I understand the minor artist as an antiheroic commonplace that must be allowed to persist in her or his difference. In the refusal to appear on the horizon of conventional historical narration, the supplement exposes and challenges a discipline's historiographical assumptions, prompting questions about how a particular artist or work is deemed relevant, valuable or important. Non-recuperative writing might therefore pose a third strategy to the two positions in tension, above. Not simply inside or outside of established systems of knowledge, the excess performed by the supplement troubles the very terms by which apparent norms are constituted, throwing the logics of value, genius, beauty or efficacy into disarray.

For conservative critics, however, the canon must be protected from such unruliness, to preserve the orderliness of the structure of valuation and the sanctity of the works conserved within its disputed province. For example, according to Harold Bloom aesthetic value is an autonomous, universal quality. Considerations of the contingency of value and the material conditions of artistic production and reception are merely symptoms of revisionist 'resentment', the defining characteristic of work by feminist, queer and anti-racist 'cheerleaders'.[31] If Shakespeare is 'the center of the canon' for Bloom and other traditionalists, Smith positions himself, eccentrically, at the dubious margin of cultural authority, and asks impertinent questions about how the terrain of culture is mapped and legitimated. Against Bloom's assertion of Shakespeare's 'palpable aesthetic supremacy',[32] it is especially thrilling to read Smith's casual disregard for *Hamlet*, staged in the course of his adaptation, *Hamlet in the Rented World* (1972). As Stefan Brecht reports, 'he feels the play is very badly written, no structure, more like a radio or tv series, [though] it can be salvaged

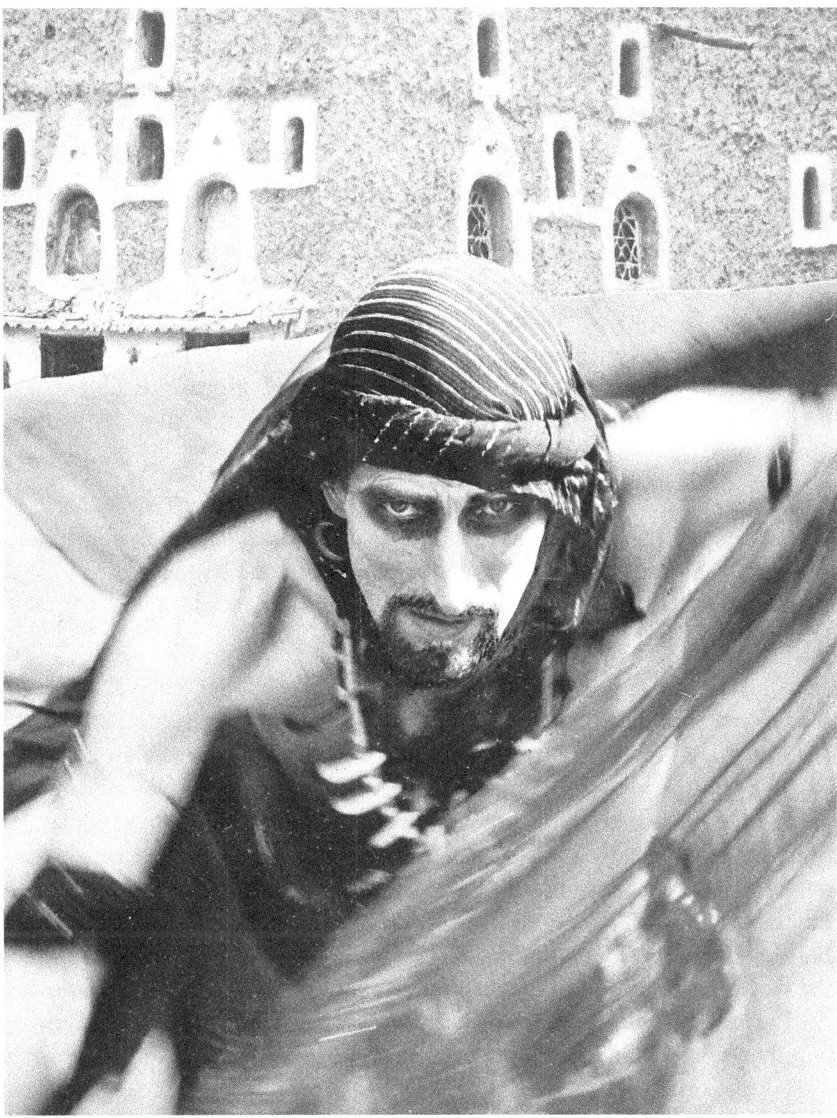

Jack Smith, *Untitled* (c. 1982–85).   **I.11**

by much cutting … He aims to play him as a fop, and very very queer.'[33] Later in the 1970s, Smith would devote several years to a distinctly camp adaptation of Henrik Ibsen's *Ghosts* entitled *The Secret of Rented Island* (1976–77). *Ghosts* has canonical status as a momentously serious instance of modernist realism, adding a curious comedic weight to Smith's decision to translate it into a performance with stuffed hippos and monkeys, explosions of glitter, ocean sound effects, and mock-*Arabian Nights* eccentricities. Moreover, 'It is timely doing *Ghosts*,' Smith states, with what might be read as portentous, apocalyptic apprehension. With reference to Osvald Alving's inherited syphilis, and his catastrophic descent into madness in the closing scene of the play, Smith adds, 'There are new strains of VD which will not respond to penicillin, you know. The play is a catalogue of wrecked lives, [of] what people have done because they were afraid of what other people would say.'[34] Smith's critiques of the canon are not merely symptoms of minority resentment, but instead ask questions about the unsettling fixity of hierarchies in canonical narration.

While Smith's campy appropriations of *Hamlet* or *Ghosts* do not dislodge the canon, he hints at how a plurality of voices begins to denaturalise the representative, universal postures of canonical works. The heretical thinkers demeaned by Bloom as the 'School of Resentment' outlined this potential in persuasive terms. In their outline of the critical project of new historicism, Catherine Gallagher and Stephen Greenblatt write,

> To wall off for aesthetic appreciation only a tiny portion of the expressive range of a culture is to diminish its individuality and to limit one's understanding even of that tiny portion, since its significance can be fully grasped only in relation to the other expressive possibilities with which it interacts and from which it differentiates itself.[35]

New historicist suspicions about the univocal sublime enable a critical account of Smith's art that does not entail recuperation through an uncritical acceptance of the terms of canonicity. Smith was expressly aware of the power relations between perceived standard-bearers of official culture and artists at the margins. He commented frequently on how art is overlooked or overwritten, especially when made familiar as a result of public scandal. 'Very often great artists are not understood,' he writes, 'even by young intellectuals in other countries. I do not understand or like the work of Fernand Léger. Do not criticize if you don't understand. Someday even I may come to like the work of Fernand Léger. I hope so.'[36]

The project of plotting out a history for marginal cultural identities therefore requires protocols that work in counterpoint to those of traditional research. Gates calls this 'autocritography': the imaginative practice of mapping alternative histories in order to constitute a minority 'discursive subject', through elective affinities with marginal figures.[37] While Gates explores this from the perspective of critical race theory, analysing the charges of the Culture Wars of the 1980s, autocritography also describes a practice of non-reproductive self-narration relevant to those of us who describe ourselves as queer. As individuals frequently removed from reproductive futurity, and often alienated from familial legacies, lesbian, gay and transgender people are especially well-placed to reinvent fantastical histories by asserting new lineages with figures who attract our attention. Plotting out a marginal ancestry, we may procure imaginative cultural heredities to prolong the affective reverberations of missed encounters with those who have preceded us. Expending energy on Smith's work and its legacies allows an autocritographical art history to shed light upon the conflicting, polyvalent and resistant culture from which he emerged. It suggests new ways of thinking about how a culture lends itself to historical analysis, and how inspiring figures lend themselves to libidinous investments. The comment on Léger implies as much, by suggesting that while he may not understand the work of the modernist painter and filmmaker, Smith assumes his mechanistic, decorative abstraction must serve its own purposes for other audiences. He therefore demurs from pursuing or emphasising his distaste, for the sake of the possibilities Léger enabled others in different situations. As Smith counsels his peers elsewhere, 'We must be humorous, fair and affectionate even while we quarrel [as] the tender part of life depends on it. We can achieve this balance because we are incredible.' By celebrating the 'incredible' possibilities of his difference, Smith emphasises his idiosyncratic combination of off-centre brilliance and the abandonment of 'pasty' credibility.[38] Such values conspire to remember queerness in terms of erotic, fraught or endangered strategies – that is, as tools for denaturalising the joy of receiving or inducing pleasure.

The effects of prosecution

As an artist who occupied himself with inventorying the grim realities of his age, Smith inevitably encountered resistance from critics, the public, and the state. This made him sympathetic to other artists in similarly embattled situations, such as Barbara Rubin, Ron Rice and John Waters, whose careers he was eager to defend. More crucially, forceful opposition imbued Smith's works with a mood of impending catastrophe, and he never tired of milking its ceremonial drama. Like the characters of Jean Genet's novels – violent, vulgar, and 'intoxicated with the tragic',[39] Smith was a figure with a ridiculously refined taste for histrionic excess, and he wore its disastrous mark like a badge of dubious honour. As Gregory Battcock writes, 'Smith speaks forcibly about the ultimate topic of every contemporary artist who grasps the implications of his actions and, through an understanding of the present and appreciation of its new knowledge, defines the existential isolation of the individual.' Battcock concludes that these encounters should testify to Smith's lasting importance for the historical witness, stating, 'For survival, the world needs such artists.'[40] Nevertheless, Smith would quickly risk becoming a cultural nobody, a social and cultural outcast teetering on the verge of financial destitution and historical oblivion. In the 1980s, several years before his death, he would describe his squalid marginality in a performance script: 'I have to live in squalor, all day long playing hide and seek with odors … No kidding folks. They love dead queers here.'[41]

Key to the centrality of catastrophe afforded in my account is the context of censorship that Smith experienced in the early stages of his career, and the lived conditions of marginalisation it caused him. After charges were brought against his film's distributor, Jonas Mekas, in 1964, the public scandal of *Flaming Creatures* became Smith's dubious claim to fame, tying him to other notorious defendants of the period. As Smith would complain, it turned his practice into a 'sex issue of the Cocktail World', but once the sensation subsided, he found himself firmly located at the margins of culture.[42] The case against *Flaming Creatures* was not an isolated legal event, but one of several crucial violations of civil liberties in the context of artistic practice in the period. It followed hot on the heels of three obscenity trials featuring high-profile defendants: City Lights' Lawrence Ferlinghetti as a result of distributing Allen Ginsberg's poem *Howl* in San Francisco in 1956; Paul Carroll and Irving Rosenthal in Chicago, for publishing ten excerpts from William S. Burroughs' *Naked Lunch* in their vanguard journal *Big Table* in 1959; and Barney Rosset at New York's Grove Press, after the publication of Henry Miller's novel *Tropic of Cancer* in 1961. In all three cases, the Supreme Court overruled the state courts' findings of obscenity, declaring each book a work of literature. Yet Smith's case fared less well.

Others have linked Smith's case to these three immediate precursors. Mekas described Smith, Ginsberg, Burroughs and Miller as artists linked by their unleashing of the 'intuitive mind'. For Mekas, one of the defendants sentenced in the case against *Flaming Creatures*, this intuitive onslaught struck a powerful chord with the forces of censorship by enabling readers 'to descend into the mind of the "lower regions" … the madman's mind, the fanatic's mind'. A movement downward, it is nevertheless imagined by Mekas to be an emergence, 'pulling man upwards … by his ears'.[43] In the hope of attending to the plight of *Flaming Creatures*, Mekas tracked the scandals – and, Smith suspected, fanned their flames – in *Film Culture* and *Village Voice*, magazines to whose pages Smith was also a frequent contributor.[44] Writing specifically of Smith's movies, Mekas notes, 'From under the ruins of the contemporary cinema, suddenly a flag was lifted up towards the sun, the flag of a great poet.'[45] Figured as an awakening, Smith's rude gesture was received unkindly by the state and, similarly, it would seem, by history.

Looking back on the debacle, Smith would recall that in the early 1960s 'it was fashionable to have a work of art in the courts', locating this phenomenon in what he terms, '[a]ll the mileage got out of Miller's books'.[46] For Henry Miller, his own work aimed at creating a 'story of art whose roots lie in massacre'. As such, he staged a fearful perspective on the fates of artists who pursue volatile modes of creative practice, anticipating Smith's own melancholic positions on the matter. While Miller is now remembered as a major figure in American literature, his *Tropic of Cancer* was originally published in Paris in 1934, by Jack Kahane's Obelisk Press (with private funding from Anaïs Nin and Wilhelm Reich), but the novel remained unpublished in America for three decades. In the 1960s, Miller became legendary in the US, yet remained marginal, excoriated by critics for the challenging subject matter of his semi-autobiographical writings. His biographer, the novelist Erica Jong remembered that when Miller contacted her in 1974, he was still considered a literary untouchable, 'doomed to live out his final decade and a half under the shadow of [an] ignoble reputation' (he died in 1980).[47] As Miller writes in *Tropic of Cancer*, 'If there were a man who dared to say all that he thought of this world there would not be left him a square foot of ground to stand on. When a man appears the world bears down on him and breaks his back.'[48] Smith concurred, stating, 'I don't want to be destroyed … and yet I want to give.'[49] Miller and Smith gesture to an intractable tension, between a giving of oneself through creative practice and the punitive responses garnered by such acts.

For Ginsberg, Burroughs and Miller, their notoriety functioned as *succès de scandales*, eventually guaranteeing their authoritative status in post-war experimental culture (Miller's literary clout was secured posthumously). Yet despite Mekas's triumphant rhetoric, the legacy of *Flaming Creatures* granted Smith 'a marginal existence lived on the edge of bohemian squalor'.[50] In terms of the material effects of his transgressions, Smith more clearly resembles the contemporary political satirist Lenny Bruce. Arrested eight times between 1961 and 1964 on account of his stand-up routines, Bruce gained notoriety, but his career never recovered. Tried on six charges in five states, Bruce was convicted of obscenity, despite petitions to the court by Ginsberg, James Baldwin, Bob Dylan and Normal Mailer. In New York in 1964, one month after Mekas's conviction for screening *Flaming Creatures*, Bruce was sentenced to three four-month prison terms on account of performances at the Café Au Go Go in Greenwich Village. He died of a morphine overdose two years later, while on appeal to the Supreme Court. Several instances in Smith's work recall Bruce's style and content, colliding surreal imagery and taboo subjects in order to ridicule moral prudery. Now-classic Bruce 'bits', like his gay cowboy in *Thank You Mask Man*, or his outrageous reading of President Kennedy's assassination in *Jacqueline Kennedy Hauling Ass to Save Her Ass* (both 1964), were played out under the sign of what he called 'art with a piece of shit in the middle'.[51] Reminiscent of these caustic turns, Smith writes in a 1964 performance script,

> If a church preacher some Sunday should say, 'A stiff dick has no conscience,' so many pussys [*sic*] would clamp up you'd think you were in a reverse explosion in a suction pump factory along the pews. Little boys would be taken home and their ears washed out with a blow torch.[52]

Like Bruce, Smith created a distinctive and often brutally funny mode of self-presentation in performance, fashioned as incisive and disquieting social critique. Both tried the patience of the state with oppositional stances on sex and sexuality; and they both suffered in their professional and personal lives on account of having their work labelled officially obscene.

Smith's legal and other struggles allowed him political insights into the libidinal economies of cultural production. Regulatory responses to his art, films, and writings incited his criticisms of the endemic abuse of the civil liberties of artists, and his anxieties were translated into the content of his performances across three decades. In an authoritative study of homosexuality and censorship, Richard Meyer argues that embattled artists often reproduce the threat and effects of censorship in their work. For Meyer, artists from Paul Cadmus to Robert Mapplethorpe give visual form to a fundamental contradiction that drives the production of lesbian and gay art. He writes, 'the prohibition of homoerotic imagery serves not only to suppress but also to provoke and produce that imagery'.[53] Meyer's reading is useful for understanding the volatile relations upheld in Smith's investment in the climate of censorship and the conferrals of obscenity upon his work. Meyer's reading also suggests a way of reading the impact of censorship upon Smith's sophisticated understanding of sexual cultures. In his writings, for example, Smith acknowledges the relations between pornography, commerce and morality, arguing that representations of sex and sexuality are crucial to the orchestrations of culture. On the one hand, for Smith, 'sexual fantasizing' allows the subject 'the pitiful means whereby the truly unpleasant difficult sex function,' consisting of sexual acts and the identities that circulate around them, 'is swathed in glamour, perversity, and ultimately, simply, interest'.[54] On the other hand, as signalled by advertising – instances of which Smith consistently incorporated into his collages – sexual representation is crucial to 'the soundness of [the] consumer economy'. Smith highlights the apparently contradictory relations between: government and obscenity legislation; the state and its manifest investments in high capitalist conditions of production; and the market economy as an enactment of 'the sex fantasies of the manufacturers':

> That is why it seems strange that municipal-manufacturing interests give [representations of sex] the bad name of obscenity. Perhaps fetishists don't furnish homes, but in being driven into social guilt the dog who is most in the

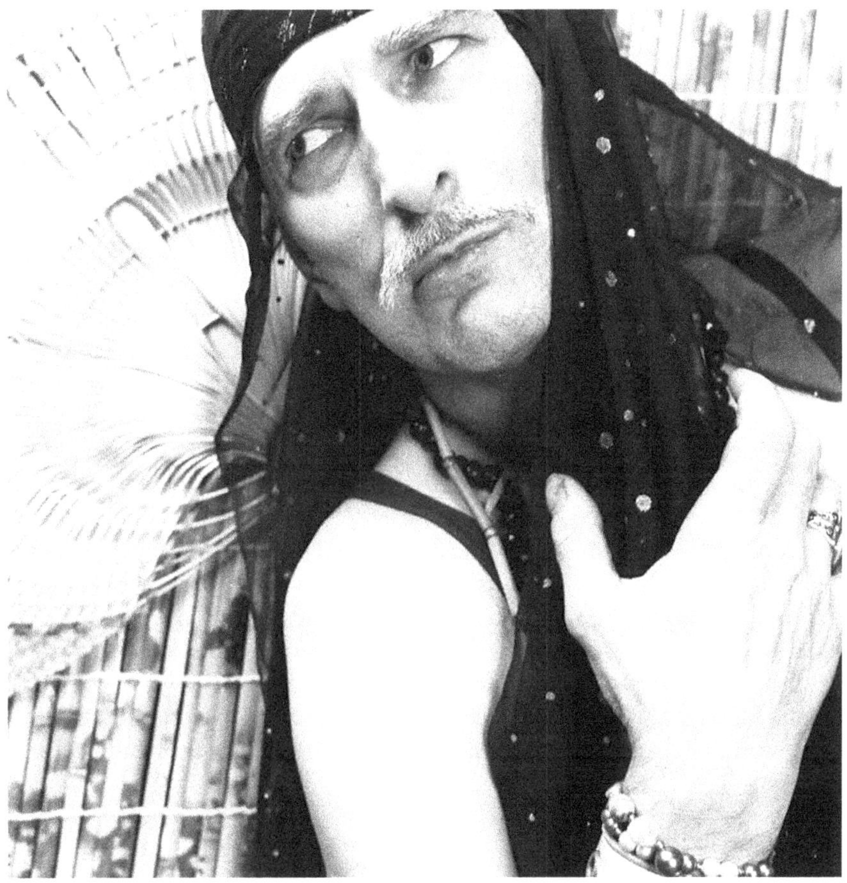

Edie Steiner, *Jack Smith* (1984).   **I.12**

unrewarding thrawl adds to his thankless and dry struggle [namely, the task of making art] … the assuming of a bad name, even the unfair premise of being a dog [whereas] the real dogs are cynical, ugly men who pay off … the police, the money collectors of the municipality.[55]

Referring to the licensing and taxation of bathhouses, strip joints, sex cinemas, pornography and suggestively erotic advertising, Smith critiques the state's investment in lucrative industries of sexual pleasure, as both a hypocritical financial gain, and a regulatory assumption of power. Smith notes, 'if there is such a thing as obscenity it is just this – the payment of funds to the police', that 'sly betrayal' of the subject's creative, sexual possibility for the sake of economic gain.[56]

In a vociferous defence of *Pink Flamingos* (1972) in the *Village Voice*, Smith further articulated his anger over the way critics sensationalise movies for the purpose of readable reviews, especially where a film exploits the tension between hilarity and filth. He writes that John Waters' movie – much like *Flaming Creatures* – risked being exploited and misrepresented as another 'sex issue of the Cocktail World', by writers whose 'public logorrhea marathons' betrayed their inability 'to recognize any difference whatsoever between comedy and sex'. He calls such writers 'devil-dykes', quickly noting that his terminology is 'not meant to imply any disloyalty to lesbians,' as the term happily describes two male columnists for the *Village Voice*, Jonas Mekas and Andrew Sarris. Despite their gender, he adds, they are nevertheless 'spear-carrying members of the hoof 'n mouth lesbian legion'. The laughter was drained from *Flaming Creatures*, he continues, by 'the kind of review that quickly boils the movie down to a checklist of the oily moments, glossily smirks over the sex novelties, and points the fairy finger'.[57] He congratulates Waters on achieving a 'gilded torrent of filth' that cannily eschewed the possibility of critics 'doing a number' on its comedy, by way of a 'nausea factor' so excessive that it 'would be too revolting [even] when described in portfolio lesbian style'. Referring to the infamous finale, in which Divine wolfs down a steaming poodle turd and regales the audience with a shit-eating grin, Smith admits that *Flaming Creatures* toed a line that was too aesthetically pleasing in comparison to the excesses of *Pink Flamingos*. Whereas Waters revealed the critics to be 'pyorrheal piranhas' – vicious, yet ultimately toothless – Smith saw his own film as falling prey to their sly betrayals, which stripped his film of its laughter by demeaning (or heralding) it as a monolith of disgusted apprehension.

'Glorious' catastrophe?

Writing in 1964, at the height of the obscenity scandal that surrounded *Flaming Creatures*, the eccentric painter Salvador Dalí was one of a number of major artists to address the challenges posed by Smith's work. In an unpublished letter to Jonas Mekas, Dalí gestured to Smith's powers:

> I am absolutely against your idea that *Flaming Creatures* is [appropriate] for everybody to see. Some erotic secrets [and] geometric solutions [are] reserved for a few only. And as the atomic bomb is the result of such secrets it was right to keep it from everybody. Nevertheless I consider *Flaming Creatures* a work of art and an excellent mystical erotic creation.[58]

Dalí's rhetoric is esoteric and overwrought, yet he highlights the peculiar incendiary force of Smith's innovations, evoking a verisimilitude between artistic experimentation, sexual excess, and the threat of disaster. Seduced by Smith's aggressive attacks on public morality, *Glorious Catastrophe* reads Smith's practice as a fruitfully ambivalent investment in crisis, exploring representations of sexuality, failure and death across art, performance, film and writing. Through critical readings of his works, I maintain that Smith's work gives precedence to unacknowledged themes in the development of performance and visual culture in the 1960s and after. These include eccentric logics of cultural production and reception such as failure, boredom, disgust, freakishness, woundedness, compulsion, paranoia, exoticism, apocalyptic tone, and other ugly feelings. If the first two chapters explore the problems that Smith poses for the writing of history, the subsequent two chapters explore the unfamiliar logics, accents and affects that Smith anatomises in his art, through close readings of key works. The final three chapters extend these previous examinations, and account for Smith's relevance for the twentieth and twenty-first centuries, and also detail some of the legacies and influences that he has bestowed on experimental culture and its analysis.

For some readers, this book's implicit celebration of catastrophe as 'glorious' might appear suspect. For Alain Badiou, the naturalising of conflict is merely a form of 'smug nihilism', and his concerns have had a profound effect on contemporary thinking around identity and subjectivity, especially in performance studies. Badiou writes, 'I do not believe the main question of our time to be that of horror, suffering, destiny, or dereliction. We are saturated by these notions, and besides, their fragmentation into [the practices of theatre] is truly incessant … Our question is instead that of affirmation, courage, of local energy.'[59] In an apparently soteriological emphasis on salvation or redemption, Badiou seems to extricate the construction of subjectivity from the fact of crisis. My mode of thinking may telescope the present and the recent past into a *fin de siècle* sensibility, conditioned by the inescapable subject position of being queer in the time of AIDS, but I am emboldened by the apocalypticism of a thinker like William Haver, who privileges the politics of historical non-transcendence. For Haver, the present and its vantages are necessarily and inescapably conditioned by the radical historicity of AIDS. Oracular gestures to its transcendence through philosophy or history are precarious in their prolepsis – 'a kind of forgetting of destitution and abjection, ultimately a forgetting or occlusion of the traumatic force of that existentiality which, in respect of the ego, is a wound'.[60] I take it as a given that a wound is neither soothed nor healed by optimistic transcendence.

In *Ethics*, moreover, Badiou argues that any theory of subjectivity that foregrounds destitution is conditioned by 'an obscure desire for catastrophe', and is thus simply an effect of 'conservative propaganda'.[61] This conflation relies on a sleight of hand, specifically his tactical inversions of critical race theory as a 'colonial encounter', and identity politics as 'a genuine perversion'.[62] By foreclosing materialist critique, Badiou ignores the possibility of more ambivalent critiques, and undermines the subject positions they may privilege. If a celebration of difference and a refusal of blinkered affirmation each constitute, for Badiou, 'at worst a threatening mix of conservatism and the death drive', it is worth asking what, precisely, is under threat, and with what practical effects, beyond the philosophical abstractions affirmed in his polemic. Queer theorists have explained the efficacy of negativity, especially for subjects who trouble the sanctity of identity, community and other consolations. As Leo Bersani writes,

> Negativity … attacks the myths of the dominant culture – the pastoral myth, for example, of sexuality as inherently loving and nurturing, of sexuality as continuous with harmonious community. Only by insisting on the bleakness, the love of power, even the violence perhaps inherent in human relations can we … begin to redesign those relations in ways that will not require the use of culture to ennoble them.[63]

For these reasons and more, Smith's art has been a powerful argument for refusing consolatory understandings of sexuality, sociality and subjectivity. If culture is depicted as being under threat from that which is properly outside it – suffering and crisis – I would hazard, after Smith, that endangering performers, audiences and institutions is a risk worth persisting in. The situations prompted by such risks are rarely fatal, though possibly disturbing, often enduring and sometimes affirmative. However, the spectrum of eventualities is hardly dependent upon an assertion of culture's volatility, or the inherent goodness of the subject.

Smith poses an uncomfortable challenge to cultural criticism and historical analysis, and his resistances can be courted as a methodology for engaging with other minor or mislaid histories. While my reading is certainly proximate to the critical praxes of scholarly queer studies, I have some reservations about the way 'queer' functions as a nomenclature for academic practices. In its unmooring from the troubled category of identity and the limiting rubric of sexual practice, 'queer' tends to become a catch-all for a nonspecific and virtually limitless conception of transgression, a byword for any practice that resists categorisation or troubles neoliberal pride. Bruce Benderson poses this thought in a characteristically ardent manner, stating that while there are individuals who identify beyond the constraints of heterosexuality, 'Unfortunately, there is no "queer" population on this planet, just an international middle class with the leisure to play language games and the feelings of guilt to need them, and an international lumpen class who'd be the first to kick our ass if we labeled them "queer".'[64] In a modification of this thesis, I use the term queer to describe specific people and their desires, and towards a definition of 'queer performance', but less so in reference to communities, ideas or effects. Queer theory's refusal of the certainties of identity politics has been crucial for broadening the previously restricted purview of scholarship, to embrace a wider range of minoritarian subjects, including readers, authors and other objects of critical study. At the same time, if translated into 'a political metaphor without a fixed referent' and a form of 'subjectless' critique,[65] 'queer' can also become an uncritical placeholder for any form of oppositional practice, in any of its critical, political, social or cultural guises. I see this as a hindrance to cultural critique, because it disregards the specifically erotic disturbances that the term 'queer' was initially deployed to celebrate. However, I hope that a turn to the erotic does not simply recuperate queer theory as, in David Eng's words, 'a metanarrative about the domestic affairs of white homosexuals'.[66]

Summaries of chapters

The possibility occasioned in Smith's investment in catastrophe depends upon a challenge, in that by setting up a risk premised upon a hostile yet fertile ambivalence, the hope for a different way of thinking may be given credence. Pursuing this account, the first two chapters explore the way Smith falls awkwardly between narratives of art, theatre and film, towards a counterhistory of cultural experimentation in the 1960s. How, I ask, is Smith's legacy useful for enacting this mode of historically invested critical address in the intersections between performance and visual culture? How does an orientation towards historicity give rise to different ideas about forces of inclusion and exclusion, and movements between discourses? How is Smith, specifically, useful in such a project? Chapter 1 reads Smith's practice towards a political appraisal of failure in the space between performance and visual culture. As such, I read the spaces of Smith's work as a homotopia of discarded objects and belittled cultural logics. Chapter 2 proposes the 'figural' condition of the artist, exploring how Smith stages this critical concept through the labour of performance, to blur distinctions between art and everyday life. As I have suggested, Smith's historical influence has been obscured, and by the early 1980s he would come to be recognised as 'the disappearing artist, Jack Smith'.[67] This chapter explores this problem through close readings of Smith's polemical pronouncements on art, theatre and history, with an emphasis on the differing legacies of Smith and his contemporaries.

Two further chapters look closely at Smith's best known films, specifically his cause célèbre, *Flaming Creatures* and his dreamy, colour follow-up, *Normal Love*. If art's work can be conceptualised as the testing of the limits of theory, how does Smith's art carry out such a labour? I attempt to answer this question by focusing on two ugly effects: disgust and freakishness. In chapter 3, disgust plays a key role in my theorising of *Flaming Creatures*, especially in relation to close readings of the ways the film was denounced in the United States House of Representatives and Senate in 1968. 'Aesthetic illusion,' Winnfried Menninghaus states, 'confuses the difference between art and reality, while disgust makes the poles completely collapse'.[68] Using a psychoanalytic framework, I pursue disgusted apprehension as an acutely performative response, towards characterising the historical specificity of Smith's representations of two modes of 'deviancy' in the 1960s, namely homosexuality and rape. Unexpected perspectives on sex and sexuality emerge as strategies that refuse critical affirmations of cohesion, identification and integration. In chapter 4, I privilege freakishness as a means of exploring Smith's performances of sexual and political identity. The historically specific phenomenon of the freak is developed as an excess of signification that holds an itinerant charge for lesbian and gay politics and performance, refusing the assimilatory promise heralded in conservative accounts of sexuality.

By pursuing the ambivalent promises fostered in glorious catastrophe, Smith's was an art that sought to celebrate the happy accidents of creative practice. As his commentators, critics and friends have suggested, Smith revelled in catastrophe with a perverse glee that flirts with morbid pathology. The three remaining chapters therefore take this book's title at its word, exploring the unique (and uniquely disturbing) proximity Smith articulated between pleasure and crisis. Chapter 5 looks to his seemingly necrophilic investment in Maria Montez as disastrous icon, and highlights the wounded bodies in her most famous film, *Cobra Woman* (1944), to dwell on the disasters played out in his camp idolatry. By exploring a film that turns on the trope of an open wound, I argue that Smith's written and performed paeans demonstrate that wounded apprehension provides a space for conceptualising the dwelling of 'camp effects' in the spaces where culture founders.

In chapters 1 through 5, Smith is cast in the role of filmmaker, performance artist, visual artist, architect, Warhol superstar, and social oddball. Chapter 6 demonstrates that Smith was a compulsive and consistent writer, despite the fact that his writings are rarely discussed in critical assessments of his work. Over three decades, Smith wrote short stories, reviews, polemics, journal entries and performance scripts, as well as a massive, overlooked cache of lists and scribbled epigrams. Premised on the peculiar, excessive character of his texts, this chapter imagines the practice of writing as tied to paranoia, frustration, failure, and desire, extending the thesis that his art reveled in the possibilities furnished by ugly feelings and unfamiliar cultural effects. Chapter 7 draws together some final thoughts on Smith's practice by examining the place of the 'exotic' in thinking about sexual and racial difference. I do so by exploring the central place he afforded the apocalyptic myth of the lost continent of Atlantis. As a hopelessly discredited fiction, Atlantis enabled a series of pseudo-scientific theses in the late nineteenth and early twentieth centuries, and became an enduring site of investment for Smith. The exoticism, imagination, and peculiar morality of the myth gives rise, I argue, to types of labour that are by turn volatile and utopian, posing a critical, 'apocalyptic' counterpoint to the assumed opposition between negativity and affirmation.

Throughout *Glorious Catastrophe*, Smith's elusive, impossible system of thought provides a platform for the elaboration of new aesthetic modes and practices, in the wake of his death, his disappearance from the archive, and his seeming reanimation in the work of contemporaries and descendents. Drawing on the historian's peculiar endeavour of shining light on the margins, this book proposes new ways of rethinking art's histories by suggesting possibilities for writing about errant, marginal, eccentric and itinerant subjects. At heart, this problem is hardly new, for the attempt to rediscover and revalue a lost cause has been a central strategy in all manner of historical projects. Papers in hand, the writer rifles history for enigmatic sparkles, for the inaudible swansong that might ignite a thought – searching for a life amid the details. In the course of our reading, 'occasionally we pick up something odd, and new', Roger Conover writes. 'We think we are reading a poem. Then something glistens.'[69] Akin to Smith's habit of collecting and recombining jetsam in his New York lofts, we too rummage through residues for scraps that catch the light. We scrutinise dispossessed finds for signs of worth and life, for a place on the mantel of culture – seduced by the muddled lights thrown, alike, from priceless gems and counterfeit jewels, or from enigmatic legends and sham histories.

Notes

1 John Vaccaro, unpublished interview with the author, New York (5 June 2005).

2 Jack Smith, 'Actavistic, action packed, action acting of PFA Hamlet, and the 1001 psychological jingoleanisms of prehistoric Rima-Puu' (1971), *Wait for Me at the Bottom of the Pool: The Writings of Jack Smith*, ed. J. Hoberman and Edward Leffingwell (New York and London: High Risk Books, 1997), p. 167.

3 Cited in Carel Rowe, *The Baudelairean Cinema: A Trend within the American Avant-Garde* (Ann Arbor, Michigan: UMI Research Press, 1982), p. 39.

4 E. P. Thompson, *The Making of the English Working Class* (Harmondsworth: Pelican Books, 1968), p. 13.

5 Walter Benjamin, 'Theses on the philosophy of history', *Illuminations*, ed. Hannah Arendt, trans. Harry Zorn (London: Pimlico, 1999), pp. 245–55 (p. 247).

6 Derek Jarman, *At Your Own Risk: A Saint's Testament* (New York: Overlook Press, 1993), p. 114.

7 Parker Tyler, *Underground Film: A Critical History* (London: Penguin, 1971), p. 82.

8 Rowe, p. xiii.

9 David Ehrenstein, *Film: The Front Line, 1984* (Denver: Arden Press, 1984), p. 23.

10 Smith cited in Uzi Parnes, 'Pop performances: four seminal influences: the work of Jack Smith, Tom Murrin – the Alien Comic, Ethyl Eichelberger, and the Split Britches Company', unpublished PhD thesis, New York University, 1988, p. 117.

11 Ken Jacobs in conversation, Kino Arsenal, Berlin (1 November 2009). Smith was a friend of Beat figures such as Huncke and Irving Rosenthal; Smith's correspondences with both writers are held in Rosenthal's papers at Stanford University.

12 Stan Brakhage, *Film at Wit's End: Essays on American Independent Filmmakers* (Edinburgh: Polygon, 1989), p. 160.

13 Jerry Tartaglia, 'The perfect queer appositeness of Jack Smith', *Experimental Cinema: The Film Reader*, ed. Wheeler Winston Dixon and Gwendolyn Audrey Foster (London and New York: Routledge, 2002), pp. 163–72 (p. 169).

14 Jack Smith, 'Art and art history', audio recording of a lecture by Smith, Forbidden Film Festival (Funnel Experimental Film Theatre, Toronto, 25–31 October 1984).

15 Jack Smith, 'The perfect filmic appositeness of Maria Montez', *Wait for Me at the Bottom of the Pool*, pp. 25–35 (pp. 26–7).

16 Ibid. p. 27.

17 Cited in Pooter, 'Review', *The Times* (1 June 1968), p. 21. See also Sheldon Renan, *The Underground Film: An Introduction to its Development in America* (London: Studio Vista, 1968), pp. 34–6.

18 Linda Nochlin, 'Why have there been no great women artists?', *Women, Art, and Power and Other Essays* (London: Thames & Hudson, 1989), pp. 145–78 (p. 146).

19 Hannah Arendt, 'Introduction: Walter Benjamin: 1892–1940', *Illuminations*, pp. 7–58 (p. 43).

20 After Smith's death, his estate handlers were engaged in a protracted legal contestation, which rendered much of his archive off-limits to researchers. Under the auspices of performance artist Penny Arcade and film historian J. Hoberman, the now-defunct Plaster Foundation initiated the bulk of this posthumous critical attention. Named after The Plaster Foundation of Atlantis, Smith's home-cum-performance space on Grand Street in the 1970s, Arcade and Hoberman's organisation was committed to four strategies in its care of Smith's estate. Firstly, the estate was preserved as a single entity. Secondly, The Plaster Foundation restored the films, primarily through filmmaker Jerry Tartaglia's efforts to remove temporary tape splices, cracked celluloid and impacted dirt from Smith's reels. Thirdly, the foundation was committed to conservation, producing colour-reversal internegatives of the restored films, and donating these to public institutions including the Donnell Media Center at the New York Public Library, and Kino Arsenal Institute for Experimental Film and Video in Berlin. Finally, The Plaster Foundation disseminated Smith's achievements, producing Smith's retrospective at P. S. 1 and four monographs. In 2004, a controversial court ruling found that Smith's estate legally belonged to his estranged sister, Susan Slater, due to the absence of a fully binding last will and testament. The court ruling enabled Barbara Gladstone to purchase Smith's estate for her influential New York gallery in 2008.

21 Rosalind E. Krauss, 'Two moments from the post-medium condition', *October* 116 (Spring 2006), pp. 55–62 (p. 56).

22 Ibid. p. 57.

23 Jack Smith, 'Letter to Heiner Ross' (1987), *Wait for Me at the Bottom of the Pool*, (pp. 149–50), p. 150.

24 Ehrenstein, pp. 20–1.

25 Ibid. p. 33. Emphasis in original.

26 John Guillory, *Cultural Capital: The Problem of Literary Canon Formation* (Chicago and London: University of Chicago Press, 1993), pp. 5–6.

27 Henry Louis Gates, Jr, *Loose Canons: Notes on the Culture Wars* (New York and Oxford: Oxford University Press, 1992), pp. 18–19.

28 Jenny Diski, *The Sixties* (London: Profile Books, 2009), pp. 3–7.

29 Alice Echols, *Shaky Ground: The Sixties and Its Aftershocks* (New York: Columbia University Press, 2002), p. 64.

30 J. Hoberman, 'The theatre of Jack Smith', *The Drama Review* 23.1 (March 1979): Autoperformance, pp. 3–12 (p. 9.)

31 Harold Bloom, *The Western Canon: The Books and School of the Ages* (London: Macmillan, 1995), p. 7.

32 Ibid. p. 39.

33 Stefan Brecht, *Queer Theatre* (Frankfurt am Main: Suhrkamp Verlag, 1978), pp. 18–20.

34 Cited in Gaby Rodgers, 'Casting by candlelight', *Soho Weekly News* (4 November 1976), p. 29.

35 Catherine Gallagher and Stephen Greenblatt, *Practicing New Historicism* (Chicago and London: University of Chicago Press, 2000), p. 13.

36 Jack Smith, 'The Astrology of a movie Scorpio' (1963), *Wait for Me at the Bottom of the Pool*, pp. 54–7 (p. 54).

37 Gates, pp. 39–40.

38 Smith, 'Astrology of a movie Scorpio', p. 56.

39 Jean Genet, *Our Lady of the Flowers*, trans. Bernard Frechtman (New York: Grove Press, 1963), p. 66.

40 Gregory Battcock, 'The New American Cinema', *Art and Literature: An International Quarterly* 8 (Spring 1966), pp. 95–110 (p. 110).

41 Jack Smith, 'What's underground about marshmallows?' (1981), *Wait for Me at the Bottom of the Pool*, pp. 137–43 (p. 137).

42 Jack Smith, '*Pink Flamingos* formulas in focus', *Village Voice* (19 July 1973), p. 69.

43 Jonas Mekas, *Movie Journal: The Rise of the New American Cinema 1959–1971* (New York: Macmillan, 1972), p. 98.

44 If Mekas took the legal fall for Smith's early political provocations (see chapter 3), Smith's performances and writings are nevertheless littered with – and to some extent predicated upon – references to his obsessive loathing of his unwelcome supporter. Labelling him 'Uncle Fishook', 'Artcrust', and a host of other ambiguously pejorative monikers, Smith understood Mekas's championing as a smear campaign. He felt Mekas was motivated by his own agenda, which was to represent Smith as an archetype of the New American Cinema, and viewed the obscenity case as part and parcel of Mekas's purportedly selfish advocacy. Smith never forgave him for apparently diminishing the power of *Flaming Creatures*, by turning it into cult artefact. This animosity condensed a set of key issues that fuelled Smith's artistic practice across three decades, constructing a convenient foil for a wider set of social and cultural frustrations, namely the twin disasters of prostituted creativity and lost artistic potential.

45 Mekas, *Movie Journal*, p. 299.

46 Jack Smith in Sylvère Lotringer, 'Uncle Fishook and the sacred baby poo poo of art' (Interview with Jack Smith, 1978), *Wait for Me at the Bottom of the Pool*, pp. 107–21 (p. 207).

47 Erica Jong, *The Devil at Large: On Henry Miller* (New York: Random House, 1993), p. 185.

48 Henry Miller, *Tropic of Cancer* (London: John Calder, 1963), p. 248.

49 Jack Smith, 'Statements, "ravings", and epigrams', *Wait for Me at the Bottom of the Pool*, pp. 151–5 (p. 154).

50 Hoberman, 'Jack Smith: Bagdada and lobsterrealism', *Wait for Me at the Bottom of the Pool*, pp. 14–23 (p. 18).

51 Lenny Bruce, *The Lenny Bruce Performance Film*, documentation of a performance at Basin Street West, San Francisco, August 1965.

52 Jack Smith, 'Red orchids' (1964), *Wait for Me at the Bottom of the Pool*, pp. 61–71 (p. 67).

53 Richard Meyer, *Outlaw Representation: Censorship and Homosexuality in Twentieth-Century Art* (Boston: Beacon Books, 2002), p. 161. Meyer's study does not extend, however, to key obscenity trials outside of the traditional history of art, and therefore does not acknowledge the censorship of films, novels and poetry in the same period.

54 Jack Smith, 'The adorable and pasty creatures: Journal notes on pornography' (1963–64), *Wait for Me at the Bottom of the Pool*, pp. 77–9 (p. 77).

55 Ibid.

56 Ibid.

57 Jack Smith, '*Pink Flamingos* formulas in focus', *Village Voice* (19 July 1973), p. 69.

58 Salvador Dalí, 'Re: *Flaming Creatures*', Letter from Arnold M. Grant Law Offices to Jonas Mekas (16 March 1964). Estate of Jack Smith, Gladstone Gallery, New York.

59 Alain Badiou, 'Theses on theater', *Handbook of Inaesthetics*, trans. Alberto Toscano (Stanford: Stanford University Press, 2005), pp. 72–7 (p. 75).

60 William Haver, *The Body of this Death: Historicity and Sociality in the Time of AIDS* (Stanford: Stanford University Press, 1996), p. 59.

61 Alain Badiou, *Ethics: An Essay on the Understanding of Evil*, trans. Peter Hallward (London and New York: Verso, 2001), p. 38.

62 Ibid. pp. 26–8.

63 Leo Bersani, 'Is there a gay art?', *Is the Rectum a Grave? And other Essays* (Chicago and London: University of Chicago Press), 2010, pp. 31–35 (p. 34).

64 Bruce Benderson, unpublished correspondence with the author, 26 November 2009.

65 David L. Eng with Judith Halberstam and José Esteban Muñoz, 'What's queer about queer studies now?', *Social Text* 84–5, 23.3–4 (2005), pp. 1–17 (pp. 1–2).

66 Ibid. p. 12.

67 Rowe, p. xv.

68 Winfried Menninghaus, *Disgust: Theory and History of a Strong Sensation*, trans. Howard Eiland and Joel Golb (Albany: State University of New York, 2003), p. 41.

69 Roger L. Conover, 'Introduction' in Mina Loy, *The Lost Lunar Baedeker* (Manchester: Carcanet, 1982), pp. xv–lxi (p. lxi).

Little triumphs of disaster: **1**
failure, boredom and excess

Time and history have proven that the sensitive souls among us have always been more vulnerable. (Cookie Mueller)[1]

In his loft performances, appearances in experimental films, or roaming the streets of New York's Lower East Side, Jack Smith was a formidable, unforgettable presence. Recognised for his formative influence on fellow artists, and notorious personality, 'Jack, the Madman of Grand Street' was eccentric, loud, abrasive and vehemently non-conformist.[2] J. Hoberman describes Smith as 'a legendary character'. 'And, even if he saw himself as plain "Donald Flamingo, just a local personality trying to make a living", he certainly didn't look or sound like anyone else,' he adds, stressing Smith's idiosyncratic mode of self-presentation as an embattled figure in the spaces of performance and everyday life.[3] The eccentricity and wildness of Smith's anti-heroic persona have often led commentators to read his practice as predominantly frivolous, campy, or obtuse. This tendency has perhaps precluded the possibility of teasing out the more demanding elements of his practice. His written and performed insights can be translucent, indistinct or baffling, but nevertheless open up new discursive spaces for reading the world. Smith distanced his own politics from the ethos upheld by gallery artists, and disapproved of institutional support or endorsement. In the wake of *Flaming Creatures* (1962–63) – its banning, seizure and what he saw as its gross critical misinterpretation – he performed his own persistent refusal to provide the market with a prized follow-up to this landmark work. Instead, he retrenched into far-flung reaches of creative experimentation, producing work that was exciting, challenging, yet perhaps unfathomable for market-oriented audiences.

This chapter focuses on the ways in which certain types of cultural practice disconcertingly evade documentation and historical analysis. The limit-text of cultural production aligns itself with other unwritten histories, such as the pedestrian rituals of pleasure, desire and survival. Smith incites unfamiliar modes of historical address that might take advantage of his marginality, which might not seek simply to insert him into dominant narratives. Instead,

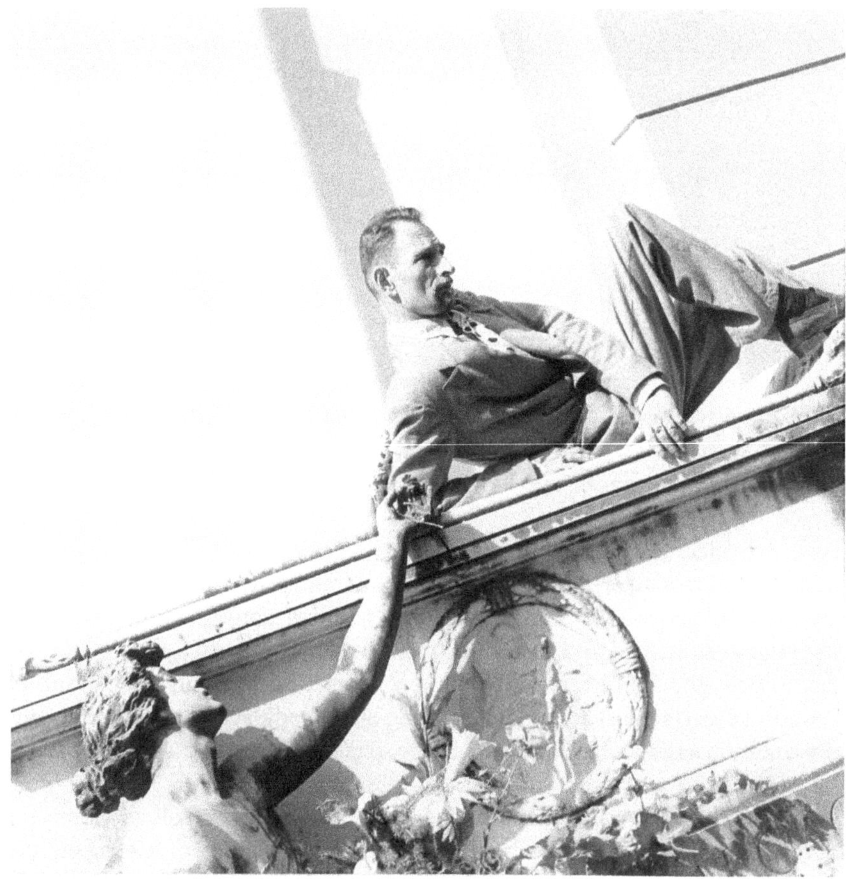

1.1   Jack Smith *Untitled* (1981).

other modes of critical attention can labour to expose the assumptions, standards and values that structure those histories. At once moronic and tragic, triumphant and vulnerable, bored and hysterical, Smith's work poses peculiar challenges to criticism. He writes that the 'romance' of a sensibility that tends towards disaster transcends the mere elaboration of style or 'technique': 'Not barely, but resoundingly, meaningfully, with magnificence, with the vigor that one exposed human being always has – and with failure.'[4] To court Smith, it seems, is to value and pursue minor experiences: failure, boredom, stupidity and self-indulgence. To disregard Smith for his espousal of these unpromising sensibilities is to decline his offer of counter-logics for the orchestration of art's possible work. On an affective level, the stakes are even higher, for to think Smith frivolous or worse is to miss the ethical imperative of his immersions in failure and crisis: the demand for concentration, for an orientation to sustain him in his faltering. Smith exploits the petty dramas of embarrass-ment, vicissitude, redundancy and boredom, staging the pedestrian trouble of a life lived under aspirations to the impossible. Such failures unveil a pathetic transparency in his performances, and elicit a distinctly perverse engagement – something like empathy – on the part of the active spectator.

Published in the *Village Voice*, Hoberman's obituary aptly describes the phenomenon that was Jack Smith: an artist who struggled against multiple adversities, from problems exclusive to makers of art to ubiquitous social challenges, and plagued throughout by imagined, near-pathological obstacles. 'I guess I thought Jack Smith would survive AIDS the way he survived poverty, landlords, neuroses, rip-offs, lack of recognition, life in New York, LSD, and the exploitation of *Flaming Creatures*,' Hoberman writes. He continues, 'it's amazing Jack lived as long as he did – but then virtually every one of his performances was about the impossibility of its own coming into existence.'[5] He emphasises Smith's 'fantastic pageantry' and underdog stamina, his mythical ability to sustain excess, hardship, exclusion, and exploitation. Along with other critics, Hoberman stressed Smith's profound importance for the New York underground, from the 1960s until his death in 1989. Dan Cameron notes that like other gay male artists on the Lower East Side such as Hélio Oiticica, Peter Hujar or Paul Thek, Smith typified the bohemian antipathy towards mainstream spaces, audiences and modes of exhibiting art, 'prefer-ring to enjoy a cultlike status within a much more rarefied group of friends and like-minded contemporaries.'[6] Smith's conspicuous placement between the historical undercurrents of visual culture, theatre and performance, and film enable an assessment of the ways histories of a period are written.

Moreover, rather than recuperate Smith into the given histories, I take advantage of his example to stage the minor tendencies that are obscured or ignored in dominant accounts of a period. In this chapter, these lesser themes include boredom, failure, excess and emotionality. My reading is informed by Catherine Gallagher and Stephen Greenblatt's account of how new historicist critiques track the flow of energies between margin and centre, high and low, rearticulating an entire range of cultural practices.[7] New historicism emerged from literary studies in the 1970s, especially in relation to Early Modern literary and theatrical cultures, encouraging a historical turn in scholarly accounts of texts and textual production. This development politicised scholarly practice, showing that the standard models for reading texts and contexts were ideolog-ically structured. After Marxist critique, on which new historicist scholarship draws, mainstream culture is understood as governed by the concerns of the ruling class, to the extent that dominant means of intellectual production are – in the words of Karl Marx – 'nothing more than the ideal expression of the dominant material relationships … grasped as ideas.'[8] By critiquing conserva-tive accounts of the writing of history and the pose of historical objectivity, historicist analysis refuses the myth of origins, linearity, and objectivity, and privileges genealogy and counter-memory as strategies for opening up contradictory readings of cultural production. This yearning for a more 'effective' history was influenced primarily by Marx, and also by Michel Foucault's turn to the radical historicism of Friedrich Nietzsche. In 'Nietzsche, Genealogy, History', Foucault writes,

> [To] follow the complex course of descent is to maintain passing events in their proper dispersion; it is to identify the accidents, the minute deviations … the errors, the false appraisals, and the faulty calculations that give birth to those things that continue to exist and have value for us; it is to discover that truth or being do not lie at the root of what we know and what we are, but the exteriority of accidents.[9]

After Foucault, cultural practice in any period can be understood as far more heterogeneous than scholarship tends to acknowledge. As Alan Sinfield argues, 'Closure is always inadequate. The complexity of the social formation and the multiaccentuality of language combine to produce an inevitable excess of meaning.'[10] As one in a series of 'turns', new historicism (and its sibling, cultural materialism, of which Sinfield is a key proponent) demonstrated the radical contingency of any mode of scholarly address. The emphasis on historicity suggested, in turn, that there are no disinterested or universal subject positions from which to read a work, an artist, or a culture. The study of performance has been profoundly influenced by this new awareness of historical specificity and critical particularity, especially in the ways that performance tends to encourage subjective critical practices that draw upon and contribute to the developments of feminism, lesbian and gay studies and critical race theory.

Smith enables a critique that privileges failure-bound tendencies, compromised affects and other marginal cultural logics. Moreover, by addressing his curious example, perhaps one moves closer to a historical method that more fully represents the diversity of a cultural moment, one replete with the enduring, the fabulous, the forgettable and the failed. In an expanded understanding of history and culture, 'major' works jostle for attention alongside a vastly expanded range of subcultural events, supplementary objects and counterhistorical voices. It is to these itinerant, volatile and elusive texts that I turn in this book. Conservative critics fear this strategy weakens the charge of the aesthetic object, while new historicism celebrates it as a powerful leveller, unsettling art's routine claims to uniqueness, transcendence, and unalienated labour. When art 'ceases to be a sacred, self-enclosed, and self-justifying miracle,' Gallagher and Greenblatt argue, 'its boundaries begin to seem less secure and it loses exclusive rights to the experience of wonder.'[11] An orientation to historicity troubles discursive limits and hierarchies, to discover a plurality of expressive possibilities within a historical archive that otherwise risks being represented as monolithic and exclusive. Against the singular, false clarity of the major work, the supplement speaks out in an obscure voice, gesturing to its own cryptic particularity at the threshold of history or culture.

The upper and lower limits of failure

In the work of Jack Smith, failure is a persistent condition for powerfully subjective responses. 'I'm sorry [but] I missed my after-breakfast nap today,' Smith announces in *I Was a Mekas Collaborator for the Lucky Landlord Underground* (1978), 'so today's adventure might not be quite [as] gung ho as necessary, but that might only make keener this sense of heightened expectation of some jungle habitat fatality.'[12] Performance studies has often asserted the necessity of failure, exploring the contradictory means by which the 'failed' object or event gives way to the production of theatrical effects, the experience of affect, or, simply, critical writing. For Sara Jane Bailes, failure in performance 'combines aspiration with resignation. It offers an ineradicably ambiguous and open-ended way of making sense, for it persists in the enactment of sustained irresolution.'[13] For Peggy Phelan, the centrality of failure to performance and its writing is symptomatic of malfunctions that condition the play of language. She writes that failure is an inevitable function of communication, rather than a problem that interrupts it. By extension, the foundering of the event of representation is less a 'scandal' than its formal apparatus, 'the constitutive force of the banal and normative theatre of the everyday'.[14] Bailes capitalises on Phelan's assumption of the centrality of failure to language and performance, arguing '[if] representation is always already the enactment of a failed promise, then to commit to that failure is to begin to perceive this condition as productive.'[15] Across the accounts given in performance studies, failure is staged as a surprisingly potent and nuanced logic of artistic and critical production.

Nicholas Ridout explains that it is the promise of failure that gives theatre and performance its social relevance. The vexed condition of the social as experienced in daily life is revealed in a performer's uncontrollable laughter (or 'corpsing'), other onstage descents into fiasco, or by embarrassment in the seats. For Ridout, the minor disasters that haunt theatre are 'capable of activating in an audience a feeling of our compromised, alienated participation in the political and economic relations that make us appear to be who we are'.[16] Performance is therefore not troubled or ruptured by the fact of failure. Rather, performance enacts, through its tendency towards disaster, the inevitability of semiotic and emotional trouble in our interactions with others, confirming Phelan's poststructuralist suspicion about the primacy of failure in social interactions. While Ridout entertains Bailes's argument about the peculiar productivity of the failed, he displaces its recuperative implications, arguing that the primacy of failure in performance 'is neither theatre's redemption, nor its undoing. Theatre', Ridout writes, 'does its own undoing'.[17] In Smith's performances, this undoing is initiated relentlessly, and sometimes apologetically, and paraded before the cringing bodies of his audience.

'"I am the Bubble Goddess", [Smith] intones, then pauses. "Tell me the truth. Has the camera started?" Close-up on his beads and beard and orange wraparound shades. "We can get better results if we are honest with each other, and you must tell me when the camera has started".'[18] From his loft shows after 1965 to late appearances in the work of other artists, such as this description of his performance in Ela Troyano's film *Bubble People* (1982), Smith's art is one that teeters at the edges of – and often plunges into – a state of failure. Moreover, Smith was not averse to acknowledging, and perversely revelling in, his own apparent failures as an artist. 'My lack of visibility was my fault', he laments in a published lecture. Nurturing his theme of self-sacrifice, he continues, 'I haven't been organized properly. I've made it idiotically easy for everyone to put me where I could be ignored … I was just squeezing art out of myself. I sacrificed my teeth, neglected my health.' Moreover, he admits, he 'didn't write those letters, didn't do any of that stuff', failures that perhaps ensured further obstacles to his delayed historical address.[19] Michael Moon describes how a sense of failure passed over from Smith's personality to his artistic practice, writing that he foregrounded, in each performance, 'the apparently inevitable judgment that it would be an unmitigated disaster, and behaved as if he … was in a state of imminent mental and emotional collapse'.[20] Rich in pity and shame, Smith's hysterical fixations are persistently choreographed around orchestrations of failure. José Esteban Muñoz argues that 'queer failure' in performance 'is not an aesthetic failure but, instead, a political refusal'.[21] In Smith's practice, failure manifests itself in at least two distinct ways that add texture to the idea of a political refusal of normative aesthetics.

At the lower limit of Smith's continuum of failure, he explores the apparent failure of performance inherent in performing what one does when one does almost nothing: turning up an hour late to his own performance, or standing in glacial stillness contemplating the shape of a pool of Blue Nile glitter – both to the enduring bafflement of his audiences. At the upper limit, as an agonist of sorts, Smith exploits failure in excess: the revelation of character in the moments when the unstable edifice of his maximalism slips, toppling over into unmanageability and crisis. This latter extreme is the human possibility made manifest in his 'Glamorous Rapture, schizophrenic delight, hopeless naiveté, and glittering technicolor trash!'[22] Both limits are derived from his adoration of Maria Montez, and from studying her failings in the art of convincing acting.

Boredom: a prelude to creativity

Central to the myth of Jack Smith are his excruciating delays, the arduous slowness of his performances, and obligatory impediments to their smooth running. Smith's magical invocations of dead celebrities and lost possibilities, and the pseudo-religious fervour of his creative inspiration, were governed in practice by frenzied overkill, but also by a relentless affirmation of tedium, slowness and boredom. In part, Smith's work asks what it is to be bored, or to be boring. What are the relationships between boredom, solitude, excess and desire, his work asks, and how is boredom located in the body of the bored witness? To an audience of art students, Smith explains,

> Making art was never supposed to be easy. It has to be *very* boring. How on earth do you think any masterpieces of the past were produced? In continuous fits of ecstasy? … No, it must be very, very boring … It must become not only boring, but really, *really*, deadly boring. And it's the person that can live with that boredom and continue to go on doing it that has the resources … to make art.[23]

Boredom as a condition of emotional life emerges as a series of readable movements in the body, manifesting itself in a litany of partially conscious gestures. This theatre of the bored body is a public marking of interior contortions, in stretches, heavy breathing, grumblings, and general agitation – visible in its pre-coded form in children moved to tears by the vertiginous frustrations of a seemingly infinite boredom. Like the physical manifestations of lust in the body's shameful blush, pounding heart and moist palms – as unspeakable longings rendered in relief – boredom's physical calls for stimulation betray the centrality of desire within its grip. For the psychoanalyst Adam Phillips, the banal crisis of a child's boredom stages the precarious realisation that she or he is waiting for an unknown something. The bored child waits for desire to present itself to an otherwise inquisitive attention. In adults, 'boredom returns us to the scene of inquiry, to the poverty of our curiosity, and the simple question, What does one want to do with one's time? What is a brief malaise for the child becomes for the adult a kind of muted risk.' The risk of boredom arises in the possibility that desire and action might not be forthcoming. A terminal crisis risks being installed in the temporary tedium of waiting. 'After all,' Phillips asks, 'who can wait for nothing?'[24]

Despite the mute recognition of the bored state as a hint of death within the experience of life, a flirtation with and mimicry of non-being, boredom also foreshadows the creative practices of everyday life. As Holden Caulfield's existential boredom in *The Catcher in the Rye* ushered forth a call to spiritual action for several generations of young readers, boredom bears the subject through the experience of tedium by engendering its own call to activity. Despite being perceived as the space of physical, mental and spiritual inaction, boredom is thus a paradoxical prelude to creativity. From this perspective, boredom signals a subjective crisis, but also functions as a declaration of the endurable, as a minor affect that may precipitate the movement towards cultural innovation. In its deictic function, boredom points the bored subject in the direction of creative inquiry, across a solitary, seemingly empty horizon. For example, Gregory Battcock ties boredom to the possibility of political action, enabling a heightened, unfamiliar engagement with art's work. In a response to films by Smith and Andy Warhol, Battcock's reading is contingent upon the political context of the 1960s, in which harassed apprehension opposes the contented pleasures of capitalist consumption:

> The use of film as a device to torment [the] audience may be understood as an intellectual challenge; certainly it forces an alert viewer to come to terms with art. This intensely human approach to art is, as usual, in direct opposition to the vast portion of the American culture which, for example, supports our ghastly involvement in Vietnam.[25]

For Battcock, Smith engenders creative involvement on the part of audiences, in contrast to the mechanisms by which commercial or mainstream culture encourages the sublimation of activity in uncomplicated and passive gratification.

Pierre Bourdieu has theorised this latter effect in a critique of the social compliance and political neutrality engineered by television, as a type of muted compliance that is distinct from my reading of boredom and frustration as preludes to creativity. For Bourdieu, television's production of pleasantly detached viewing is a technique for hidden censorship or symbolic violence, through the repetition of received ideas, and the exclusion or banalising of relevant or unpleasant information. These functions are enabled by television's high-speed transmission of information emptied of political complexity. 'Communication is instantaneous because, in a sense, it has not occurred,' he writes, 'or it only seems to have taken place. The exchange of commonplaces is communication with no content other than the fact of communication itself.'[26] For boredom to be a prelude to creativity, therefore, there needs to be a kernel of possibility that resides in the experience, that distinguishes it from the symbolic violence of an uncontented communication of emptiness. Smith's emphasis on the representation, exploitation and precipitation of boredom in performance gestures to his interest in a mode of artistic labour that does not shy from meagre affects and relatively unexamined experiences. He stages the political ramifications of the minor, in place of the grander, seemingly more authentic emotions produced in modernist art and culture, partly because they have been depoliticised in their incorporation into mainstream modes of cultural consumption.

Glamorous rapture

If Smith pursued failure in practices that tested the lower limits of performance – for example through boredom – his work also tested the potentiality of failure in excess, where performance topples over into a kind of volatile rapture. Photographic documents of Smith's performances show him and collaborators reading from scripts, and exploring performance material in an improvisational way. One such image shows Smith performing with Maria Antoinette of John Vaccaro's Play-House of the Ridiculous, as Noxzema, and Warhol superstar Tosh Carillo as 'a dead belly dancer' (see figure 1.2). The performance, *Brassieres of Atlantis* (1969) was subtitled 'A Lobster Moon Brassiere Pageant', and given six midnight showings at The Plaster Foundation of Atlantis. In the script, Smith specified the fantastical setting of the piece as 'Ten million B.C. in the prehistoric Brassiere Atlantis of the future. A volcano-pyramid provides the background of the pageant. In front of it and to the right is a spectacular pile of garbage.'[27] As Smith reads from a script, the belly dancer feigns exotic death and Noxzema looks on quizzically. 'Not only are [performers] kept from memorizing lines,' Smith states elsewhere, 'but they are encouraged to make a hash of it,' as though such a revelation could

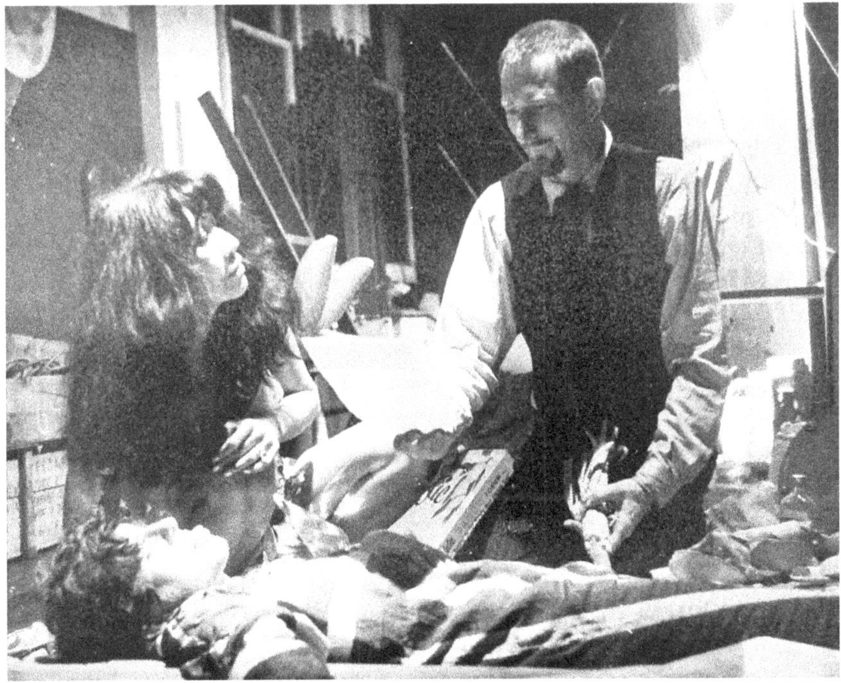

Jack Smith, *Untitled (Jack Smith in 'Brassieres of Atlantis')* (c. 1970).   **1.2**

be staged most powerfully in the moments where theatrical pretence tips over into excess, embarrassment and failure.[28]

In a treatise on acting, written as a press release for *Hamlet in the Rented World* (1971), Smith outlined a set of theses derived from watching Maria Montez movies from the 1940s. He defines his technique as 'actavistic', a neologism that lays emphasis on the atavistic, instinctive part of life that may exceed conventional acting. In his excess, Smith stages the revelation of the performer's fraught subjectivity as a 'Theatre of Lascivious Intrusion', pointing to maximalist elements that are conventionally suppressed in the theatre. Smith writes, 'We do have revolutionary ideas about acting and we are testing them on the world's most abused plays.'[29] Theatrical naturalism relies upon the suspension of disbelief in order to keep in play the unstable fictions of plot and character, suppressing the tendencies through which performers break out of character. However, like his contemporaries in the experimental theatre of New York, such as Julian Beck and Judith Malina's Living Theatre, Smith courted happy abuses of theatrical convention.

As Stefan Brecht recounts, in *Gas Stations of the Cross Religious Spectacle* (1971) and other pieces Smith 'read from a sheet … as awkwardly as possible, stumbling, inexpressively, dully, with an admonition not to engage in a fucking staring contest'. Repudiating the audience for actually watching the work, Smith challenges the conditions upon which theatrical spectatorship – and perhaps visual representation at large – is predicated. Moreover, Smith and his fellow performer 'part of the time acted serious, like carny-fakers, part of the time laughed, giggled or smiled as though "breaking up", making the put-on explicit … to escape the ridicule of identification with the act'.[30] Borne on the experience of these excesses, Smith contends, 'if an actor just stands on stage and thinks, the audience knows what he's thinking and it is more direct and clear than memorized lines. Ultimately, memorized speech is possibly the least dramatic thing that can happen on the stage'.[31] The celebration of a canon of works and the tendency towards honorific treatment of such texts in naturalism seemed to have drained potential innovations from the practice of theatre, Smith argued: 'actually a discovery could be made every day by anybody, if the Western [tradition] of having great plays to be memorized wasn't making mynah birds of us all'.[32] Smith urges himself and his collaborators to innovate, to channel failure, and to fall apart, in pursuit of a more thoroughly 'dramatic' quality in art.

The triangulation of theatre, art, and its others was a crucial discursive formation in the 1960s. The formalist art historian Michael Fried famously held that anti-theatrical, modernist art suspends its objecthood in favour of a 'presentational' sensibility, whereas 'incurably' theatrical art aspires to discover and project objecthood as such, by foregrounding its contingency upon the space and the spectator.[33] Smith's example complicates these art-historical assumptions about theatricality, not least for the way he demonstrates that Fried's account of the theatre was anachronistic. Stephen Bottoms notes that Fried underestimates the contemporary theatre's forgetting of physical context in the production of meaning.[34] Moreover, Smith suggests that his practice interrupts equivalences between performance and visual culture in other interesting ways. Fried's rhetoric upheld the anti-theatrical prejudice, using it to demean minimalist (or 'literalist') sculpture and its apparent apprehension of the viewer's particularised body. Fried was unconcerned with performance art or body art, which was nevertheless beginning to creep into galleries at the moment of his essay's publication in 1967. However, his critique of minimalism functions as a smokescreen for farther-reaching anxieties about art as a dignified convention whose autonomy was under attack from an expanded field of production. In the late 1960s, performance art and body art had begun to emphasise the centrality of corporeality to the production and reception of art. As Amelia Jones has argued, it was body art that forcefully called into play the particularity of its audiences.[35] In the late 1960s, works by Carolee Schneemann, Vito Acconci, Bruce Nauman and others were regularly programmed in galleries and other art spaces, requiring a new critical nomenclature that integrated performance into the changing artistic landscape. In the early 1960s, Smith's work prefigured this development, acknowledging the various means by which performance and visual culture addresses its audience.

Fried distinguished the authentic quality of art – its 'presentness' – from the corrupt objecthood of lower aesthetic forms. The presence inaugurated by minimalism 'is basically a theatrical effect or quality – a kind of *stage presence*'. In the course of his vilification of theatre and safeguarding of art, Fried presents 'theatricality' as a trans-historical fact, defined as the antithesis of the values held to be uniquely essential to artistic practice. Similarly, by protecting the humanistic underpinnings of the canon, he defends the anxious violability of value, truth and beauty. Invoking the time-honoured fantasy of art's finitude, Fried's offensive achieves a crescendo with the histrionic declaration, 'The success, even the survival, of the arts has come increasingly to depend on their ability to defeat theatre.'[36] His polemic sequestered many forms into this degraded landscape, including minimalism, theatre, and, implicitly, body art and performance art as emergent discursive formations. In his work, however, Smith usefully differentiates theatre from emergent practices. Smith argues that his technique 'would seem to be saying let's *not* pretend, [and] this could affect thinking', accounting for the specific conventions of theatre and theatricality in the moment of his own innovations.[37] Or, as he told Gerard Malanga, 'acting is only a substitute for a real person … If you are lucky enough to get a real person into your movies [then] acting won't be necessary, but real people usually end up in other walks of life'.[38]

Smith's aspiration to the radical foregrounding of the performer's subjectivity in performance is posited against theatre, despite Fried's assertion that the revelation of the individuated beholder is the *ne plus ultra* of theatrical representation. Smith's form 'rests on the premise that everybody already is a fine actor, that everybody in fact uses drama every moment of their lives, and that it's the fault of theatre that nothing of this can survive … because of the way that the drama is stamped out of everything on the stage', through the contemporary theatrical convention that disavows the rich subjective life of the performer.[39] Smith's celebration of the theatricality of everyday life wrenches theatre from its inverse relation to creativity and dignity – the false opposition set up by Fried – yet also suggests that in its contemporary formulation, theatre and performance have some way to go before its claim to political effects can be secured. In this, he anticipates yet troubles Jacques Rancière's statement that 'Every spectator is already an actor in her story', where performance is a third term in the circuit set up between performer, spectator, and the work. The theatre is anticipated as a form 'whose meaning is owned by no one, but which subsists between them, excluding any uniform transmission, any identity of cause and effect.'[40]

A rarely shown and little-known film, Smith's *Song For Rent* (1969) neatly enacts the relation between the failure to perform and the counterintuitive production of meaning as a third term, with the potential to produce enigmatic, affective responses in the viewer. Smith is rolled out onto the stage in his loft, to Kate Smith's rousing rendition of Irving Berlin's 'God Bless America', from the 1943 war movie, *This is the Army*. Elaborately bedraggled, Smith sits in a wooden wheelchair, posing as his alter ego, Rose Courtyard. Wearing a bright red fright wig and a papier-mâché mask over the lower part of her face, Rose waves to her audience, attempting to keep hold of the objects bundled in her arms – a scrapbook with a rubber chicken secreted in its pages, decorative corns-on-the-cob, an open can of Campbell's chicken gumbo soup, a heart-shaped chocolate box, and other improbable, evocative detritus. Each tumbles periodically to the floor, over inert legs bound in plastic bags and adhesive tape. The soundtrack is excessive in its own way – the patriotic fervour of Kate Smith's voice is emphasised by the song's harmonies, strings and horns. Against this florid backdrop, Jack Smith mugs and flusters. In the final shot of the film, the camera focuses on his gorgeously enamelled, glittering eye, which offers forth a streaming, solitary tear.

Responding to the work of Smith's protégé Robert Wilson, Craig Owens explores the anti-theatrical effect of foregrounding the performer–spectator relation, despite Fried's assertion that this relation is the modus operandi of theatre. Considering the development of performance after Bertolt Brecht and Antonin Artaud, Owens states, 'Theatrical representation establishes itself in that rift which it alone creates between the tangible *presence* of the performer

and that *absence* which is necessarily implicated in any concept of imitation or signification.'[41] In creating that gap, imitation – the 'theatrical signified' – questions and revitalises the relation between viewer and performer.
Owens notes that after Brechtian distance, which exaggerates the rupture,
and Artaud's cruelty, which annihilates it, performance no longer lays claim
to a theatrical signified located beyond the audience's individuated, bodily
encounter with the event. Owens's historical account of theatrical engagement decentres Fried's crude negation of theatricality. Whereas for Fried, the
emergent mode of engagement institutionalised by minimalism was merely
a vulgar solicitation, Owens understands the displacement of representation
and the privileging of embodied response as a formative assault upon the
subject. Wilson, and by extension Smith, 'does not intend to provoke articulate
response: rather, [his work] argues the poverty of those systems through which
such a response might be formed – primarily language, but also all processes
of logical thought according to which we … come to terms with experience'.[42]
While theatrical convention constructs the performer as a perpetual stand-
in, a mimetic placeholder for an absence located outside the space of representation, Smith refuses traditional theatricality by shifting from a referential
mode to an apparently immediate one. Or, as Owens writes, 'The performer
no longer stands for anything other than himself.'[43]

In Wilson's early works such as *The Life and Times of Sigmund Freud* (1969)
in which Smith performed, the collapse of fictional representation is partly
dependent on what Leo Bersani calls its 'monstrous' duration (each performance lasted 12 hours). For Bersani, the piece stages a confusing levelling of
its constituent parts. No particular moment in Smith's performance 'seemed
designed to be more dramatic or more significant than other moments', with
the result that the audience is 'unable to locate any salient moments at all
in a pleasingly or maddeningly drawn out movement or episode'.[44] Bersani
describes this excess as a perverse dwelling at the peripheries of cultural
practice that (like desire) refuses assimilation into the grand narratives of a
culture. For Smith, Wilson borrowed his techniques but quickly transformed
them into a 'mindless' practice, reconstructing himself as a 'behemoth …
armoured with the adoration of the Museum of Modern Art' – a damning
condemnation of Wilson's apparent assimilation into the mainstream of
artistic practice.[45] Drawing out the theatrical encounter to a barely unendur-
able duration, and locating it in a space that resists the conventions associated
with institutional theatre, Smith's more clearly resistant practice turned the
table on the false sense of immediacy that performance is often understood
to rely upon. The difficulty of watching causes the artificiality of the set-up to
return to the scene with a vengeance, confirming the fraught subjectivities of
the people involved, and revealing the highly mediated condition of the space
in which relationships are produced.

An unmistakeable aura of menace

While participating in postmodernism, Smith's attraction to a flawed glamour pervaded by minor affects and experiences perhaps reconstructs outmoded tropes, including emotionality, authenticity and autobiography. Refusing what David Hopkins calls the 'conceptual purity' of art in the 1960s – and an attendant 'puritan iconophobia' in its histories – Smith's contradictory investments conspired to efface the memory of his importance in the period.[46] His interests perhaps imply that, in the context of the 1960s, his artistic sensibility appears outré, a seemingly regressive position tied to 'expression', as an aesthetic category thrown out with the unfashionable practices of the previous decade. Harold Rosenberg observes that expressivity had become an embarrassing affectation by the end of the 1950s. Before the turn of the 1960s, 'the pervading acridity of the years immediately following the war brought on by memories of the war dead, the return of the mutilated, the images of the death camps, of Hiroshima, had been largely dissipated. The feeling of crisis was no longer pressing, no longer *popular*'.[47] This decline conformed neatly to the 'pedantic formalism' of Clement Greenberg, and his disciple Michael Fried. For Smith, however, distance from the years of war, and a national boom in economic security were not sufficient to assuage the sense of looming disaster – from the macro-political urgency of Cold War isolationism and the war in Vietnam, to the proximate threat of homophobic violence and marginalisation in the years before the decriminalisation of homosexuality.

Perhaps Smith is a *passéiste*, or else his emotionality anticipates the aggressive vitality of punk, which would explode onto the New York scene around 1974. In his emotionality, Smith may foreshadow 'the solipsism, the neurosis, the cosmetic rage' of punk, in Dick Hebdige's authoritative formulation.[48] Either way, in his emotional translation of social concerns into the stuff of artistic labour, Smith stages a tension between his progressive politics and an aesthetic allegiance to other historical times. His disappearance from the archive of 1960s art was perhaps consolidated by the privileged position of crisis in his work – the elaboration of subjective destitution in his performance style, and the attraction to emotive engagement in his audiences. By focusing on the disasters of theatrical representation, and signalling the trouble this poses for historicity, Smith stages a series of turns in the development of contemporary art after 1960 – some of which were perhaps fateful or less than fortuitous.

In an essay originally published in *Film Culture*, Jonas Mekas describes Smith's *Withdrawal from Orchid Lagoon* (1970), reading his plangent slowness amid the wreckage in explicitly melancholic terms. The performance is described as a lament for lost possibilities, staged in the detonated space of Smith's downtown loft. Leaving The Plaster Foundation of Atlantis in the early hours of the morning, 'when all the theatres had been closed and over ... all the ugly, banal, stupid theatres of the world', Mekas describes the performance as 'final burial rites' consisting of activities played out as if to mark, or mourn, 'the end of civilisation'. 'Only Jack Smith was still alive,' he writes, 'a madman, the high priest of the ironical burial grounds, administering last services here alone and by himself ... very painfully conscious of it all, the sadness himself, the essence of sadness himself.'[49] In more disinterested tones, Hoberman concurs, reading the work as a critical exploration of 'entropy, decay and collapse' – an experience tinted with 'an unmistakeable aura of menace'. Hoberman continues, 'The evocative music, the lateness of the hour, the slowness of the action, combined to create an elastic framework that ... encompassed all mishaps and delays – in fact, anything that happened – into the framework of Smith's art.'[50]

In a reading of the same event, Stefan Brecht describes the space of the Plaster Foundation of Atlantis as a graveyard, echoing Mekas's suggestive account of Smith's saintly lament in a morbid landscape. He remembers a 'minor votive screen in the background, with empty bottles in the niches. A toilet with junk in it, including a crippled, perhaps headless doll. Old, small Christmas trees with hardly any needles left. Feathers, wire netting, a string of colored lights.' Amid the desolation there is a ramshackle wooden, architectural structure. After several hours of painstakingly slow and deliberate performance by Smith, the audience is petitioned to help him complete the piece. Brecht and the two other remaining audience members take to the stage to assist Smith in his rite, burying the 'crippled' doll in a makeshift mausoleum of heavy wooden planks. He describes the procession as 'definitely squalid, a sentiment for orphanage among the merest means.'[51]

For this reason and beyond, Smith's performance work is considered the apotheosis of 'queer theatre' in Brecht's formulation. For Brecht, queer theatre is a minority cultural logic that participates, implicitly, in some elements of the Marxist definition of postmodernism. As such, queer theatre is 'derisive low comedy and burlesque',[52] mimicking Fredric Jameson's diagnosis of postmodern art as digesting low culture while repudiating modernist assumptions of depth. However, for Brecht, queer theatre refuses a key element of Jameson's analysis, namely his diagnosis of a dulling of grand emotions such as suffering and alienation – 'the waning of affect' – in favour of indifferent modalities. For Jameson, the high emotions are replaced by a proliferation of 'decorative' or other surface intimations, which find their archetypal representation in the 'gratuitous frivolity' of Warhol's serial canvases.[53] In Brecht's characterisation, queer theatre seems to refuse this dominant tendency by courting an 'heroic paradox', revelling in the low – camp excess, the tawdry glamour of old Hollywood, and other cultural detritus – while at the same time rehearsing its 'nuance of despair and dejection, as [though] the universal comedy were tragic'.[54] This orientation is 'queer' as the producer is seduced by 'the beauty possible under these conditions, the beauty of the low, the evil and the ridiculous', while painfully conscious of the 'artifice' of staging affect. For Jameson, postmodernism is a periodising hypothesis that comes about in the refusal of modernism; as such, postmodernism is characterised as repudiation, 'a virtual deconstruction of the very aesthetic of expression itself'.[55] As such, Smith courts the waning of affect by producing boredom, but also produces affectively charged performances, maintaining a difficult relation to the emergent scholarly discourse of postmodernism.

A video document called *Midnight at the Plaster Foundation* (1970) further demonstrates Smith's investment in negated, 'expressive' artistic labour. The twenty-minute document records a section from *Claptailism of Palmola Christmas Spectacle* (1970–71), and clearly shows how Smith staged his works not as presentations or collaborations, but as violent collisions with audience members and fellow performers.[56] Performed in his Grand Street loft, the piece starts with Smith railing at Abbe Stubenhaus, his assistant from 1967 to 1973, who stands against an exposed brick wall on the makeshift stage. 'Stay there and restore it!' Smith shouts, his authority undermined by his ambiguously gendered attire of a dark sweater with a white brassiere worn over the top. In the background, we hear scratchy emanations of kitsch 78s much like the collaged soundtrack to *Flaming Creatures*. Maddened by Stubenhaus' apparent incompetence, Smith continues to scream, needling him with angry directions: 'What the fuck are you doing? You're not concentrating!' Attempting to deliver a line according to Smith's clashing directions, the performer's inevitable failure is met with more enraged chastisement: 'You're not yelling! You're *still* not yelling!' Smith's loud voice has a grating, aggressive intonation. 'Follow one direction I give you!' When Stubenhaus does so, Smith savages him regardless: 'But the tape is already *ruined*! You didn't milk it! You didn't *dramatise* it!' Audience members entering from the street interrupt the hostile baiting, and are confused by the contradictory demands Smith channels through his assistant. 'It's free to come in,' he tells them, 'but you have to pay 50 cents'. Gesturing wildly, and shouting, Smith returns to directing the performer on stage, only to turn back to the audience members to remind them, loudly, 'If anyone wants to go to the bathroom, please ask for the Lucky Nun of Nua Nua and give her a dime, and she will show you where the bathroom is.' An appeal from a billboard sign in the background shouts, incongruously, 'AT EASE GENTLEMEN.'

Rustling the pages of his script, and attempting to concentrate with visible difficulty on the task at hand, Smith raises an imposing hand high and throws back his head. Pausing between each shouted word, and waving or pointing throughout, he proclaims, 'You. Can. Stare. Into. The. Eyes. Of.' The pronunciation of the last word trails away, wretchedly, and with it the hopes for syntax, sense, and resolute meaning in the broken line. He pauses for an uncomfortable length of time before continuing, emphatically: 'Now. Good. See. What. The. Future. Holds. In. The. Future. Of. Your. Dreams!' He glares at the script. His gestures are now careful, yet pained and baffled. He looks up to hold the audience in an uneasy stare, tensing his brow into a morose expression. Returning his eyes to the script, he slowly reads, 'You must admit you do have problems. You don't know all the answers. You need help. You. If you can't admit.' Smith turns the page to find he has lost his place. 'Well, that, uh.' He bites his finger and shakes his weary head. 'My mind just wandered off,' he confesses, looking bewildered and sad. Lamentably, he adds, 'Well, there was a reason for it. I started off on the wrong page.' His frustrations are played out on fellow performers in the lead-up to his own monologue, only to confound the audience with his own failure to complete the performance or pursue a planned structure for the work.

Looking into the lens of the Portapak, and checking the recording on a closed-circuit monitor, he directs the cameraman to pan. 'Please get the trees. Please. *Pleeeeease*.' Positioning a small, glittering, plastic Christmas tree on the stage, he points to it and implores, 'Put this in the middle of the screen.' Addressing the audience again, his apologetic tone is emboldened in an apparent attempt to salvage or at least continue the performance. He shouts, 'But you must wait your turn! Several people were trampled last week. But you must wait your turn! You must have your dimes ready. Remember to forget, not to forget to remember. No staring contests. You. Must. Have. Your. Dimes. Ready. Have your dimes ready!' The delivery is painfully slow, disordered. Fluctuating in tone and pitch, he interrupts his monologue with sighs and angry sounds. The sense is tragic, even pitiful. 'Your dimes, your dimes, *your dimes*!' He continues until the music changes, not fortuitously, in the midst of his repetitions, stopping the accumulations of intensity and command. His flow is lost, and he offers up a final, destitute 'your dimes'. It is an apologetic gesture of resignation, tinted with bathos by the rambunctious, happy soundtrack. Admonishing himself for the mess he has made of the show, he asks himself aloud, 'Everything is in the wrong place. How can you make so many wrong decisions?'

As Gerald Rabkin noted in a review of Smith's *The Secret of Rented Island* (1976) published in the *Soho Weekly News*:

> The work contains a manic intensity which despite its outrageous disregard [for] audience sensibility finally … transcends boredom. It is one thing to be bored by incompetence, another to have one's limits of tolerance tested … [Smith] perseveres and will not be deterred despite the pain for performers and audience. As always, he follows his own impulses, rewriting the theatrical rule as he goes, oblivious [to] what can or can't be done.[57]

As the reviewer explains, the audience members exposed to the two different methods may have a difficult job of distinguishing between a performer testing one's limits of cultural pleasure, and a genuinely tedious performance. The former culminates in the failure to produce consumer satisfaction, confounding an assumption about pleasure in the theatre. Boring performance, however, lacks the delivery of pleasurable sensations it aims to induce. 'The results, however, are dangerously similar,' Rabkin observes. This ambiguity registers in various responses to Smith's precarious exercise. In an open letter to the *Village Voice* in 1967, one complainant writes, 'There are beautiful accidents in art … but there are numberless ludicrous accidents, and Smith's aleatory fumblings are certainly ludicrous and … infinitely boring.'[58] Specifically, he lambasts the presentation of 'the unutterable tackiness of bathos-laden drag queens at an impoverished homemade ball', and other manifestations of 'the dreary dime-store altar of Jack Smith'. Also writing in the *Soho Weekly News*, Don Shewey protests of a later performance,

> This is not what I expected from [Jack Smith] … I expected charismatic perfor-
> mance, virtuosity, fantastic and distilled dementia … No such thing. Just a
> dreary, bitter melancholic with no zest, no fun, a fantastic record collection and
> a twisted mind, perched on the edge of the abyss and sifting through fragments
> of an ancient fantasy he can no longer communicate.[59]

The reviewer's response is not unexpected, for to demand 'virtuosity', 'zest' and other reasonable yet conservative requisites for inducing cultural pleasure is to underestimate the challenge Smith posed to those very conventions. Never-theless, the critic's pejorative account usefully signals the modes of self-presen-tation, including the foregrounding of slowness and boredom, which Smith channelled into an enduring performance practice. While formalist criticism asked that artists concern themselves exclusively with what is given in visual experience, Smith was busy plumbing the viscera of cultural and emotional life. Smith's performances carry out specific cultural work, while also calling into question the critical conditions in which it circulated. Shewey's response is particularly interesting as it demonstrates how the context responds to Smith's work, in aesthetic as well as cultural terms.

In performances such *Claptailism of Palmola Christmas Spectacle*, we see Smith apparently taking out his frustrations on his hapless aide and audience, as if unleashing angst-ridden accumulations of privation and outrage by baiting generous performers and paying publics alike. During the perfor-mance, dimes are mentioned as the fee to use the bathroom, but the refer-ence is removed from its original context. Repeated ad nauseam, its original meaning drains from the utterance and the phrasing takes on an emotive force. It no longer signifies a formal instruction, but evokes a sense of pathos that is bound up with its delivery, mimicking the frustration with which he demands concentration from Stubenhaus, and precise handling of the camera by the technician. As his entreaties to the audience lose their signification through repetition, similarly the invocation of personal experience loses its integrity as a delivery of autobiographical detail. On this relation between interactions with Smith in his personal life and their emergence as the material for performance, the artist Penny Arcade recalls,

> I had a huge fight with Jack because he wanted me to come and sew everyday … He was furious [when I refused] and told me I couldn't go to his performance, and so I go to the performance shrouded in coats, hiding in the back … and I'm sitting there frightened that he's going to see me … And he comes out and his first line is 'So you didn't want to sew!' … Everything that's going on in his life becomes the performance and it doesn't really matter what he's talking about because he's just using it as a way to alleviate the pressure and somehow travel through the anxiety … In the end, the whole thing was about survival, it wasn't about self-expression … The goal was to alleviate some pressure.[60]

The contrast, set out in this conversational account, between 'survival' and 'self-expression' marks a clear distance from the emphasis on form in early performance art, laying the onus on the integration of daily experience into the stuff of artistic practice. Smith emphasises the traumatic, interpersonal dynamics encountered in everyday life, staging performance as a putatively cathartic project, with the hope that it might (in Arcade's words) 'alleviate some pressure'.

However, relying on the memories and opinions of colleagues can be difficult, methodologically. As Jen Harvie argues, 'versions of the "same" memory' may serve different cultural functions: on the one hand, 'memories may validate identities that have been historically marginalised or oppressed', while, on the other hand, 'memories may … omit or forget features that trouble the image of itself a community is trying to create'.[61] As Warhol would recount, Smith used to say that he performed 'for the therapy, because he couldn't afford "professional help," and … wasn't it brave of him to take psychoanalysis in such a public way'.[62] Smith's statement is a joke at his own expense, a comic distancing from the 'expressive' function that haunts his practice. In the interview with Warhol's assistant, Gerard Malanga, Smith delivers a similar statement, wryly skewing a benign question about career prospects into a query into Smith's emotional stability. Malanga asks, 'What are your immediate plans?' 'Well,' Smith replies, 'I have got to try to pull myself together'.[63] Both quips signal two strata of his performance work that mark it as out of synch with the dominant codings of the period, namely his foregrounding of emotionality, and by extension, the similarly stigmatised quality of theatricality.

Smith's manic scapegoating of others fuelled his emotional life and art practices, and shaped the peculiar morality he modelled around them. As we have seen, these included collaborators, audiences, and peers. His friend Ronald Tavel writes,

> Jack berated fate all his life, acknowledged but indulged his madness, ate up his energies in poison-pen letters, poison telephone messages, and fury at every runaway hit and arts grant on the grapevine as his private, paranoiac mythology well implies … But, on sufficient occasion he saw and let us see those greedy crustaceans shuttle through the cerulean gaze of gilled Lamurians; he let us glimpse all that 'gilded' gimcrackery as the anima and animus of his antediluvian recall.[64]

Smith's paranoid antagonisms crucially extended to the paying public, whom he railed against for their 'pasty' adherence to convention – sexual, aesthetic and otherwise – and for their assumed conspiracy in the normalisation of culture. Smith's agonising procrastinations and interruptions were thus part of an assiduous refusal of conventional modes of aesthetic pleasure, denying that tepid satisfaction – ordinary, compliant consumption – on the part of the audience. As such, he administered cruel lessons to the passive consumers of dictated pleasures. This tendency constitutes a minor history in the development of performance and visual culture in the 1960s. While, after Fried, minimalism refigures the temporality of perception and the physicality of encounters with art, the minimalist object is incapable of prompting a fuller articulation of the conditions of subjection – of, that is, the subject's constitution and regulation by networks of power. Smith, however, would habitually torture his audiences with a seemingly interminable waiting for action, with the courting of abandonment at every step, alongside proclamations on how terribly everything was turning out on stage. Smith would suggest that by so doing, he concentrated the audience down to its most receptive core, weeding out any pasty normals to have wandered in off the street, and cultivating the lazy received habits of the underground hangers-on. Making no bones about exploiting the 'scum of Bagdad audience'[65] for his own experiential, ostensibly purgative purposes, he would end performances by forcibly ejecting the few remaining stragglers from his loft. No goodbye. No goodnight. No thanks for borrowed time. Smith would simply stand, turn his eyes to his weathered crowd, and with his nasal drawl rising to a caterwaul, he would scream, 'get out I don't need you – Get out … OUT!'[66]

Notes

1 Cookie Mueller, *Walking Through Clear Water in a Pool Painted Black* (New York: Semiotext(e), 1990), p. 148

2 Jonas Mekas, *Movie Journal: The Rise of the New American Cinema 1959–1971* (New York: Macmillan, 1972), p. 395.

3 J. Hoberman, 'Obituary: Jack Smith, 1932–89', *Village Voice* (3 October 1989), p. 74.

4　Jack Smith, 'The perfect filmic appositeness of Maria Montez' (1962), *Wait for Me at the Bottom of the Pool: The Writings of Jack Smith*, ed. J. Hoberman and Edward Leffingwell (New York and London: High Risk Books, 1997), pp. 25–35 (p. 30).

5　Hoberman, 'Obituary', p. 74.

6　Dan Cameron, 'It takes a village', *East Village USA* (New York: New Museum of Contemporary Art, 2005), pp. 41–64 (p. 43).

7　Catherine Gallagher and Stephen Greenblatt, *Practicing New Historicism* (Chicago and London: University of Chicago Press, 2000), pp. 10–11.

8　Karl Marx, 'Communism and history', *Selected Writings*, ed. David McLellan (Oxford: Oxford University Press, 1977), pp. 171–9 (p. 176).

9　Michel Foucault, 'Nietzsche, genealogy, history', *Language, Counter-Memory, Practice: Selected Essays and Interviews*, ed. Donald F. Bouchard (Ithaca: Cornell University Press, 1977), pp. 139–64 (p. 146).

10　Alan Sinfield, *Cultural Politics: Queer Readings* (London and New York: Routledge, 2005), pp. 36–7.

11　Gallagher and Greenblatt, p. 12.

12　Cited in Uzi Parnes, 'Pop performance: Four seminal influences: The work of Jack Smith, Tom Murrin – the Alien Comic, Ethyl Eichelberger, and the Split Britches Company', unpublished PhD thesis, New York University, p. 64.

13　Sara Jane Bailes, 'Some slow going: Considering Beckett and Goat Island', *Performance Research*, 12.1 (2007), pp. 35–49 (pp. 47–8).

14　Peggy Phelan, *Unmarked: The Politics of Performance* (London and New York: Routledge, 1994), p. 32.

15　Bailes, p. 48.

16　Nicholas Ridout, *Stage Fright, Animals, and Other Theatrical Problems* (Cambridge and New York: Cambridge University Press, 2006), pp. 93–4.

17　Ibid. p. 13.

18　C. Carr, *On Edge: Performance at the End of the Twentieth Century* (Middletown: Wesleyan University Press, 1993), p. 78.

19　Jack Smith, 'Remarks on art & the theater', *Historical Treasures*, ed. Ira Cohen (Madras and New York: Hanuman Books, 1990), pp. 111–36 (pp. 125–6)

20　Michael Moon, 'Flaming closets', *October* 51 (Winter 1989), pp. 19–54 (p. 50).

21　José Esteban Muñoz, *Cruising Utopia: The Then and There of Queer Futurity* (New York and London: New York University Press, 2009), p. 177.

22　Smith, 'The perfect filmic appositeness of Maria Montez', p. 26.

23　Jack Smith, 'Art and art history', cassette-tape, audio recording of a lecture by Smith during the Forbidden Film Festival (Funnel Experimental Film Theatre, 25–31 October 1984), Toronto.

24　Adam Phillips, *On Kissing, Tickling and Being Bored: Psychoanalytic Essays on the Unexamined Life* (London and Boston: Faber and Faber, 1993), p. 79.

25　Gregory Battcock, 'The new American cinema', *Art and Literature: An International Quarterly* 8 (Spring 1966), pp. 95–110 (p. 104).

26　Pierre Bourdieu, *On Television*, trans. Priscilla Parkhurst Ferguson (New York: New Press, 1996), pp. 25–9.

27　Jack Smith, *Drawings, Photographs and Ephemera from the Collection of Maria Antoinette and Edwin Ruda* (New York: Mitchell Algus Gallery, 2003), p. 18.

28 Jack Smith, 'Actavistic, action packed, action acting of PFA Hamlet, and the 1001 psychological jingoleanisms of prehistoric Rima-Puu' (1971), *Wait for Me at the Bottom of the Pool*, p. 166.

29 Ibid. pp. 165–6.

30 Stefan Brecht, *Queer Theatre* (Frankfurt am Main: Suhrkamp Verlag, 1978), p. 15.

31 Smith, 'Actavistic, action packed', p. 165.

32 Ibid. p. 167.

33 Michael Fried, 'Art and objecthood', *Art and Objecthood: Essays and Reviews* (Chicago and London: University of Chicago Press, 1998), pp. 148–72 (pp. 153–7).

34 Stephen J. Bottoms, *Playing Underground: A Critical History of the 1960s Off-Off-Broadway Movement* (Ann Arbor: University of Michigan Press, 2004), p. 127.

35 Amelia Jones, *Body Art / Performing the Subject* (Minneapolis and London: University of Minnesota Press, 1998), p. 15.

36 Fried, p. 163.

37 Smith, 'Actavistic, action packed', p. 165.

38 Gerard Malanga, 'Interview with Jack Smith', *Film Culture* 45 (Summer 1967), pp. 12–6 (p. 15). Emphasis in original.

39 Smith, 'Actavistic, action packed', p. 166.

40 Jacques Rancière, *The Emancipated Spectator* (London and New York: Verso, 2009), pp. 15–17.

41 Craig Owens, '*Einstein on the Beach*: The primacy of metaphor', *Beyond Recognition: Representation, Power, and Culture*, ed. Scott Bryson *et al.* (Berkeley, Los Angeles and London: University of California Press, 1992), pp. 3–15 (p. 3). Emphasis in original.

42 Ibid. p. 7.

43 Ibid. p. 4.

44 Leo Bersani, *A Future for Astyanax: Character and Desire in Literature* (London: Marion Boyars, 1978), p. 281.

45 Smith, 'Remarks on art & the theater', p. 111.

46 David Hopkins, *After Modern Art, 1945–2000* (Oxford and New York: Oxford University Press, 2000), p. 177.

47 Harold Rosenberg, *The Anxious Object* (Chicago and London: University of Chicago Press, 1966), p. 264. Emphasis in original.

48 Dick Hebdige, *Subculture: The Meaning of Style* (London and New York: Routledge, 1979), p. 28.

49 Mekas, *Movie Journal*, pp. 393–4.

50 Hoberman, 'The theatre of Jack Smith', p. 7.

51 Brecht, pp. 12–13.

52 Brecht, p. 9.

53 Fredric Jameson, *Postmodernism, or The Cultural Logic of Late Capitalism* (London and New York: Verso, 1991), pp. 10–11.

54 Brecht, p. 9.

55 Jameson, p. 11.

56 The performance is not named, but clearly resembles *Claptailism* as summarised in Brecht, pp. 13–14

57 Gerald Rabkin, 'Bizarre survivor: Review of *The Secret of Rented Island*, Collation Center', *Soho Weekly News* (11 November 1976), p. 28.

58 Martin Last, 'Flim-flam man: An open letter about Jonas Mekas', *Village Voice* (30 November 1967), p. 4.

59 Don Shewey, 'The flame goes out', *Soho Weekly News* (18 June 1980), p. 59.

60 Penny Arcade, unpublished interview with the author, New York (18 May 2005).

61 Jen Harvie, *Staging the UK* (Manchester and New York: Manchester University Press, 2005), p. 41.

62 Andy Warhol with Pat Hackett, *POPism: The Andy Warhol '60s* (New York and London: Harcourt Brace Jovanovich, 1980), p. 32.

63 Malanga, p. 16.

64 Ronald Tavel, 'Maria Montez: Anima of an antediluvian world', *Flaming Creature*, p. 100.

65 Jack Smith, 'Taboo of Jingola' (1972), *Wait for Me at the Bottom of the Pool*, pp. 102–5 (p. 102). Smith's 'Bagdad' refers to the fictionalised, poetic geography conjured in Golden Age capers like Raoul Walsh's *Thief of Bagdad* (1927).

66 Jack Smith, 'Rehearsal for the destruction of Atlantis' (1965), *Wait for Me at the Bottom of the Pool*, pp. 90–5 (p. 94).

2 'Beyond self-disappearance': Jack Smith and art's histories

Lady of the legless world I have refused to go beyond self-disappearance. (Gregory Corso)[1]

Despite the reformulation of art and theatre as expanded fields of production in the 1960s, Jack Smith troubles the accounts given of the work that matters in the period. Smith positioned himself on the margins of historical narration, exposing and confirming his own volatile position by relentlessly castigating the art establishment, including curators, gallerists, archivists, critics, artists, scholars and art college faculty. Smith was unwilling to accommodate his practice to the apparent needs of institutions or the marketplace, and fuelled this intractable situation by publicly decrying their enduring failure to acknowledge his achievements. This chapter focuses on Smith's practice in terms of his public statements on production, reception and criticism, towards a political account of the discourse on art and theatre, and a historiography of the minor. I ask how Smith's peculiar example allows us to think differently about critical discourse and its effect on the legacies of specific artists. According to Smith, processes of historical narration are categorically repressive, punitive, and delimiting of artistic labour and the dissemination of knowledge. In his own paranoid imagining of critical practice, he states:

> The art is sucked out of everyday life until it is dreary and ugly to pay for the latest useless jewel of technology which sucks up the imagination in place of art … It began [with] the newspapers … They were mixed in with the interests that were [invested] in the trivialization of the populace. Anyone not representing the viewpoint of cretin novelty consumerism was picked apart in their pages.

In a shift of terms from the general to the specific, Smith discusses his treatment at the hands of the art establishment. Lamenting his own abuse in the third person, the prime victim of the destruction of art is a beleaguered subcultural avenger:

> There was somebody called Jungle Jack who they tried to pick to death even tho he was only an artist … I think he saw art as ideas that should be distributed

to the public rather than some treasure that could be bought by an individual. Anyway him they attacked.[2]

Bearing Smith's polemical stance in mind, how can we read his work as necessarily falling wide of historical narration? How is his work a limit that throws light on – and perhaps interrupts – the critical discourses of art history and theatre studies?

This chapter approaches 'the artist' as a figural condition, proposing that Smith's artistic persona has been central to the ways in which he is represented (or otherwise) in accounts of art after 1960. I argue that through such an approach, the historical and cultural polyvocality of a period (namely, the 1960s) is rendered in further relief. Adrian Rifkin shows how history stages the artist as an object of discourse, articulating the implicitly theatrical relation between the persona and her or his work as a kind of mise en scène. Such stagings highlight the historical possibilities for an artist's emergence as an object of discourse, by placing them against the backdrop of ongoing politics of valuation. For Rifkin, this effect condenses the subjectivities of artist and historian; writing shades this historiographical relation with the 'artifice' often implied by theatrical staging.[3] Rifkin notes that the strategic construction of a specific artist will necessarily display symptoms of the culture that she or he is deemed to represent.

When this construction involves a canonical artist – in Rifkin's case, the nineteenth-century painter Jean-Auguste-Dominique Ingres – such a status is 'only secured at the risk of some strange and interesting violences being done to one or another of his possible histories, or stagings'.[4] Ingres' status was confirmed in the 1940s, when scholars argued his paintings symbolised the integrity of political identity at a time of conflicted national politics, underscoring a belief in truth and art at the heart of tradition, political imagination and the revolutionary spirit. The figural condition of the artist, as a 'fetish' securing colonial heritage, masculine privilege, national identity, or tourist economies (in the context of the state support of museums), reveals itself to be 'a utopian identity which is also a shelter from the shocks of history'.[5] I argue that the figure of the artist at the vital limits of a history reveals even more pressingly the assumptions and imperatives of critical practice.

In a late public statement entitled 'Remarks on art & the theater' (1989), Smith positioned himself as a casualty of the culture industry. The transcript is an aggressive attack on the vampirism of collectors, collaborators, curators and disciples. 'I've been influential … in the most god-awful way,' Smith railed, 'I mean I didn't want this, to create a race of prostitute drag queens. I'm ashamed of it.'[6] As his health failed him, Smith intensified his outrage at the economic inequalities between performer and audience, and the implied injustice of contributing to the development of art only to be relieved of any personal gain. Intermittently, Smith was afforded the critical respect that was due an artist of his experience. Yet Smith was frequently maddened by cursory reference to him as a 'seminal' artist: he would reply, acerbically, that his seminal status did not pay his rent. Courting this position, Smith states, 'I'm not going to stand on this stage in front of all these healthy yuppies … [and] entertain them [when] I'm the only one in the room without teeth.'[7] This propensity towards martyrdom registers in Judith Jerome's ironically understated description of Smith as 'more than a little self-sacrificial' in his public persona.[8] Designating 'criminality' as 'the only American response to real art', he rages, 'I was knocking myself out … to make this stuff. And I always assumed that people would see this and have pity on me and give me at least the support of not stealing from me. They didn't'.[9]

In a version republished in the catalogue for *In a Different Light* – a group show of queer art co-curated by Nayland Blake and others – the editors have edited out apparently offending passages. Elsewhere, Blake writes that the danger in trying to make art-historical sense of Smith is that 'he will be made to fit into the polite parody pantheon that American culture reserves for those it posthumously defangs'.[10] Despite this reservation, Smith's unpleasant statements about AIDS and community-based support are notably absent from the version reprinted in Blake's catalogue. In the earliest transcript, Smith states:

> This raging pest from the Gay Men's Health Crisis … has no right to just go to anybody's home, but she just came over. The poor creature, her life was so empty that she had to join the gay movement to pester AIDS victims in order to have a social life … I thought I had to entertain her, and she let me talk and chatter and rave on.[11]

Unsavoury as his reactions read, his embittered generalisations on community care and his use of the maligned phrase 'AIDS victims' are instances of the harsher side of Smith's insights into abuse, the state of gay culture, the myth of community, as well as other themes persistently grappled with in his expansive oeuvre. 'It's the inarticulate person that's going to cause you trouble, more than a malevolent or evil person', he adds, in an idiosyncratic take on Nietzsche's realisation that 'the harm of the good is the most calamitous of all harm.'[12] With an air of menace, Smith remarks of community support workers, 'I'll be ready for the next one.'[13]

By calling upon anecdotal and other representations of a subcultural icon like Smith, the historian may explore the historiographical implications of another mode of critical attention, honouring instead of apologising for Smith's 'defiant aesthetic lower-depthism'.[14] Remembering his friend, the novelist Gary Indiana writes,

> The world he lived in had a terrifying lack of boundaries. Within his hermetic realm Jack was utterly logical and everything he did made perfect sense.

Outside that magic kingdom he was quite mad, and though his madness was essentially benign it could wear you out. How far you would let Jack take you into his world was the same sort of scary challenge that drugs presented.[15]

Benign or otherwise, I hope to avoid obscuring the gaps and smoothing over the discrepancies in Smith's practice, pronouncements and critical-historical reception. Similarly, I am keen to avoid the lure to desexualise Smith, which strikes me as a salient characteristic of Mary Jordan's compelling documentary *Jack Smith and the Destruction of Atlantis* (2006). Alternative modes of reading enable a 'wilfully anachronistic projection', re-reading history against the grain of orthodoxy through a practice Rifkin calls 'ana-historesis'.[16] Characterised by his own polemical, outraged relation to the disciplinary formation of art history, Smith enables an ana-historesis of performance and visual culture in the 1960s.

The curious forgetting of Smith in current attempts to assess art of the 1960s is dependent, perhaps, on a restricted vision of the diversity of practices in the period. It also points to a scholarly simplification of the politics at work in marginal practices. Francis Frascina notes the fact that 'readings of art and theory since the 1960s have continued not only to single out a conventional canon and traditional categories but also to minimise a dialectical relationship between culture and politics'.[17] The slide from view of a host of important artists is a symptom of this trend.

In terms of Smith, the combination of several distinctive tendencies present him as a problematic figure for the fluid techniques of art-historical rendering: his unapologetic queerness; his vociferous critiques of art and art history; his rejection of finite and commodifiable forms of production – of 'some treasure that could be bought';[18] and his generally inappropriate politics. Blake argues that the art-historical denial of Smith's politics exposes the discourse on the 1960s as functioning to trivialise art itself, complicit as it may well be with capitalism's disregard for the ethical.[19] So, by privileging the narratives that give historical currency only to that art which evacuates social or political efficacy from its own rationales of production, the authorised histories of the 1960s cordon off politically indeterminate and culturally uncontainable modes of artistic labour. Blake observes that 'Smith's activities left him in the paradoxical position of exerting great influence on a cultural scene that he was largely written out of'.[20] Smith was not oblivious to this insider/outsider contradiction. As Smith wrote of his own historical legacy, 'I take life's offerings 10 years 20 years too late never quite on time to stubbornly hold out against … obvious truths … until I see their peculiar meaning for me … I accept all missing out if it means keeping my crazy honesty.'[21]

Performance and visual culture

Smith endured a challenging relation to histories of performance, partly conditioned by the marginal discursive position of performance in major histories of art. Shannon Jackson has argued that the disciplinary transformations of art history into visual culture studies, and theatre studies into performance studies, retain different models of heterogeneity and interdisciplinarity, because of the crucially antagonistic place of theatre in these two reformulations. While, in the 1960s, theatre was beginning to be seen as conservative or 'stodgy' for performance studies, it was perceived as 'subversive' for art in the same moment. Theatre could not aspire to the medium-specificity that modernist art criticism had privileged, and was therefore seen as a form of dissidence, even before theatre's postmodern turn. 'Performance from this history,' Jackson writes, 'looks less like its own specific medium than the means by which visual media undo their specificity. From this view, performance is not so much a parallel field to visual culture, but a mechanism by which art history begins to cultivate the sensibilities of visual culture.'[22] Jackson observes a series of parallels, discontinuities and contradictions between the study of art and performance after 1960, such that the dominant histories or disciplines are not dominant in the same way or with the same effects.

In critical surveys of 1960s art, the history of performance is neatly triangulated around three sites: Happenings, the Judson Dance Theater, and Fluxus. The history that poses Jackson Pollock's drip-painting practice as the origin for Happenings constitutes part of a well-established narrative of 1960s performance. Certain problematic elements are necessarily downplayed in this narrative fantasy, such as the individualistic sentiments, gritty sensibility, and avowed theatricality of Happenings, despite the angst mythologised in Pollock's artistic persona. Allan Kaprow's mythic *18 Happenings in 6 Parts* (1959) pointed towards a paradigm shift, from the hegemony of academic painting to a seemingly new and unprecedented type of work. Reading Pollock's canvases as a theatrical environment created through the painter's expansive gestures, Kaprow specified the effect on the viewer as one of assault. Envisaging the rejection of painted canvases for temporal manipulations of objects, Kaprow sanctioned the use of furniture, food, neon lights, smoke, water, movies and other unfamiliar materials, towards an emergent medium. He writes, 'Not satisfied with the suggestion through paint of our other senses, we shall … disclose entirely unheard-of happenings and events, found in garbage cans, police files, hotel lobbies; seen in store windows and on the streets; and sensed in dreams and horrible accidents.'[23] Intriguingly, Smith is rarely considered in terms of Happenings as a crucial development in performance-oriented art of the 1960s, despite his use of similar materials and affects.

The study of theatre and performance has acknowledged the centrality of emotion, affect, narrative and other qualities deemed unfashionable in art history. Moreover, their centrality to art of the 1960s has persisted despite calls to rethink pop art and other major tendencies as straightforwardly cool and commodified. For example, Thomas Crow reads Warhol's paintings of electric chairs in terms of the contemporary agitation over the execution of the writer Caryl Chessman in 1960, and thus as 'almost expressionist' in their attempt to register 'the open sores in American political life'.[24] Similarly, Claes Oldenburg's attraction to ugliness and decay found early expression in his environments, including *Store* (1961), a Lower East Side shop filled with oversized, hand-painted plaster replicas of commercial objects, including mannequins and delicatessen cakes. The project presented life as happened upon – in shop windows, for example – in place of the attempt to transmute experience into abstraction. 'If you're a sensitive person', Oldenburg writes, 'and you live in the city, and you want to face the city and not escape from it you just have to come to grips … with the landscape of the city, with the dirt of the city, and [its] accidental possibilities.'[25] However, within the development of pop art as a critical logic, the persistence of existentialist tropes is understood to be less important than the emphasis on superficiality, expressive indifference and serial production. Oldenburg's rather monstrous sculptures are conveniently rewritten as banal, Warholian paeans to booming post-war commerce.

Judson Dance Theater is central to narratives of performance in the 1960s. It has been mythologised by Sally Banes as a 'heroic, egalitarian collective' that confirms the history of the 1960s as a period of fortifying dissent, emerging from an artistically inclined political left.[26] 'In any full account of the period,' Crow writes in his survey of 1960s art, 'the impact of [Judson's] reflective, proto-feminist variant of avant-gardism needs to be set against the far more prominent example offered by Warhol's contemporaneous factory,' tying the collaborative principles of the new dance to the communal labour Warhol engineered to produce his celebrated screen prints.[27] Similarly, Fluxus artists including George Brecht, George Maciunas, Yoko Ono and Nam June Paik, are lent critical authority for their refusal of the object in favour of the event, as a critique of formal autonomy and capitalist modes of distribution that govern the art market. Notably, David Hopkins establishes a seemingly untroubled correlation between Fluxus and Happenings, in terms of their intermedial pledges, refusals of commercial value, and attempts to close the gap between art and life, despite the vigorous ideological disagreements between the two camps.[28] The coincidence of performance with painting and sculpture in these dynamics has resulted in the concomitant art-historical privileging not of performance and its position as an art form, but of the co-operative performance practices signified by Judson Dance Theater, Fluxus and Happenings. In the American context, other artists whose performance work is immediately valued are almost exclusively those who rejected medium-specificity as a defining aspect of their practice, permitting assimilation through other work: Robert Rauschenberg, Robert Morris, Joseph Beuys or Bruce Nauman. In Daniel Wheeler's survey of post-war art, for example, Rauschenberg's are imaginatively described as 'some of the first performance pieces created by a visual artist', and codified as one more instance of his being 'on the prowl for bigger canvases and a broader palette'.[29] Thus, critically well-received practitioners working solely in performance or other time-based media in the 1960s are those artists whose practices support the mobilisations of a dominant critical apparatus, such as Neo-Dada, pop or minimalism.

A crust like Warhol

For Walter Benjamin, the 'cultural treasures' that endure historical memory 'owe their existence not only to the efforts of the great minds and talents who have created them, but also to the anonymous toil of their contemporaries'.[30] His statement acknowledges the value of the major artists of a period, yet asserts a reciprocal relation between this status and an expanded series of contemporary individuals and objects of study. Politically invested scholarship must invest itself in the latter, for as Benjamin asserts, 'nothing that has ever happened should be regarded as lost for history'.[31] If representative narratives of the 1960s are contingent upon the messy, irrational, failure-bound practices left unfigured in authoritative accounts, a paramount example is Andy Warhol's early dependency upon Smith's formative example. In the first half of the 1960s, the Lower East Side was the crucible of avant-garde practice in New York, home to thriving experimental film, performance and theatre scenes. Smith's influence over experimental artists on the Lower East Side was confirmed by his unorthodox appearance and eccentric personality, at a historical moment when the 'superstar' was a nascent cultural phenomenon that could inspire and confirm one's influence. A friend of Smith's in the 1960s, the poet Rene Ricard confirms the strict polarisation of interest among those living and making work on the Lower East Side. 'It's strange to look back and remember how in the early '60s film aesthetics seemed so neatly split between Warhol and Jack Smith,' he writes. 'The apparent antithesis made an entire and rich culture … And at one point they were equally famous.'[32]

In the New York underground, Warhol's early celebrity was dependent on the success of his films and the notoriety of his superstar entourage. In the early 1960s, Warhol was perceived as shadowing Smith's achievements in these areas, as it was his example as a filmmaker that Warhol happily admitted to following in his own film work. In 1966, when asked which filmmaker he admired most, Warhol replied, 'Jaaaacck Smiiiittttth … When I was little, I always … thought he was my best director … I mean, just the only person I would ever try to copy … and now since I'm grown up, I just think he makes the best movies.'[33] Smith performed in a number of Warhol's films, starring in the unfinished epic, *Batman Dracula* (1964), and sat for a striking, underexposed screen test in 1965. Smith's entourage of 'creatures' patently set the model for Warhol's Factory, and key creatures including Mario Montez, Beverly Grant, Marian Zazeela, Tosh Carillo, Francis Francine and Joel Markman would leave Smith's Cinemaroc Studios to take up temporary residence in Warhol's silver haven.

Lawrence Rinder notes that the 'superstar' was Smith's innovation, as was 'the very idea of Warhol's Factory – an avant-garde, Bohemian simulacrum of the traditional Hollywood studio, consisting of an ensemble of essentially replaceable stars and starlets presided over by a charismatic auteur'.[34] Asked by Glenn O'Brien, 'Who invented the word *superstar*?' Warhol replies, 'I think it was Jack Smith.' 'And who were the first superstars?' 'They were all Jack Smith stars.'[35] Warhol's *Camp* (1965) acts as an extended dramatisation of this influence (see figure 2.1). A series of vaudeville-style acts filmed on 16 mm in the Factory, *Camp* includes a vignette by Montez in a plaid housedress, who shakes it 'like jelly on a plate' to *I Wish I Could Shimmy Like My Sister Kate*. Looking dapper, Smith hovers in the background, chatting to Carillo and refusing to take his place in the evening's superstar turns, until a slow and mesmerising drift to a Lucite-fronted Art Deco cabinet, out of which Smith retrieves a *Batman* comic, in reference to Warhol's unfinished film. Acknowledging the importance of the performers over and above the quality of the filmmaking, Warhol delighted in *Camp*'s status as 'a bad movie'. 'The technical work is terrible,' he added, 'but the people are so fantastic.'[36]

Warhol accompanied Smith on an excursion to film *Normal Love* in 1963, during which he filmed his first movie, a newsreel of Smith at work. In *POPism* Warhol remembers, 'Jack Smith was filming a lot … and I picked something up from him for my own movies – the way he used anyone who happened to be around that day, and also how he just kept shooting until the actors got bored'.[37] Indeed, this would become the defining characteristic of Warhol's practice as a filmmaker, and, moreover, the crux of his public persona. Later in his memoir, he writes, 'the more you look at the same exact thing, the more the meaning goes away, and the better and emptier you feel', suggesting a continuum between the techniques he learnt from Smith and the style he would nurture in his self-presentation.[38] Writing about the 1960s, Warhol outlines his debt to Smith as a precursor, and sketches the crucial modification he applied to Smith's example – as an exploiter of cultivated boredom and of personalities that gravitated towards him – to arrive at his own persona of evacuated subjectivity. Michael Moon notes that Smith's idiosyncratic personality, as presented in writings and performance, 'fits the alternately glacially ironic and self-distancing but also aggressively "deviant" and exhibitionistic milieu of New York pop culture of the '60s, a culture that first centred around Smith but soon shifted to Warhol.'[39] However, Smith's cack-handed vacancy

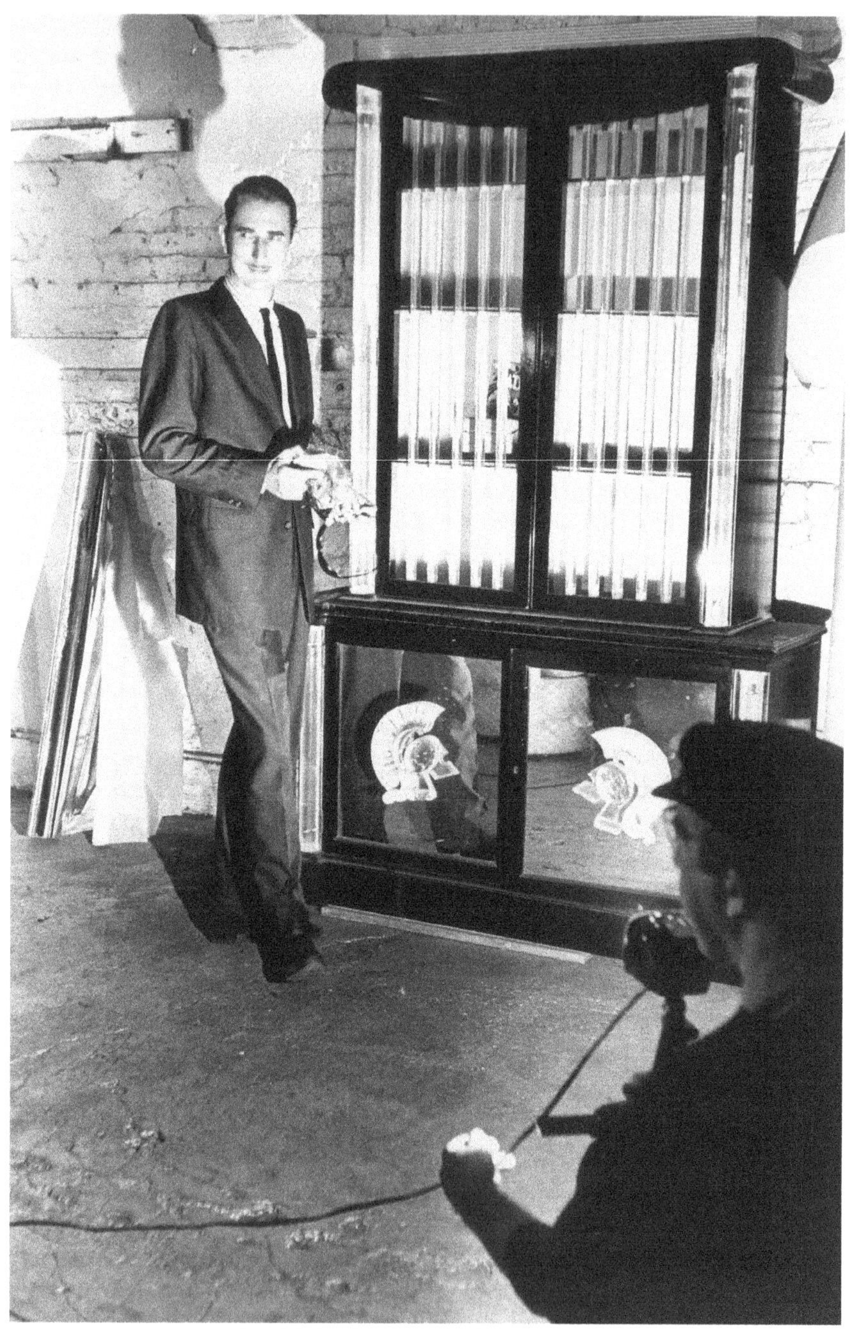

2.1 Fred W. McDarrah, *Filming 'Camp' at the Factory* (1965).

and aesthetic volatility are borrowed and ironicised in their mutation into Warholian passivity. This appropriation and transformation marks the explicit contrast between Warhol's machine-like, ice-cool candour, and the extravagant, half-crazed glamour of Jack Smith.

The stark difference in attitudes is one reason why the two figures would have greatly different receptions by the art market. This informed Smith's intense dislike of Warhol, whom he described as a 'crust', referencing the defining horror of 'crustaceousness' institutionalised by minimalism and pop art.[40] Elsewhere Smith states, 'They [gallerists and collectors] just threw money at Warhol because he conformed exactly to what Americans want', namely acquiescence to high capitalism and the market economy.[41] In contrast to Warhol's acquiescence, Smith states, 'I don't mind a certain amount of trouble'. The 'pasty cheerfulness of capitalism … can only produce a crust like Warhol,' he adds. 'I don't want to be too happy'.[42]

While Warhol's *Death and Disaster* series (1962–64) presented a disturbing vision of American life and its ways of death, his early intimations of political and cultural destitution were substituted for more palatable imagery after 1964, in a move greeted with gallery approval and marked commercial gain. Warhol's success was also contingent upon a shading of his homosexual visibility; as Richard Meyer argues, 'Warhol's fixation on celebrity and popular culture, for example, became ever more central to the subject matter of his early-1960s art. His homosexuality, on the other hand, was displaced from … the register of the explicit to that of the encoded.'[43] As a result, Warhol resorted to a kind of double-identity, between his friendlier painting practice and the psychosexual theatre of his Factory film work. While Warhol's film and performance-related work remained relatively indigestible in the gallery market, works such as *Blowjob* (1963) and *Chelsea Girls* (1966) nevertheless assured him his growing underground reputation. Having secured his priority in the market Warhol partially returned to uncomfortable content in painting in the 1970s, in the *Oxidation Paintings* (1978) made by urinating on metallic pigment, and the explicit screen prints, *Sex Parts* (1978). However as Jennifer Doyle argues, his enduring fascination with pornography and other troublesome tendencies are marginalised or ignored in museum surveys of his work.[44] This is most likely an extension of the *cordon sanitaire* Warhol erected around his sexuality identity. Gavin Butt shows that as Warhol began to take control of his public persona, from 'abject swish' to a more acceptable, commodified projection, he produced 'a critically sanctioned "Warhol" that depended on the forgetting of his earlier, more recognisable homosexuality.[45] Death, sexuality and experimentation became curiously *avant* to Warhol's own avant-garde project, marking a kind of cultural outpost where Smith's cultural disturbances were to be more unmanageably located.

Smith's denunciations of Warhol were the basis for a whole range of imaginative terms for describing the decline of art and his own disastrous placement in its histories. In a journal entry in the early 1960s, Smith wrote of his recurrent critical hallucination, admonishing what he feared to be the inhibitive, regulatory agenda of the art establishment, namely their project to 'resurrect the tired aging corny outmoded moldy hateful fuck idea … [of] a world's accretion of centuries and centuries of moldiness'.[46] Asked to define his use of the term, Smith stated in an interview, 'Moldy is something that is very lush and gaudy and colourful and primitive and a bit old, but it could also be very new and have all those qualities … like fans or feathers … or color combinations [that] create a sort of moldy effect like orange and pink.'[47] Plaster and crusts are themes that run through his writings about the state of art and cultural history. 'Crust' tends to denote the normative standards of artistic production denounced by Smith and epitomised in Warhol's ambivalence. It describes a compromised superficiality that Smith ostentatiously described himself as falling prey to – a hypocrisy pardoned by his own gratuitous nonsensicality, and enduring abandonment to 'personal tweakiness'.[48] 'Pasty' concepts, upheld by the tradition of polish and crust, include the cult of artistic competence, the privileging of rationality in art, and narrative logic. Pasty artists allowed their work to be translated into critical sense, in order to uphold the vampiric status of 'critichood'.[49]

Smith stages these inventions and slippages in a vivid response to a 1966 exhibition by Walter de Maria. In his cryptic though favourable review, Smith rehearses the idiosyncratic aesthetic mythology that he would nurture throughout his career. The review implicates the contemporary move towards a polished aesthetic within a strangely sophisticated account of objecthood, framed in terms of philosophical and metaphysical notions of the body. Minimalism is decried as the institutionalisation of a cult of the 'crustaceous', and demonised as representing a host of repressive, even terrifying disciplinary conventions. His review suggests sculptures de Maria was exhibiting at the time, for example *Museum Piece* (1966), a highly polished steel object in the form of a swastika, with hollow tracks along its arms, through which a large steel ball could be rolled. The shiny surfaces and rectilinear forms of *Museum Piece* reference the polish and weight of minimalist sculptures by contemporaries such as Donald Judd. If Judd and de Maria anticipated the viewer to engage in a physical way with their works, the collision between childish play and the imposing symbol of Nazism demanded a careful negotiation of one's participation, unlike the more clearly convivial engagement that the minimalist cubes and other objects might have invited.

Museum Piece also suggests the semiotic slippage that the swastika underwent in its transformation from an ancient Jain and Hindu sign to the stigmatised totem of the Third Reich. Smith suggests a complicated relation to the Christian use of symbols. In paranoid displacements of authority from art institutions to the Church to the ubiquitous political intrusions of capitalism, Smith states that in foregrounding the crucifix as a sculptural object over and beyond the suffering body, the state naturalised an aesthetic of 'dry-cleaning fetishism, and the object became more and more plastered in response to the demands of liquor manufacturers and their henchmen the courts'.[50] Stripping the wounded body of Christ from the cross to leave the enduring symbol of the cruciform structure, the Church inaugurated a distillation of sculptural form that led to the 'specific objects' of the minimalists. The cruciform shape represents an overlaying of two rectangles, and Smith defines the rectangle elsewhere as 'the preferred shape of capitalism' (evidenced in its centrality to architecture, which supports the prime evil of 'landlordism').[51] He continues that a historical accumulation of 'crusts' – from the symbolic forms of Christianity to the mounting 'polish' privileged in the art world – has worked to 'inundate my sensibilities and set obstacles to artistic development'. Smith set out to combat this with his own brand of excessive representation, 'a florid peak of wealthy marination, such as I will have to chip at all my life for the sake of my soul'.[52] For Smith, polish amounts to a state of optimum finish, implying a type of finiteness that sits at a tangent to the open-ended, anarchic, 'florid' quality that he strove for in his films, performances and writings. If de Maria's *Museum Piece* inverted the minimalist concealment of subjectivity, Smith celebrates and borrows this strategy. Throughout his practice, Smith dresses the labour of artistic production in a permanent state of crisis without resolution.

Smith was fully aware of the discrepancies between his practice and the prevailing codes that were being developed and formalised in the period. Despite traversing proximate terrains, Warhol was able to maintain a workable relation between experimental practice and mainstream success. Smith lacked the ironic emotional detachment and resolute careerism of the new breed of young New York artists, and reference to his work almost never occurs in authoritative surveys of visual culture in the period. Confidently defining 'The Sensibility of the Sixties', Irving Sandler noted a decided shift from the 'hot, dirty, hand-made, direct-from-the-self' look of the 1950s to the 'cool, clean, mechanistic, and distanced-from-the-self' look of the following decade.[53] The cusp delineated by Sandler, 1958–62 is also the period of the crystallisation of Smith's practice, from his early ventures in single-reel film to the visceral onslaught and garrulous sexuality of *Flaming Creatures*. With the arrival of Frank Stella's work in the late 1950s, art was seen as capable of rejecting illogic, illusion and allusion for the priority of symmetry, impersonality and repetition. Along with Robert Rauschenberg and Jasper Johns, Stella's work was seen as uncompromisingly at odds with the intuitive improvisations of Jackson Pollock and Willem de Kooning, clearing a path for pop art and minimalism in the early 1960s. According to Sandler's narrative, in the 1960s artists rejected the expressive concerns of the 1950s with the new agenda of an anti-subjective, anti-expressionist practice.[54] This account privileged the palpable calm of John Cage's Zen Buddhism, the programmatic logics of R. Buckminster Fuller, and the vacant cool of Warhol's feigned prostitution to the allure of commodity and celebrity fetishism. In lurid contrast, with his battalion of 'pasty cutie pie chorus creatures sprawled screaming on the layers of [a] 12 foot high cake,' Smith was anything but 'cool.'[55] I argue that his vociferous restating of a tortured relation to art and art history must be taken into account in considering the historical placement of Smith's work.

The thrill of vampirism

In October 1984, Smith arrived in Toronto to show *Flaming Creatures* and other films, and give an accompanying artist's lecture at the Forbidden Film Festival, a weeklong event organised at The Funnel Experimental Film Theatre. An organiser remembered his surprise when Smith arrived without any films, to which Smith retorted, 'Why would you need the moldy films when you've got me?'[56] Instead, Smith presented a performance, *Brassieres of Uranus*, which included several collaborators including musicians, actors perched on ladders, a small exotically garbed child and a brassiere-making workshop. The show was photographed by Edie Steiner, and documented as a short film by Midi Onodera. A separate photo-shoot was organised by Steiner in her studio.

Titled 'Art and art history', the lecture he presented is an excellent summary of Smith's unflinching views on the relation between the work of artists and the prominence attributed to successive generations by academics, critics and curators. The audio recording is an important, unacknowledged document that can be read alongside several of Smith's other idiosyncratic, late proclamations on the machinations of art history. Discussed earlier, 'Remarks on art & the theater' was presented as part of a discussion with William Niederkorn, Jim Neu, Ann Wilson and others at the *Double Symposium on Acting* on 19 August 1989, one month before his death on 25 September. His presentation was transcribed and published by Niederkorn in his newsletter, *The True Comedy Planet*, and later reissued in two different forms. Smith's comments in 'Remarks on art & the theater' tally with many of the sentiments presented at the Toronto 'Art and art history' lecture, of five years earlier.

In his lectures, Smith stuck by his preoccupations without irony, as transparent and uncompromising principles for the production of art. His ideological positions were confirmed by several decades of his perceived abuse by artists, curators and critics – the remorseless persecution anxiety allegorised in his self-portrait, above, as 'Jungle Jack'. For Smith, the boundary between aesthetic and moral conceptions was slippery. His aesthetic ideas were almost indivisible from his dogmatically held moral pronouncements, specifically on the tendency for curators and artists to steal work from predecessors, and re-present it uncredited. Smith saw this as the key reason why he had been forgotten. It was, to him, a double-pronged attack, on the part of ethically depleted and artistically undernourished younger artists, as well as the critical and academic establishments that nurtured their cannibalism and raised their products to the level of cult objects. To the artists congregated to hear his contribution to the symposium in New York, he railed,

> I don't think that any of you realize sufficiently what you are up against ... That's what [is] being pushed in the schools: Vampirism ... The way it's being taught: some really powerful personage or work ... [is] dangled in front of [students]. Then they are fertilized by this ... [Tutors are] not showing them, molecule by molecule, how to make the art. They're substituting the system [with] exposing [students] to some artist, and the more soaked in tragedy and failure that person is whose art they're dangling in front of [them] the better, because then it enhances the thrill of vampirism.[57]

Smith is implicitly criticising the rise of the formally trained artist, and the vogue for Neo-Dada in the 1960s and after. The impact of Marcel Duchamp's 'readymades' was paramount in American art after expressionism, such as the paintings of Johns and Rauschenberg, and later works by Robert Gober and Sherry Levine. Duchamp finally settled in New York in 1955, and the rediscovery of Dada was confirmed as a major trend in New York by William Seitz's *The Art of Assemblage* exhibition, which opened at the Museum of Modern Art in 1961. However, for David Hopkins, Neo-Dada artists working in assemblage 'arguably repressed [Duchamp's] bodily preoccupations' in favour of an 'aesthetics of indifference'.[58] Such work played into the hands of the art establishment by being smartly aware of European modernism, while its fresh, new look fit the demands of the thriving post-war art market. 'Such metaphorical fine-tunings to the tradition of the readymade have turned into a rather monotonous end-game,'[59] Hopkins adds, noting a deadened repetitiveness that Smith himself drew attention to through his caustic account of artistic development as sustained by the potent yet ultimately shallow 'thrill of vampirism'. This arguably reached its apotheosis – strategic or otherwise – in the 1980s, when artists such as Jeff Koons capitalised upon the abandonment of political purchase by privileging ingratiation over disruption, reifying his public identity as a high-priced commodity.

Smith's Toronto lecture was unscripted, and delivered at an excruciatingly slow pace. Short phrases and individual words are punctuated with Beckettian silences – hesitations, delays, *ums* and *aahs*. Syllables are drawn out to the brink of intelligibility. Certain lines of thought are suddenly expounded with newfound vigour, only to unravel, thin out, and vanish as if without trace. The trying slowness ties his lecturing into a continuum with his performance practice, in which Smith would draw out tasks and poses for hours on end, 'puncturing long silences only with occasional cryptic non-sequiturs about penguins,' Gary Indiana remembers, 'or a startling piece of extremely bad nutritional advice.'[60] Interspersed in these comical yet alluring oratorical oddities are thought-provoking commentaries on his experiences as an artist on the margins of historical narration. 'Art is not forced on people,' Smith argues, 'it has always come from the people.' After a long, awkward pause, he continues,

> And it is not a reversal of the ancient, you know, and eternal purpose of art. Art is not something to, you know [*long pause*] superimpose over everyday life. If it's any good it has always come from everyday life. But the ideas about art are so perverted that it's become a guessing game. One year it's confused with Katharine Hepburn's jaw-line. Another year, this year it happens to be, uh, it's being mistaken for, um [*long pause*] a grosser kind of sleaze than has ever been imagined before … As a matter of fact, in this perverted time of art that we've evolved, uselessness is the most prized quality – the more spectacular and idiotic and useless the better.[61]

Central to Smith's portrayal of the system of valuation is the contingency of art's appraisal by the establishment. By extension, he is highly critical of the institutional privileging of 'idiotic', politically benign work, a tendency towards – in Blake's words – the 'domestication and trivialisation of art itself, as part of capitalism's relentless trampling of the humane'.[62] Blake's phrasing is astute, for it highlights the connivance Smith identifies between cosmetic values and commercial success. This connection is represented by Smith's reference to more transparent high capitalist strategies of market fetish, suggested by Hepburn's stylised beauty. It is meaningful that Smith's frame of reference for regimes of pleasure is that of mainstream Hollywood. Moreover, the Hollywood he refers to is a manifestly outdated one; kitschily, he valorises a star whose celebrity was confirmed in the early 1930s, but who was seen to be past her critical prime by the late 1950s. His idiosyncratic reference to a usurped cultural moment is a foundation of Smith's thought and practice. The idea that an industrial complex such as Hollywood would be governed by censorship of production and dictated towards the engineering of consumer desire is a familiar one. However, Smith's deployment of an acute understanding of these processes as the basis for an artistic practice – and as a method of critiquing the art establishment – was unique. Smith's scrutiny of the systems by which he saw his life's work devalued was framed in relation to an otherwise negligible subplot in the Hollywood narrative: the short-lived career of Hepburn's contemporary, Maria Montez, and the latter's usurpation by another little-known star, Yvonne de Carlo.

Despite or because of his ambivalent relations to the art establishment, Smith stressed his position as a self-instructed artist. He attended classes in filmmaking at CCNY in 1956 where he met Ken Jacobs and Bob Fleischner. He also attended a course on witchcraft at the New School in an attempt to understand the occult implications that some commentators perceived in his work.[63] Smith's development was crucially impacted by his commitment to innovative modes of self-education. In 1956, Jacobs and Smith taught themselves the finer details of filmmaking by watching a reel of Joseph Cornell's *Rose Hobart* (1937), which Jacobs had borrowed (he was Cornell's studio assistant at the time). He and Smith 'looked at it in every possible way: on the ceiling, in mirrors, bouncing it all over the room, in corners, in focus, out of focus,' Jacobs remembered. 'It was just like an eruption of energy.'[64] Similarly, Smith learnt about art history by attending free lectures at the Frick Museum. He states, 'I went to those lectures for months and months until I could figure out the rest, and that was how I was then able to make storytelling compositions with my still camera, which [were] then used in the filmmaking.'[65] This schooling was consolidated by afternoons spent at the Metropolitan Museum of Art, especially with works by his favourite painters, Jean-Honoré Fragonard and Paolo Veronese. Of the latter's *Mars and Venus United by Love* (c. 1576), he states, 'It's the most beautiful painting I've ever seen', its flattened perspective, painstakingly disorganised arrangement of bodies, and skewed scales perhaps informing the compositional strategies that characterise his strikingly cluttered photographs of the early 1960s.

Of his other favourite, he continues, 'Fragonard is the spirit of Baroque. It's not called Baroque, but it's the direct continuation of it. There is no Baroque theatre anymore. Hollywood was the Golden Age of Baroque.'[66] He took his pleasures from works such as Fragonard's whimsical yet dramatic painting *The Progress of Love: The Lover Crowned* (1771–72), on permanent display at the Frick. In his attention to such works, he understood and adapted the traditional definition of the transformation from Renaissance to baroque style, as defined most authoritatively by Heinrich Wölfflin in 1888. For Wölfflin, at the turn of the sixteenth century Italian artists such as Bernini, Michelangelo and Raphael began to introduce elements that dissolved the formal certainties of High Renaissance composition in painting and sculpture. 'Renaissance art is the art of calm and beauty', he wrote. 'Its creations are perfect: they reveal nothing forced or inhibited, uneasy or agitated.' However, producing a different effect, baroque art 'gives us not a generally enhanced vitality, but excitement, ecstasy, intoxication.'[67] Softening the classical rigidities of the Renaissance, baroque art is described as a kind of non-style, a fluid anti-category of artists that are difficult to place other than in contrast to prior and later formal styles. Smith saw a kind of freedom in this historical example of formal dissolution, and laid claim to Wölfflin's account in order to imagine himself as a latter-day baroque artist. If Hollywood had abandoned the 'ecstasy [and] intoxication' of baroque painting, Smith would manifest these disquieting forces in his own films and performances.

Embittered by what he saw as superficiality and frivolity of public taste, Smith emphasised his own self-tutoring as a foil to the ethical corruption harboured by the academy, and the cult of young artists produced and savoured in the market. The new breed of intellectually nourished, theoretically bolstered artists emerged from university fine art programs, and were regaled by Smith with unflappable contempt. In a paranoid construal of the academic privileging of postmodern forms, his writings and lectures often criticise techniques such as appropriation and the industrial delegation of production. Smith fought these developments by deploying his own personal experiences as fables: allegories of enforced prostitution to the underground and its apparently fiendish guardians (in Smith mythology, the likes of Jonas Mekas or Susan Sontag). This adversarial position against theory might appear reactionary, yet Smith anticipated a critical backlash against postmodernism in the 1990s. Donald Kuspit argues that the emergence of postmodernist techniques in the early 1960s denied the therapeutic imperatives of modernism, stripping progressive art of its emotional history in order to replace it with a glamorous but cynical narcissism. 'Appropriation art', Kuspit writes, 'is expressed as a feeling of déjà vu and a sense of art's loss of significant human purpose – its inability to afford an important perspective on the lifeworld … [W]hatever the morbid nostalgia of appropriation touches turns to stone'.[68] Smith had been held hostage to such morbid medusas, from the rent-stealing landlord to the grand thief 'Uncle Fishook' lurking in his underground vault of sugar zombies.

In a more progressive formulation than Kuspit's, Bruce Benderson argues that the drive towards cerebral modes such as conceptual, appropriation and 'neo-situationist' art severed the prior link between art, intellect and desire, 'substituting instead suspicion, cynicism, and puritanical prohibitions for what could be force, relevance and intense pleasure'.[69] However, appropriation can enable politically incisive, libidinal art, from Gran Fury's restating of AIDS statistics in their activist installation *Let the Record Show …* (1987) to Ron Athey's staging of Pierre Molinier's erotic self-portraits in *Solar Anus* (1999). Before appropriation could be rethought as an activist practice, however, Smith's persecution anxieties gave birth to a new handmaiden of the Lobster. Squeezed out of art programmes around the country, under the sway of the vampire artist-academic, the cannibalistic student proffered forth its hateful new fetish, the 'sacred baby poo poo of art'.[70] As early as 1964, Smith would rail against 'the new cutie-pie nonchalance' produced by 'the self-limitation school of art', which he recognised as the new mainstream of artistic production.[71]

'You would not have to be fertilized by anyone else if you knew how to make [art] yourself,' he continues. The image of fertilisation recurs obsessively in his proselytising on art-making and art education. Smith refused to find pleasure in his influence on other artists, mainly because he saw himself consistently eluding financial recompense for his contributions. He rails,

> That's the main problem of your life. If you are making any kind of art … then of course you get weary of all the damned duplicating, pilfering … You cannot go through an institution of any kind without some glaring theft … Anybody will tell you that. Ask anybody. It's always been that way.[72]

Similarly, in response to Niederkorn's suggestion that 'there were still lots of people whom you helped', Smith replied aggressively, 'I don't want to help them. I'm sorry they were helped … It's only swept me under the carpet and made my life lousy'.[73]

In a scribbled introduction to a performance entitled *The Pirate and the Penguin*, written during the 1980s, Smith fumes:

> It makes me ill to go on and on supporting a system, Jonas Me-crustism and pork barrel Mamaism, that represents the theatrical vampirism of the community through [the] squandering, in mid-air, of fortunes squeezed from the public, on management-class plane trips to the South of France and on mostly lame theatre flown in from all over the world for runs so brief that none but the same 100 art school cripples ever see it.[74]

Extolling his perfunctory socialist inclinations, he continues, 'The way funds are spent only robs the public of theatre art. If there are theatres whose concern is to make a direct exchange of theatre art for public support then I am interested in talking business with them. I am in the phone book.' In a later draft of the introduction, also held in his archive, Smith further inflames his censure of the performance establishment, aiming it more precisely at emerging, 'fertilization-hungry' artists, whom he sees as dominating the scene, or at least the attention of its celebrants. 'Fertilization always occurs in some variation of the apprentice system', he continues, and this process inspires the vampirism of critics and gallerists. Their selective celebration of artists, and entailed denigration of marginal practices 'only subtracts art from the communities they occupy like tourists'.[75] Here, the ethics of artistic labour are indelibly fused with the life goals of the artist. Those of the marginal artist are shown to be doomed to failure, a condition of the market's terminal descent into corruption. In his 'Remarks on art & the theater', he laments, 'Americans never made art'. 'We want to get rid of [art],' he continues, 'stamp it out, rape it. Just like we have raped this country. You can't indulge in something like that and say it isn't hatred.'[76] He refers, obliquely, to the support of methods of industrial production in minimalist sculpture, and to the refusal of subjective display and the hand of the artist in conceptual practice. Each is tactically misread as a personal affront to Smith's grandiosely personal ways of working.

The parable of the fresco painter

In the 'Art and art history' lecture in Toronto, Smith recounts an episode from his penultimate trip to Europe, to participate in Germano Celant's film festival, *The Restless Language*, in Genoa in the summer of 1981. His visit was documented by a striking series of portraits by the Italian photographer Nanda Lanfranco, in settings including a cemetery and a beach (see figures 2.2 and 2.3).

In Genoa, Smith recalls, he encountered an octogenarian fresco painter, and in the lecture this meeting is recounted as a parable. 'Fresco painting', Smith explains, 'was painting on wet plaster and the pigment would soak into [it] and became part of the wall. In other words then it wouldn't crumble away. It will be there as long as the wall is there, uh … It's in the plaster, you know. It's

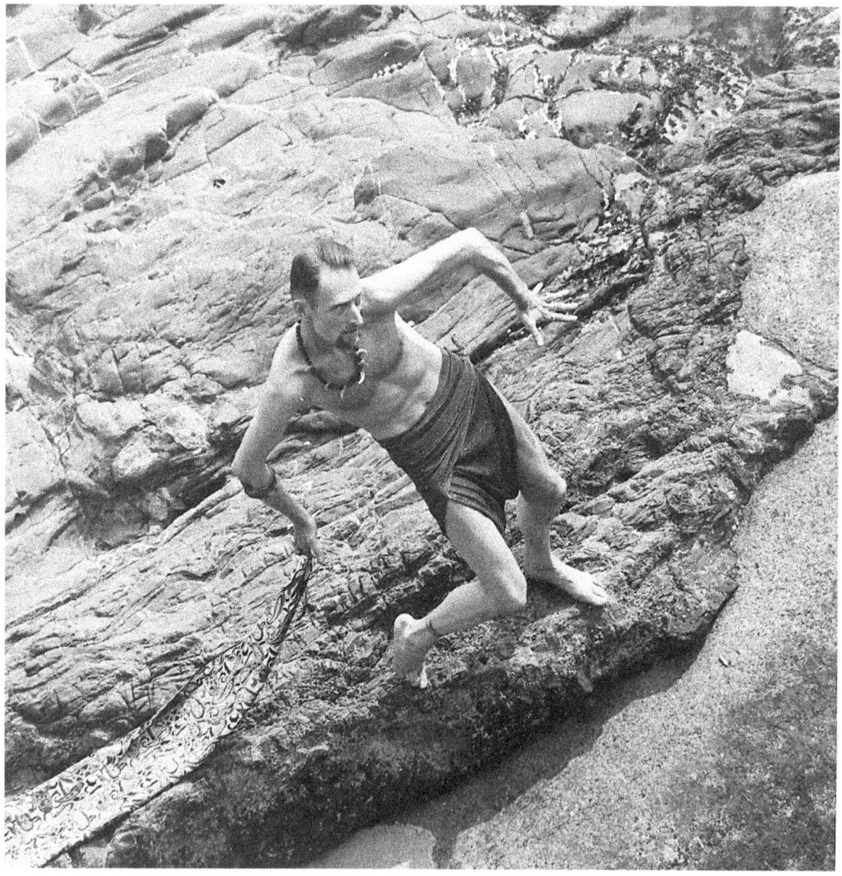

2.2   Jack Smith, *Untitled* (1981).

a wonderful thing, a damn good reason for fresco.'[77] His statement collapses several key themes in the Smith lexicon. As a metaphor for the depth and durability of artistic integrity, fresco constitutes an organic model of artistic labour. This is in contrast to the superficial Warholian 'crust' of painting, which conspires apolitically with the free market economy. The extended parable also indexes the recurring theme of a lost idyll based on imagined tropical or otherwise 'exotic' pseudo-historical imagery, parodying scholarly objectivity through the relaying of dubious facts about the development of art history. His concoction also allows him to explain his dream of a socialist utopia, based on the idea of a junkyard as a marketplace of ideas. 'Wonderful things can come from commerce', he told Sylvère Lotringer, 'but not from capitalism.'[78]

In the parable of the fresco painter, recounted at some length, the elder is imagined as slavishly working on a fresco, unaided by the luridly described,

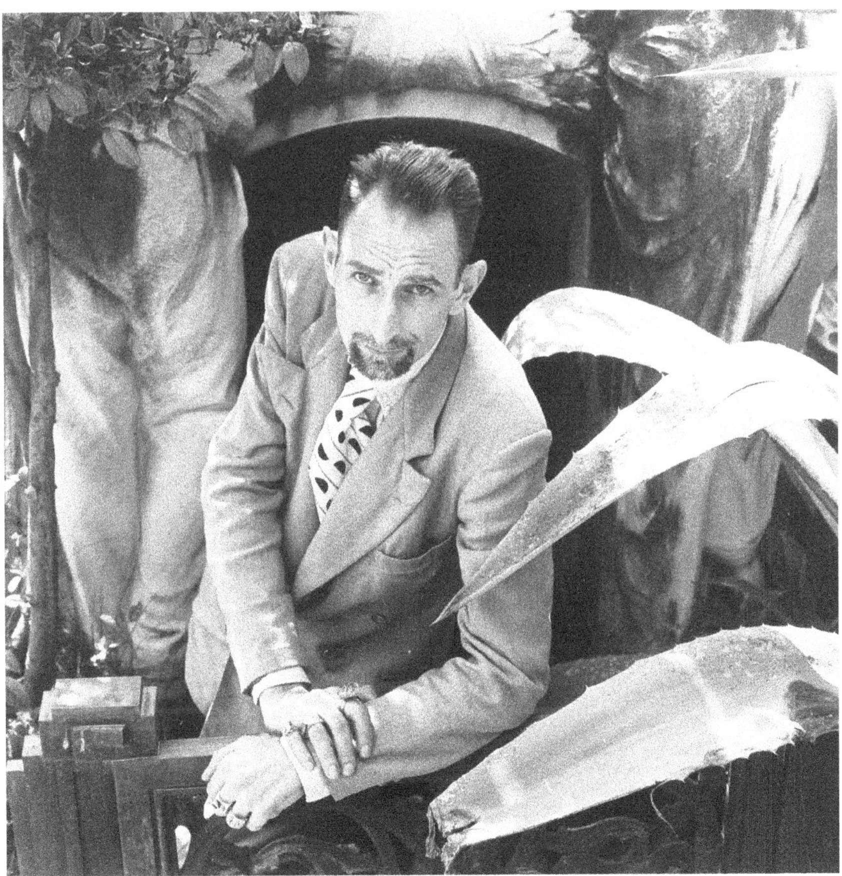

Jack Smith, *Untitled* (1981).   **2.3**

young male students that surround him. 'I thought I was hallucinating but all these people were standing around watching this old man having to go and fill buckets of water and take them back to where the work was being done.' Inevitably outraged, Smith helps the aging painter lug pails of water across the courtyard, mixing it with sand and plaster. Describing the scene, and his highly symbolic horror at the laziness of the younger artists, Smith elaborates on his memories to expound a theory of the development of the plastic arts:

> I myself have not approved of art since the Thirteenth Century when I think it became crustaceous. And it was directly caused by the Catholic Church luring the best painters out of fresco to make, uh, illuminated panels for altars, and they made this, you know, very profitable and glamorous so they got artists to stop making frescoes.

Armed with a small amount of formal training and a florid imagination, Smith improvised on these resources by adapting discursive categories and other cultural texts to describe the ideas he intuited about art: its history, making, teaching and criticism. By castigating all art after the Middle Ages, he contradicts his frequent celebration of baroque painting. Nevertheless, his propositions are spontaneous, inventive and obscure – comical in their excess, and mordant in their paranoid wit. He composed a set of misquoted assumptions

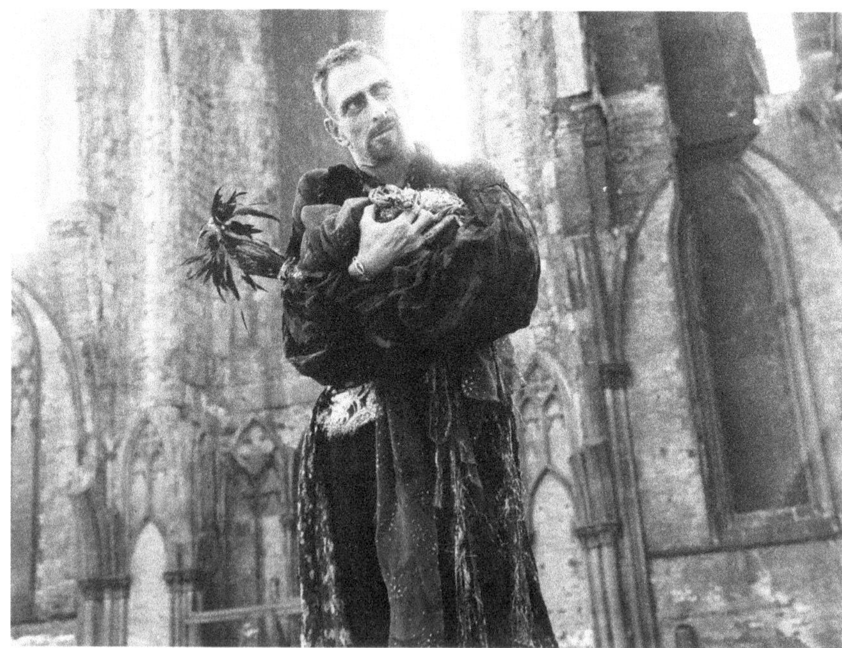

2.4   Jack Smith, *Untitled (from 'I Danced with a Penguin')* (c. 1983).

to be deployed usefully, in college lectures, essays and other tirades, as well as in his performances.

Smith's sojourns in Europe provided a vantage to describe the frustrations and hindrances that he felt in New York – those apparently deliberate privations handed down by a conspiratorial master signifier. 'Have you ever driven through the German countryside? It's art,' he told Niederkorn. 'There are rows of crops in stripes, winding gently around the curves of the hills. In stripes!' He adds, 'Farming is very close to making art. It's much closer than a lot of things.'[79] Smith made three trips to Europe in the 1970s and 1980s. During his first trip, in 1974, Smith stayed in Cologne, in Sigmar Polke's studio, with Katharina Sieverding and Klaus Mettig, and also at the home of experimental filmmakers Wilhelm and Birgit Hein. The latter remembers organising surgery on Smith's sinus, which he could not afford without health insurance in New York. Hein recalled Smith expressing his gratitude to the surgeon and nurses by giving them small bamboo sculptures that he worked on while recovering in hospital. During the two nights Smith stayed with the Heins, Birgit Hein's mother, E. Michelis, documented this sojourn in a series of brilliant portraits of Smith in Egyptian drag. The Heins were enthusiastic about Smith's influence in Germany. Wilhelm Hein stated his work was crucially influenced by his 'great heroes', Smith and the Austrian filmmaker and performer Otto Mühl – a provocative combination to be sure. Of his work with Smith on the documentation of *Moses* (1974) in Cologne, Hein writes, 'I was only a recording machine (perhaps a good one) but it is 100% Jack's work.'[80] When Smith finally overstayed his welcome in Germany, he travelled to Amsterdam to visit the filmmaker Babeth van Loo. He also spent several months in Italy, presenting a performance slide show at Fabio Sargentini's Galeria L'Attico in Rome, the site of influential exhibitions including Jannis Kounellis' *Untitled (12 Horses)* (1969). Smith returned to New York in early 1975.

For his first international appearance, Smith had been brought to Cologne to perform at *Kunst Bleibe Kunst (Art Remains Art)* at Kunsthalle Köln, a series programmed as part of the exhibition *Projekt '74: Aspects of International Art in the Early 1970s*. Others involved in *Projekt '74* included the French conceptual artist Daniel Buren and major proponents of American and European performance art of the late 1960s and 1970s, such as Vito Acconci, Joan Jonas and VALIE EXPORT. While in Cologne, Smith was commissioned to give a short performance, which was documented as a series of stills, and as an edited film for the WDR television programme *Kino 74*. The ten-minute performance film was directed by his German host Birgit Hein, and prefaced with clips from *Normal Love*. Hein's mini-documentary was a partner film to her profiles of Kenneth Anger (1973), Kurt Kren (1978) and Andy Warhol (1981). Gwenn Thomas photographed the intervention in Cologne Zoo (see

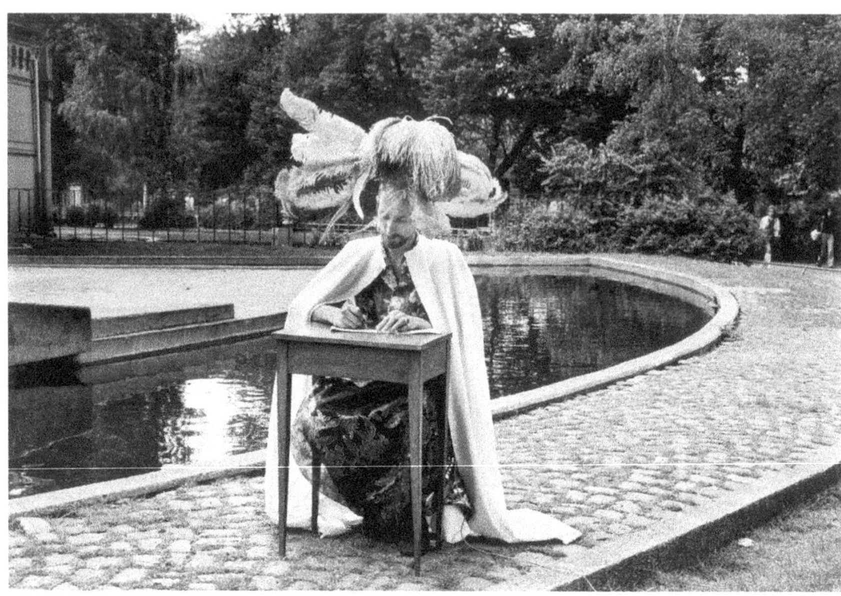

2.5   Jack Smith, *Fear Ritual of Shark Museum*, Cologne Zoo (1974).

figure 2.5), and Smith arranged her images as a cartoon strip titled *Fear Ritual of Shark Museum* (1974) for Willoughby Sharp and Liza Bear's vanguard magazine, *Avalanche*.[81] Bear, Sharp and Thomas had flown to Cologne for the festival, to report on it as a cover story for the magazine.[82]

In the performance at Cologne Zoo, Smith sits at a park-bench writing cheques, and wears an elaborate feathered headdress, a floral shirt and linen suit. In a nonchalant, off-kilter voice, he sings the opening lines to *I'm Going to Sit Right Down and Write Myself a Letter*, a pop ballad first made famous by Fats Waller in 1935. In the next section, Smith sketches equivalences between the evils of landlordism and the way in which museums kill off the spirit of art. 'Here I am collecting rent checks from the monkeys … Here is one from the monkey to the eagle', he shouts, waving the payments owed the predator by the caged animals. 'Art should be free. Everything should be free, and it could begin with art', he states in the performance. The sad fate of the museum is decried as a 'place [that] is like a morgue all day long. Then they snap shut at five pm'. Instead, Smith demands, 'put something interesting in it and stay open until five in the morning!' His polemic is a gloss on F. T. Marinetti's 'Manifesto of Futurism' (1909), which compared museums, libraries and academies to mausoleums: 'cemeteries of empty exertion, calvaries of crucified dreams, registries of aborted beginnings!'[83] The phenomenon of landlordism is characterised in Smith's rant as the interminable and seemingly illogical event of 'pay[ing] the rent that can never be paid', as a correlative to the museological

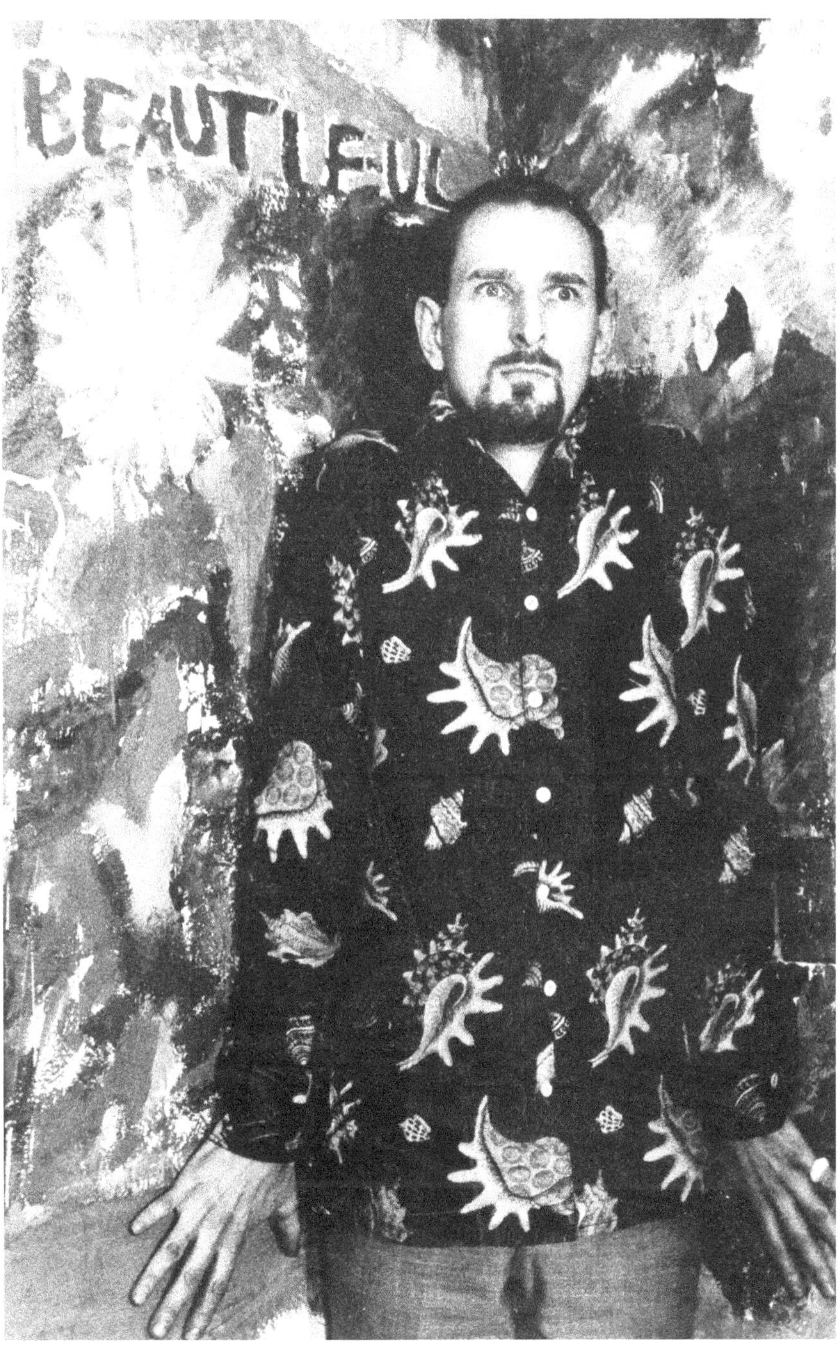

Jack Smith, *Untitled* (c. 1970). **2.6**

practice of flattening out differences between works to strip them of their critical purchase.

Despite his railings against the art establishment, intermittently Smith did rely on gallerists, curators and patrons. It is interesting to note that although Smith had a tortuous relation to the art establishment, he did manage to sustain short relationships with gallerists who supported his work, especially in Europe in the 1970s. The Cologne visit was organised through Hildegarde Lutze, a German gallerist based in New York. Smith met Lutze earlier in the year, when she had invited him to perform *Sacred Landlordism of Lucky Paradise* at a gallery owned by Rheinhard Onnasch, a dealer of works by diffi-cult American artists such as Ed and Nancy Kienholz. In New York, his most important source of establishment support was his financial agreement with Isabel Eberstadt, a patron to Smith and other underground artists including John Vaccaro. Eberstadt was an author and New York socialite, the daughter of poet Ogden Nash, and wife of fashion photographer Frederick Eberstadt.

At the invitation of the performance historian Elisabeth Jappe, Smith returned to Europe in 1977, to give a performance called *Irrational Landlordism of Bagdad* at the Cologne Art Fair. Smith's made a final trip to Germany in 1983, during which he presented a performance titled *I Danced with a Penguin*, at Kampnagelfabrik Theatre, Hamburg. Although the run was only sched-uled for two nights, Smith stayed in Germany for three months.[84] His trips to Europe are especially interesting as he was specifically invited to present performances, even if his notoriety stemmed from the legacy of his film work, especially *Flaming Creatures*.

Focusing on Smith's idiosyncratic takes on art and art history enables a theoretical and historical consideration of Smith that does not retain the hope that he might fit. Instead, I am interested in a methodology that takes into account his radical insights without politely overlooking his political or historical misfires. This approach might capitalise on his irreducible differ-ence without betraying the internal contradictions of his work. Indeed, by cataloguing the discomfiting contradictions of a culture, Smith stages the fallout from the inevitable failure of a critical pretence to rationality. As such, he is what Ralph Rugoff usefully calls a 'rear-guard artist', a documenter of a 'brutalist libidinal circus' who struggles for recognition amid or against more palatable designations.[85] Unlike the triumphantly inclined front line of the *avant*-garde, the *derrière*-garde artist leads audiences away from the transcen-dental forefront of cultural advancement, backwards into a thrillingly material, regressive space. 'No education, nothing, no advice, no common sense in my life,' Smith complained of his lot as an artist and as a subject, 'an insane mother I mean, no background, nothing, nothing, and I have to make art, but I know that under these conditions the one thing I had to find out was if I could think of a thought that had never been thought of.' For Smith, the project of making art is categorically the attempt – destined towards glorious catastrophe – to do something new, to insert a worthwhile thought into an incomplete world. Despite his difficulty as a person, and his categorical refusals of conservative definitions of cultural pleasure, he entertained hopes about art, truth, success and beauty. His perverse faith was dependent on a little burst of sanity, a hunch or hope that if an artist struggles against the essential incompleteness of the world, it will redress the balance of power by securing a historical place for one's labour. 'Whatever new thoughts you can think of that the world needs,' Smith protested, 'will be automatically clothed in the most radiant language imaginable.'[86]

Notes

1 Gregory Corso, 'Notes after blacking out', *The Happy Birthday of Death* (New York: New Directions, 1960), p. 11.

2 Jack Smith, 'Dehumanize and grab' (1979), unpublished journal, n.p., estate of Jack Smith, Gladstone Gallery, New York.

3 Adrian Rifkin, *Ingres, Then and Now* (London and New York: Routledge, 2000), pp. 1–3.

4 Ibid. p. 8.

5 Ibid. p. 10.

6 Jack Smith, 'Remarks on art & the theater', *Historical Treasures*, ed. Ira Cohen (Madras and New York: Hanuman Books, 1990), pp. 111–36 (p. 126).

7 Ibid. p. 127.

8 Judith Jerome, 'Creating the world to be created: Karen Finley and Jack Smith', *Women and Performance: A Journal of Feminist Theory* 10.1–2 (1999), pp. 135–54 (p. 139).

9 Smith, 'Remarks on art & the theater', p. 132.

10 Nayland Blake, 'The message from Atlantis', *Flaming Creature: Jack Smith, His Amazing Life and Times*, ed. Edward Leffingwell, Carole Kismaric and Marvin Heiferman, the Institute for Contemporary Art, P.S.1 Museum (London and New York: Serpent's Tail, 1997), pp. 168–83 (p. 170).

11 Smith, 'Remarks on art & the theater', pp. 134–6. See Jack Smith, 'Historical treasures: Remarks on art & the theater', *In a Different Light: Visual Culture, Sexual Identity, Queer Practice*, ed. Nayland Blake, Lawrence Rinder and Amy Scholder (San Francisco: City Lights Books, 1995), pp. 287–93.

12 Friedrich Nietzsche, *Ecce Homo*, trans. Anthony M. Ludovici (Mineola: Dover Publications, 2004), p. 136.

13 Smith, 'Remarks on art & the theater', p. 135.

14 Stefan Brecht, *Queer Theatre* (Frankfurt am Main: Suhrkamp Verlag, 1978), p. 27.

15 Gary Indiana, '"Insistent director", Jack by popular demand: Jack Smith in retrospect', *Artforum* 36 (October 1997) p. 67.

16 Rifkin, *Ingres*, p. 132.

17 Francis Frascina, *Art, Politics and Dissent: Aspects of the Art Left in Sixties America* (Manchester and New York: Manchester University Press, 1999), p. 135.

18 Smith, 'Dehumanize and grab', n.p.

19 Blake, p. 182.

20 Ibid. p. 177.

21 Jack Smith, unpublished statement, estate of Jack Smith.

22 Shannon Jackson, 'Performing show and tell: Disciplines of visual culture and performance Studies', *Journal of Visual Culture* 4.2 (August 2005), pp. 163–77, (pp. 172–3).

23 Allan Kaprow, 'The legacy of Jackson Pollock' (1958), *Essays on the Blurring of Art and Life*, ed. Jeff Kelley (Berkeley: University of California Press, 1993), pp. 1–9 (pp. 7–9).

24 Thomas Crow, 'Saturday disasters: Trace and reference in early Warhol', *Modern Art in the Common Culture* (New Haven and London: Yale University Press, 1996), p. 61.

25 Cited in Barbara Haskell, *Blam! The Explosion of Pop, Minimalism, and Performance 1958–1964* (New York: Whitney Museum of Art, 1984), p. 22.

26 Sally Banes, *Greenwich Village 1963: Avant-Garde Performance and the Effervescent Body* (Durham and London: Duke University Press, 1993), p. 35.

27 Thomas Crow, *The Rise of the Sixties: American Art in the Era of Dissent 1955–69* (London: Everyman, 1996), pp. 126–8.

28 David Hopkins, *After Modern Art 1945–2000* (Oxford and New York: Oxford University Press, 2000), pp. 104–10.

29 Daniel Wheeler, *Art Since Mid-Century: 1945 to the Present* (London: Thames and Hudson, 1991), p. 133.

30 Walter Benjamin, 'Theses on the philosophy of history', *Illuminations*, ed. Hannah Arendt, trans. Harry Zorn (London: Pimlico, 1999), pp. 245–55 (p. 248).

31 Ibid. p. 248.

32 Rene Ricard, '"No dice", Jack by popular demand: Jack Smith in retrospect', *Artforum* 36 (October 1997), p. 68.

33 David Ehrenstein, 'An interview with Andy Warhol' (1966), *I'll Be Your Mirror: The Selected Andy Warhol Interviews, 1962–1987*, ed. Kenneth Goldsmith (New York: Carol & Graf, 2004), pp. 63–70 (pp. 66–7).

34 Lawrence Rinder, 'Anywhere out of the world: The photography of Jack Smith', *Flaming Creature*, pp. 139–51, (p. 144).

35 Glenn O'Brien, 'Interview: Andy Warhol' (1977), *I'll Be Your Mirror*, pp. 233–64 (p. 245). Emphasis in original.

36 Cited in J. Hoberman and Jonathan Rosenbaum, *Midnight Movies* (New York and London: Harper & Row, 1983), p. 69.

37 Andy Warhol with Pat Hackett, *POPism: The Andy Warhol '60s* (New York and London: Harcourt Brace Jovanovich, 1980), p. 31.

38 Ibid. p. 50.

39 Michael Moon, 'Flaming closets', *October* 51 (Winter 1989), pp. 19–54 (p. 37).

40 Sylvère Lotringer, 'Uncle Fishook and the sacred baby poo poo of art' (Interview with Jack Smith, 1978), *Wait for Me at the Bottom of the Pool: The Writings of Jack Smith*, ed. J. Hoberman and Edward Leffingwell (New York and London: High Risk Books, 1997), pp. 107–21 (p. 116).

41 Smith, 'Remarks on art & the theater', p. 123.

42 Lotringer, p. 119.

43 Richard Meyer, *Outlaw Representation: Censorship and Homosexuality in Twentieth-Century Art* (Boston: Beacon Books, 2002), p. 125.

44 Jennifer Doyle, 'Queer wallpaper', *A Companion to Contemporary Art since 1945*, ed. Amelia Jones (Malden and Oxford: Blackwell, 2006), pp. 343–55.

45 Gavin Butt, *Between You and Me: Queer Disclosures in the New York Art World, 1948–1963* (Durham and London: Duke University Press, 2005), pp. 110–18.

46 Jack Smith, unpublished journal, c. 1961–63, p. 73, estate of Jack Smith.

47 Gerard Malanga, 'Interview with Jack Smith', *Film Culture* 45 (Summer 1967), pp. 12–16 (p. 16).

48 Jack Smith, 'The perfect filmic appositeness of Maria Montez' (1963), *Wait for Me at the Bottom of the Pool*, pp. 25–35 (p. 30).

49 Ibid. p. 29.

50 Jack Smith, 'Ammonia pits of Atlantis: Evil in the art world, or Walter versus the giant knick-knacks' (1966), *Wait for Me at the Bottom of the Pool*, pp. 97–101 (p. 98).

51 Lotringer, p. 117.

52 Smith, 'Ammonia pits of Atlantis', p. 99.

53 Irving Sandler, *American Art of the 1960s* (New York: Harper & Row, 1988), p. 60.

54 Sandler, p. 60. Jonathan D. Katz has complicated the concealment of subjectivity in the work of Johns and Rauschenberg. See, for example, his catalogue essay in Jonathan D. Katz and David C. Ward, *Hide/Seek: Difference and Desire in American Portraiture* (Washington: Smithsonian Books, 2010), pp. 37–45.

55 Jack Smith, 'The astrology of a movie Scorpio' (1963), *Wait for Me at the Bottom of the Pool*, pp. 54–7 (p. 54).

56 Many thanks to Gordon W. for sharing his memories of Smith's visit.

57 Smith, 'Remarks on art & the theatre', pp. 123–5.

58 Hopkins, p. 43.

59 Ibid. p. 64.

60 Indiana, p. 67.

61 Jack Smith, 'Art and art history', audio recording of a lecture by Smith, Forbidden Film Festival (Funnel Experimental Film Theatre, Toronto, 25–31 October 1984).

62 Blake, p. 177.

63 David Ehrenstein, *Film: The Front Line, 1984* (Denver: Arden Press, 1984), p. 26.

64 Cited in J. Hoberman, *On Jack Smith's Flaming Creatures and other Secret-Flix of Cinemaroc* (New York: Granary Books, 2001), pp. 126–7.

65 Smith, 'Art and art history'.

66 Smith, 'Remarks on art & the theatre', pp. 119–20.

67 Heinrich Wölfflin, *Renaissance and Baroque*, trans. Kathrin Simon (London: Collins, 1984), p. 38.

68 Donald Kuspit, *The Cult of the Avant-Garde Artist* (Cambridge and London: Cambridge University Press, 1993), p. 106.

69 Bruce Benderson, 'Surrendering to the spectacle', *Sex and Isolation and Other Essays* (Madison and London: University of Wisconsin Press, 2007), pp. 60–75 (p. 60).

70 Lotringer, p. 107.

71 David Brooks, 'Free association interview with Jack Smith – April 23rd, 1964', *Film Culture* 77 (1992–93), pp. 24–33 (p. 32).

72 Smith, 'Art and art history'.

73 Smith, 'Remarks on art & the theatre', pp. 132–3. This section was similarly excised from the edition reprinted in Blake's catalogue to *In a Different Light*.

74 Jack Smith, hand-written introduction, 'The Pirate and the Penguin', unpublished manuscript, estate of Jack Smith.

75 Jack Smith, redrafted version of 'The Pirate and the Penguin'.

76 Smith, 'Remarks on art & the theatre', pp. 131–2.

77 Smith, 'Art and art history'.

78 Lotringer, p. 115.

79 Smith, 'Remarks on art & the theater', p. 131.

80 Wilhelm Hein, unpublished correspondence with the author, 31 March 2011.

81 Jack Smith, 'Fear ritual of shark museum', *Avalanche* (December 1974), pp. 26–7.

82 Thanks to Gwenn Thomas for providing information about the event.

83 F. T. Marinetti, 'The founding and manifesto of Futurism', *Marinetti: Selected Writings*, ed. R. W. Flint (New York: Farrar, Straus & Giroux, 1971), pp. 39–44 (p. 43). Thanks to Slava Mogutin for this observation.

84 Birgit Hein, Klaus Mettig, Petra Korink and Elisabeth Jappe discussed Smith's trips during a panel at the Exile Gallery, Berlin (1 November 2009).

85 Ralph Rugoff, 'Mr. McCarthy's neighbourhood', *Paul McCarthy* (London: Phaidon, 1996), pp. 32–87 (p. 37).

86 Smith in Lotringer, pp. 114–15.

Flaming Creatures and **3**
the burden of disgust

The only way to avoid the horror of horror is to give in to it. (Jean Genet)[1]

Jack Smith's *Flaming Creatures* (1962–63) erupted into the cultural landscape at a loaded historical juncture. While the Motion Picture Production Code was more or less redundant by 1961, enabling relatively more graphic movies to enter circulation, the reception of *Flaming Creatures* immediately anticipated a backlash against sexual cultures during the symbolic cleanup of New York, launched in preparation for the 1964 World's Fair. In the United States Supreme Court, Chief Justice Earl Warren confirmed that *Flaming Creatures* was to be regarded as obscene, stating clearly, 'This film is not within the protections of the First Amendment.' Warren characterised the film as 'utterly without social value [and] substantially beyond customary limits of candor in representing sexual matters [such that] the dominant theme of the material taken as a whole appeals to the prurient interest.'[2] The reception of the film – its formal obscenity and subsequent placement in congressional discussions of its official status as a source of disgust – explicitly demonstrated the disruptive effects of Smith's work. *Flaming Creatures* intervened in a series of continuing historical struggles, between subjective articulations by the sexually misbegotten, and their policing under dominant moral codes.

In film, prose and performance, Smith unflinchingly rejects the possibility of unproblematic sexuality thought separate from the threat of deprivation, danger, denial and death. As such, Smith exposes the fragility of the ego and the destitution of the cultural structures that condition it, that 'perfect Swan Lake of wrecked lives.'[3] His explorations of sex, death and other disasters in *Flaming Creatures* are considered here under the potent sign of disgust, as an affective force that has powerful implications for the study of performance and visual culture. In a journal he kept during the filming of *Flaming Creatures*, Smith lists a series of titles for 'Doomed Movies'. Interrupted by the reminder, 'You must make a fantastic spite movie', the list signals the centrality of death and disaster to his filmmaking, and includes such potent rejects as 'To Be Truly Dead', 'Climax of the Nothing Period' and 'Dead Flesh Comes to Life',

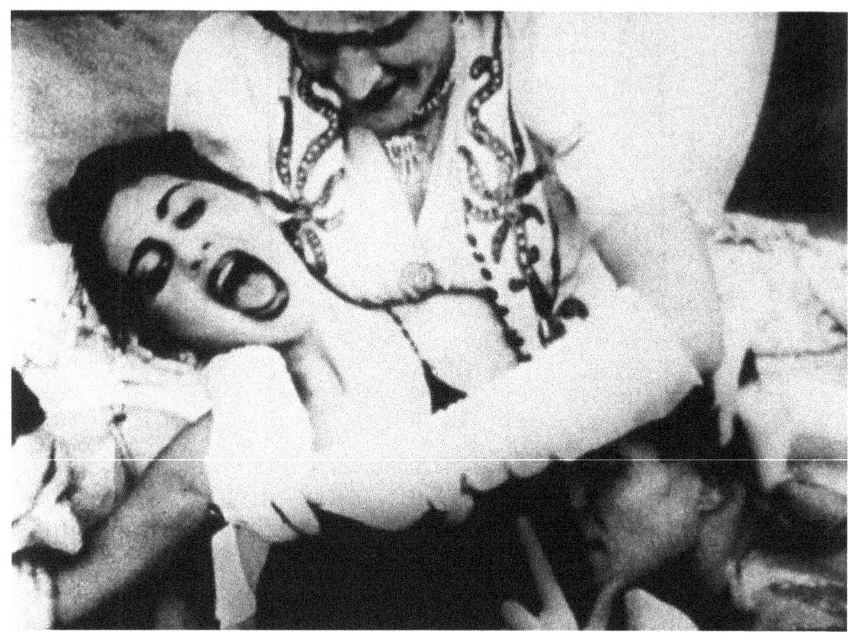

3.1   Jack Smith, *Flaming Creatures* (1962–63).

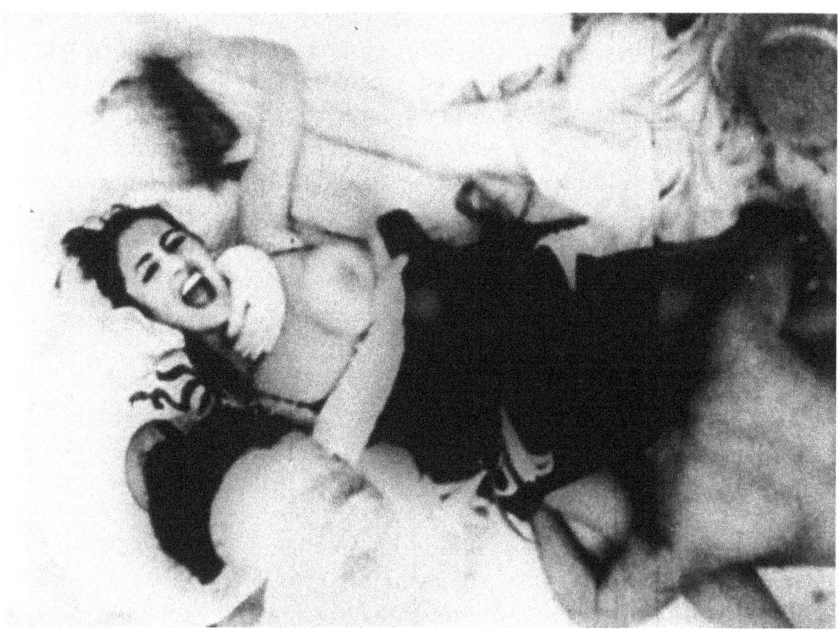

3.2   Jack Smith, *Flaming Creatures* (1962–63).

interspersed with reminders of his 'moldy obsessions' such as the gilded remains of 'M. M.' (Maria Montez).[4] Colliding kitsch with horror, Smith devises ambivalent confusions between pleasure and pain, desire and death – other rejected titles include 'Poetry & Hepatitis' or 'Blossoms and Beatings'. By staging 'social death', as the mortification of the subject through shame, guilt, or stigma, Smith also comments on the contemporary position of the queer in the early 1960s, in an age before the decriminalization of homosexuality, or the partial liberalization of public perspectives on gendered, sexual, racial or class difference.

Might there be political mileage in exploring the unseemly underside of identity politics? I argue that *Flaming Creatures* is important because its difficulties might be celebrated for what I call the *burden* of disgust. Disgust emerges as a contradictory effect in the encounter with art: disgust is both repulsive and attractive; the opposite of the aesthetic, yet its paradoxical condition of existence. Disgust, and its siblings, indignation, revulsion, and other ugly sentiments are perhaps surprising preoccupations for the study of art. However, I will argue that disgust is not alien to the register of the aesthetic, but, rather, constitutes both its upper and lower limit.

As *Flaming Creatures* shows, Smith was no stranger to the attractions of seemingly unpalatable spaces and practices. Moreover, since the 1960s the reception of art has continually returned to the threat that pleasurable effects might devolve to the experience of the disgusting or the sexually disturbing. As evidence of this fact, we might look briefly to the art criticism of a connoisseur of the disgusting, the late Republican Senator for North Carolina, Jesse Helms. His political statements are a useful barometer for the prevalence of disgusted apprehension in legislative and other responses to contemporary art. In a series of presentations to Congress in July 1994, three decades after congressional discussion of the offences of *Flaming Creatures*, Helms sought to restrict Federal funding for art that involved a host of seemingly unanticipated perversions, namely 'mutilation or invasive bodily procedures on human beings dead or alive; or the drawing or letting of blood'.[5] This was intended as a reworking of the notorious Helms Amendment of 1989, which prohibited Federal support for works that were sexually explicit or deemed as having anti-religious sentiments. 'Mr. President,' Helms stated, 'I have tried, without success, to establish in my own mind [why the media is] obsessed with trying to prove that black is white and white is black, and that disgusting, insulting, revolting garbage produced by obviously sick minds is somehow art, and that this art is worthy of being subsidized and rewarded by and with grants of Federal funds.' The exemplary targets of his brickbat included 'photographs of a naked homosexual with a bull whip protruding from his rear end, or a naked woman on a stage, her body covered with chocolate, or photos of mutilated human corpses, or blood soaked towels dispatched on a pulley over the heads of an unsuspecting audience terrorized by such a surprising development'. Helms caricatures works by Robert Mapplethorpe, Karen Finley, Joel-Peter Witkin, and Ron Athey, and suggests that they epitomise the underside of the aesthetic, the nadir at which point art falls into 'filth'. Such artists are debased by their investments in maligned modes of production, in Helms' unsavoury description of his targets not as artists, but as 'human cockroaches'. These attacks took up the conservative mode of congressional attacks initiated in discussions of *Flaming Creatures* in 1968, which indicted Smith's work as evidence of 'the sick climate in which we are now suffering'.[6]

The compulsion to engage with the messy, adulterated and disgusting qualities of lived experience is a crucial aspect of Smith's artistic strategy. Creative work that questions its own completeness – and its own naturalised elevation into the realm of the aesthetic – encourages new approaches to the labours of art and of research, usefully contesting naturalised assumptions within academic, legal and popular discourses about art. In the final moments of this chapter, this enables the idea that Smith was committed to the elaboration of art as a structure that fails, and that this ties into his intuitive relation to contemporary theories of sexuality, identity and desire. Psychoanalysis necessarily becomes a useful apparatus for exploring his work, especially after Jacques Lacan's persuasive account of the subject as a structure that comes into being through failure and disaster, countering the conventional logic of subjectivity as pristine except for the pathological situations that derail it. In a turn to psychoanalysis, I borrow jouissance towards a formulation of the interplay of pleasure and disgust, desire and death, in Smith's work.

Various aspects of Lacan's critique recall Smith's project. These include Lacan's refusal of affirmative imaginings of sexuality, his theoretical metaphysics of negativity, his style of critical vacillation in the seminars, and a foregrounding of difficulty, tension and conflict in the play of desire. Throughout this book I am invested in the ways Smith's work allows a revaluation of unfamiliar logics of cultural production, including the seemingly unexamined aspects of art, sex and other ambivalent phenomena. The work of jouissance arises in this chapter as a term for discussing the body and its perhaps unpalatable desires, in relation to different orders of subjective catastrophe. The ways in which the work's offences register in official modes of reception is a crucial method for measuring its effects. I twin these commentaries with a series of theoretical discussions of the power of disgusted apprehension. In Lacan's poststructuralist psychoanalysis, for example, jouissance takes the 'beyond' of Sigmund Freud's 'pleasure principle' as its point of departure, and translates it into a discursive effect.[7] For Freud, the reality principle demands the postponement of satisfaction, and necessitates the tolerance of unpleasure, while the death drive is the force that seeks to lead the subject back to a prior, more primary state of things, sustaining the annihilatory fantasy of returning (in death) to inorganic substance. Both are signalled by the compulsion to repeat experiences that are antagonistic to pleasure and constructive life, represented by his infamous analogy of the child's replaying of the mother's traumatic departure in the game of *fort-da*.[8]

As a means of accounting for how the death drive undercuts the urge towards pleasure, jouissance refers to the self-shattering that occurs in the subject, not so much as a break in the prior stability of the desiring self, but rather as a sign for the fact that subjective coherence has always already been precluded. Although notoriously circuitous in his accounts of key principles, Lacan gives his most precise definition of jouissance in an untranslated lecture of 1966:

> What I call jouissance … is always in the nature of tension, in the nature of a forcing, of a spending, even of an exploit. Unquestionably, there is jouissance at the level of which pain begins to appear, and … it is only at this level of pain that a whole dimension of the organism, which would otherwise remain veiled, can be experienced.[9]

The work of jouissance, therefore, confirms the essential volatility of a desiring body caught in the grip of the drives. The writings of Jean Genet epitomise this volatile gesture; building on the sentiment introduced in this chapter's epigraph, in *Our Lady of the Flowers* (1943) he writes that in the solitary depths of an autoerotic debauch, 'I was plunged to the mouth in horror. The horror entered me. I chewed it. I was full of it.'[10] Genet and Smith both populated their works with the erotic lives of subjects at the margins of living, and encountered powerful resistance to their artistic indiscretions. Moreover, Genet's film *Un Chant d'Amour* (1950) was the only other underground film that provoked heated debate in congressional hearings in 1968.

Smith understood that experiences in cultural life are conditioned by horror, dissimulation, disappointment, and failure. He was particularly attuned to the construction of non-normative sexualities as deviant, as well as to the subversive potential of performance to disrupt illusions of cultural stability. As suggested above, his work anticipated challenges posed to the assumed safety of the aesthetic in the Culture Wars of the 1980s and 1990s. In *Flaming Creatures*, drag queens sniff flowers, dance coquettish dervishes across the frame, and flagrantly lift their dresses to flaunt male genitals. At the close of the film, for example, two figures are shown twirling pleasantly in a perfunctory waltz, as the shot from above reveals a pair of rolled tights masquerading as one queen's transvestite breasts. A multitude of couples join the fray, waltzing and carousing in front of the painted flowers used as the film's sole backdrop. A woman sniffs a lily, and the camera pans down to a man's face buried in her crotch; close-ups appear of another woman's hairy armpit. With a rose between his teeth, Mario Montez dances across the frame like a widowed giantess, his monumental frame draped in veils of black lace.

Throughout the film, bodily conjugations take place without the depiction of erection or penetration, so that the categorically 'sexual' is displaced by a confusing democracy of erotic play. The exception to the rule of apparently infantile mischief is the hungry violence of the pivotal rape scene. Nevertheless, this and the rest of the film attest to Smith's fascination with the excluded elements of lived experience, from the unspoken commonplace of sexual violation, to deviations too outlandish for any disciplinary science. The portrayals of defamiliarised eroticism and public sex in *Flaming Creatures* highlight the assumed positions of its queers, vamps and vampires as moral and sexual outsiders. Because they break strictures governing gender and sexuality, they perform a specifically social death, placing themselves outside the boundaries of an imagined community of the normatively sexed and gendered general public. Viewers of the document may temporarily locate themselves outside a cultural norm only for that exile to be safely revoked through reaffirmations of spectatorial distance from the alien bodies onscreen. However, the personas caught on film are destined to an inconsolable and permanent social death, as symbolised in the corpse in drag's ascension to the living death of vampirism near the end of *Flaming Creatures*. Indeed, Smith would later burlesque the film's power to symbolically mortify its creator by association, changing its name to *Respectable Creatures* on the can in which the film was carried, on a transatlantic flight in 1974, for fear that the original title's notoriety would cause him to be arrested on arrival in Germany.[11]

While the central gang rape may produce revulsion in some reviewers, it was Smith's explorations of homosexuality that have secured the lasting notoriety of *Flaming Creatures*. If, as Gavin Butt has argued, the male artist is a historical figure that has tended to call its own sexuality into question, as 'a subject of sexual and epistemological uncertainty', the crisis of artistic masculinity is most pressingly compromised when such labours explore the limits of taste and decency.[12] In the 1960s, the rumoured or admitted homosexuality of certain male artists had a profound impact on the reception of performance and visual culture. While some artists worked to straighten up their queerness, Smith obstinately reinforced the readable signs of his sexuality. Moreover, Smith did not merely flaunt his sexuality, but explored its politics in a challenging way, using film, writing and performance to foreground the seemingly disastrous relations between desire, disgust and death. As a contemporary critic noted, *Flaming Creatures* consisted of 'images of individual personalities completely destroying existing ideas of how … people and things should appear on the screen', in order to tap into the historical tensions of 'a time when man has moved towards the destruction of the individual by society and the destruction of society by nuclear holocaust'.[13] Inevitably, by being able to incite such powerful readings, Smith's film also encountered strong resistance from conservative defenders of culture.

'The monster vice'

Made on a shoestring budget of around $300, and filmed on stolen reels of Perutz Tropical film, *Flaming Creatures* premiered at midnight, on 29 April 1963, at the Bleecker Street Cinema on New York's Lower East Side. The film was shown alongside *Blonde Cobra*, his earlier collaboration with Ken Jacobs and Bob Fleischner. Police harassment was a regular feature of underground screenings, and in the following year showings of *Flaming Creatures* would be prevented by force at legitimate venues including Gramercy Arts and the Tivoli Theater, and other spaces hired by Jonas Mekas for use by filmmakers of the New American Cinema. *Flaming Creatures* was greeted with its first signs of trouble several months later, causing a furore when it was banned from the third international Experimental Film Competition in Knokke-le-Zoute, Belgium in December 1963. The decision became newsworthy when a small group of American filmmakers stormed the projection booth, and projected Smith's banned movie onto the face and body of Pierre Vermeylen, the Belgian Minister of Justice, who had attempted to quell the small riot that broke out at Mekas's instigation. The event was widely reported in the European press, and the scandal seemingly followed Mekas and his entourage to New York.[14]

Flaming Creatures was one of four films – alongside Genet's *Chant d'Amour*, Kenneth Anger's *Scorpio Rising* (1964) and Andy Warhol's *Blue Movie (Fuck)* (1968) – that demonstrated the limits of legal permissiveness towards the underground.[15] By extension, they staged the persistence of taboos against visual representations of sexuality in the 1960s. Published in 1963, the year *Flaming Creatures* was first screened, John Rechy's *City of Night* explored the tensions that homosexuality reveals between expressions of public and private morality. Both Smith and Rechy argued that homosexuality, promiscuity and other non-normative practices might reveal the limitations of traditional sexual morality, and provoke a subjectively elaborated moral code. Rechy writes,

> The only immorality is 'morality' – which has restricted us, shoved into the dark the most beautiful things that should glow in the light … Yet this unreasoning world ignores the true obscenity of our time: poverty, repression, the blindness to beauty and sensitivity – *vide*, the sneaky machinations of our own storm troopers – the vice squad.[16]

Indeed, Smith was no stranger to the 'sneaky machinations' of the vice squad. On 3 March 1964, at the New Bowery Theater, St. Marks Place, Mekas presented *Flaming Creatures* alongside Warhol's benign newsreel, *Andy Warhol Films Jack Smith Filming Normal Love* (1963). Police raided the screening, impounding both reels, the projector and screen, and arresting the projectionist, manager, and ticket-taker.[17] Unfortunately, Warhol's film was lost when police confiscated the sole print.

People of the State of New York vs. Kenneth Jacobs, Jonas Mekas and Florence Karpf was heard before a three-judge panel in the Criminal Court, and expert witnesses including Allen Ginsberg, Susan Sontag and filmmaker Shirley Clarke defended the artistic merit of *Flaming Creatures*. Ten days later, Mekas was arrested on a new count, for screening *Un Chant d'Amour* at a benefit for the *Flaming Creatures* defence fund. A further screening of *Flaming Creatures*, alongside *Scorpio Rising*, was raided later in the month. Mekas and Jacobs were convicted on the charge of obscenity, and each received suspended prison terms of 60 days in the New York City workhouse in June 1964. However, unlike the charge against *Scorpio Rising* – banned on the same day as *Flaming Creatures* in a separate ruling in Los Angeles – the ruling against Smith's film has never been reversed. The ruling was upheld at the New York Appellate Court, and on 11 October 1966, the United States Supreme Court was unable to reach a verdict, and screenings of *Flaming Creatures* remain technically illegal in 22 states.

Between 1966 and 1968, *Flaming Creatures* continued to re-emerge at the centre of legal and political skirmishes. In the weeks after the first 'teach-in' against the Vietnam War, at the University of Michigan in early 1966, *Flaming Creatures* re-entered public consciousness, thanks to its placement at the centre of a series of on-campus wrangles. At the University of Michigan in the same year, police raided a screening of the film, confiscating the print. Police also disturbed screenings at the University of New Mexico (1966), the University of Texas (1966, in an event organised by the Students for a Democratic Society), and the University of Notre Dame (1968). After the latter, the Emeritus Dean of Notre Dame Law School wrote to the *Washington Post* on 20 September 1968, writing that to condone the movie's exhibition would be 'to close one's eyes to vice'.[18]

The film also became a new site of political leverage on account of Justice Abe Fortas' move to reverse the Criminal and Appellate Court decisions against the film, in the Supreme Court hearing in October 1966. This became a politically volatile issue when President Lyndon B. Johnson nominated Fortas for the position of Chief Justice in 1968. Smith's film became an instrument of right-wing retaliation against Johnson's ailing Democratic administration, as lobbyists critiqued Fortas' position on *Flaming Creatures*, representing his sympathy for Smith's film as an indictment of civil libertarianism. As Senator Robert C. Byrd (WV) stated, Fortas' politics signalled 'the current permissiveness … that has come increasingly to characterize the U.S. Supreme Court in the last decade'.[19] As documented in the *Congressional Record* for 1968, *Flaming Creatures* was discussed extensively in presentations to the United States Senate and House of Representatives, on five separate occasions from July to September.

In the first congressional address on the issue of *Flaming Creatures*, on 22 July 1968, Representative John R. Rarick of Louisiana introduced a long discussion on Fortas' judiciary record on obscenity. 'Mr. Speaker,' Rarick began, 'Abe Fortas has earned his role as Mr. Obscenity, based on his extremist notions that the parents and society in general should have no power or right to establish a pattern of morals or dignity'.[20] *Flaming Creatures* was discussed alongside a list of 25 other instances in which Fortas was deemed to be lenient on pornography. Charles H. Keating, Jr and James J. Clancy of Citizens for Decent Literature (CDL) led the extensive presentations to the House. Later renamed Citizens for Decency through Law, CDL were an anti-pornography lobbying group based in Smith's home state of Ohio. Keating and Clancy showed that between 1966 and 1968, Fortas had participated in every decision in which the United States Supreme Court had heard challenges to State and Federal obscenity decisions. Of the 26 cases that came before the court, 23 decisions had been reversed. Of the three remaining cases, one decision had been upheld (namely, the obscenity of Genet's *Un Chant d'Amour*). In the other two cases, the appeals were deemed 'moot' – that is, the court refused to pass judgment, therefore the earlier convictions still stood. One of the moot appeals involved the sale of pornographic materials to minors; the other was the case against *Flaming Creatures*.

In Clancy's lengthy statement, *Flaming Creatures* was described in disparaging terms and conflated with a range of other artefacts, including 20 pulp paperbacks (with titles such as *Shame Agent, Orgy House*, and *Sex Life of a Cop*), 12 books aimed at BDSM enthusiasts, a series of pornographic photographs, 8 strip-tease movies, and 11 'girlie' and 'nudist' magazines. In the House of Representatives, Keating attacked the nomination of Fortas to the position of Chief Justice, stating, 'in June 1967, the curtain rang down on the performance of the United States Supreme Court during the 1966 October term [when the case against *Flaming Creatures* was heard]. By their actions the community standards of 13 states were upset'.[21] Keating contrasted Fortas' support for *Flaming Creature* to his ruling against Genet's movie, banned after a screening was prevented at University of California, Berkeley in 1964. Keating noted that *Flaming Creatures* 'depicted a 7–minute rape scene, acts of oral intercourse, fondling of the female vagina and breasts, masturbation of the visible penis, and the like, some of which were suggested but never shown in the film *Un Chant d'Amour*'.[22] He reiterated the comparison between the two films, noting that while the dreamy evocations of fellatio and sodomy in *Un Chant d'Amour* provoked a Superior Court judge to rule that it 'is nothing more than hard-core pornography and should be banned', none of the scenes 'approached the offensiveness of *Flaming Creatures*'.[23]

On 1 August 1968, the *Chicago Tribune* reported that 5 members of the Senate Judiciary Committee viewed three of the films under discussion, including *Flaming Creatures*, noting 'Even some of the strongest backers of Fortas found the movies filthy and disgusting'.[24] Keating was one of the most outspoken denouncers of Smith's work, and a crucial influence on Smith's cultural and historical marginalisation. Keating described Smith's film as part of 'this Nation's growing obscenity problem', and he attacked Fortas' vote against the Supreme Court decision by saying that the 'evidence is all around us that this Nation in 1967 has embraced the monster vice'.[25] Keating pursued anti-pornography attacks on films, books and magazines until the 1980s, including high-profile lawsuits against Russ Meyer and Larry Flynt. His biographers suggest that Keating's work as a 'warrior in the fight against filth' was part of a strategy to gain a public national status after an earlier mark against his reputation, when he was investigated for espionage and 'fraud against the government' by the Atomic Energy Commission in 1956.[26] However, despite being known in the 1950s and 1960s as 'Mr. Clean' on account of his anti-pornography crusades, Keating was disgraced when charged in a major fraud and racketeering scandal in 1989, receiving a ten-year prison term in 1992.

In Congress, the discussion around *Flaming Creatures* and related offences passed swiftly from the House of Representatives to the Senate. In the ensuing filibuster, Senators John L. MacLennan (AR) and Strom Thurmond (SC) denounced Smith's work to secure the attempt to hobble Fortas's nomination. On 27 September 1968, MacLennan described the film to the President by saying 'it makes one sick to look at it. It is despicable. Depraved acts are displayed in the film'. Moreover, he misrepresented the legal status of Smith's film by arguing, 'to legalize this filth is to support and sustain the attack that these filth manufacturers are making … We cannot sustain and maintain the character of this Nation if we demoralize and immoralize the youth of this country'.[27] At the suggestion of Senator John C. Stennis (MS), Thurmond organised a private congressional screening of *Flaming Creatures* for senators and the President. Tellingly, Smith's film was shown alongside a fourteen-minute film of a striptease, and two reels of hardcore pornography. Thurmond's 'Fortas Film Festival' collapsed the three types of film under the homogenising moral rubric of the pornographic, deploying the concept against Fortas as a symbol of the slackened moral principles apparently marshalled by progressive politics. Of Smith's film, Thurmond observed specifically, 'it is very significant to note that Justice Fortas stated in this case that he would have reversed the lower court decision'.[28] Indeed, Fortas was the only Supreme Court Justice who voted to reverse the conviction of the exhibitors of *Flaming Creatures*.

By attracting the attention of senators and the President, Keating had been extremely influential in his mobilisation of *Flaming Creatures* as a symbol of the grip that vice had apparently taken over American culture and society in the 1960s. The group he co-founded, the CDL, was a highly effective lobbyer for greater state control over the production, exhibition and distribution of pornography in the decade. Notably *Flaming Creatures* was a rallying point in the CDL's crusade for 'decency'. In an account in *Newsweek*, Keating stated, '[t]hat movie was so sick … I couldn't even get aroused'.[29] In his brilliant non sequitur, Keating deems that the film's inability to arouse him deprives *Flaming Creatures* of the meagre value attributed even to pornography, as if its recuperation as an aid to masturbation would at least secure its place within a culturally degraded system of value.

Homophobic revulsion

After Keating's proclamation of *Flaming Creatures* as a profoundly 'sick' artifact, I ask what, precisely, is the sign of the movie's sickness? The disgusting emerges as a shifting, ghostly quality in the film, and the terms of its excitement of displeasure are described repeatedly yet evasively in presentations by Keating and others. The film exerts a mildly nauseating affect for me in Smith's footage of lips sliding across themselves in greasy black accumulations, to pucker up for slimy air-kisses. Yet the question of which sequences induced disgust in the early 1960s is starkly attested to by comments published at the time. Writing for the *Saturday Review* in 1963, Arthur Knight called *Flaming Creatures* a 'faggoty stag-reel' in which '[e]verything is shown in sickening detail, defiling at once both sex and cinema'.[30] Homosexuality is positioned centre-stage in Knight's description, and cited as a spur to disgusted apprehension. For Knight, the excess of *Flaming Creatures* not only compromises the work itself, but also demeans the safety of both the sexual and the cinematic within a fragile cultural order. A further viewer (a municipal judge) described the film as 'a smutty purveyance of filth [that] borders on the razor's edge of hard-core pornography'.[31] This horror signals both contemporary viewers' arrivals at a traumatic border, one where performances of homosexuality, gender confusion and uncoded erotic play enact a return: namely, the eruption of disgust, whose identity the aesthetic is fantasmatically relied on to suppress.

Keating and the CDL were sensitive to the perceived threats posed by homosexual pornography. In *Perversion for Profit* (1965), a propaganda film that Keating produced to warn of the dangers of vice, the narrator George Puttnam states, 'Through this material today's youth can be stimulated to sexual activity for which he has no legitimate outlet. He is even enticed to enter the world of homosexuals, lesbians, sadists, masochists, and other sex deviants … This moral decay weakens our resistance to the onslaught of the Communist masters of deceit'. Amid shots of salacious reproductions from 'girlie' and physique magazines, readings from pocketbooks, and other 'smut', Puttnam declares, once exposed, 'the insatiable curiosity of youth will cause him to delve deeper and deeper into this grotesque material until his utter depravity is complete'.[32]

If the 'sickness' and 'utter depravity' signaled by the opponents of *Flaming Creatures* is the homosexuality that pervades much of Smith's work, how and with what effects did the film incite homophobic opposition throughout the decade of its creation and scandalous release? Leo Bersani has given a convincing reading of the threat posed by homosexuality, which focuses on the panic and disgust that homosexuality has often been privileged with inducing. In 1987, Bersani famously critiqued redemptive reinventions of sex by proposing the celebratory maxim: 'To be penetrated is to abdicate power'.[33] Displacing the apparent offence of this statement, his early writings inverted the phobic horror of the humiliation of anal penetration, rendering it as 'the terrifying appeal of a loss of the ego'. By affirming the possibilities opened up by the penetration of the anatomically male body, he perversely rejoices in the political potential of 'constitutive masochism' as the modus operandi of sexuality. 'If the rectum is a grave in which the masculine ideal … of proud subjectivity is buried,' Bersani writes in a classic formulation, 'then it should be celebrated for its very potential for death.'[34] Bersani's rhetoric is that of shattering, exploding and otherwise rupturing or breaking up; as such, 'death' for Bersani is to be understood as a loss of balance between the life drive and the force of jouissance, but also as actual death – a bodily crisis which culminates in some process of evanescence, in dematerialisation, or even suicide. Indeed, beginning with *Flaming Creatures*, Smith's films and performances evidenced a striking fascination with death and decay, through the recurring motifs of reanimated corpses, vampires, mummies and other figures of the undead. In his work he collided such imagery with homoeroticism. The place of death in the queer imagination is a site of contestation, not least because AIDS literalised the symbolic proximities between queerness and finitude. However, there may still be some critical leverage in Bersani's claim that non-reproductive sexual practices enact the breakdown of the self, shattering its imposed coherence into erotic intensities. This proposition manifests itself, here, in my reading of homosexuality, crisis and difference in Smith's work, as a mandate to ask questions about the tenability of different writings on the body and aesthetics, when inserted into queer theory's imaginings of the self.

To be sure, *Flaming Creatures* is a homoerotic palimpsest. The film's participants are always scantily clad in thrift-store apparel, with their faces obscured by veils or masks. At the close of the first sequence, the camera surveys an orgy of fleshy contiguities, panning from a face down legs and torsos to a fleshy body. Smith's camera follows a man's arm down to its grip on another's flaccid penis, which it vigorously shakes, the frame stilling on its movement for some four seconds. After a short cutaway to ghostly pale footage of another queen in comedy facial contortions, the film returns to a much denser image, closely focused on the lips and nose of Francis Francine (Frank di Giovanni) – a Coney Island 'hermaphrodite star'[35] and Smith superstar who appears as a haggish queen with an ornate spray of white lilies. Another queen applies lipstick while a thick soft penis rests on her shoulder, in the upper left corner of the shot. Her gyrating lips brush towards and across the cock, using it compositionally as a framing device, and membering it as lure.

The central bodily motifs are lips, tongues, limp dicks and swollen breasts, initiated in the opening credits where a woman poses with her tongue flaccidly pushed over her teeth and lips. Accompanied by emphatic lip-smacking sounds, Francine's androgynous voiceover is laid over the arrangements of performers enthusiastically applying lipstick with increasing fervour. 'A fabulous new heart-shaped lipstick that shapes your lips as you colour them,' Francine states. In an ensuing conversation with Francine in the voiceover, Smith intones in his nasal drone, 'Is there a lipstick that doesn't come off when you suck cocks?' 'Yes,' Francine replies, 'indelible lipstick. It stays on and on.' In a droll misinterpretation, Smith asks, 'But how does a man get lipstick off his cock?' Here, Smith's play with gendered signifiers slips neatly into verbal intimations of homosexual intimacy. He suggests the historical conflation of the reality of male homosexuality with the fantasy of the penetrated man's inevitable emasculation. He also collides sexual practices with a stylised blithe spirit that has often been a mainstay of gay male systems of representation. Indeed, while scandal, censorship, and attributions of obscenity would pursue Smith throughout the 1960s, he was also involved in more frivolous orders of criminal trouble, which matched his propensity for queeny affectation. In one such anecdote, Smith was sent to Bellevue for psychiatric observation in 1962 after being arrested for the ambitious and characteristically flamboyant crime of 'attempting to shoplift a department store's entire display of costume jewelry'.[36] Smith's diverse criminality metaphorised the familiar tension between serious outrage and lightweight faggotry, as staged in the scene of lipsmacking tomfoolery in *Flaming Creatures*.

Questioning other confusions about the 'real or potential political impli-cations of homosexuality', Bersani's critiques the pastoralising impulse that structures redemptive reinventions of sex. He argues that the lived reality of sexual practice is often uncritically raised to the political dignity of 'semiotic guerrilla warfare'.[37] For example, he shows that the (now lost) bathhouses of New York and San Francisco are theorised as chimerical signifiers of liberal experimentation, in apologetic disavowals of their function as a spatial organi-sation geared towards maximising physical pleasure. Elsewhere, William Haver reiterates Bersani's suspicion by stating, 'it is neither political, episte-mological nor moral subjects who know the unbearable sweetness of the fuck.'[38] Countering pastoral mythologies, Bersani writes that the strategy of 'performing sex as *only* power' – or, indeed, as only frivolity – 'is a salvational project, one designed to preserve us from a nightmare of ontological obscenity, from the prospect of a breakdown of the human itself in sexual intensities'.[39]

Challenging Michel Foucault's assertion that homophobia responds to the threat of new social relations, Bersani describes penetration as a more powerfully disturbing threat to the heterosexual imagination, where the ego is overwhelmed in its internal complex by a *'jouissance* of exploded limits'.[40] Central to his thesis is the convincing allegation that to blame homophobic anxiety on the threat of new social relation – rather than apparently frightening sexual acts – is ultimately disingenuous about homosexuality and the violence it inspires. Under the rubric of the pastoralising project, '[homophobic] revulsion, it turns out, is all a big mistake: what we're really up to is pluralism and diversity, and getting buggered is just one moment in the practice of these laudable humanistic virtues'.[41] Rather than herald the possibilities opened up by new social relations, Bersani re-imagines the moment of climax – the unbearable sweetness of the fuck – as that ecstatic suffering into which the subject might plunge when pushed towards and beyond a certain threshold. He extrapolates this disastrous image as the root of phobic responses to male homosexuality, which becomes useful for analysing the erotic threat posed by bodily representation.

It should be added, however, that I doubt Foucault is being disingenuous about the horror that anal penetration inspires. Instead, by reading the figure of 'the homosexual' as 'an historic occasion to re-open affective and relational virtualities, not so much through the intrinsic qualities of the homosexual, but due to the biases against the position he occupies', Foucault attempts to disentangle the concept of homosexuality from a particular sexual act, so that the first does not stand as the ineluctable truth of the other.[42] Foucault challenges his readers to think a future for homosexuality that does not replicate the violent conflations enacted by the homophobic majority, in which the body of the gay man is reduced to the fact of his penetrability. Under what historical conditions has the homosexual become intelligible, Foucault asks, and with what effects? And how can these effects be reconstituted by challenging the ways in which homosexuality produces meaning for a culture? Nevertheless, Bersani's essay is the most convincing account of the revulsion male homosexuality inspires, and is therefore relevant to a study of *Flaming Creatures*, as a film that incited such violently homophobic opposition throughout the decade of its creation and scandalous release.

Bersani's project is partly premised on the stigmatisation of powerlessness within a masculinist economy of representation. He critiques the apparently inevitable conflation of feminine sexuality with bodily passivity – and thus of submissive sexualities with emasculated destitution, loss of ego and death. The male heterosexual fantasy of feminine desire as a self-destructive appetite for losing sight of the self is correlated with the similarly phobic fantasy of anal penetration. This potent fear finds conscious form, he writes, in the 'seductive and intolerable image of a grown man, legs high in the air, unable to refuse the suicidal ecstasy of being a woman'.[43] Bersani critically stages the unmistakable misogyny of this fear of violation, a conservative fantasy that condemns the penetrated bodies of women and gay men alike to the nowhere of symbolic mortification.

Contemporary mainstream representations rehearsed similar anxieties, of course. Sal Mineo's character Dov Landau indexes this confusion in Otto Preminger's film *Exodus* (1960) when he describes his treatment at the hands of concentration camp guards: 'They used me,' he cries, 'like you use a woman!' His exclamation suggests that penetrated women and men suffer the mutual mortal indignity of being barred from the burden of masculinity. *Flaming Creatures* deploys this residual, phobic image, despite the fact that the film does not directly figure anal penetration among its catalogue of sexual performances. Gavin Butt argues that the spectral image of anal penetration has a tendency to haunt queer art, even where abstraction would seem to reasonably preclude sexualised readings. In a convincing analysis of the vanishing point bracketed by concentric rings in Jasper Johns' combine painting *Target with Plaster Casts* (1955), for example, 'even though not represented within the field of vision, it is the anus, connoted through metonymic association, which forms the locus of an imaginary homoerotics of the male body'.[44] This process of metonymy reminds us of another promiscuous slide into signification: the tendency for spectacles of homosexual intimacy to conjure the fantasy of anal sex. *Flaming Creatures* readily stages this potent tendency, procuring a relation between sexualised performances in the field of vision – men touching each other's genitals, or dancing together in drag – and the invisible event that ghosts it, namely the hidden performance of a man penetrated by another man.

The scandal of disgust

It was an article by Susan Sontag published in the *Nation* magazine in 1963 that confirmed the wider public reputation of *Flaming Creatures*. Her reading shoehorned the film into her general theory of metaphor, and the essay soon found its way into her first collection, *Against Interpretation*. 'There are no ideas, no symbols, no commentary or critique of anything in *Flaming Creatures*,' she writes in this inaugural text. For Sontag, aesthetic space is the space of pleasure, distinguished from moral space, which retains the 'imperative about taking a position towards one's subject matter'. Sexual pleasure, she asserts, is the prime location towards which 'it isn't necessary to have a position'.[45] Her essay culminates in the general theme of her work – from this early point until her troubling work on AIDS in the late 1980s – that in place of an hermeneutics we need an erotics of art: but not, it would seem, a politics of representation. Sontag's enfeebling of Smith – her insistence that 'In good films, there is always a directness that entirely frees us from the itch to interpret' – refuses the possibility of approaching *Flaming Creatures* as a political text: one that harbours a richness that would facilitate ethical-critical thinking.[46]

As D. A. Miller argued of Sontag's writing, in the year of Smith's death in 1989, '[the] claim for the precession and superiority of form over a content whose main function is to justify the elaboration of artistic or literary devices is of course a familiar one.'[47] He notes that this strategy was rendered particularly problematic in Sontag's later writings. In *AIDS and its Metaphors*, Sontag argues that military metaphors abstract the suffering of people with HIV/AIDS, but she effectively strips the disease of its epidemiological immensity. By demeaning the material implications of metaphor, she argues that 'even an apocalypse can be made to seem part of the ordinary horizon of expectation [which] constitutes an unparalleled violence that is being done to our sense of reality, our sense of humanity'.[48] Sontag obscures the details of suffering, and the activist responses that so usefully deployed militaristic imagery, towards a conceptual account that is unsympathetic to the linguistic inventiveness of those threatened by illness. Abstracting Smith in her earlier essay, Sontag colonises his film and its performances by recasting representation as an apparently untroubled labour. She writes, 'there is not only moral space, by whose laws *Flaming Creatures* would come off badly; there is also aesthetic space, the space of pleasure [in which] Smith's film moves and has its being.'[49] Filth and defilement are cordoned from the work as the underside of a maintainable moral space: one that can be policed through a faulty assertion of the aesthetic realm's – and hence the subject's – apparent immunity from it. She achieves this distinction by refashioning the film as a 'rare modern work … of joy and innocence,' refusing its sexual complexity, and undermining the threat it poses to conventional morality.[50]

Against Sontag's refusal of sexual politics, *Flaming Creatures* can be mobilised as a text that acknowledges sex as inevitably haunted by the bodily threat of failure and disgust. Branden Joseph confirms Smith's fixations with disgust, decay and death, through a convincing comparison between his ventures in film and writing and the fragmented Beat novels of William S. Burroughs. For both, he writes, 'there is always a confluence of decay – bodies leaking or coming apart and ultimately ending in death – and a polymorphous desire that … literally streams out in all directions.'[51] For Smith, then, sexual pleasure is an eerily terminal experience that insistently points to loss of ego, pre-empting Bersani's later account of the shattering of the subject. In an interview in 1967, Smith considered the sordid content of much of his work, telling Gerard Malanga: 'Well, a lot of unpleasant things exist [in the world] … among which is the pornography in everyone's soul … In other words, voluptuous vagaries and so forth are all part of humanity simply as we know it.'[52] Among these 'unpleasant' eventualities, disgusted apprehension plays a central role.

In a monograph on the topic of disgust, Winfried Menninghaus accounts for its significance as a condition of the production of meaning in philosophy, art and culture since the eighteenth century. For Menninghaus, disgust constitutes the upper and lower limits of pleasure. The lower limit is a vomitive clearing-away conjured by a crisis of self-preservation in the face of inassimilable otherness, its prime object being the encounter with the corpse. Beauty's upper limit is characterised as the surprisingly similar voiding of content caused by the sickening excess of pleasure one confronts in extreme satiation. Aesthetic space, for Menninghaus, is therefore grounded in an 'abysmal' assumption by which the beautiful tends, in and of itself, to become disgusting. Menninghaus argues that 'the often-conjured inexhaustibility and indeterminacy of aesthetic experience can thus be read as a remedy to the radical finiteness of disgust, since disgust not only defines and threatens the aesthetic realm from the outside, but, due to beauty's self-sickening tendency, has always already infiltrated its interior structure.'[53] As such, aesthetic space is a volatile condition, whereby the borders of the disgusting surround and condition the locus of pleasure.

Flaming Creatures confirms this reading, by performing disgust as the extreme counter values of the aesthetic, and trafficking the affect into its visible centre. Elsewhere, Smith's experimental prose confirms his fascination with representations of monstrosity, the body's functions and its fetid remains, especially in collision with the ridiculous. His artist writings are littered with narratives of botched corporealities and unsublimated interiors, minor epics of disgusting zones and sordid encounters that contextualise their parallel, cinematic manifestation in *Flaming Creatures*. 'The white pig of the Medina' (1967) is one such tale. It is the story of a syphilitic whore, housed in a brothel whose 'atmosphere of keif dreams … the White Pig gave up chunks of her putrefying body to maintain,' where vultures 'brazenly squat around [her] slowly putrefying dream pretending to be somewhere else … "I'm a woman with morals," she would squall while being flipped over on her stomach [as] her flaccid, grayish white anus collapsed with a crash'.[54] This and other fables give free reign to Smith's flights of fancy, offering grim accretions, fatal irregularities and interrupted wholes. Throughout, he often proffers a detail or two to send a quiver through the firmest stomach. While Smith's literary efforts are often seemingly disregarded as juvenilia, this potentially implicates childishness and the child as guardians of the survival of perverse pleasures in the forcibly civilised field of aesthetic play. In art and performance after Smith, disgust similarly arises in unexpected and itinerant ways. As Ralph Rugoff notes of Paul McCarthy's work, for example, 'In watching his tapes, I have learned that there is something surprisingly nauseating about the simple image of a family-sized bottle of ketchup gushing into a bucket.' Like other minor spectacles of despoliation in McCarthy's work, this vivid event elicits a revulsion that perhaps reflects our 'uneasiness with spontaneous emissions', issuing forth from bodies or their surrogates.[55] In Smith's film, nauseating affects emerge in a litany of places, from chocolate smears of lipstick, to the overwhelming central representation of gang rape.

The shittiest lust

In one striking exchange about the problem posed by *Flaming Creatures*, the Speaker of the House asked James Clancy of the Citizens for Decent Literature, 'Is it your experience … that material of this kind would cause a person of unbalanced mind, psychotic mind, to create acts of violence?' 'Yes, sir,' Clancy replies on behalf of CDL. 'Aren't women and children the usual victims?' John William McCormack asks. 'Oh, yes, sir,' replies Clancy.[56] This suspicion of the corrupting influence of pornography was a central motif in congressional presentations against the excesses of *Flaming Creatures*. In addition to concerns about the homosexuality represented in the film, representatives and senators expressed outrage at the possibility that *Flaming Creatures* – and pornography in general – might inflame violent desires in its audiences. In a length instance of fear mongering, Keating argued that instances of rape had risen by 34% between 1960 and 1966, and asserted that 'the girlie magazine problem' was a major factor in this development. Spurious evidence was provided to the House of Representatives; for example, Keating described an incident in Burbank, California in which a 12–year-old girl was 'raped … by a 20–year-old boy with a girlie magazine in his hip pocket' as a causal link between the consumption of pornography and violence against women.[57]

Nevertheless, the excesses of the gang rape in *Flaming Creatures* can be relied upon to provoke unsettling affective responses in viewers, from unease, to indignation, to outright revulsion. If Sontag attempted to strip the film of its political charge, I seek to rethink the ways in which *Flaming Creatures* enacts a range of possibilities for political investment, not solely in order to defend its ambitious, unabashed, and quite unprecedented queerness, but also in more politically ambivalent spaces. I argue that the rape scene is not simply a sorry slippage in Smith's sexual politics, nor a symptom of the implicit misogyny sometimes attributed to male homosexuality. Rather, it is an exploration of a set of questions about the condition of lust and desire, and a troubling commentary on what could be understood as the tendency of sex and sexuality towards disaster.

The centrepiece of *Flaming Creatures* is a series of frozen tableaux, beginning with a scene composed around a dirty foot, as a grimy fetishistic object in the far foreground. The shot alternates between Francine's puckered glare, and the luscious pout of Sheila Bick shrouded by white lilies. Francine's compulsive looking pre-empts the eventual segue into the violent and relentlessly long rape scene, the central event of the film. Before Francine seizes her prey in a half-hug-half-stranglehold from behind, the two rock together for a curious moment, the held woman fanning herself wistfully. Suddenly, the grip tightens into an attack. A hand is placed on her ample breast and her face animates into a scream, one she will maintain for the six long minutes of the rape that she endures. Her howls mix with the campy plucked strings and concubine serenades of Smith and Tony Conrad's soundtrack. Joined by other attackers, a hand releases her other breast from its brassiere and the camera focuses on its vast jiggle. Hands and faces cover her body and slowly lift her negligee to reveal her genitals, fan-hand flailing. A queen joins her on the floor, and is similarly ravished, but her face remains playful, unlike the convincing horror of the raped woman's enduring violation. Smith persistently constructs these pairings of horror and play, of feigned violence and believable violation. Similarly, when the attack is disturbed by a fortuitous earthquake, Bick and another woman (Judith Malina) swoon together in pseudo-lesbian consolation. An earthquake does not disturb the rape as such, but rather accompanies it, emulated in the shake with which the camera records deep close-ups of skin, body parts, and the borders of clothes, returning relentlessly to the enigmatic motif of the madly shaken breast of Sheila Bick. As the scream-sounds cease, she stands and sways in a histrionic stagger, right breast still hanging outside her black slip. The Living Theatre's Judith Malina, holds her from behind in an embrace that directly mimics the hold with which the rape scene started. The couple dash backwards out of the frame. As violins rise up in an exhorting flourish, the exhausted woman is consoled by a coruscating caress across her exposed breast, again mirroring the violent jiggling that serially punctuated the rape.

Flaming Creatures is structured by the persistent representation of shaken body parts. Breasts and flaccid penises are shaken in antagonistic display, as alluring objects but also as wilted, useless appendages. Refusing to sexualise the breast as lure, Smith also fails to valorise the penis as an object of sexual empowerment, dismantling its sacred armature as the mark of threat or privilege. The penis and the breast are rendered exhausted remnants: interchangeable and volatile in the ennui of their sexless shake. The shake emphasises each as a site of confusion, figuring a destabilising function that plunges the viewer into the fold between disgust and laughter. The trope of the shake in *Flaming Creatures* is a space of – or gap in – representation that registers the slippage between consolation and assault in relations between bodies. This enigmatic quality works to undermine the subject's handle on the assumed gulf between violence and consolation. The viewer is thus 'shaken' in her or his assumptions about the codes one wields in encounters with the bodies, desires and sexual practices of others.

After a few moments more of lovingly ambivalent body-jostles, the two women share a kiss amid a cascade of flowers and detritus. Violence and intimacy collide as Smith's camera performs a space in which the gulf that separates them is no longer assured. The assumed discrepancy between cruelty and consolation becomes disconcertingly hazy. After Lacan, such a crisis may reveal the play of jouissance within the attempt at loving. Jouissance arises here because interpersonal relations depend upon the threat of an 'unfathomable aggressivity from which we flee'.[58] The subject vacillates before the crisis of a desire to lose oneself in the other. This violence is not simply a pathology, but a structural element of language, and therefore of sociality. As if to allegorise this crisis of identification and self-loss, in *Flaming Creatures*, Malina continues to kiss her ravished lover, who lays spent and motionless after the ordeal of her disastrous sexual encounter. With her legs and arm to the side, Bick mimics the throes of some pale death.

My description risks aestheticising the rape around which *Flaming Creatures* is seemingly structured. Jennifer Doyle notes that the 'operatic gang rape … may seem to betray feminism … and to firm up the commonsense suspicion of gay culture as secretly misogynistic'. However, Doyle wonders if it could be read as a politically progressive representation. As a 'farcical' representation of 'the disasters of heterosexual culture', Smith's film might also operate as a 'quite profoundly feminist' representation, she adds.[59] Doyle argues that gay male economies of representation might 'create an alternative cinematic space for women' by the very fact that such works are read as primarily 'gay'. 'Because she is framed by a gay male context, she gets to be something other than the straight sex object,' and therefore confronts punitive conventions about the gendering of desire.[60] I pursue Doyle's thought here, to see what Smith's film might tell us about the historical relations between feminism and sexual politics, and to ask how, specifically, the nauseating rape scene may be something other than an anti-feminist representation. Indeed, as Craig Owens noted, 'the myth of homosexual gynophobia remains perhaps the most powerful obstacle to a political alliance of feminists and gay men'.[61] Curiously, this obstacle obscures the foundational link between misogyny and male homophobia in Western culture. The political purchase of Smith's rape scene can be elaborated upon with reference to a striking argument between the literary critic Kate Millett and the novelist Norman Mailer. In the early 1970s the two writers wrestled with the question of whether or not an appalling representation of women signals the play of unexamined misogyny.

In 1970, Millett published *Sexual Politics*, a landmark feminist study of twentieth-century literature by male novelists. In the course of her analysis, Millett forcefully critiqued Mailer, D. H. Lawrence and Henry Miller for what she saw as their misogynist representations of women. She countered their anti-feminist sexual politics with a celebration of the novels of Jean Genet, offering a pointed contrast between heterosexual male posturing – as a 'pathology of virility' – and the progressive politics that male homosexuality might enable.[62] In *Our Lady of the Flowers* and other novels, Genet provided a 'painstaking exegesis of the barbarian vassalage of the sexual orders', Millett writes, providing the groundwork for Doyle's similar conclusions about films by Smith and Warhol. By portraying 'the power structure of "masculine" and "feminine" as revealed by a homosexual, criminal world', Genet's gay male underworld 'mimics with brutal frankness the bourgeois heterosexual world', exposing its inadequacies through a kind of hypersexual burlesque.[63] However, Mailer, Miller and Lawrence seemingly write without political self-awareness, confirming instead the most repellent and unjust tendencies of their culture. She writes,

> What Miller did articulate was the disgust, the contempt, the hostility, the violence, and the sense of filth with which our culture, or more specifically, its masculine sensibility, surrounds sexuality. And women too; for somehow it is women upon whom this onerous burden of sexuality falls.[64]

This explains the degradation of female bodies and desires that characterises Miller's *Tropic of Cancer* and later books. For Millett, Miller collapses sex with dirt, violence and scorn, as a result of his inability to find a critical foothold from which to view his own inscription within a compromised sexual politics. A soiled embodiment of 'the American manchild', Millett's Miller is 'malignant', 'neurotic' and a latent homosexual.[65] Miller is a passive conduit for the most disastrous effects of heterosexual culture; his rapacious, nearly autobiographical protagonist channels his culture's excesses into the women he penetrates, redoubling the 'dirt, violence and scorn' of patriarchy.

A more sympathetic critic than Millett, the novelist Erica Jong attempted to reconcile the thrill of reading Miller with her anxious relation to his legacy. A Jewish woman, Jong saw the mythic misogynist and anti-Semite as a doubly ambivalent literary guru (after her debut novel was published, Miller was her most vocal supporter and, later, a friend). Jong finds a progressive feminist compromise between her distaste for Miller's *blagueur* pose – his sexism, narcissism and caricatures of Jews – and her triumphant identification with his authorial liberation from the niceties of liberal humanism:

> [Miller] does not say people must always be happy and free of suffering. He does not expect to have no ugly feelings or violent thoughts. He accepts all the extremes of life – the rape fantasies and the murderous thoughts as well as tenderness and affection – and his acceptance gives the reader the gift of self-acceptance.[66]

Like Genet in Millett's reading, Jong affords Miller a critical perspective on the potentially disastrous stuff of fantasy. I suggest that Smith's film retains a similar critical leverage. *Flaming Creatures* stages Smith's anti-humanist criticality, recasting the catastrophic conflation of heterosexuality, filth and violence as something other than inevitable. In its pursuit of unpleasant desires, and pleasing antidotes, the film suggests an opening onto different social relations, posing tentative possibilities for political engagement with art, and with the world.

Norman Mailer was quick to publish a retort to *Sexual Politics*. In 1971 he savaged Millett in writing, under the pretence of defending Miller from what he saw as the feminist critic's 'lack of fidelity to the material she read,' in a book characterised by a style in which 'the yaws of her distortion were nicely hidden by the smudge pots of her indignation.'[67] Over and above his exertions to denigrate Millett, Mailer evocatively describes the horror of sex and the depths of disaster plumbed in Miller's representation of 'the great ocean of the fuck'. For Mailer, reading Miller, 'There were mysteries in trying to explain the extraordinary fascination of an act we can abuse, debase, inundate, and drool upon, yet the act repeats an interest – it draws us toward obsession, … full of the shittiest lust.'[68] He argues that any representation of sex as disastrous necessarily offers a critical perspective on sexual politics, regardless of its writer's gender or sexuality.

Between Millett and Mailer's vociferous polemics, desire is mutually represented as tending towards disaster – even if both writers did so towards different ends. Millett's critique aimed to reclaim the bodies of women from what she reasonably saw as exploitative: that is, the deploying of female bodies as a screen onto which the potent fears and anxieties of heterosexual masculinity might be projected. Mailer's nearly slanderous rejoinder exacerbated the violence Millett uncovered in his writings. However, by defending Miller, he pointed to an interesting thought, namely that his famously prurient 'fascination' was not aimed at the bodies of women, but rather at the relationships that heterosexual desire sets up and exploits. *Flaming Creatures* pre-empts this angry conversation between Millett and Mailer, forcefully representing the heterosexual dyad as a relationship grounded in disaster. The rape scene stands as a powerful representation of heterosexual crisis. Defamiliarised through drag, non-linear narrative, and dizzying camerawork, the rape scene burlesques heterosexuality, giving a potent form to what Mailer terms, above, an act 'full of the shittiest lust'. Although lust is sometimes represented as pleasure, reciprocity and joy, Smith demonstrates that it can tip quite readily into catastrophe, blurring the already hazy distinction between sexual pleasure and disgust.

Despite the challenges Smith posed to mainstream values, he was consistently appalled by the strategies by which mass culture sought to defang his political achievements. Smith suggested that this was achieved by taming the excesses of his film, or by curbing the difficult forms of laughter that his outlandish representations might have sought to induce in viewers. The friction between seriousness and comedy is pronounced in *Flaming Creatures*, and my reading may risk overstating Smith's investment in negative affects. In a recent interview, Jonas Mekas stressed the contradictory qualities in both Smith's personality and artistic practice, and suggested a nuanced account of the pleasurable frustrations in *Flaming Creatures*. In the course of our discussion, Mekas described Smith's sense of the '*maudit*' (or the damned), his 'irreverence' and 'unpredictability'; each extend to Smith's reorganisations of affects and emotions – especially, for Mekas, of sadness and laughter, which the remainder of this chapter seeks to consider. Mekas describes Smith's evocations of sadness as 'desperate', distinct from depression or gloom: 'not a normal person's sadness … no, it's existential … it's pushed to ecstasy.'[69] Smith's explorations of laughter in *Flaming Creatures*, Mekas explains, are similarly 'complex': 'again, his humour is pushed to some other level … outsiders don't see it. That's why the senators could not see it; the police could not see it. Nothing for Jack was normal.'

I asked Mekas if he thought critics had been too literal in our readings of *Flaming Creatures*, and of Smith's writings about his work: 'Yes. One-directional', he replied, 'while Jack was always more complex. Our relationship was also complex.' Indeed, the complexities in their tumultuous friendship began because Smith was prevented from testifying in the obscenity trials prompted by *Flaming Creatures*. 'But I was not in charge', Mekas explained. 'It was not up to me who was going to testify. But he was very unhappy about it'. Emile Zola Berman's legal defence strategy ensured Mekas and his co-defendants received suspended sentences, rather than the feared outcome of lengthy prison terms. 'Jack, very innocently, though he could just go in and tell [the judge] … what it was all about. But that's not how the courts work'. Mekas sympathises with Smith's belief that *Flaming Creatures* should prompt laughter from its viewers, but doubted he could instruct the court in its perverse humour. 'Jack himself always said that it should not be taken too seriously … But that's not how [the courts] saw it.'

Misquoted Laughter

In an interview in the late 1970s, Smith stated of *Flaming Creatures*, 'I started making a comedy about everything that I thought was funny. And it *was* funny. The first audiences were laughing from the beginning all the way through. But then *that writing* started.' Smith refers to the essay by Sontag, and blames the film's fate on her account. 'It turned [*Flaming Creatures*] into a magazine sex issue', he adds.[70] Smith bemoaned what he saw as the abuse of his prime work, including the ways in which it suffered at the hands of the critics and, ultimately, the public – who disarmed its laughter, and directed the work's aggressive power against the artist. As such, he testifies partly to an apprehension of critical exploitation – by Sontag and Mekas – yet more clearly and extensively by the judicial and legislative processes that sullied the film's reputation. Nevertheless, anxieties about his own mistreatment would persist as a paranoid trope that characterised Smith's artist statements throughout his tortured career. His statements can also be read as a misapprehension of the audience's laughter, an unreliable assurance – however sincere or knowing – of their conflict-free amusement at early showings of *Flaming Creatures*.

In *Flaming Creatures* and elsewhere, Smith relentlessly ran bleak thoughts into animations of nut hilarity, despite later apologias for his own apparent failures. *Flaming Creatures* performs rogue itinerancies within the space of art's work, misquoting the experiences of bodies from their volatile manifestations in, or as, desire. As a prime motivator of intimate reactions within the encounter with art, disgust could be said to bring the subject to a standstill, to stop it in its tracks. In opposition, laughter does not refuse the subject's orientation towards the event, but frames it, gives it space. Either way, Menninghaus writes, 'Disgust … and laughter are complementary ways of admitting an alterity that otherwise would fall prey to repression; they enable us to deal with a scandal that otherwise would overpower our system of perception and consciousness.'[71] The collision between laughter and disgust is a familiar one, and a prerequisite of farce, slapstick and gross-out comedy. The collision staged in Smith's work is one that foregrounds the certainty of failure, shame and embarrassment in our dealings in the erotic, no less than in love's counterpart, rejection. Desire, here, is parenthesised by horror and laughter, bound in the push-me-pull-you rhythm of the drives towards life and death. *Flaming Creatures* does so in a manner that can perhaps be thought of as a structural mimicry of an erotic principle: by allowing us our laughter, he saves us from shattering.

Throughout this chapter, I have sought to address the intensity of Smith's investment in his iconic movie *Flaming Creatures*, and the pain that its mistreatment caused him. The banning of the movie was clearly the defining event of his career, and a whole cosmology of effects can be traced to this landmark event. The disgust it inspired in others confounded Smith's faith in the underground, yet also secured his commitment to the fact that art might retain a power to unsettle the securities and platitudes of contemporary life. 'Movies aren't just something … I came to', Smith states, 'they are my life'. Smith's filming sessions were events where his indulgence was so powerful, and the limits between art and the everyday so blurred, that the camera deemed superfluous to the performances it documented. He continues,

> After *Flaming Creatures* I realized that [it] wasn't something I had photographed; Everything really happened … [T]hose were things I wanted to happen in my life and … we really lived through it; you know what I mean? … It was just almost incidental that the camera was around. In other words, if it had happened before the camera was invented, it would have gone on much the same way it did.[72]

Here, Smith struggles, tellingly, in his attempts to articulate how, in performance, the theatricality of the event relates to a putatively 'external' reality. Smith's suggestive statement – that the incidents would have been enacted with or without the camera's presence – complicates the relation between his film- and theatre-based performance work, but also imply a documentary impulse in his filming. In his account, the events had a life of their own, such that the recording is considered secondary to the status of the performance, in its own tangled relation to reality. Indeed, Marc Siegel has theorised Smith's film work in relation to the notion of witness, to read his process as a mode of queer documentary practice. Arguing that 'gay historiography has tended to ignore the importance of queer cultural expressions as a kind of documentation', Siegel reads *Flaming Creatures* to expose a scholarly refusal to invest itself in the problematic excesses of sexual representation, including the forgetting of less familiar – or indeed less palatable – histories of queer lives.[73] Siegel's essay is a progressive critique of the lesbian and gay canon, specifically its anxiety in the face of creative work that hints at 'an eroticism that is always beyond the reach of representation.' This seemingly impossible project aims 'not solely to document that we really do and did live like that, but also to proliferate queer challenges to the normalization of erotic life'.[74] However, by attempting to record that which is always beyond the form that pursues it, the attribution of the term 'documentary' to the work in question might undermine such challenges. The normative presentational strategies entailed in documentary's efforts to record – and therefore to contain – can be too easily refigured (or recuperated) as a classificatory function. The concept of a misquoting of experience, suggested by Smith's own words on the filming, may avoid these implications, while also fostering his pursuit of a new language of cinematic practice that would collapse the boundaries between typically distinct forms of experience and figures of resistance.

The film historian James Stoller describes Smith's imagination as 'a principle unto itself' in that his work 'sets its own terms, and locates itself beyond the terms of conventional praise – or blame. Whatever process [that] has to happen for something to become culture hasn't happened with Jack Smith'.[75] Exercises denoted as the supplements of culture are never productive in a manner that would comply with the demands of market capitalism. Episodic, interstitial and eccentric, Smith's efforts do not result, in 'culture' as we have come to learn it. This resistance to colonisation by culture is grounded in Smith's hatred of capitalism, and his perverse thought on beauty: that in ugliness one finds the dim sparkle of some yet-unthought splendour; and that in beauty one finds a semblance of apposite horror. The desire for beauty is reconceived as the romancing of monstrosity, a courting of the multiple deaths that shadow daily experience.

Practices that feign the work of jouissance – through confusions of the work of disgust and laughter – function by misquoting a possible source, repeating its crisis in ambivalent erotic situations. The idea of a staging of the work of self-loss on a structural level may be invoked to signify such coexistences of the method and the break – a persistence that is without, or at least against, production. Unlike attempts to represent a life in its horrific details – a prime example being the AIDS memoir – stagings of the work of jouissance propose misquoted sites of suffering, translated from lived experience with all the certainties of slippage and mutation that 'translation' signifies. While memoirs do not function as 'authentic' records of real experience, their novelistic form often roots such literary productions within a more familiar tradition of representation – one premised on the assumption that the writer may usefully and exactingly portray the details of a particular social reality.

In the grip of the work of jouissance, however, the performance of cultural failure takes place only to lose itself amid its own tentative crackle. This culmination is distinct from the theatrical convention by which the event rises to a representation of fracture, to be resolved in climax or closure. Rather, the work that rehearses its own jouissance is a movement to collapse proper, where the event attains its paradoxical form: not finished but abandoned. The work that gestures towards jouissance engulfs its own form, pushed to the point at which it no longer coincides with itself. While the disgusting object can be vomited up, or laughed away, jouissance is repeatedly externalised, and each time only partially. Like trauma, the work of jouissance offers the subject no mastery. If the proposal seems hopeless, it is perhaps a status derived from this work's own fostering of the irrational in the face of crisis, its own acute propensity to summon ridicule, to be coped with – as Smith coped with his own disastrous lot – in catastrophic laughter burdened with disgust. His fostering of jouissance at a practical level engages methodological conflict, and explains his uncanny ability to refuse, avoid and interrupt the practices of historical recuperation. *Flaming Creatures* played a significant role in discussions about cultural values in the 1960s, and in some ways set a precedent for subsequent furores around pleasure, desire, decency and other loaded concepts. Careful analyses of the movie – including its repercussions and legacies – enable plenty of theoretical and political possibilities. These are both enabled and undercut by the status of *Flaming Creatures* as a work that is conditioned by what I have described as a structure that fails. The inevitability of misfires, which characterises writing, is played out in the volatility of practices that rehearse the work of jouissance, and is also redoubled in the partial responses commanded by such works. Oppositional scenes of critical response might usefully dwell in the spaces where culture seems to founder. These sites are made all the more conspicuous by their proximity to death, disgust, disease and other bodily disasters.

Notes

1 Jean Genet, *Our Lady of the Flowers*, trans. Bernard Frechtman (New York: Grove Press, 1963), p. 84.

2 Cited by Senator Strom Thurmond (R-SC) in 'Supreme Court of the United States', *Congressional Record* 90:2 (30 September 1968), p. S28775. Warren was an influential figure, widely known as the Chairman of the President's Commission on the Assassination of President Kennedy (1963–64).

3 Jack Smith, 'Lobotomy in Lobsterland' (1965), *Wait for Me at the Bottom of the Pool: The Writings of Jack Smith*, ed. J. Hoberman and Edward Leffingwell (New York and London: High Risk Books, 1997), pp. 81–8 (p. 84).

4 Jack Smith, unpublished journal (1961–3), p. 199. Jack Smith Archives, Gladstone Gallery, New York.

5 Senator Jesse Helms (R-NC), 'Amendment No. 2396 to the Excepted Committee Amendment', *Congressional Record* 81:7 (25 July 1994).

6 Charles H. Keating, Jr, Remarks to the House, 'Justice Fortas and a Matter of National Concern', *Congressional Record* 90:2 (4 September 1968), p. H25565.

7 Jacques Lacan, 'The transference and the drive', *The Four Fundamental Concepts of Psycho-Analysis: The Seminar of Jacques Lacan, Book XI*, ed. Jacques-Alain Miller, trans. Alan Sheridan (Harmondsworth and New York: Penguin, 1979), pp. 183–4.

8 Sigmund Freud, 'Beyond the pleasure principle', *On Metaphysics*, ed. James Strachey (London and New York: Penguin Books, 1991), p. 322.

9 Cited in Nestor Braunstein, 'Desire and jouissance in the teachings of Lacan', *The Cambridge Companion to Lacan*, ed. Jean-Michel Rabaté (Cambridge: Cambridge University Press, 2003) pp. 102–15 (p. 103).

10 Genet, p. 97.

11 In the 1980s, the title *Respectable Creatures* was also retrospectively given to a collection of fragments filmed between 1950–66, which brings together an early, playful parody of Maria Montez in *Arabian Nights* (1942) and footage from a carnival in Rio de Janeiro. His friend Ela Troyano clarified the origins of the title in a conversation in Berlin in March 2009.

12 Gavin Butt, *Between You and Me: Queer Disclosures in the New York Art World, 1948–1963* (Durham and London: Duke University Press, 2005), p. 49.

13 Sheldon Renan, *The Underground Film: An Introduction to Its Development in America* (London: Studio Vista, 1968), p. 36.

14 J. Hoberman and Jonathan Rosenbaum, *Midnight Movies* (New York and London: Harper & Row, 1983), pp. 50–9.

15 Tyler, p. 47.

16 John Rechy, *City of Night* (London: Granada Publishing, 1964), pp. 72–3.

17 J. Hoberman, 'The big heat: Making and unmaking *Flaming Creatures*', *Flaming Creature: Jack Smith, His Amazing Life and Times*, ed. Edward Leffingwell, Carole Kismaric and Marvin Heiferman, The Institute for Contemporary Art, P.S.1 Museum (London and New York: Serpent's Tail, 1997), pp. 152–67 (p. 162).

18 Clarence Manion cited in Senator Strom Thurmond (R-SC), 'Nomination of Justice Fortas', *Congressional Record* 90:2 (11 September 1968), p. S31397.

19 'Supreme Court of the United States', *Congressional Record* 90:2 (30 September

1968), p. S28785. Byrd was a former member of the Ku Klux Klan, and in 1994, as Chair of the Appropriations Committee, he would lead an attempt to defund the National Endowment for the Arts, in response to a performance by Ron Athey in Minneapolis.

20 Representative John R. Rarick (LA), 'Abe Fortas opposed by Citizens for Decent Literature', *Congressional Record* 90:2 (22 July 1968), p. E22717.

21 'Justice Fortas and a Matter of National Concern', p. H25563.

22 Ibid. p. H25564.

23 Ibid. pp. H25562–3.

24 Cited in ibid. p. H25551.

25 Ibid. p. H25565.

26 Michael Binstein and Charles Bowden, *Trust Me: Charles Keating and the Missing Billions* (New York: Random House, 1993), pp. 86–9.

27 'Supreme Court of the United States', *Congressional Record* 90:2 (27 September 1968), p. S22717.

28 'Supreme Court of the United States', *Congressional Record* 90:2 (30 September 1968), p. S28775.

29 Cited in Hoberman, 'The big heat', p. 164.

30 Cited in J. Hoberman, *On Jack Smith's Flaming Creatures and Other Secret-Flix of Cinemaroc* (New York: Granary Books, 2001), p. 38.

31 Hoberman, 'The big heat', p. 164.

32 Quotations from the *Perversion for Profit*. For a discussion of the movie, see Whitney Strub, 'Perversion for Profit: Citizens for Decent Literature and the Arousal of an Antiporn Public in the 1960s', *Journal of the History of Sexuality* 15.2 (2006), pp. 258–91.

33 Leo Bersani, 'Is the rectum a grave?', *AIDS: Cultural Analysis / Cultural Activism*, ed. Douglas Crimp (Cambridge and London: MIT Press, 1988), pp. 197–222 (p. 212).

34 Ibid. pp. 220–2.

35 Jack Smith, audio documentation of untitled performance, 56 Ludlow Street, 1962–64, *Les Evening Gowns Damnées* (New York: Tony Conrad's Audio ArtKive/ Table of the Elements, 1997).

36 Branden W. Joseph, *Beyond the Dream Syndicate: Tony Conrad and the Arts after John Cage (A 'Minor' History)* (New York: Zone Books, 2008), p. 233.

37 Bersani, p. 207.

38 William Haver, 'Really bad infinities: Queer's honour and the pornographic life', *Parallax* 13 (October–December 1999), pp. 9–21 (p. 11).

39 Bersani, p. 221. Emphasis in original.

40 Ibid. p. 217.

41 Ibid. p. 219.

42 Michel Foucault, 'Friendship as a way of life', *Foucault Live: Collected Interviews, 1961–1984*, ed. by Sylvère Lotringer, trans. Lysa Hochroth and John Johnston (New York: Semiotext(e), 1996), pp. 308–12 (p. 311).

43 Bersani, p. 216.

44 Butt, p. 160.

45 Susan Sontag, 'Jack Smith's *Flaming Creatures*', *Against Interpretation and Other*

Essays (New York: Farrar, Straus & Giroux, 1967), pp. 226–31 (p. 229).

46 Sontag, 'Against interpretation', *Against Interpretation and Other Essays*, pp. 3–14 (p. 7).

47 D. A. Miller, 'Sontag's urbanity', *The Gay and Lesbian Studies Reader*, ed. Henry Abelove, Michèle Aina Barale and David M. Halperin (New York and London: Routledge, 1993), pp. 212–20 (p. 212).

48 Susan Sontag, *AIDS and Its Metaphors* (London: Penguin, 1988), p. 93.

49 Sontag, 'Jack Smith's *Flaming Creatures*', p. 231.

50 Ibid.

51 Joseph, p. 254.

52 Gerard Malanga, 'Interview with Jack Smith', *Film Culture* 45 (Summer 1967), pp. 12–16 (p. 14).

53 Winfried Menninghaus, *Disgust: Theory and History of a Strong Sensation*, trans. by Howard Eiland and Joel Golb (Albany: State University of New York, 2003), p. 33.

54 Jack Smith, 'The white pig of the Medina' (1967), *Wait for Me at the Bottom of the Pool*, pp. 73–5 (pp. 73–4).

55 Ralph Rugoff, 'Mr. McCarthy's neighbourhood', *Paul McCarthy* (London: Phaidon, 1996), pp. 32–87 (p. 49).

56 'Justice Fortas and a Matter of National Concern', p. H25554.

57 Ibid. p. H25565.

58 Jacques Lacan, *The Ethics of Psychoanalysis, 1959–1960: The Seminar of Jacques Lacan, Book VII*, ed. Jacques-Alain Miller, Book VII, trans. Dennis Porter (London and New York: Routledge, 1992), p. 186.

59 Jennifer Doyle, *Sex Objects: Art and the Dialectics of Desire* (Minneapolis and London: University of Minnesota Press, 2006), p. xxv.

60 Ibid. p. 72.

61 Craig Owens, 'Outlaws: Gay men in feminism', *Beyond Recognition: Representation, Power, and Culture*, ed. Scott Bryson *et al.* (Berkeley, Los Angeles and London: University of California Press, 1992), pp. 218–235 (p. 219).

62 Kate Millett, *Sexual Politics* (London: Virago, 1977), p. 22.

63 Ibid. pp. 18–9.

64 Ibid. p. 295.

65 Ibid. pp. 303–13.

66 Erica Jong, *The Devil at Large: On Henry Miller* (New York: Random House, 1993), p. 131.

67 Norman Mailer, 'The raging affair: Kate Millett and Henry Miller', *The Time of Our Time* (London: Little, Brown and Company, 1998), pp. 773–90 (p. 774).

68 Ibid. pp. 785–6.

69 Jonas Mekas, unpublished interview with the author, New York (8 September 2011). Subsequent statements by Mekas in this section are from this source.

70 Sylvère Lotringer, 'Uncle Fishook and the sacred baby poo poo of art' (Interview with Jack Smith, 1978), *Wait for Me at the Bottom of the Pool*, pp. 107–21 (p. 107). Emphasis in original.

71 Menninghaus, p. 11.

72 Cited in Sally Banes, *Greenwich Village 1963: Avant-Garde Performance and the Effervescent Body* (Durham and London: Duke University Press, 1993), p. 94.

73 Marc Siegel, 'Documentary that dare/not speak its name: Jack Smith's *Flaming Creatures*', *Between the Sheets, in the Streets: Queer, Lesbian, Gay Documentary*, ed. Chris Holmlund and Cynthia Fuchs (Minneapolis and London: University of Minnesota Press, 1997), pp. 91–106 (p. 92).

74 Ibid. pp. 104–5.

75 James Stoller, '16mm', *Village Voice* (7 December 1967), p. 37.

Innocent monsters and *Normal Love*   4

To the general public … [You] think we are naughty to look at bodies, think about our orgasms, apply the processes of our intellect and imaginations to determining what the body's needs are, to be led by our bodies … Most of the terrible tensions of your life come from the discrepancies between what your bodies ask of you and your crabbed gratifications. (Jack Smith)[1]

Jack Smith was keenly aware of the psychic cost of sublimation. He was particularly fond of denouncing the consumers of mainstream culture for their hypocrisies, and their consolatory persecutions of sexual outsiders. After *Flaming Creatures* and the affront it posed, Smith set about filming *Normal Love* (1963–64) as a satire on heterosexuality that imagines it as a mundane submission to social and economic pressures. Filming began in July 1963, in the grounds of the painter Wynn Chamberlain's country house in Old Lyme, Connecticut, and continued in John Vaccaro's large loft on Great Jones Street in Manhattan. Smith edited some of the rushes, according to evocative notes in his journals, but the film was left definitively unfinished. Written in red lipstick on marble, the cast list boasts several performers reprising appearances from *Flaming Creatures*, including Angus MacLise, Francis Francine and Mario Montez (see figure 4.1). These superstars were joined by a further host of underground figures, including Andy Warhol, the (then heavily pregnant) Beat poet Diane di Prima, ukulele songster Tiny Tim, the actress Beverly Grant (see figure 4.2), theatre-maker John Vaccaro, and filmmaker Naomi Levine. Smith defied the convention to fix scenes in a definitive sequence, and reels were recombined in makeshift, fluid forms and presented in live performances throughout his life.

Writing in his journal, Smith notes the key elements of the work: the 'HORRORS OF DEATH', 'innocent monsters' (a phrase lifted from Charles Baudelaire), 'creatures … trailing over the hillside', 'regeneration', and a poetically imagined denouement of sorts, in which 'Death in an Iron Door Clangs Shut/ in [the] form of a Broken Heart'.[2] In journal notes made after wrapping the shoot, he remembers the surrogate heterosexuals in the movie clowning

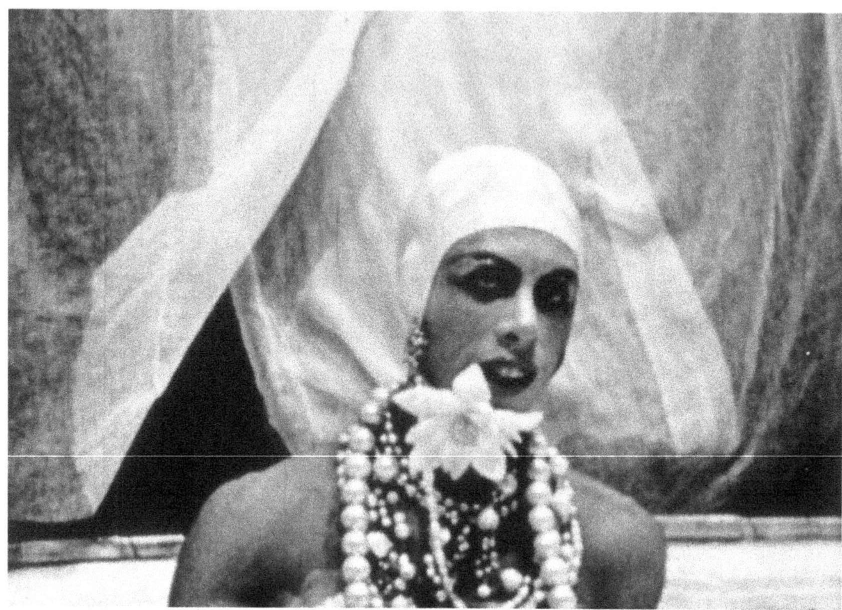

4.1   Jack Smith, *Normal Love* (1963).

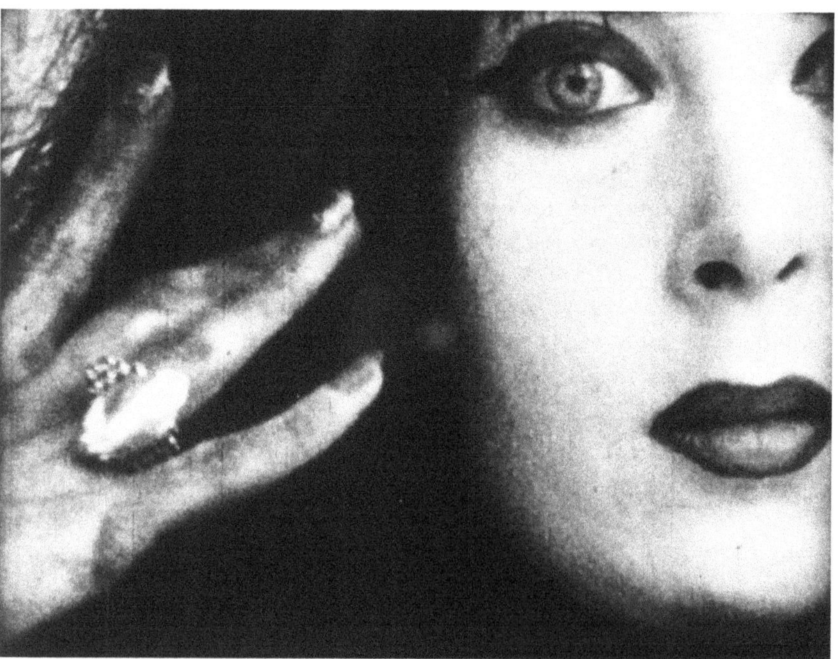

4.2   Jack Smith, *Normal Love* (1963).

atop a giant cake designed by Claes Oldenburg, 'whereon they wasted their afternoons in the service of the forces of banality – the horror beneath the dreary, pasty face of everyday life of police protection and the sex fantasies of the manufacturers'.[3] For Smith, normative sexuality includes but exceeds heterosexuality, and is conditioned by the market forces of advertising. Later in the same journal entry, he condemns the 'Plutocrats whose proper function is finding new uses for plastic and the utilization of nubile young girls … to tease extra pennies from a public which is happily milked for the sake of a steady flow of acquiescently grinning air-brushed darlings'. As such, the conditioning of desire by market capitalism results in the compulsory fantasy of a perfected dream world, consisting exclusively of beautiful couplings, comfortable sex and uncomplicated genders. Smith concludes that these techniques cause the public to be 'shocked by images of partners without textureless faces, shocked by the uselessness of anything but cut-out, rigidly self-conscious beings smiling pleasantly, displaying a product and fainting with rapture all at the same moment'.[4] The implication is that this also results in a mode of cultural reception that rejects representations of sexuality that admit to the ugly and the unclean, to pain and defilement as conditions of our desiring interactions with the bodies of others. As argued in the previous chapter, *Flaming Creatures* admitted this without shame, and with facetious strokes of comedy, and for these offences it struck a negative chord with a cultural orthodoxy that rails against such indiscretion. Hence the fuss made by censors over the film, resulting in court action and a public scandal that was ultimately detrimental to Smith and to – as he called it – 'the dull but honest *Flaming Creatures*'.[5]

In a wonderful turn of phrase, J. Hoberman describes Smith's aesthetic in *Normal Love* as 'glamour-encrusted povera', hinting at Smith's use of everyday substances – Coca-Cola, milk, Halloween costumes and cheap jewellery – towards a vivid evocation of other possibilities.[6] P. Adams Sitney confirms the work's vivid beauty and sensuality, stating, 'Of all the film-makers of the mythopoeic stage of American avant-garde film, Jack Smith was perhaps the most gifted with imaginative powers.'[7] Sitney positions *Normal Love* at the apex of Smith's 'ravishing' mythopoeisis, as a venture that renders identity ambivalent through an esoteric aspiration to mystery, mythology and metamorphosis. Indeed, Smith teases layers of performance in circles that fall short of narrative, building luminous images that culminate in a nebulous, indefinable *cri de coeur*.

After the 'sickeningly pasty reception in New York of *Flaming Creatures*,' Smith committed himself to facetiously acknowledging the apparent demands of the dominant culture, by 'shooting a lovely, pasty, pink and green color movie that is going to be the definitive pasty expression.'[8] Although he actually planned and began filming *Normal Love* before the backlash against *Flaming Creatures* (which kicked off with the first police raid in March 1964, eight months after he commenced shooting the new project), the legal fallout must have enabled him to critically reformulate the political implications of the new directions his filmmaking had started to take. The first sequence of *Normal Love* introduces the viewer to Smith's favourite Superstar of Cinemaroc, Mario Montez in gaudy drag regalia. As a luridly extravagant drag mermaid, Montez lights candles and incense around a portrait of his namesake, Maria, adorned in a frame and set atop a shrine or temple, similar to the ones Smith installed and nurtured in his apartments. Smith's camera travels its slow zoom, to reveal the Technicolor Mermaid. Deliriously beautiful in a crimson dress, she reclines in a circular floral spread in a paddle-pool filled with milk. The sequence is dominated by red hues, a theme completed by the red plastic cherries he suggestively mouths. Further scenes are similarly ordered through a dominant colour – green, red, pink or yellow – each presiding swathe flashed through with flecks of white lights, deep earth and painted skin.

Colliding sensual drag and 'pasty' aesthetics, Smith articulated the contradictions between an underground, dissident politics and the conservative expectations of his audiences. How, then, does *Normal Love* crystallise emergent political and theoretical knowledge about sexual dissidence? Like much of Smith's work, it does so in contradictory, partial, intuitive ways, not least because in the 1960s the discursive tools were barely available to assist in articulating a coherent political representation. Indeed, as Alan Sinfield reminds us, '[t]hat's how representation works: we make our cultures by negotiating more and less satisfactory images,' because even faulty or partial visibility will produce modes of subcultural address that 'bring notions of queerness, however inadequate, into everyday popular interest'.[9] As such, Smith's film does not represent or produce a coherent polarisation between conformity and deviance, but nevertheless stages compensatory improvisations on personal, historically specific questions.

By following *Flaming Creatures* with his lyrical, unfinished film *Normal Love*, Smith staged official culture's ambivalent displacements of freakishness – and other forms of indeterminacy – away from rigorously maintained norms. *Normal Love* includes several veiled references to *Flaming Creatures*, such as the recurrence of a prosthetic nose (worn by Joel Markman, the vampire starlet from *Flaming Creatures*), and the aggressive courting of a woman that replicates his earlier film's notorious rape scene; elsewhere, as performers frolic on a jetty, a dirty foot is pointed at the camera, mimicking the licking of feet that prefaces the rape scene in *Flaming Creatures*. I argue that *Normal Love* emerged from the aftermaths of Smith's previous work, *Flaming Creatures*, specifically its mauling by critical and legal apparatuses. By situating Smith within the context of subcultural practice – the gay milieu of early 1960s New York, as the segue between Beat and Hippie countercultures – Smith and other queer artists produced work that articulated a historically specific realisation that 'culture' as traditionally formulated did not speak to them, or on their behalf. As Raymond Williams noted in 1958, the dominant class controls the transmission of cultural practice, producing a selective tradition whose representations will inevitably be 'related to and even governed by the interests of [that] class'.[10] The dominant culture therefore produces and normalises criteria based upon texts that suit the values it has an interest in supporting. In the context of Smith's work, such values are those that pertain to – and restrict – the politics of gender and sexuality, identification and communion. Borne on his abuse in the aftermath of *Flaming Creatures*, Smith did not seek to insert himself into the culture as it was contemporaneously structured, opting rather to produce works that spoke to his interests and those of his peers. In this way, *Flaming Creatures* and *Normal Love* referred to – and indeed helped to constitute – the developing pre-Stonewall gay subculture. His opting out of a properly participatory relation to culture does not preclude resentment at marginalisation. A subcultural orientation may be dissident, but the subculture is still thoroughly 'ideological' in character, often re-inscribing the cultural values that its participants strive to solve in provisional ways.[11]

In Smith's idiosyncratic worldview, art is persistently brought into play to stage his perspectives on sex and his related fixation on decay and death. His resentment of conventional morality – of 'generations and generations chained to a bed'[12] – were staged daily to the brink of madness, and always stopped short of the totality of politics. Nevertheless, his work maps out a shifting cartography of available points of resistance and knowledge. The politically discomfiting sign of the 'freak' is developed as an excess of signification, a variation on Sue Golding's figure of the 'pariah', that may hold an itinerant charge for sexual politics, refusing the assimilatory promise heralded in conservative perspectives. For Golding, the pariah designates a body whose sexuality is marked by the threat of exile, difference and death, a force of otherness that retains the possibility of overcoming crisis through a spirit of collective bravado. Disavowing assimilation, the pariah embodies queerness as 'our quantifiable strangeness and unclassifiable curiosity slip-sliding around sex itself', as a mark of distinction radicalised in the time of AIDS.[13] Against such celebrations of the thrill of difference, Alice Echols has argued that paeans to the body of the outcast in queer theory might install a 'hierarchy of perversion', with adverse political effects. She adds that the revisionist fascination with non-normative practices obscures the historical efforts to oppose the labelling of lesbian and gay bodies as deviant, and might also privilege the experiences of middle-class white men, who have often been allowed greater freedom to safely transgress sexual conventions. Echols also argues that the romance of the queer outlaw underestimates the very real threat posed by supposedly assimilatory lesbians and gay men.[14] Echols' criticisms are sensitive to the material implications of revisionist theories of sexuality, and I acknowledge her concerns by focusing explicitly on the historicity of the freak as a subject position performed in specific subcultural contexts.

The freak as an exilic figure of contingent sexual difference enables me to track a less familiar trajectory of crisis in the 'neurotic gothic sex-colored world' of New York in the pre-history of gay liberation.[15] A cultural pre-history of non-affirmative sensibilities may therefore pre-empt or foreshadow the influence of later, AIDS-inflected theory. Moreover, I echo Richard Dellamora's convincing argument that the symbolic twinning of homosexuality and catastrophe is confirmed in the horror, grief and loss wrought by AIDS in the 1980s, but is set up much earlier, at least before the end of the nineteenth century.[16] The emergence of a public culture of homosexuality in the 1980s perhaps relied upon the pre-existence of a relatively private culture of crisis, insularities that were periodically breached by scandal, persecution, and various types of institutional and social violence. It was upon this history that lesbian, gay and transgender cultures premised their emergence. Or, as Gore Vidal succinctly put it in 1949, 'One must have a tragedy to have a literature'.[17]

The grip of freakishness

In *Normal Love,* our distinctions between the 'pasty normals' and characters designated as freaks are continually open to challenge. While some characters mime the vacuity and tedium of heterosexuality in Smith's characterisation, other characters oppose this normative prison of the same through costume, play and other theatrical effects. Peopled with 'pasty normals' as well as uprooted flaming creatures, *Normal Love* evokes pathos, jaded humour, troubled sexuality and literary beauty in equal measures. Courting us with magic, with illusions of desire, belonging and death, the film teases our ties to received emotional, physical and spatial certainties. The Mummy character in the film is a seemingly remote creature that stands outside Smith's damning representation of heterosexuality as a tired and tragic coupling. Angus MacLise's Mummy evokes an easy pathos, as a timid incarnation of a horror type traditionally represented as threatening and terrifying. Unlike the Werewolf, who playfully overpowers the Mermaid and teases her with pleasures before removing her to some unstated elsewhere, the Mummy in *Normal Love* is a passive figure towards whom characters devote compassion. They feel sorry for him, take care of him, treating the pitiable undead like an out-of-town wallflower, to be consoled by the concern of thoughtful strangers. Momentarily released from his identity as the locus of disgust, of putrefaction and blind enmity, Smith's Mummy enters a fugitive kind of community, however transitory, comic and eventually untenable such belonging might be. Inevitably, his horror is returned to him in the second reel. In an eerie sequence, the camera focuses on the revelation of his eye, and fabric bandages are peeled and lifted to reveal a gaping mouth. The image is deathly, moribund, and terminally disconcerting.

As examined in the previous chapter, Smith's explorations of sex and sexuality relentlessly drift towards the messy, unpleasant and unpalatable underside of pleasure. In relation to *Flaming Creatures*, I argued that Smith poses the crucial influence of the experience of jouissance, the force that dissembles the drive towards aesthetic unity and subjective coherence. These ideas draw upon a century of psychoanalytic accounts of desire. For the Freud of *Beyond the Pleasure Principle*, in his departure from clinical psychoanalysis towards a metaphysical theory of the psyche, the hypothesis that the mental apparatus endeavours to reduce excitation is re-imagined as under constant threat from both the reality principle and the death drive. The freakishness that Smith tends to imagine can therefore be reconsidered not as eccentric, deviant imaginings of life at the margins of the social, but as a quality that is central to the play of desire in the constitution of the contemporary subject. Smith's affronts to the mythical consolations of pleasure can therefore be extended by deploying a series of his grim performance-based ventures as parables of Freud's thoughts on the death drive.

Smith's short film entitled *Hot Air Specialists* (1983) performs the abiding rule of Freud's thesis with characteristic bathos, and unflinchingly comic performances of sexual disgust and deferred aggression.[18] The film shows Smith in his often-reprised role as the scare-queen courtesan, Rose Courtyard, star of his earlier film *Song For Rent* (1969). Dressed in a red gown and gloves, bijoux jewellery and a blood-red tangle of hair, Smith's vibrant face is caked with layers of make-up. Rose entices a greasy, dishevelled, cross-eyed john who has dropped by to engage in some unwholesome liaison. She seduces him with feigned coyness, grimly tonguing a dried tropical flower, as the camera performs lip-centric paeans to Rose's pout-laden, paint-clogged, gender-variant seduction. With mock-virginal affront, Rose reproaches his clumsy advances with intermittent slaps, and punishes his gaucheness with a purse-wallop, protecting the burden of her questionable purity. Despite her disingenuous castigations, the tongue-tied punter makes a final over-zealous move, pulling down her shabby neckline to reveal a hairy chest in the place of the heaving, porcelain bosom he had, perhaps, quixotically imagined. In a scene of masterful gross-out excess, the john vomits uncontrollably, issuing forth chunky liquids over Rose's hairy chest and knotted wig. He continues to gag into her lap, heaving out nasty chicken-soup emissions that pool in the crinoline between her legs.

The death drive, in Sigmund Freud's foundational account of psychoanalysis, exists in opposition to the life instincts, which are categorically sexual. In Smith's oeuvre, the two forces are as tangled as Rose Courtyard's vomit-stricken wig, as the life drive is challenged by the death drive at every turn. For Freud too, death and the erotic are inextricably linked by this tension; hence Freud poses the 'dualistic view of instinctual life … [in which] two kinds of processes are constantly at work … one constructive or assimilatory [the life drive] and the other destructive or dissimilatory [the death drive].'[19] The daemonic force of the death drive short-circuits the rational-humanist assumption that the 'natural' in man is a pulse or compulsion only towards perfection and the 'good', inhibited solely by external dangers. In *Hot Air Specialists*, the revelation of the disgusting beneath the patina of beauty and promise of pleasure – however unconvincing Rose's beauty and its entailed promise might be – perhaps confirms Freud's thesis that an internal movement purely towards 'intellectual achievement and ethical sublimation' is to be dismissed as the stuff of benevolent illusion.[20] Smith thoroughly destabilises any promise of clean and productive congress between the two (grim) players in the tryst. Any semblance that normality might reasonably be recovered is vanquished in the thwarted conjugal scene.

This opposes the traditional understanding of non-normativity as a rerouting of normal sexual and other functions from their correct or natural path towards wholesomeness and coherence. The terms used to describe sexual difference in pathologising terms – deviation, perversion, obscenity (the ob- or off-scene) – imply the unnatural or unexpected directions in which desire can be driven, when subjects find themselves in the grip of freakishness. 'The majority of freaks are forced into the most unnatural of lives,' Tod Browning warns in the prologue to his movie *Freaks* (1931). 'Therefore, they have built up among themselves a code of ethics to protect them from the barbs of normal people.'[21] Released in 1932, *Freaks* was rapidly taken out of distribution after the revulsion it aroused in audiences. Re-released in 1963, the year Smith made *Normal Love*, it acquired cult status in college campus and art-house screenings, and held a special resonance for the burgeoning counterculture. Smith never stated his affection for Browning's movie, but his writings are littered with references to 'pinheads', 'freaks' and other notable centrepieces; moreover, the conniving beauty's name – Cleopatra – cannot have gone unnoticed by Smith, bearing in mind his persistent Egyptophilia. More importantly, *Flaming Creatures* and *Normal Love* brought together social outcasts to translate such a 'code of ethics,' as intuited by Browning, into an anti-aesthetic forging tentative, partial ties between people of extravagant and eccentric difference. Like Browning's cult movie, *Flaming Creatures and Normal Love* are notable for their mutual nihilism. Smith's imagining of humanity as destitute and painful was represented with characteristic wit, even if its comedy was lost on some viewers. Browning's film, on the other hand, left little space for comedy. His approximation of reality is governed by a horror of life that is not restricted to those spurned by the forces of 'nature' or good fortune. In *Freaks*, the pure of intention meet with disaster. Agents of malice are in turn punished at the hands of the good, with forcible mutilation and death. These variant but complicit injunctions on the bodies of the charitable and devious alike are signalled in the climactic act: the extensive and violent gamut of tortures inflicted on the body of Cleopatra, by the avenging freaks. For her wickedness against the duped midget protagonist, Hans, and the entailed crime against the community of freaks who retaliate on his behalf, the blonde beauty is reduced to an incapacitated vision of shrieking horror, on show for the terror and ambivalent delectation of a paying public.

However, despite its similar proliferation of 'freaks', Smith's *Normal Love* refuses narrative and thematic resolution. As I will gesture to through comparisons to two contemporary plays – Edward Albee's *Who's Afraid of Virginia Woolf?* (1962) and Mart Crowley's *The Boys in the Band* (1968) – despite the pleasure afforded by forward-thinking narrative explorations of difference, linearity in this period seems to entail problematic resolutions. While there is fun along the way, the experience ends leaving a sour taste in the mouth. In Browning, Albee and Crowley's documents, which bookend *Normal Love*, linearity reproduces and affirms conservations assumptions about sexuality and sociality that the works themselves might have served to rethink. However, exploring scenes of encounters between generic characters appropriated from B-movie mythology, Smith's movie eschews narrative development and closure, instead staging a series of events that work to demonstrate how a subject might attempt to make a liveable life in a time of privation. His itinerant, improvisatory characters include the Werewolf, Mummy, and Beverly Grant's Cobra Woman; and fantastical characters such as John Vaccaro's White Bat, or Mario Montez's Mermaid in thrall to a haunting Spider, later doused in Coca-Cola by the Werewolf in a mud pit.

Freaks occupies a legendary position in the history of midnight movie culture. In its re-release in the early 1960s, the film's title underwent a shift in signification as a result of the newly versatile, hipster term 'freak', and the film's subject matter struck up an unexpected relation with Beat writing's evocative narratives of social alienation, sexual freedom and cultural experimentation. According to Steven Watson, the term 'Beat' itself 'originally derived from circus and carnival argot, reflecting the straitened circumstances of the nomadic carnies', forging a further, etymological relation between these different species of social outsiders.[22] Screenings of *Freaks* in the 1960s consolidated post-Beat adherents' identifications with the symbolic figure of the outcast. Browning's film attempted to historically locate the horror invoked by the unusual bodies that populate his film, describing the manner in which, 'In ancient times anything that deviated from the normal was considered an omen of ill luck or representative of evil.' The prologue continues:

> Gods of misfortune and adversity were invariably cast in the form of monstros-
> ities, and deeds of injustice and hardship have been attributed to the many
> crippled and deformed tyrants of Europe and Asia. History, religion, folklore
> and literature abound in tales of misshapen misfits who have altered the world's
> course. Goliath, Calaban [*sic*], Frankenstein, Gloucester, Tom Thumb and
> Kaiser Wilhelm are just a few, whose fame is worldwide.

Similarly, Philip Core writes, 'Throughout history there has always been a
significant minority whose unacceptable characteristics – talent, poverty,
physical unconventionality, sexual anomaly – render them vulnerable to
the world's brutal laughter.' Core borrows the same terminology to suggest
that the pariah bodies of queers are marked by their difference, extending
Browning's observation that a parallel was often procured between subjective
difference and external markers. Core continues that sexual outsiders '[hide]
their mortification behind behaviour which is often as deviant as that which
is concealed,' bringing together the themes of physical discrepancy, sexual
deviation and social death, explored throughout this chapter.[23]

In tracing the excess of perceived limits of subjection, *Freaks*'s original
release brought Browning vilification and scandal, destroying his career in a
manner that prefigures the effect that *Flaming Creatures* would have on Smith's
nascent public career thirty years later. The similarity is extended through the
mutual irony that their respective scandals, in fact, also secured the secret
fame of each, confirming their own cult notoriety and the status of their
respective films as legendary (and until recently, elusive) curiosities. 'Never
again,' Browning's film announced, 'will such a story be filmed, as modern
science and teratology is rapidly eliminating such blunders of nature from the
world. With humility for the many injustices done to such people (they have
no power to control their lot) we present the most startling horror story of the
abnormal and *the unwanted*.' Smith unwittingly took up this challenge. Like
Freaks, Smith's films are populated by collections of misfits with ambiguous
genders and unusual bodies. Browning's sideshow freaks – midgets, pinheads,
amputees and bird-girls – undergo a translation into Smith's coterie of flaming
creatures, his collection of local personalities, drag queens, hermaphrodites,
junkies, Coney Island drag show scenesters, and other colourful degenerates.

Imagining the queer as freak

In a collection of essays entitled *Freakshow*, Albert Goldman characterises the
mood of the 1960s in a telling manner that usefully collapses the emergent
cultural enterprises of that decade with the developments forged by Smith's
example. Reclaiming the term as a constructive category of pop-cultural
labour, he writes,

> I have recorded the [1960s] as monstrous and fascinating, bizarre and theat-
> rical, stirring and ridiculous – as, in a word, a freakshow. I like that word.
> Its ambivalent charge of affection and contempt, its forbidden frankness and
> disarming familiarity make it a token of this era's queer spirit and the flaming
> creatures it has hatched.[24]

Interestingly, the phrase 'flaming creatures' would appear to have, by 1971, entered countercultural argot, even though Smith is only mentioned in passing in Goldman's book. Moreover, one such reference fleetingly disparages Smith's work in trifling terms, as 'limp perversion in campy costumes'.[25] While the phenomenon of the freak emerges in the 1960s in part as a counterhegemonic masculinity derived from the strategies of the burgeoning gay rights movement, Goldman disparages this specific history, representing Smith's work as both pathological and tame.

Writing notes on the filming of *Normal Love*, Smith described his creatures 'all incandescently amok, no control over themselves – their souls glowing thru their skin. And their eyes burning with the desire to give & the realization of our common helplessness. Tragic twisted faces – Labrynths [*sic*] for a tormented minotaur'.[26] In this context, the subject who self-identifies as a freak borrows and soothes the ugly history of those unfamiliar bodies that have, historically, been labelled as freakish by a frightened majority. The assumption of freakishness by non-normative subjects assumes the burden of difference, stripping it of its obscenity and laying claim to it as an unfamiliar state of dignity. Smith's freaks are therefore a compensatory invention, produced by minority subjects in response to a desire or to be different from the majority, coloured by a need to do so together. Freakishness conjures a peculiar form of sociality, as a temporary release from marginalisation and persecution, which is revoked as one returns to other modes of social participation. *Normal Love* enacts these movements between the mainstream and the margin, harassment and identification, and articulates the joy of freakishness while acknowledging the threat of disaster. Such disasters are those that haunt all forms of sociality, not least marginal communities, as well as the perceived difficulties of reintegrating after the serious play of freakishness has run its course. Smith's film is careful to show that the dream of transcending the social through serious play is prone to the reality principle, not least because the possibility of exemption from sociality is conditioned by the threat of social death – exile and abandonment – and in limit-cases, physical injury, punishment, incarceration and biological death.

Conditioned by such experiences in daily life, queers have been resourceful in constructing new ways of coping with the threat of disaster. One counterintuitive tactic is to emphasise one's perceived difference, writing 'internal' differentiations upon the skin of the body, partly to burlesque the assumptions of the mainstream. In order to do so, a grab bag of cultural references – celebrities, B-movie characters, sideshow monstrosities, criminals, undesirables, outcasts – is corralled into the development of new identities. As Marybeth Hamilton writes, in a study of Little Richard's highly sexualised performances in the mid-1950s, 'freak' was not simply pejorative, but also 'an historically specific social identity' taken up by lesbians and gay men, as a means of appropriating the subcultural tradition of the carnival sideshow.[27] This appropriation enabled self-styled 'freaks' to denigrate heterosexual norms as passive and conformist, and to celebrate homosexuality as a liberated, empowered mode of sexual dissidence. In the context of the late 1950s and 1960s, this gesture tapped into the emergent civil rights movements, and consolidated the shift towards new models for subjectivity based upon a refusal to apologise for sexual difference. Hamilton notes that the political efficacy of the freak was compromised by the late 1960s, especially in the context of black arts and culture, as the mainstream capitalised on its difference and appropriated its effects as consumer-friendly kitsch. Nevertheless, the appropriation and resignification of freakishness prefigures the feminist appropriation of hysteria in art of the 1970s towards an attempt to strip an outmoded diagnostic category of its patriarchal charge, and the later appropriation of 'queer' as a proud designation in the 1980s.

By gesturing to the articulation of 1960s modes of erotic self-fashioning and belonging, Smith disrupts the popular myth of the Stonewall riots of 28 June 1969 as the foundational event of gay liberation. George Chauncey has mapped the development, over the first half of the twentieth century, of the production of modern male homosexuality, through social, commercial and other forms of distinctly gay male culture in New York. Chauncey tracks the kinds of relationships that men created in this context, forging communal ties and social identities beyond the reductive logics of isolation, invisibility, and internalisation. As such, his book forcefully counters the lore that Stonewall occasioned an explosion into visibility of a new culture for gay men in New York, which then paved the way for the emergence of lesbian, gay and transgender radicalism. 'The "gay world" actually consisted of multiple social worlds, or social networks,' he writes, 'many of them overlapping but some quite distinct and segregated from others along lines of race, ethnicity, class, gay cultural style, and/or sexual practices.'[28] Stonewall enabled the public construction of a recognisable sexual politics, which was further confirmed over a decade later, in the early 1980s, through the activist cultures that emerged in response to AIDS.

Chauncey does not, however, acknowledge the role art played in the development of marginal communities and topographies, ignoring the use of cultural representation to produce and sustain the emergent gay 'worlds' of the pre-Stonewall era. This is despite his argument that gay social life involved the development and dissemination of 'gay folklore', by 'claiming historical allegiance [to…] a tradition on the basis of innumerable individuals and idiosyncratic readings of texts', such as the films of Judy Garland or Bette Davis, or the songs of Cole Porter.[29] Similarly, he downplays the compensatory production of representations by the dominant culture, which limit and police performances of social and sexual dissidence.

Difference and assimilation

Since the 1950s, the heterogeneous field of lesbian and gay studies has at times refused to question the tyranny of the normal over 'anomalous' bodies, practices and desires. At the close of *Normal Love*, one character – ostensibly a freak – takes a histrionic revenge on the normals, razing them from their icing-laden promontories with a watergun. They cascade with clumsy extravagance, overacting their decadent death-throes as they topple down the cake's layers to lounge, as dead, in still lives of tacky restfulness. Douglas Crimp theorises Smith's work as being crucial for refusing easy distinctions between sexual and other identities, restating this work's urgency in a time when 'normalization [is] the battleground of queer political struggle.' For Crimp, the art of Smith – as well as of Warhol, the Kuchar brothers, and others – does not attempt to reflect a 'historical gay identity', but, rather and more importantly, Smith's contribution is crucial 'because it disdains and defies the coherence and stability of all sexual identity.'[30] As such, by refusing coherent distinctions between groups, and defying the necessity to fully reify character in his films and performances, works such as *Normal Love* support Crimp's thesis that the queer work 'we deserve' – in a time of contested rights, invaded privacies, and cultural assimilation – is that which actively refuses to categorise and define our desires.

Historically, lesbian and gay culture has often suppressed uncomfortable designations in the name of assimilatory politics. The 'pre-history' of American gay liberation is often represented as the movement towards a radical politics of visibility, whereby marginalised individualised refused the mandate of cultural silence by appropriating the techniques of direct action gleaned from the civil rights movements, and were thus mobilised into political action. As John D'Emilio argues, for example, in the mid-1960s '[t]he counterculture sought a revolution in consciousness, [a] transformation of self that would create a personality, ethics, and style of living consistent with the political and social criticism of the New Left'.[31] This pursuit, however, lent itself to the formulation of ideals that could be aspired to, and these were consolidated as models for the newly constructed gay visibility. This tendency that has been described as 'homonormativity', a compulsive force that works, in Sara Ahmed's suggestive phrasing, to problematically 'straighten up queer effects,' at the expense of those whose bodies, practices or desires resist or impede assimilation.[32]

Up to and after Stonewall, the gay rights movement would repeatedly fall prey to such normative agendas, markedly failing to support or provide for apparently unassimilable queers: transgender, bisexual, sadomasochist, elderly, or disabled people, as well as a further host of wilfully uncategorisable perverts. Esther Newton argues that despite their representation as intrinsically dissident, lesbian and gay cultures have historically organised themselves according to normative codes of group control, withholding legitimisation from those that trouble the standards of a specific sexual subculture. 'Those who have not joined the social group or merged their individual deviance with the cultural norms are considered the *real* deviants,' she writes, marked as different through processes of exclusion and re-stigmatisation that replicate, hypocritically, the dominant culture's prior threat of marginality.[33]

Throughout the 1960s, this assimilatory drive passed over into emergent artistic styles and identities. As testified to by the coding or obscuring of sexuality in the work of Andy Warhol, Jasper Johns and Robert Rauschenberg, the artistic avant-garde suppressed its sexuality in favour of abstraction's evacuation of subjectivity. Similarly, Nayland Blake notes, as the margin became the cultural mainstream, repressing its queerness, so too did queers begin to repress and overcome the assumed sexual dissidence of homosexuality.[34] In its urban manifestation, the purported radicality of homosexuality was often co-opted in favour of the bourgeois aspirations of the emerging gay market. As a result of his excesses, Smith's work has always struck an awkward relation to the developments of gay culture. 'I took my program to a gay theatre and [the manager] couldn't understand how it was gay', he complains. 'If I wasn't discussing exactly how many inches was my first lollipop then it wouldn't be anything they'd be interested in.'[35] As an emergent cultural formation in the late 1960s, lesbian and gay theatre began to breach the surface of mainstream recognition, and at the same time formalised its assumptions about what it deemed to be properly suited to its specialised venues, constituencies, and audiences.

Dissident lesbian and gay theatre practitioners did, however, persist in their work through the 1970s and 1980s. Charles Ludlam's Ridiculous Theatrical Company is one such example, borne of Smith's influence. As Ludlam writes of his 1976 play *Caprice* (starring Mario Montez in his last performance for over thirty years): 'I showed the gay world, and gay people were the ones who were most offended. Some thought it was great and understood it; others thought that we should only be presenting a so-called positive image of gays.' Demonstrating Smith's anti-assimilatory influence, Ludlam adds, 'I would never stoop to presenting a positive image – of anything.'[36]

Performing difference

My discussion of the queer as freak runs a familiar discursive risk, namely the danger of essentialising homosexual difference by labelling the queer as necessarily a social or cultural outsider. The critique of essentialist arguments was developed in Marxist feminism of the early 1980s, and was appropriated by queer theory to analyse the faulty reasoning that bolsters phobic imaginings of the hidden truths and origins of homosexuality. Michèle Barrett argues that essentialist positions are frequently reductionist, for they subsume complex phenomena (for example, class) to biological determinants; such arguments are also empiricist, because they assume that social behaviour are caused by a limited set of observed factors.[37] By rendering social arrangements to be biological or otherwise 'natural' givens, the ideological and political roles of these arguments are inevitably reactionary as they frame contingent phenomena as transhistorical, universal and monolithic. However, the familiarity of the threat of essentialism relies upon discursive problems that have formed around the deployment of the term in writing about gender and sexuality. Teresa de Lauretis notes that identity politics often falls back on 'self-righteous' charges against those who are deemed guilty of falling prey to essentialism, while obscuring the question of an 'essential difference' between, say, feminist and anti-feminist politics. However, 'the essential difference of feminism lies in its historical specificity,' de Lauretis argues. An understanding of difference, essential or otherwise, must take into account the particular conditions of emergence that shape discursive objects and fields of analysis, as well as 'the erotic component of its political self-awareness [and] the absolute novelty of its radical challenge to social life itself'.[38] Thus, the apparent problem of essentialising the queer as freak in *Normal Love* can be reframed by focusing on the question of the specificity of this formulation, accentuating representations of social and cultural difference in the context of specific historical conditions of emergence, recognition and deployment.

In an interview in 2005, Penny Arcade explained how performance-oriented play arose from the collaborations of marginalised individuals in New York in the 1960s. Talking about the serious play explored by figures including herself, Smith, Vaccaro and others, she says,

> Everybody performed all the time. It was a way of entertaining yourself and entertaining your friends. But it wasn't self-conscious, it wasn't like somebody was *on* all the time, it was a way of mediating your own personality. We didn't have any model for the kinds of people we were. We were freaks in the real sense that we were not normal and we were pegged as not being normal, in school and by our families, and we were here in New York being not-normal together … The other side of feeling different and weird and awful and alienated is feeling special, right? So you … make yourself feel better by making yourself special.[39]

Combative, erotic, and alienated from sociality as well as the history of dramatic representation, the freak is thrown into a state of crisis. The subject finds oneself adrift from viable precedents with which to identify. The compulsion to perform imagines the estranged subject pushed towards performance. Or, as Arcade archly concludes, confirming the relation between alienation and the necessities of performative self-invention: 'Healthy balanced people do not become performers. They don't need to.' The outcasts who find themselves driven to serious play are not freaks by nature of their queerness, but choose freakishness as a style because their physicality, attitudes, desires or predilections conspire fortuitously with the specificities of the geographical and historical locales in which they find themselves.

The creatures in *Normal Love* bear these improvisatory, happily 'unhealthy' orientations towards the situations they occupy. Each seriously playful mise en scène arises from the freakish state of grace described by Arcade. In the green sequence towards the middle of the first reel, Arnold Rockwood's character faux-maniacally gnashes his gnarly joke-store teeth. Painted, masked and wrapped in rags, Rockwood pursues Diana Baccus. Having playfully cavorted with an Arabian consort, by whom she is smilingly ravished, she engages Rockwood with a cream pie in the face. As such, the sequence invites a string of poached film references, including Lon Chaney's mangy terror, the overplayed silent Orientalia of 1920s Douglas Fairbanks vehicles, and Marx Brothers visual buffoonery. Playing reference against reference, Smith choreographs mass cultural signs to produce connections and circuit-breaks that fall as if at hazard. Each interruption seems to trip equally by association and non-association. Smith's repetition of outdated cultural material could produce a hermetic realm, but instead it supports what Arcade implies to be the constructive self-satisfaction of a communal life 'in New York being not-normal together'. With the pie squeezed onto his face, Rockwood falls out of character, not laughing or otherwise maintaining the forced inanity of his earlier mode of play; he takes off his silver mask, and cleans his plastic teeth, his face that of a disappointed, hurt or frustrated child interrupted in fantasy's sway. Once cleaned up, Rockwood returns to form and eagerly resumes his chase. The crisis of non-communication is averted by consolidating a sense of community among otherwise estranged individuals.

These bodies, painted, playful, childlike and retaliatory, do not refuse or overcome identity but, rather, perform the need for new modes of social comportment based on play, mess, ambiguity and ambivalence. In the harem scene, strewn lazy and sated, the human flotsam of *Normal Love* lay draped in chiffon along a timber jetty by coastal waters. Some smoke, or lie close to one another. As harem, its figuring is undercut by the putative stillness of the scene, so that the staging resembles the aftermath of some bloodless massacre, reinforced by the human skull tickled by a skinny bald boy, David Sachs. As such, they also revoke the jubilant promise of the sexual. Watching each other engaging in the unproductive ventures of lazing, smoking, swooning, they open up temporary spaces for new ways of being together, in communal modes that are not defined by social convention. For the few moments they play together, striking draped poses on the windswept jetty colonnades, the freaks enjoy the pleasures afforded by their difference.

Viragos, freaks and fairies

In the United States in the 1950s and 1960s, specific types of knowledge were deployed in order to sustain a punitively rigid distinction between homosexuality and heterosexuality. The period can be characterised as the interval between the popularisation of Freudian psychoanalysis in the 1930s and the removal of homosexuality from the American Psychiatric Association's *Diagnostic and Statistical Manual of Mental Disorders* (the *DSM*) in 1973. Psychoanalytically inflected writings in this period often rely upon an assumption of the debilitating proximities between homosexuality and infantile sexuality. The vogue for Freud's theories on sexuality worked to simplify his clinical position, such that it became commonplace to describe homosexuality as interrupted psychic development, in which the child's polymorphous perversity fails to achieve 'normal', adult genital sexuality. Moreover, in the 1960s, a set of assumptions derived from ego psychology structured deeply problematic mainstream understandings of the desire in lesbian and gay cultures to refuse or redefine normative sociality. While some subjects were terrorised by these accounts, others capitalised on the indictments levelled at them for their perceived transgressions. In order to explain the implications of Smith's celebration of difference, I explore two contemporary texts that staged the way in which homosexuality troubled the mainstream.

In a long and detailed critique of the homosexual stranglehold on American theatre, published in 1965, Donald Kaplan documents contemporary fears about the effects of homosexuality on culture. A psychiatrist and contributing editor to the *Tulane Drama Review*, Kaplan cites the 'alarm' registered by critics and audiences alike, and offers a telling account of contemporary prejudices about homosexuality in the 1960s. If homosexuality 'has always hovered about the theatre', Kaplan writes, 'current theatre materializes this specter' in productions that are 'literal', 'simplistic', 'puerile' and 'obscene'.[40] Owing to the influence of gay playwrights – Edward Albee, Tennessee Williams and William Inge – Kaplan argues that theatre itself has taken on the key characteristics of homosexuality. He describes the homosexual sensibility – and by extension his 'ideologic style' – as governed by 'behavior without responsibility', where '[i]ntelligence, discrimination, and reason … have little status' on account of a delegation of moral values in the narcissistic services of immature defiance.[41]

By claiming that the theatre had to defeat homosexuality, Kaplan proposed a skewed counterpoint to Michael Fried's contemporary polemic against the apparently defiling influence of the theatre upon the plastic arts.

For Kaplan, the tension between George and Martha in Albee's play *Who's Afraid of Virginia Woolf?* stages the homosexual male's pathological attempt to master his anxiety. In the play Albee supposedly creates a world where infantile pleasure can triumph over the primacy of adult (hetero)sexuality. Kaplan produces this reading through a critical sleight of hand, describing the adulterous liaison between the unsympathetic virago, Martha, and her husband's posturing yet feeble colleague, Nick, as the 'sexuality of the parental bedroom'. In Albee's fantasy, Kaplan suggests, this 'is no match for the multifarious derivatives of George's oral aggression, anality, voyeurism, masochism, and procreative reluctance'. The account hardly squares with Martha's vitriol in the play, evident in the litany of ball-breaking statements that culminate in her admission, to George: 'I'm loud and I'm vulgar, and I wear the pants in this house because somebody's got to.'[42] In Kaplan reading, however, in the denouement of the play, '[t]he *enfant terrible* [George] again triumphs over the cocksmen of the outside world, and the nursery is preserved'.[43]

Kaplan conveniently casts George as a latent homosexual, a stand-in for the playwright who writes to wreak havoc on heterosexuality. Nick and Martha are represented as a wholesome heterosexual couple placed under duress by George's deluded narcissism. This reading is obscured by Kaplan's forgetting of the narrative device of the play (Martha pretends to have a son who is away at college) and his misrepresentation of the deeply ambivalent power relations between George and Martha. These omissions shore up his hollow reading of George triumphing by way of 'tactics of pregenital perversity'.[44] In the play, the cocksman apparent, Nick, is harangued by Martha as an impotent 'flop' in the bedroom,[45] thus deflating the triumphant thrust of his 'parental sexuality'; Nick's cuckolded wife, Honey giggles, sleepwalks and vomits her way through the play, yet has lured Nick into marriage with a phantom pregnancy. Kaplan argues that the homosexual always 'sides with the victim against the oppression of God or society' (represented by the heterosexual unity), but it is unclear who the 'victim' in this play might be, and which one – in what is clearly a catalogue of disasters – the audience inevitably sides with. Regardless, the gay playwright's urge is deemed symptomatic of an 'ideologic style' in which he 'does not champion humanity, but merely himself', a neat get-out clause for the confusion upon which the play capitalises for its enduring dramatic effect.

Nevertheless, Kaplan supposes that George is paradoxically more victimised and yet more triumphant than the three other characters in the play. For Kaplan's reading to function, George must enable the homosexual audience – or at least the homosexual playwright – to identify with him. Yet if George performs little triumphs – over Martha by 'killing' her imaginary son, and over Nick by compromising his marriage to Honey – his parlour games are deeply pyrrhic victories, and hardly afford him the moral high ground required by 'the homosexual' and his 'ideologic style'. Moreover, if *Virginia Woolf* enables the homosexual playwright to attain 'lawless', narcissistic salvation at the expense of his desperate resentment of heterosexuality, why did the predominantly heterosexual audience indulge Albee in his hysterical shadowboxing? 'The homosexual ideology perpetrates the fraud of rebellion without revolution,' Kaplan concludes, 'of gain without the responsibilities of sacrifice.' Unlike the heroic democracies articulated in the playworlds of Samuel Beckett, George Bernard Shaw, or Bertolt Brecht, he argues, in theatre under the sway of homosexuality 'the curtain falls and returns us to a world unaltered and uninspired. The experience,' he adds, 'is humiliating.'[46] Kaplan is unwilling to ask if this experience of humiliation is interesting or familiar. If the feeling of humiliation that Albee orchestrates feels familiar for an audience, it seems to point to the disasters of heterosexuality when constrained by petit bourgeois, capitalist-oriented sociality, as do the plays of another homosexual 'ideologist' of the period, Tennessee Williams. In the subsequent issue of the *Tulane Drama Review*, Lee Baxandall criticised Kaplan's essay, yet upheld his suspicions about the effect of homosexuality upon writing. He argues, 'a homosexual viewpoint may make some special contribution [but] it is less generally valid, balanced, and embracing than is the best pondered heterosexual outlook, given a world in which the homosexual still is despised and persecuted.' Aiming at a more progressive account of the homosexualisation of American culture, Baxandall continues, 'The homosexual vision is not in itself debilitating; what hurts is not to have it set in the broadest perspective.'[47] For Baxandall, homosexuals can make a special contribution to culture – but only, it would seem, if they are heterosexual.

I have focused on Kaplan's essay at some length because it demonstrates a contemporary account of assumptions about homosexual difference, which complements my reading of Smith's celebration of the possibilities inaugurated in freakishness. Indeed, as Stephen Bottoms has noted, homophobia was a crucial strategy in straightening out the theatre, a compensatory response to the deathgrip that homosexuals were believed to have stolen over theatrical production in the period.[48] Albee's play was a convenient whipping boy for this moral crusade. Finally, Kaplan's article also points – albeit obliquely – to the way in which Albee's play effectively lampooned heterosexuality, while also gesturing to a subversive possibility for queers, who may escape the seemingly inevitable disasters of hetero socialisation. Albee's representation of the heterosexual couple is a potentially dissident one, counter-figuring the heterosexual as freak. However, the play mockingly represents heterosexuality as a failed social identity, while also pointing to an absent figure excluded from its disastrous field of power relations: the homosexual, the 'specter' which so clearly haunts Kaplan's phobic account of the contemporary theatre. The freakish heterosexuals in the play, however, hold no transgressive charge but, rather, excoriate each other through their inability to imagine another form of sociality beyond one tied up in oppressive tendencies – misogynist, exploitative, emasculating, and resentful of forbidden pleasures. The social relations in *Virginia Woolf* are clearly played out under the spell of Martha's godlike father – Nick and George's employer; having prevented George's cultural production before the beginning of the play (by blocking the publication of his autobiographical novel about patricide) the patriarch produces and sustains the excruciating devolution of sociality towards disaster.

Similarly, Smith used to epigram letters and other ephemera with the pithy aphorism, 'When you have police everything looks queer,' effectively reproducing the notion that deviation is created and sustained by the very powers commonly perceived to prevent them.[49] Another iconic play of the period, Mart Crowley's *The Boys in the Band* also figures this logic, but focuses on the production and display of explicitly homosexual subjectivities. As one contemporary reviewer wrote, Crowley's play was so vicious that it made *Virginia Woolf* 'seem like a vicarage tea party'.[50] Like Albee's play, *The Boys in the Band* is peppered with camp repartee, and relies on a vindictive parlour game for its emotive force. In both setups, fragile camaraderie devolves into savage verbal attacks and desperate power play over the course of one fateful evening. The host of the party, Michael is a swishy neurotic ruined for normal love by an overbearing mother. He sustains much of the camp laughs of the play, and implodes spectacularly at the close of the evening after inducing his friends into public and humiliating confessions. His guests are a coterie of gay 'types'. Nevertheless, they are all empathetic characters, each marred by a problem that defines their personality. Michael's confidant, Donald is sweet, but plagued by his professional failures. Larry is promiscuous, but locked in a monogamous relationship with Hank, an assimilatory figure whose butchness places him on the bare perimeter of the closet. Emory is a flaming yet sexless queen, who professes his love of Maria Montez and provides many of the best quips. Harold is an 'ugly, pockmarked Jew fairy' and a sharp-tongued, hilarious, self-hating bitch, to boot.[51] The object of many barbs, Cowboy is a dim but sincere hustler, gifted to Harold on his birthday. However, the spur of much of the tension is the gate-crashing heterosexual, Alan. His distraught arrival prompts suspicions among the guests, and his supposed latency becomes the target of Michael's cruel and manipulative parlour game. The game is the dramatic vortex into which the other characters are drawn, with compelling and sometimes excruciating results.

Whereas *Virginia Woolf* takes pleasure in a humiliated vision of heterosexual coupling, Crowley's play stages homosexuality as a series of available (yet inevitably disastrous) subject positions. 'Oh, no! NO! It's beginning!'

Michael cries, as the narrative reaches fever pitch and the guests leave him in Donald's consoling, tranquilising arms. 'The liquor is starting to wear off and the anxiety is beginning! … Oh Jesus, the guilt! I can't handle it any more. I won't make it!'[52] Michael's histrionic implosion is all the more striking for the speed with which he recovers his composure. Crowley suggests that homosexuality is frequented by the threat of dissolution, as a subjective volatility that can be shored up by linguistic and other assaults.

The anxious roll call of disastrous subject positions culminates in Michael's infamous line, 'You show me a happy homosexual, and I'll show you a gay corpse.'[53] As a representation of gay life before Stonewall, it played directly into the hands of conservatives, as demonstrated by a contemporary statement – from the *Catholic Film Newsletter* – that the film adaptation 'comments with wit and passion on the desolation and waste which chill this way of life.'[54] If in 1968 *The Boys in the Band* represented the contemporary phenomenon of the queer as freak, it appeared barely inhabitable. The queer may be a freak (a term bandied about frequently in the play), but the fairy attains happiness only in death, even if he seeks solace in the meantime through psychoanalysis, promiscuity, alcoholism, medication and sadistic wit. I suggested earlier that linear narrative may encourage moralistic denouements that have troubling inevitabilities when deployed towards representing queers. *The Boys in the Band* also suggests that by the end of the 1960s, the short-lived possibilities of queerness as a lived personification of innocent monstrosity had simply run its course. Contained by the mainstream, queers could be represented as freaks, with amusing results, but at the risk of re-inscribing the subjective crises that the phenomenon set out to challenge. I should add that I am a great fan of *Boys in the Band*, but my enjoyment of and affection for the play and film are difficult to square with my uncertainties about its political efficacy.

However, *Normal Love* is a valiant example of a cultural artefact that both articulates the power of the freak as a figure of sexual self-designation in the early 1960s, and evades the tendency of narrative closure (or the will of the mainstream) to appropriate and contain the possibilities inaugurated in the phenomenon. In the film, outsiders test the occupations of space enacted by the bodies of others, such as in the encounter between the Werewolf and the Mermaid in the first reel. The two frolic together in the shallows of a bank of rich mud, and as he holds her playfully, he lifts her up and over, losing his balance, careening into the deeper mess of the bog. He leans into her head, the two by now laughing and screaming, and pulls off her wig. Holding her, he feeds her from a Coke bottle, and pours the rest of its contents over her face and chest. The Mermaid flutters her lashes, laughs, rearranges her soiled seashell brassiere, and the Werewolf lifts her from the quagmire lagoon to carry her in his arms, mud falling everywhere, her cumbersome ladytrail saddened with dirt. The mud that saturates the scene of play is posed in counterpoint by the quick succession to a languorous Mermaid drifting in a bath of pristine milk.

'Hunt the human flies,' Charles Ludlam counsels. 'Avoid the average man and cultivate the freak, not because you like abnormal people, but from the scientific attitude that it is from the abnormal that we learn.'[55] There is no glory in my catastrophes, only banality; but there is some relief in identification with the catastrophic incidents that make up the lives of others, and especially those of the dead. There is solace in holding up the evidence that another has translated the details of personal disasters into the events of art. In defining a fictitious lineage for one's own lot, the subject set adrift finds succor in the knowledge that the disasters others have made of their lives have not been compounded by a failure of imagination. While a life, love, career, faith or future has fallen apart, the subject of such catastrophes has endured the partial and piecemeal aftermaths of a simple but urgent question: how does one make something of something else, or of oneself? (But the hours, which I thought would be largely a matter of blotting from my mind all thoughts beyond today, become, instead, a time that culminates in violence.) In the 1960s, Smith's films, performances and other works relate to the iconic works of the decade, and also those that lingered for nostalgic or camp consumption. Yet Smith's efforts also work through their limitations in order to rethink the inhibitions, assumptions and compulsions that make a life feel more or less livable. By expending energies on unconventional, alien, and seemingly dismal possibilities for self-sustenance, in a world fraught by danger and disaster, his ardent pursuit of difference frames the attraction unto strangeness as an ethical mandate. These are the counterlogics of life, art and politics that this work tends to invoke. As such, Jack Smith offers his audience the chance of living at a remove from perfection, in the diffuse and opportune register of the perverse. His gifts are noticeably barbed, and costly, which is not to say they are unwelcome.

Notes

1 Jack Smith, 'The astrology of a movie Scorpio' (1963), *Wait for Me at the Bottom of the Pool: The Writings of Jack Smith*, ed. J. Hoberman and Edward Leffingwell (New York and London: High Risk Books, 1997), pp. 54–7 (pp. 54–5).

2 Jack Smith, 'Journal notes on *Normal Love*' (1963–4), *Wait for Me at the Bottom of the Pool*, pp. 45–9, (pp. 45–8). In the film *Blonde Cobra*, Smith states '"Life swarms with innocent monsters." Charles Baudelaire'.

3 Jack Smith, 'The adorable and pasty creatures: Journal notes on pornography' (1963–64), *Wait for Me at the Bottom of the Pool*, pp. 77–9 (p. 77).

4 Ibid. p. 78.

5 Jack Smith, 'Statements, "ravings", and epigrams', *Wait for Me at the Bottom of the Pool*, pp. 151–5 (p. 153).

6 J. Hoberman, 'Treasures of the mummy's tomb: The lost films of Jack Smith', *Film Comment* (November-December 1997), pp. 42–5 (p. 45).

7 P. Adams Sitney, *Visionary Film: The American Avant-Garde, 1943–2000*, third edition (Oxford: Oxford University Press, 2002), p. 337.

8 Smith, 'The astrology of a movie Scorpio', p. 55.

9 Alan Sinfield, *Out on Stage: Lesbian and Gay Theatre in the Twentieth Century* (New Haven and London: Yale University Press, 1999), pp. 270–1.

10 Raymond Williams, *Culture and Society: Coleridge to Orwell* (London: Hogarth Press, 1987), pp. 320–1.

11 Dick Hebdige, *Subculture: The Meaning of Style* (London and New York: Routledge, 1979), p. 16.

12 Jack Smith, 'Lobotomy in Lobsterland' (1965), *Wait for Me at the Bottom of the Pool*, pp. 81–8 (p. 81).

13 Sue Golding, 'Pariah bodies', *Sexy Bodies: The Strange Carnalities of Feminism*, ed. Elizabeth Grosz and Elspeth Probyn (London and New York: Routledge, 1995), pp. 172–80 (p. 172).

14 Alice Echols, *Shaky Ground: The Sixties and Its Aftershocks* (New York: Columbia University Press, 2002), pp. 142–4.

15 Jack Smith, 'Belated appreciation of V. S.' (1964), *Wait for Me at the Bottom of the Pool*, pp. 41–3 (p. 42).

16 Richard Dellamora, 'Queer apocalypse: Framing William Burroughs', *Postmodern Apocalypse: Theory and Cultural Practice at the End* (Philadelphia: University of Pennsylvania Press, 1995), pp. 136–67 (p. 161).

17 Gore Vidal, *The City and the Pillar* (London: Abacus, 1997) p. 154.

18 The date of *Hot Air Specialists* is unclear, although Ronald Tavel remembers lending Smith a chandelier in 1983, which can be seen prominently in the film. Tavel offered this information in a discussion at the Kino Arsenal in Berlin in March 2009. Critics including J. Hoberman questioned the authorship of the film, arguing that its narrative is uncharacteristically linear.

19 Sigmund Freud, 'Beyond the pleasure principle', *On Metaphysics*, ed. James Strachey (London and New York: Penguin Books, 1991), p. 322.

20 Ibid. p. 314.

21 This and further quotes are from the prefatory warning to *Freaks*, as transcribed from the reissued DVD of the film. Emphases appear (capitalised) in original.

22 Steven Watson, *The Birth of the Beat Generation: Visionaries, Rebels, and Hipsters, 1944–1960* (New York: Pantheon Books, 1995), p. 3.

23 Philip Core, 'From *Camp: The Lie That Tells The Truth*' in *Camp: Queer Aesthetics and the Performing Subject, A Reader*, ed. Fabio Cleto (Edinburgh: Edinburgh University Press, 1999), pp. 80–6 (p. 81).

24 Albert Goldman, *Freakshow* (New York: Atheneum, 1971), pp. xiv–xv.

25 Goldman, p. 352.

26 Smith, 'Journal notes on *Normal Love*: July 23, 1963', *Wait for Me at the Bottom of the Pool*, pp. 45–9 (p. 45).

27 Marybeth Hamilton, 'Sexual politics and African-American music: Or, placing Little Richard in history', *History Workshop Journal* 46 (Autumn 1998), pp. 161–76 (p. 171).

28 George Chauncey, *Gay New York: The Making of a Gay Male World, 1980–1940* (London: Flamingo, 1994), p. 3.

29 Ibid. pp. 283–8.

30 Douglas Crimp, 'Getting the Warhol we deserve', *Social Text* 59 (Summer 1999), pp. 49–66 (p. 64).

31 John D'Emilio, *Sexual Politics, Sexual Communities: The Making of a Homosexual Minority in the United States, 1940–1970* (Chicago and London: Chicago University Press, 1983), p. 225.

32 Sara Ahmed, *Queer Phenomenology: Orientations, Objects, Others* (Durham and London: Duke University Press, 2006), p. 173.

33 Esther Newton, *Mother Camp: Female Impersonators in America* (Chicago and London: University of Chicago Press, 1979), p. 51. Emphasis in original.

34 Nayland Blake, 'The message from Atlantis', *Flaming Creature: Jack Smith, His Amazing Life and Times*, ed. Edward Leffingwell, Carole Kismaric and Marvin Heiferman, the Institute for Contemporary Art, P.S.1 Museum (London and New York: Serpent's Tail, 1997), pp. 168–83 (p. 182)

35 Sylvère Lotringer, 'Uncle Fishook and the sacred baby poo poo of art' (Interview with Jack Smith, 1978), *Wait for Me at the Bottom of the Pool*, pp. 107–21 (p. 112).

36 Cited in David Kaufman, *Ridiculous! The Theatrical Life and Times of Charles Ludlam* (New York: Applause, 2002), p. 237.

37 Michèle Barrett, *Women's Oppression Today: Problems in Marxist Feminist Analysis* (London: Verso, 1980), pp. 12–3.

38 Teresa de Lauretis, *Figures of Resistance: Essays in Feminist Theory*, ed. Patricia White (Urbana and Chicago: University of Illinois Press, 2007), pp. 183–4.

39 Arcade, Penny, Interview with the author, New York (18 May 2005).

40 Donald M. Kaplan, 'Homosexuality and American theatre', *Tulane Drama Review* 9.3 (1965), pp. 25–55 (p. 28).

41 Ibid. pp. 36–7.

42 Edward Albee, *Who's Afraid of Virginia Woolf?* (Harmondsworth, Penguin Books, 1965), p. 94.

43 Kaplan, p. 35.

44 Ibid. p. 35.

45 Albee, p. 111.

46 Kaplan, p. 55.

47 Lee Baxandall, 'The theatre of Edward Albee', *Tulane Drama Review* 9.4 (1965), pp. 19–40 (pp. 39–40).

48 Stephen J. Bottoms, 'The efficacy/effeminacy braid: Unpicking the performance studies/theatre studies dichotomy', *Theatre Topics* 13.2 (2003), pp. 173–87 (pp. 175–6).

49 Jack Smith, 'Statements, "ravings", and epigrams', *Wait for Me at the Bottom of the Pool*, pp. 151–5 (p. 151).

50 Clive Barnes, 'Review: *Boys in the Band* opens Off Broadway', *New York Times* (Monday 15 April, 1968), p. 48. The two works have frequently been compared, for example in Crayton Robey's excellent documentary film, *Making the Boys* (2009).

51 Mart Crowley, *The Boys in the Band* (Harmondsworth: Penguin Plays, 1968), p. 46.

52 Ibid. pp. 89–90.

53 Ibid. p. 91.

54 Cited in Ben Brantley, 'Review: As the boys return, the party isn't over', *New York Times* (21 June 1996).

55 Charles Ludlam, *Ridiculous Theatre: Scourge of Human Folly: The Writings of Charles Ludlam*, ed. Steven Samuels (New York: Theatre Communications Group, 1992), p. 162.

5 The deaths of Maria Montez

Shall we seek the sanctuary of my den of cutthroats and thieves, and see how much mileage we can get off a dead star tonight? (Jack Smith)[1]

After fifteen minutes of confusing, minor plot upheavals, amid the staged simplicity of a township of island people, a white man and his young, loin-clothed companion ascend a treacherous incline of exotic palms and brilliant coloured foliage. The shot changes to an island vista, a lost city that sprawls to the right, massaged to the left by a frothing coastline, and topped by the ominous mass of a seething, wooden volcano. In the brush that foregrounds the panorama, the two figures emerge – Kado, played by the popular Asian child-star of the 1930s, Sabu; and his friend and master, Ramu, played by Jon Hall, a poor man's Errol Flynn. Both feign surprise at the landscape, in all its tawdry splendour. The scene cuts to a woman's hand holding up another's wounded wrist to the screen. Looming large, almost centred in the frame, are two purple-red scabs, nestled in creases of skin. These are not scars, but open and unhealing wounds. The lip of the right-hand hole is skirted by a filmy, white accretion, a seepage of the spirit glue that holds on the fake lesion. 'Have you ever wondered what that meant?' asks a wistful off-screen voice. The shot shifts to Maria Montez, who shakes her beautiful head, a little too intently. 'All my life,' she replies, wooden and moronic like the vista. She is still shaking, slightly glazed. The angle shifts to take in the important face and head of the elderly woman who holds Montez's wrist; in her attractive mid-Atlantic burr, she announces a further revelation, in a film full to the earlobes with startling disclosures: 'I am your grandmother, child. These people are *your* people. You were born here!' 'I don't believe it,' Montez stammers, amid a short tango of facial expressions, each nominally conveying her compelling, ham-fisted confusion. As she speaks, her bold shoulders shift with the wringing of her hands, just outside the frame. The grandmother continues, 'My daughter was your mother. She bore twin girls. At the age of a year you were both submitted to the sting of King Cobra. You, the natural born ruler, almost died from the venom, while Naja, your sister, proved immune. So she became High

Priestess, while you, the supposed weakling, were to be destroyed after the island custom.'

Robert Siodmak's *Cobra Woman* (1944) turns on the image of a wound that will not heal. In the scene described above, the good sister, Tollea, bears the mark of an open wound, two glistening red punctures on her wrist. Unhealing, her cuts signify both a separation and a troubled belonging: namely the marking by (and as) failure that caused her exile from Cobra Island, and the omen that she must return, to save its inhabitants from her sister's genocidal rage. The wound that her evil twin overcame, Tollea still bleeds from. The ancient snakebite functions here as fate sealing, an ambivalent sign that bestows difference, yet also ensures the possibility for overcoming that fateful separation. It is, after all, a multiple wound: two teeth puncturing one body, these twin-cuts are redoubled on a different – yet identical – body (Montez plays the parts of both Tollea and Naja).

For Smith, *Cobra Woman* held the ambivalent honour of being 'the best and worst Hollywood movie ever made'.[2] As a movie, it is both singularly awful and entirely typical of the vehicles that Montez took first billing in. Its plot is overburdened by its twists and turns, as well as by its leading lady's overacting, yet also reveals further burdens, namely its possible reference to lofty texts in classical drama. Specifically, the wounded body of Maria Montez indexes the catastrophe suffered by Philoctetes in Sophocles' classical play. *Philoctetes* and *Cobra Woman* are both concerned with perpetual wounds brought about by ill-fated encounters with snakes, resulting in exile, and the ensuing compulsion to enter into a resolution of fates via a return that opens onto an ambiguous future. Philoctetes and Tollea wear their taints upon their sleeves. Like *Philoctetes*, *Cobra Woman* turns on a future created by a fatalistic altercation with a snakebite. Indeed, the film is punctuated by images of snakes: the actual cobra, unconvincingly cut into the film before each dancing scene; a lumbering plastic snake; and a variety of costume jewelsnakery, including the apparently menacing 'cobra jewel', upon whose implied powers rightful rule relies. In Sophocles's play, the wounded warrior Philoctetes is a desolate figure wracked with consuming pains, the permanent effect of having been bitten by an accursed snake as punishment for trespassing on holy ground. Homeward-bound on a ship, Odysseus and his men grow weary of Philoctetes and his unrelenting cries. Sickened by the stench of his wounded leg, his crew abandons him on an uninhabited island. Ten years on, alone and wracked by pains, the wound has not healed and still oozes blood. Blind to the curse set upon his stricken body, but mortally aware of the disgust he inspires, Philoctetes's suppurating wound acts as cipher for a communicative space that refuses communion. Both texts pose the wound kept open as the sign of an unresolved enunciation. As Philoctetes states, '[It] is not the pain of what is past that stings me, / but the prospect (as I see it) of the sufferings /

that I must still face.'[3] Or as the interlocutors of *Cobra Woman* put it, of Tollea's anomalous wound, 'Have you ever wondered what that meant?' 'All my life.' A speaking in progress, each wound is an effect that still bleeds meaning. The wound demands a speaking to counter the failures of the culture from which each protagonist has been expelled.

As Smith's obsession with Montez demonstrates, the cut in the body provides a space for conceptualising the dwelling of camp effects in the spaces where culture founders, in sites made conspicuous by their proximity to death, disease, disgrace and other bodily disasters. The inevitability of misfires, which characterises speaking, is emphasised in the happy glut of significations and contradictory enunciations that queer performance enacts. As I characterise it, queer performance runs high and low into each other in strategic or creative ways, to destabilise the authority of the mainstream and revitalise the minor. Moreover, queer performance emphasises the peculiar force of the damaged, faulty or marginal body. It celebrates woundedness by pointing to the failures of normative culture, explicitly framing the ways that the mainstream fetishises death and disaster in veiled terms. Such practices are queer in a historically specific sense. Cultural studies has shown that subcultural practices appropriate mainstream objects and deploy them towards oblique, resistant ends. As Dick Hebdige writes, subcultures enact a struggle within signification: 'a struggle for possession of the sign which extends to even the most mundane areas of everyday life.' Hebdige is referring to punk's powerfully 'illegitimate' appropriations – of safety pins as a fashion accessory, for example – whereby a banal object takes on 'secret' meanings for a subordinate group, as 'a resistance through style'.[4] This reading usefully extends to the queer subcultural appropriation of trashy, dated Montez movies, which held such an evocative charge for a range of gay male artists in the 1960s. The reading of Smith's work as subcultural text also gestures to the enduring legacies of his practice, for subsequent generations of viewers. This development of a subcultural ethics of wounded recognition is one suggestion of how the act of reassessing Smith's work, as well as his critical reception and influence on others, is part of a wider rethinking of art's histories.

In my understanding of Smith's work, the imperative towards failure and seemingly hysterical 'self-critique' circulates around the concept of the open wound. This is significant, for the latter provides a way of re-reading the discourse around modes of production by lesbian, gay and transgender artists, specifically the seemingly exhausted domain of camp. First and foremost, Montez allowed Smith a medium to channel his intensely melancholic and nostalgic fantasies of a better time and place. His perspective upon the world was a profoundly dark vision, as testified to in his performance in Beth and Scott B.'s film *Trap Door* (1980), in which he laments, 'Man is essentially brutal by nature. So is woman. Brutality stalks the streets, lurks behind the walls of seemingly respectable faces. We are supermen among sadists.' Similarly, in his final performance, Smith embodies the spirit of death in Ari Roussimoff's feature film *Shadows in the City* (1990), alongside other trash-infused stars of the New York underground including Taylor Mead, Annie Sprinkle, Kembra Pfahler and Nick Zedd. Montez vehicles enabled a tentative yet heady flight of fantasy for Smith: an escape from the brutality of the city, the privations of poverty, and the ever-present threat of creative exploitation. Inane yet ravishing, her films provided an idyllic space that was nearly beyond appropriation, as a movie genre so disastrously compromised as to be almost safe from recuperation.

My argument thus entails reading sites of libidinal investment as hieroglyphs, signs laced with the gaps that efficacious communication resists. These signs function as the props of an enormous dereliction, calling attention to their own failures (including camp's resistance to critical discourse) as well as to greater disasters that conceal themselves – however partially – in the registers of official culture. Our meagre identifications in queer performance and camp effects, therefore, foster the failures that condition our encounters with the bodies of others, in and through language. But in their excessive signification, in their extravagant flaunting – of doomed bodies, open wounds and broken signs – such practices might retain the thought of some other form of meeting, a precarious kind of speaking. I argue that queer performance, or rather our negotiations of their traces as readers, may thus constitute a mode of representation that frontloads its own proximity to failure. Or as Smith states in his performance *I Was a Male Yvonne de Carlo for the Lucky Landlord Underground* (1982), 'The communication breakdown of Jingola … This is the only way these desert disasters come to pass. Not knowing the process of talking or working. Their bodies, as well as the entire community, will soon be covered by drifting sand.'[5] The content of Smith's statement is emphasised by its juddering, broken syntax. He imagines communication as a compensatory ideal that functions by repressing the inevitability of breakdown, and counters this by staging the fact of incommunicability in his performances. As John Durham Peters argues, the fantasy of communication as the dream of a successful transmission of internal content inhibits the hard work of both interpersonal connection and the construction of community. 'Too often,' he writes, '"communication" misleads us from the task of building worlds together. It invites us into a world of unions without politics, understandings without language, and souls without bodies, only to make politics, language, and bodies reappear as obstacles rather than blessings.'[6] Through the example of Smith's investment in Montez's faulty representations, I ask how a failure of communication may enable – rather than foreclose – bold ideas, novel connections, and other possibilities.

Raging and flaming

Maria Montez is a marginal personality in the history of 1940s cinema. She was born María Africa Vidal de Santo Silas y Gracia, in Barahona in the Dominican Republic in 1912. Her father was Consul General to Spain, and sent her to a Catholic convent school in the Canary Islands, after which the young María worked as a model in London, New York and San Francisco,

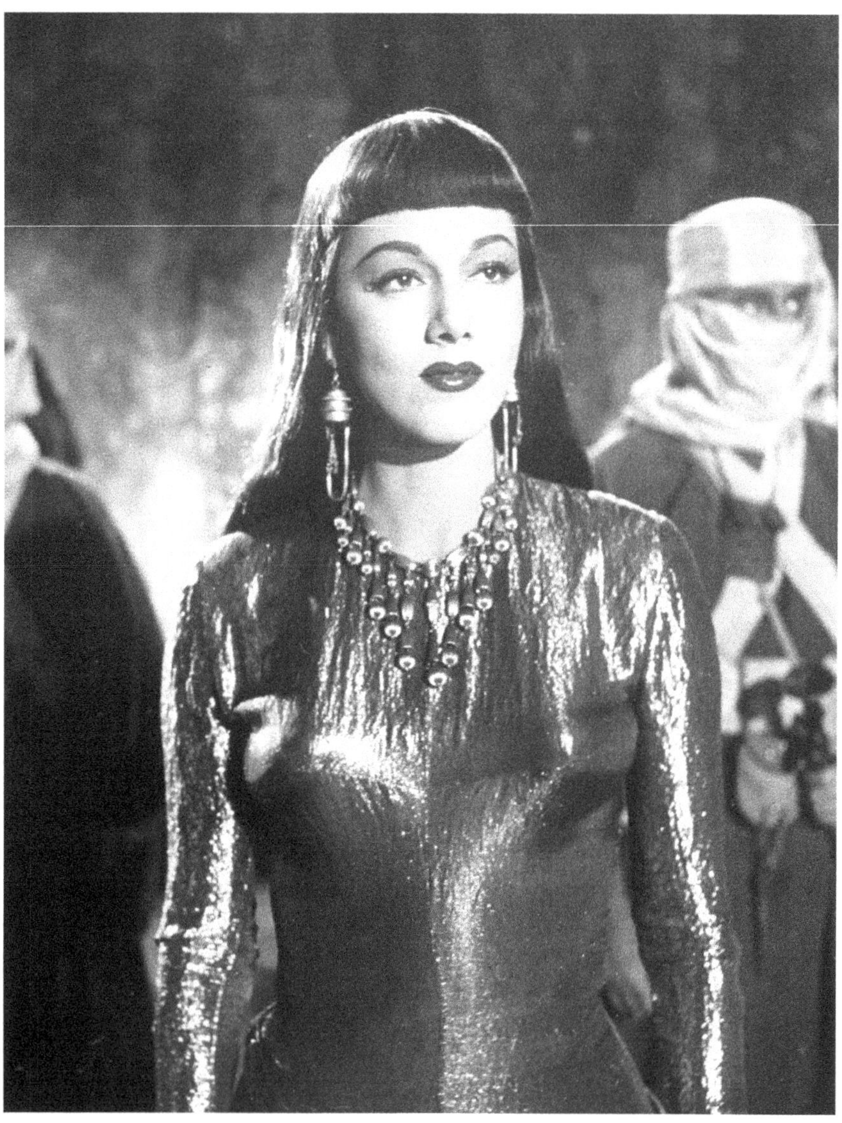

5.1   Peter Stackpole, *Maria Montez* (1947).

before striking fame as a young starlet in Hollywood. Montez was famous for her smouldering beauty, and for the curious languor of her acting style. In America, she was a transitory star around whom a number of Hollywood whimsies were created, yet she also had a short career in 'respectable' French films in the late 1940s, such as Bernard-Roland's *Portrait of an Assassin* (1949), also starring Erich von Stroheim. After emigrating to Paris, Montez counted Jean Cocteau among her admirers, and he became a close friend in the last years of her life. Her husband, the French actor Jean-Pierre Aumont writes in his memoirs: 'Maria and [Cocteau] belonged to the same race. Both of them moved easily between the confines of the real and the unreal. Both of them were familiar with messages from the beyond, ghosts, and premonitions'.[7] Montez cultivated this mystical propensity, creating a screen presence that framed her transcendent beauty with an evocatively performed vacancy. This jarring tension shone through her celebrated absence of acting skills.

According to Ronald Tavel, Smith built a series of shrines to Montez, 'to oversee and share his confidential life; and he literally prayed to her daily for artistic inspiration, and claimed it was she who instructed him to place her altar itself at the center of *Normal Love* … "Hearing is obeying," [Smith] intoned'.[8] Smith got the idea to erect the altar after hearing that Montez herself had built a private chapel inside her Beverly Hills mansion, to safe-keep a statue of Saint Anthony of Padua, the patron saint of lost things, lost souls and missing persons. Her films would translate into an almost magical resource for Smith. Her example 'stoked up crucial energy for his countercapitalistic impulses [and was] the inspiration for some of the more breathtaking urges in the live one-madman shows especially – urges that would impel Jack to self-critique under his breath, "Gilded, Gilded"'.[9] Moreover, the trash cinema of Maria Montez occupies a curious role in the development of avant-garde performance in the 1960s. Draped in lamé and studded with sequins, Smith's contemporaries such as Jackie Curtis, Holly Woodlawn, Candy Darling, Mario Montez, Margo Howard-Howard, Agosto Machado and Alexis del Lago created extravagant drag styles cribbed from the glamour of 1940s Hollywood starlets – Montez, and also Lana Turner, Veronica Lake, Hedy Lamarr and Dorothy Lamour. Founders of the Play-House of the Ridiculous in 1965, John Vaccaro and Ronald Tavel met at a Montez screening at the Beaver Cinematheque in New York. Together, Vaccaro, Tavel and Smith would attend arduous twelve-hour marathons of her films, revelling in the tropical excess of *Cobra Woman*, and other daft epics such as *Arabian Nights* (1942), *White Savage* (1943), *Gypsy Wildcat* (1944) or *Siren of Atlantis* (1949).

Montez was a crucial influence upon Smith for her professional achievements, but he also expended vast energies on the trials of her short life. Key among these latter details were her relationship with her husband, Jean-Pierre Aumont, and her apparent feud with another little-known starlet of the 1940s,

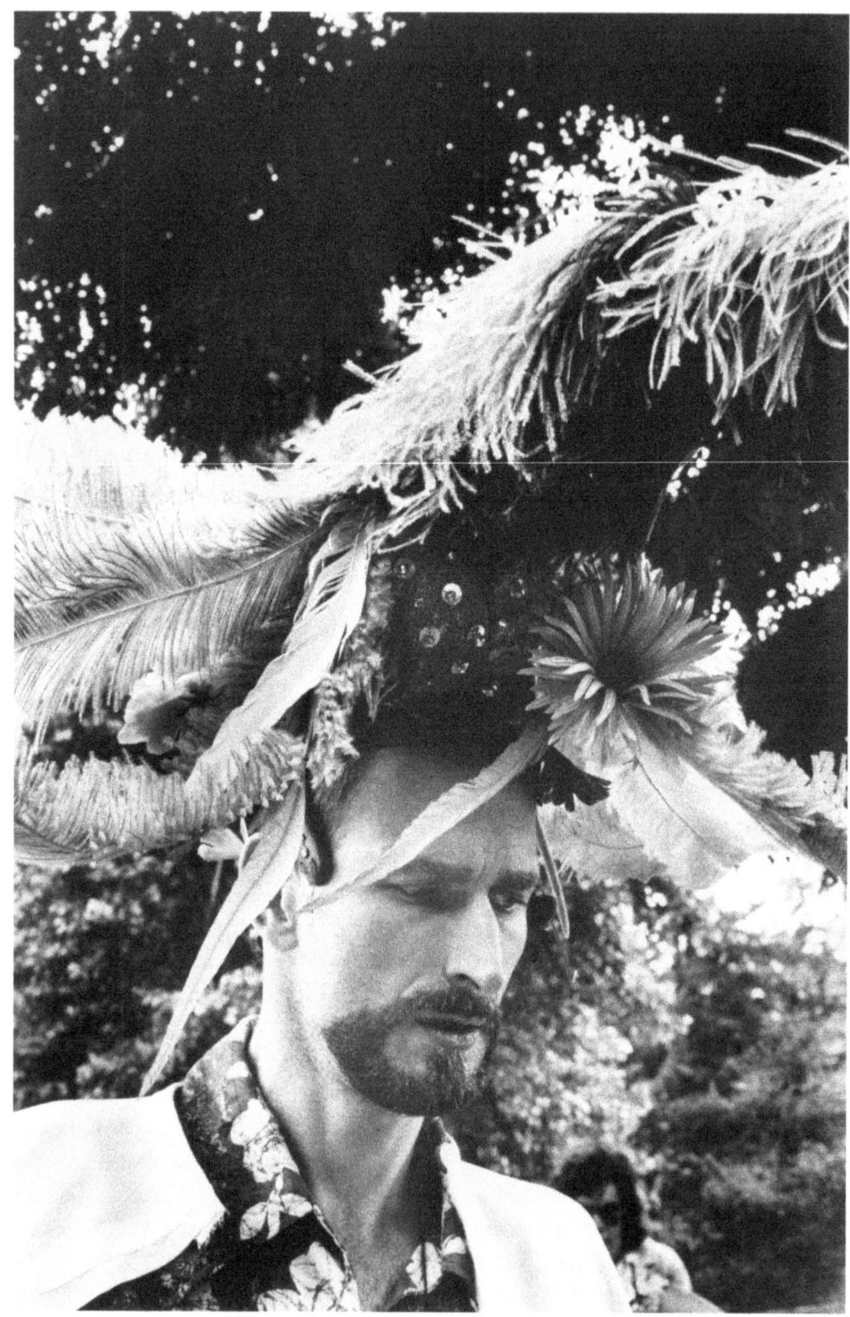

5.2   Jack Smith, *Fear Ritual of Shark Museum*, Cologne Zoo (1974).

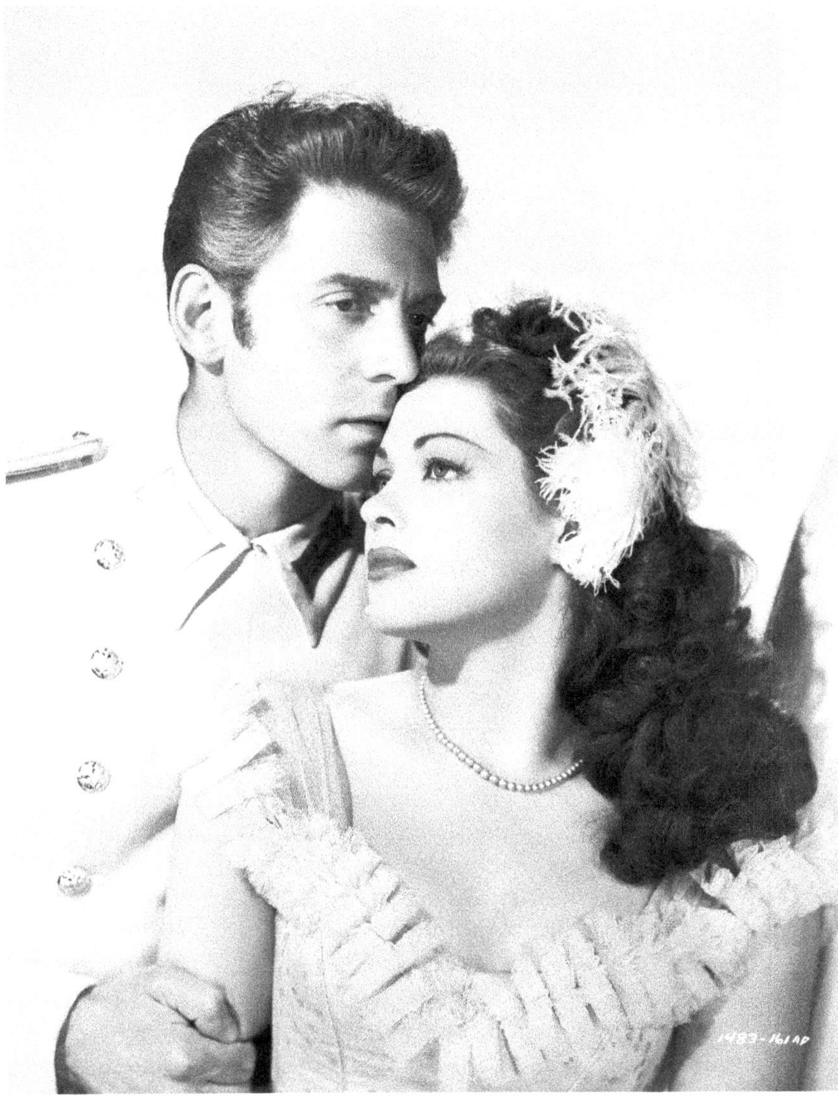

Actress Yvonne de Carlo and actor Jean-Pierre Aumont on the film set of *Song of*   **5.3**
Scheherazade, directed by Walter Reisch in USA in 1947.

Yvonne de Carlo. Aumont recounted the situation that caused the rift between
Montez and de Carlo. In 1947, he was lent by Metro Pictures to another studio,
Universal, 'where Maria was the reigning queen,' to star in *Song of Scheher-
azade*. He writes:

> However, it was not with her that they intended me to work but with Yvonne de
> Carlo, whom they were trying to set up as a rival to Maria. At that time it was

the policy of all the studios to create such oppositions among their stars under contract. Thus, Debbie Reynolds was brought in to replace Judy Garland, Gregory Peck to oppose Clark Gable, Ava Gardner to supplant Lana Turner. If a star did poorly at the box office or became difficult, [a] replacement was right there to take over.[10]

For Smith, de Carlo was thus a potent symbol for the exploitation of the Hollywood star system and, by extension, the shaky morality of the art market. In performances and writings, Smith would decry de Carlo as a place-holder for a larger set of professional difficulties and perceived betrayals. Her name appears in performance titles such as *I Was a Male Yvonne de Carlo for the Lucky Landlord Underground* (1982) at the Museum of Exotic Aquatics in New York. In Cologne some years earlier, Smith would tell the audience of his performance *Irrational Landlordism of Bagdad* (1977) that despite the best intentions of artists, 'the stairway to socialism is blocked by the Yvonne de Carlo Tabernacle Choir … This is the rented moment of exotic landlordism of prehistoric capitalism of tabu'.[11] Vehement railings against de Carlo were a persistent feature of Smith's performance antics, and his fury at her betrayal of Montez would not wane even when her career had long since fizzled. After its publication in 1987, Smith would read aloud de Carlo's autobiography in performances, and add his own biting commentaries, to the amusement or befuddlement of his audience – many of those in attendance would have had little or no memory of de Carlo, except perhaps her tenure as an actress in the 1960s TV sitcom *The Munsters*, or her appearances in Stephen Sondheim musicals on Broadway in the 1970s.[12] Her name was even adapted to a neologism – 'Yvonne de Carloism' – used by Smith to describe guilty acts of duplicity or ingratiation on the part of himself or other artists.

Juan Suárez has persuasively documented the crucial influence of 'low' or pop culture on avant-garde film in the period. In his Marxian reading, the films of Smith, Andy Warhol and Kenneth Anger stage a three-way intersection between gay identities, mass culture, and Euro-American avant-gardism, towards a new model of subcultural activism. Suárez argues that in his turn to Montez, Smith articulates how an otherwise mundane interest in the products of the culture industry could be appropriated as an oppositional practice. Outdated or otherwise maligned products such as *Cobra Woman*, he suggests, which become 'indigestible by the social order' when they outlive the moment of their production, are borrowed and 'awakened for more authentic and participatory forms of cultural and social life'.[13] To the degree such works exhibit 'tawdriness, vulgarity, and bad taste', the greater their subcultural use-value.[14]

From underground cinema to Happenings and the emergent pop aesthetic, this was less a symptom of the avant-garde artist's perversity than a signal of avant-gardism's guerrilla inversions of conventional taste and value. Tavel foregrounds Montez's impact on certain groundbreaking artists of the 1960s, specifically Smith, for whom she was a 'literally continuous preoccupation':

> Mantling himself in her, laying claim to her in fandom's name and nature of both wholly identifying and being violently possessive, Smith saw her as the maker of all art and, in the process of projection … revisited her in all the beauty he intended to create in his life. Thus at times, metaphorically, every pertinent phenomenon was screened through her.[15]

Montez has also, of course, had notable detractors. A star of Andy Warhol's *Chelsea Girls* (1966), 'Pope' Ondine wrote a rambling counter to Smith's enduring adulation, disparaging Montez as 'a very limited film personality,' and 'a star of what – Grade C Desert Melodramas'. More damningly, he slanders her cult as peopled by 'transvestites [who] have taken up [her] rather paltry existence and blown it up to the same size as their own … egos'.[16]

Performance and autobiography

'The perfect filmic appositeness of Maria Montez' is a classic Smith text, published in *Film Culture* just before *Flaming Creatures* was first screened. It is an elegy to Montez, upon whom Smith confers – with sincere adulation – the title of 'the World's Worst Actress': 'hilarious to serious persons, beloved to Puerto-Ricans, magic for me, beauty for many, camp to homos, Fauve American unconscious to Europeans'.[17] His adoration of Montez is more than ironic pantomime; rather, she is an iconic figure whose working-through in oddball prose allowed Smith to critique public conceits of taste and value, and conventions of cultural pleasure. He privileges the 'delirious hokey' of her acting, the way that 'one of her atrocious acting sighs suffused a thousand tons of dead plaster with imaginative life and insight'.[18] Smith is unusual among artists for the way in which he used his personal admiration for Montez (as fetish) and compensatory demeaning of Yvonne de Carlo (as nemesis) as enduring spurs to creativity. It demonstrates how autobiographical concerns influenced his practice, especially in writing and performance. As such, he cultivated a perverse failure to distinguish between himself and his work.

The use of autobiographical content in performance reached its apotheosis in the 1990s, in explorations of identity politics by performance artists such as Karen Finley, Ron Athey, Tim Miller or Robbie McCauley. For Marvin Carlson, however, autobiographical performance is a historically rich mode that has fulfilled different functions across various periods. He notes that theatrical performances by celebrities '*in propria persona*' were a common feature in nineteenth-century theatre, citing billings of Buffalo Bill (as himself) in live and film features, where such performances produced spectatorial pleasure through tactical confusions between character, role and identity.[19] However, after 1960, the prevalence of autobiographical performance produces meaning differently, Carlson argues, when the poststructuralist interest in the construction and revelation of subjectivity affords these tactical confusions with a unique valence that was unavailable to audiences in earlier historical moments. By the late 1960s, autobiographical performance enacted a further challenge, critically positioning the performance of self between the discursive traditions of theatre and art. Carlson writes, 'If traditional theatre was inhospitable to [autobiographical performance] on the grounds that it seemed to deny the imaginative, mimetic basis of art, performance [art] was inhospitable on the quite different grounds that autobiography introduced textuality and narrativity into the abstract, non-matrixed actions that characterized the body art of such performers as Chris Burden, Bruce Naumann [*sic*], or Vito Acconci.'[20] It would seem that Jack Smith's autobiographical, desire-led performance practice operated in a troublesome position between these two resistant imperatives, anticipating the return to autobiography in the work of a younger generation of artists in the 1980s.

Smith's commitment to autobiographical performance bears upon two related conditions: firstly, a sense that, as Carlson observes, there was a historically contingent critical purchase in the medium, as it enabled the performing subject to interrogate and reject the frequently formalist assumptions of both art and theatre in the early 1960s; secondly, Smith was perhaps emboldened by the psychic weight afforded by being a disconcerting presence on the street, as an unabashed and flamboyant homosexual man in the years before both the increased political recognition afforded lesbian and gay experience after 1969, the decriminalisation of homosexuality in New York in 1977, and the passing of a gay rights bill (barring discrimination against lesbians and gay men) in 1986. As Neil Bartlett notes, the power of autobiographical performance for queer subjects – and particularly drag queens – derives from their translation of a 'climactic indignity' suffered in the street into a 'triumph of gesture' in the theatre. 'Their survival skills on stage,' he states, 'are continuous with their survival skills in life.'[21] Smith is classic in his refusal to distinguish between 'survival' on the streets and in his performances, creating a continuum in which he provoked and sustained failure at every turn.

If Smith's practices are contradictory, he was nevertheless a keen theorist of his own work, even if in sometimes veiled terms. Smith's explanations in 'The perfect filmic appositeness of Maria Montez' signal the manner in which mutual principles are spread across the various modes of his practice: writing, performance and film. Smith writes that the reluctance to admit of her validities is a refusal of the cultural significance of failure: 'we cause their downfall (after we have enjoyed them) because they embarrass us, grown up as we are and post adolescent / post war / post graduate.' Emboldened by their privileges, audiences laugh at Montez and resent the 'rainbow colored gates' of her embarrassing celluloid world.[22] Smith refuses to legitimise the sincerity of good acting, or the seriousness of intelligent plots: 'I don't feel nonsense in movies is a threat to my mind since I don't go to movies for the ideas that arise from sensibleness of ideas.'[23] For Smith, ideas do arise, but not as direct transferrals from the work's legible surface. Meaning issues from the encounter with a temporal phenomenon, allowing for what he terms forms of 'resolution', attainable only through physical processes, sensitive identifications whose limits, it would seem, mimic the threshold of the magical.

As such, Smith's comments on Montez's acting skills function as decoys for self-analysis. David Packman confirms this argument, observing that another early text by Smith (a commentary on the movies of Josef von Sternberg) 'serves as well as a delightful introduction to the sensibility evidenced in his own *Flaming Creatures*'.[24] His artist writings allow him to refuse the introversion of self-criticism while signalling the developments he was ushering forward in both underground film and experimental theatre. Carefully written observations of bad movies and lousy acting materialise in his film and performance work as self-conscious attempts to act, and obsessive requests that the audience convince him he is even actually performing. 'The worst thing of all is that nobody thinks I'm acting … at all … If you couldn't move in your theater seats

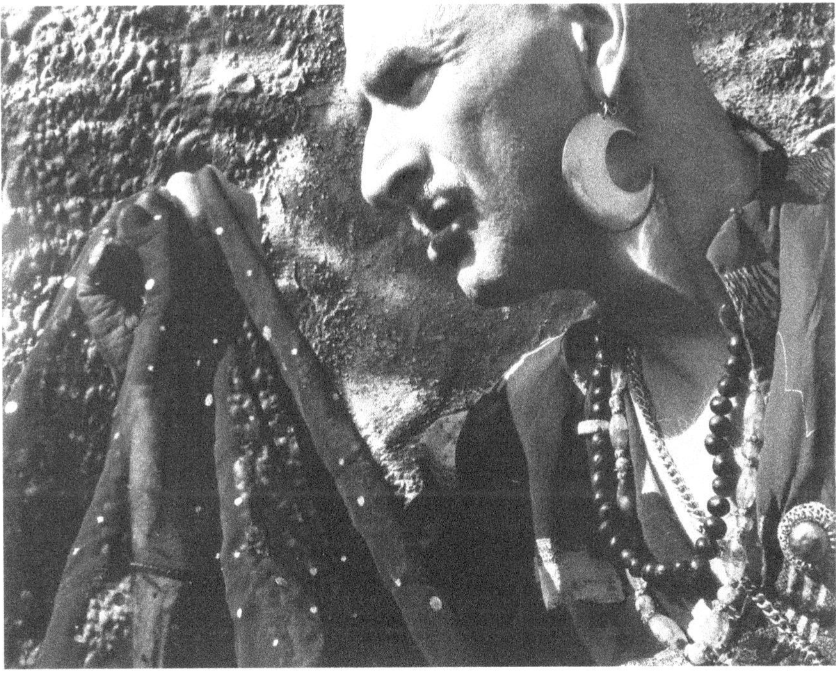

Jack Smith, *Untitled* (c. 1980).   **5.4**

… if you couldn't tear your eyes off of the actor, then it must be good acting.'[25] Smith collapses an audience's fascination for the unravelling of catastrophes on stage with the normative values afforded skilled acting in the theatre.

Montez clearly epitomises Smith's anti-aesthetic, because by failing to act competently, she allows for something 'genuine' to be caught on film, 'a personality that exposes itself'.[26] Inept acting is 'a technique for revelation … with people as their unique selves, not chessmen in a script.'[27] This is the crux of Smith's practice, for if his performance persona is a calculated performance of self, Smith deploys performance as a tool to define a politics: one that is not impeded by the intrusion of nonsense, eccentricity and failure. As Quentin Crisp wrote, an artist's skill is hardly central to the elaboration of one's style but is valuable simply as 'a colorless fluid in which to suspend a monstrous ego'.[28] Writing specifically of the films of the 1940s, the camp icon adds that the undermining of skill in favour of insincerity, exaggeration and excess – in overcooked performances by Montez as well as her contemporaries – worked to heighten rather than undermine the pleasure to be achieved by audiences. 'What audiences went to see was not an act of impersonation,' Crisp continues, but the 'triumph of cast-iron personality over the hazards of life, desertion, betrayal, misunderstanding, and death.'[29]

Like her contemporaries, Montez may have achieved 'intensely devotional' followers, Peter Evans writes, yet this adoration is limited to 'a narrower circle of kitsch and camp idolaters.'[30] As one such idolater, Smith loved Montez for opening up of a whole range of expressive possibilities, through the overturning of technique for the realm of 'inept approximation'. This dimension of self-presentation, accepted as a virtual mantra by the practitioners circulating around the Play-House of the Ridiculous, culminated in Smith's privileging of the sincerity of trash over the false magic of value. Michael Moon describes Smith as 'one of the most accomplished and influential but least known producers of the extremely theatricalized, densely materialist version of urban gay male social and artistic practice that has to this point been recognized, studied, and theorized chiefly under the extremely reductive rubric of "camp".'[31] Ransacking Montez's onscreen achievements, Smith plundered the potentially campy contradictions of her failures in the art of convincing acting: an excess of theatricality and intrusions of apparent authenticity; intensity and superficiality; the mindlessly self-evident and implausible self-contradiction. Fabio Cleto writes,

> It is precisely [the restless] holding together of antitheses that makes camp irreducible to a set of features, for it works by *contradiction*, by *crossing* statements and their possibilities of being. Intentions, seriousness and their correlates (politics and agency) are there, and yet they are only present in a queer articulation: not one that will concede itself as classifying tool, but rather as a puzzled, questioned issue.

As such, 'both *failure* and *betrayal* can be traced as features of all camp effects, as part indeed of its own activation and horizon of possibility.'[32] Charles Ludlam confirms Cleto's description when he writes that the thrust of camp – like its weird sister, the Ridiculous – lies in 'Admiring what people hold in contempt [and] holding in contempt things that other people think are so valuable,' adding, 'it's a fantastic standard' for living.[33] Seeking inspiration in these pleasurable collisions, Smith's fascination was inevitably framed by the ambivalent tragedy of Montez's lurid fall, from Hollywood grace into obscurity and early death.

'Whatever is near you is near death!'

In September 1951, Montez died at her home in Paris, aged 39. An overdose of weight-loss medication brought on a heart attack, which caused her to drown in her hot paraffin bath.[34] At the time of her death, Smith was nineteen, and working as an usher at the Orpheum Theatre in Chicago, where a series of commemorative screenings turned him onto his lifelong obsession with the raging and flaming star. That star fetish should be intensified by death is nothing out of the ordinary, and in fact a crucial trope in the workings of popular culture. This public tendency was monumentally confirmed when James Dean was killed in a car wreck in 1955. As J. Hoberman writes,

> [The] smashed racing Porsche in which Dean perished was purchased by a young Los Angeles couple who exhibited it in a bowling alley, charging customers a quarter to see it, half a dollar to actually sit in the driver's seat and touch the bloody, misshapen steering wheel. Apparently 800,000 tickets were sold. Meanwhile, bolts and screws salvaged from the wreck went their separate routes like pieces of the True Cross.[35]

The 'Dean cult' enacted a morbid public interplay between the cachet of celebrity martyrdom, and the macabre revelation of desire's intensification in sensational death. Such investments were revealed as the popular cultural compulsion to monumentalise the distinctly unglamorous relics of Dean's epic dying, as if his body's celebrants hung on to its traces for dear life. The allure of his saintly figural body depends on a tension between his coolly detached glamour and the rich possibilities for projection and identification opened up by the perfection of his screen image.

Despite the pleasures of such investments, Caryl Flinn writes that such grisly preoccupations in camp practices must be considered in terms of assaults directed at bodies, and especially those of women. This observation is important, considering the ghosting of my thoughts by the wounded body of Maria Montez. Iconic camp effects including Robert Aldrich's *Whatever Happened to Baby Jane?* (1962) are characterised by Flinn as exercises of aggression and ridicule, 'necro-romps' that play out an 'excess of consumption, a wasted production that is literalized by [and] on female bodies'.[36] Displacing the 'perverse democratization' of signs purportedly at play in queer work, Flinn argues that camp 'may collude unwittingly with a dominant culture that seems increasingly bent on doing damage to the female body'.[37] I want to argue that a tonality of camp's work – as flaunted in Smith's attachment to Montez – is the pleasure it affords in calling attention to the internal failings of mainstream (heterosexual, Anglo-centric) culture. This criticality extends to his representations of and fascination with the fantastical failings of the body of Maria Montez.

Peering disdainfully down at those enveloped in her silver glow, Montez's screen quality triggered Smith's excessive investment in a series of otherwise unremarkable vehicles. Publicity for her movies played into such perverse investments, by describing her as 'Daughter of Eve with the soul of Satan', 'Ravaging the souls of men with the lash of primitive hate … and the call of pagan love,' or the 'Pagan witch, no man could tame – or resist!'[38] Predicated on these racially conspicuous representations, the 'dotty splendour' and 'magnificent lunacy' of Montez's Technicolor extravaganzas sent a generation of children and homosexuals into ecstasies of pleasure.[39] Moreover, Montez's conspicuous Dominican lilt indexes a distinctly racialised body. In the celluloid confections Smith pleasured himself with, Montez would be seen riding out to 'exotic' or 'tropical' adventures throughout the 1940s, often alongside actors of colour such as Sabu or the 'mysterious' Turhan Bey.[40] As Mekas wrote in an advertisement published in the *Village Voice* in 1963, 'Jack Smith describes the voice of the late Miss Montez as having an inexplicable accent, a composite of French (from her husband Jean-Pierre Aumont), Spanish, Greta Garbo, and Dracula – as a matter of fact the same accent and rhythm as Bela Lugosi, filled with implications of the mythical kingdom of Transylvania.'[41] Montez's status as a woman of colour persisted in the tenor of her voice, marking her difference from other stars of the period who passed convincingly, such as Rita Hayworth (born Margerita Carmen Cancino). Montez, on the other hand, could not pass, failing – or refusing – to overwrite her *Latinidad*.[42]

This conspicuousness manifested in the roles she played in the films that would captivate Smith and his friends. Tavel argues that they provided a sense of escapism that was magnified for 'those who, watching a cowboy and indian movie, identified with the indians, and with third-world persons, be they Islander, Arab, or Asian' and a host of 'second-class citizens' including women and queers, 'minorities, the loner, the sexual outlaw'.[43] Directed by Greg C. Tallas, *Siren of Atlantis* (1949) evocatively condenses the tendency of 1940s Hollywood to conflate Montez's racial difference with voracious sexuality and morbid 'pagan love'. She plays Antinea, the immortal queen of Atlantis, who lures the stranded lieutenant St Avit with murderous desire. Antinea is a man-eater, seducing her suitors and encasing them as statues of gold, to produce an undead coterie of (in one character's words) 'scattered souls from ill-fated expeditions, tossed up by the sandy waves of the Sahara into the mountainous heights' of the lost continent. Companioned by a panther, and surrounded by betrothed soldiers and embalmed lovers, Antinea wraps herself in diaphanous lamé, and sleeps in a giant conch shell retrieved from the seas into which Atlantis is doomed to fall. Her hapless lovers fall prey to the sultry mantrap and her fruity monologues. 'Don't pretend to hate me!' she pleads, wearing a bejewelled bustier and an alluring smile. Played by her off-screen husband, St Avit is duly persuaded of her charms, for 'desire is as bright as the sun!' In an overblown scene, which precipitates his death, St Avit's right-hand man Morjhane challenges Antinea, exposing her cruelty: 'You feed on death … cursed with the joy of killing.' He continues,

> You're sustained only by the beauty that you find in your mirror, but I look into your eyes and what I see there is ugliness, a soul merciless and cruel, a heart withered and evil, twisted like the root of an ancient tree. Wrapped and sheathed in your gold you're as old and as dead as the mummies … in their sepulchres, from whom you claim your heritage. Whatever is near you is near death!

In *Siren of Atlantis*, Montez is the exemplary femme fatale, a classic Holly-wood representation that highlights the troubling assumption of female desire as ravenous and deadly. A woman's desiring body is conflated, here, with a seemingly trans-historical threat of catastrophe. Smith parodied Montez's character in the film as 'Siren of the Cretan Cookoo Cult', in a disastrous narrative of a 90–year-old decaying starlet called Mavis Davis, 'universally acclaimed as the loveliest corpse … to have somehow not have been born yet' who ends the horrific short story as 'the turd in the coffin' swarming in 'blonde maggots'.[44] *Siren of Atlantis* was also the basis for the imagined Montez vehicle *Siren of Babylon*, a concoction Gore Vidal narrates in the first four chapters of his novel *Myron* (1974). In the novel, the transgender hero Myron/Myra Breck-inridge follows Smith's example, enshrining Montez after becoming enrap-tured at the sight of 'the Priestess of the Sun'.[45] As eroticised outsider, and an available idol for the sexually misbegotten, Montez's screen roles emphasised her potential as a redeemer of the alien, as empowering figure for those that saw themselves as lost or powerless amid the ravaged sprawl of modernity.

As demonstrated by this chapter's epigraph, Smith would introduce perfor-mances by parading his morbid attachment to – and merciless plundering of – the legacy of Maria Montez. As such, he aped – and exploited – the erotic investment in death and dying that mass culture harbours. So, while camp practices are often enacted in relation to the excesses or failures of women's bodies – Judy Garland's substance abuse, Dolly Parton's breasts, or Montez's accent – the energies openly invested in these effects serve a parodic function, burlesquing the excesses and failures that characterise the (barely) sublimated abuses inherent in mainstream culture. For Jennifer Doyle, strategies such as these go some way towards explaining 'why many of the most significant gay male artists of the twentieth century frequently put women in their work, not only as iconic placeholders for an idealized, deconstructed, or camp version of femininity but as crucial allies in the attempt to make a livable life out of a world organised against the minority sexual object'.[46] In this critical formulation, the gay male artist seeks out the failings in mainstream representation, and works to exploit their political implications for subjects at the margins of culture.

Smith's artist writings are littered with textual fantasies about the partial resurrection of corpses, perverse imaginings of the death of beauty – and of specific (female) beauties: Montez of course being a frequent casualty to these desires. One such text is 'The memoirs of Maria Montez, or wait for me at the bottom of the pool', a Burroughsian fable published in 1963–64. It is composed as a fictional account of a day of filming with the Queen of Technicolor, fantasised as having continued her Hollywood studio career beyond her death in 1951. The bathtub in which she drowned is imagined as a pool at whose side a deathly love scene is being filmed: 'The dust settled', he writes. 'O finally! Maria Montez was propped up beside the pool which reflected her ravishing beauty. A chunk fell off her face showing the grey under her rouge … The chunk of putrid meat in the pool showed up in all the shots.'[47] In the text, Smith illustrates the cultural disavowal of proximities between death and desire with grisly detail and misplaced humour. He critiques the appropriation of the sexual by the machinery of the culture industry, and orchestrates a textual cinema around the lurid collapse of beauty. Montez's decomposing body, marshalled into cosmetic proxy for a lost or defiled 'value', signals the darkness of shame and denial lurking beneath conventional images of sexuality. His imagined environment is one saturated by death, and serially punctured by disappearance: 'The decor hangs down in tendrils and dust settles over all. There are strangled bodies hanging in the tendrils … The set disappears in shadows, disappears in scaffolding. Miss Montez has disappeared from view.'[48] The death imagined in the text is an all-encompassing one, a negation that revokes the permanence of all that its would-be film conditions. 'Rushes come back that no one remembers taking', he writes, 'Rushes of blank film, of sets not on the lot, of empty, ruined, demolished sets … Endlessly long shots of deserted … preworld Monte Carlo ballroom sets empty'.[49]

As a parable of the artistic context within which Smith's work was being produced and presented, the text threatens its object (the missing film) with disappearance. The disagreeable object that beggars belief and logic is substituted by the cultural product it seeks to displace – namely the empty beauty maintained over and against that which would invoke illogic or horror. 'The leading man realizes he has been duped at the bottom of the pool,' duped not by death but by the cultural apparatus sustaining the reception of art, which sequesters death beyond the frame of the thinkable. Andrew Ross notes the 'necrophilic economy that underpins the camp sensibility, not only in its resurrection of deceased cultural forms, but also in the way in which it serves an ambivalent notice of mortality to the contemporary intellect'.[50] Smith's camp ponderings of the wounded body of Maria Montez are an instance of such an investment, feigning an inappropriate desire on the part of the artist. Smith eagerly concurs in the soundtrack to Ken Jacobs' *Blonde Cobra* (1959), where he screams: 'This corpse is obviously dead … I'm ravishing the corpse, ravish, ravish, ravish, ravish, ravish, uuuuh necrophilic longings, necrophilic fulfilment!'[51] Yet the insinuation of this monstrous gesture – quiet hands sliding far, running fast to the bodies of the dead – also encourages his more telling allegation: that the underpinnings of the age of formalism as a cultural logic are indeed repressive, not just of unacceptable artistic practices but also of the problematic politics signalled by them.

Necrophilic longing, uh, uh, uh

For Jennifer Doyle, the event of producing or consuming the work of art is particularly invested in disaster when it broaches critical questions about sex and sexuality. Doyle's *Sex Objects* is persistently invested in moments of hermeneutic collapse, in which readers mistake the differences between books and bodies, texts and lives. Describing these promiscuous encounters as 'sodomitical' scenes, she writes,

> [The] sodomitical possibilities inscribed within the scene of producing and consuming art [can be read] as activities that allow … a physical intimacy defined by something other than the imperative to reproduce, as a scene in which the pleasures of representing sex outstrip the epistemological drive to figure sex out.[52]

Akin to this criminal scene of physical consort, Philippe Sollers provides an equally visceral description of the non-producer of culture as similarly sodomitical. In the literary establishment of the 1960s, critical convention dubs writers of experimental literature as 'castrati, impotents, fetuses': 'Their writings are sterile, disembodied, unreadable; their authors are decadent mandarins, fat women incapable of birth, larvae – in a word, just the opposite of what a novelist's function demands: a narrative virility able to rape nature effortlessly, a creator, a *procreator*.'[53] Doyle's image of artistic endeavour as a grotesque coupling between bodies in neglect of procreative necessity is prefigured in several ways by Sollers' statement, issuing from the same 'sodomitical' gesture. Monstrously underdeveloped (fetuses, bestial larvae), sterile and barren, deviant or effete, Sollers' experimental writer is deemed a failure by culture – a perverter of form, power and faculty – incapable of the forcible reproduction of Nature stipulated in the demands of productive culture. Sardonically imagining the masterful producer of authentic culture as an industriously dutiful rapist, in the same stroke Sollers effectively draws on the disgust aroused by the avant-garde and/or sodomy. The latter dyad's excess is complicated, here, by the masquerade of each in maligned (feminine, emasculated) incapacity, a political refusal of the exultant Author's proud and persuasive masculinity. Smith capitalises on the sodomitical possibilities of experimental culture, raising Montez's wounded body to the status of fetish, and framing this investment as resistant, excessive and necrophilic.

Sexual catastrophes and monstrous genders have long been a central part of the allure of mass culture, especially when catastrophe or monstrosity befalls the bodies of famous women. In his scathing assessment of studio extravagance and off-screen depravity, in *Hollywood Babylon*, the underground filmmaker Kenneth Anger writes that in the 1920s, 'Professional do-gooders would brand Hollywood a New Babylon whose evil influence rivaled the legendary depravity of the old … Yet while the country's organized cranks screamed for blood and boycott, the public, unfazed, flocked to the movies in ever-increasing multitudes.'[54] The first chapter of Anger's acidic lingering in Hollywood casting-couch sleaze and other scandals is filled with images of Golden Age stars in florid, Orientalist settings, such as the gargantuan Babylon reconstructed for D. W. Griffiths' 'Sun Play of the Ages', *Intolerance* (1916), which fell into disrepair and was destroyed three years later. The ensuing sections of Anger's books catalogue the suicides, addictions, abuses, indulgences, 'organ talk', and other sources of squalid intrigue that befell the demimonde and its tabloid-soiled stars. He writes,

> Aside from the scandals which made the papers, Hollywood has always had its own supply of inner-sanctum scandal tales, prattle that livened the boredom between takes, but never saw the light of a gossip column. Depression insecurity brought out the worst in the Bitch Goddess: stars struck out at stars, directors inveighed against directors, front-office men trashed everyone in sight.[55]

Despite the disasters Montez suffered, on film and in life, her contemporaries fared even less well. Anger's demonising of the excesses of 1940s femmes fatales perhaps appears collusive with the fact that the machinery of Hollywood – and the mainstream culture over which it held such sway – terrorised those actresses who transgressed against its moral dictates. Two movie actresses who suffered most spectacularly under this protocol in the 1940s were Lupe Vélez and Frances Farmer, seemingly archetypical sexual and moral outsiders. Vélez, the 'Mexican Spitfire', would apparently embarrass her husband (the original *Tarzan*, Johnny Weissmuller) and outrage general decency by 'flash[ing] her charms at Hollywood parties by flinging her dress over her head'. Anger adds, mordantly, 'she was always innocent of lingerie'. In 1942, pregnant with the actor Harald Maresch's love-child, and pursued by tabloid scandal, Vélez took an overdose of 75 Seconals, and was found dead in her fake hacienda on North Rodeo Drive, with her head in the toilet.[56] The campy horror of Vélez's death directly influenced New York artists in the 1960s, including José Rodríguez-Soltero's film *The Life, Death, and Assumption of Lupe Vélez* (1966) starring Charles Ludlam and Mario Montez; Warhol's slightly earlier *Lupe* (1965) featured Edie Sedgwick in the eponymous role.

Described by Anger as 'sensitive and highly strung', Frances Farmer was the subject of continued persecution by press and studio bosses.[57] In 1943, while on probation for drunk driving, Farmer dislocated a studio hairdresser's jaw with a sucker-punch and lost her sweater in a nightclub brawl. On arrest, she was dragged topless through the lobby of the Knickerbocker Hotel, a notorious Hollywood hangout. In custody, Farmer signed her occupation as 'Cocksucker'.[58] After sentencing, Farmer was led out of court in a straitjacket, and subjected to the gruesome ordeal of three months of daily insulin injections, allegedly followed by a 'therapeutic' frontal lobotomy. Her mother Lillian Farmer had signed her fateful commitment papers, blaming her daughter's apparent insanity on 'World Communism'.[59] In opposition to Anger's bitchy vilifications, however, Smith sought refuge in zealous over-identification with the camp legends of Montez and other spurned actresses of the 1940s. As Flinn suggests, camp identification may condense and homogenise a litany of disastrous events by abstracting the specific contexts in which subjects are abused, bodies wounded, and lives destroyed. Despite its ghoulish humour, Anger's archive romanticises these effects, whereas Smith broods over them, and invests them with a kind of care, nursing their failures with sodomitical, faux necrophilic longings. In his creative importunities, Smith performs disastrous attempts to break the fall of his idol, Maria Montez, and soothe her failures with glamour.

The promiscuity of language

For Susan Sontag, writing in 1964, camp is, indeed, a 'grave' matter for it 'converts the serious into the frivolous'. Its critical prowess, she argues, arises from its ability to stage culture as 'a seriousness that fails', a straying of creative fantasy from the realm of beauty and truth, into the volatile space of irresponsibility.[60] In an attempt to muddy the ditch that Sontag runs between the serious and the frivolous, I have focused on Smith's fascination with the wounds and deaths of Maria Montez, and briefly acknowledged the contingent histories of other Hollywood starlets. Smith does not simply recuperate Montez's famously silly ventures as overlooked works of successful textual appropriation. Neither, as Sontag might have it, is Smith driven by the meagre pleasure afforded by being irresponsible in the space of art. Rather, his investment in bodies and objects that are fantastically prone to failure mimics a seditious effect, one specifically at stake both in certain practices of performance, and in camp's precarious political charge. The purportedly necrophilic investment in the gilded remains of dead stars can be read as a repeated attraction to the wound, specifically, to the wound that cries out, as a textual resourcefulness that facilitates different types of critical labour. As Smith asked, in the essay on Montez mentioned earlier, 'Why do we object to not being convinced – why can't we enjoy phoniness? … because it holds a mirror to our own, possibly.'[61] His elegant mangling of residues of dominant culture apes the failings of language, as the order of signification that bestows value to systems of representation, power on certain bodies, and meaning to their products.

The formal effects at work in queer texts – including those that collect under the register of camp – are, therefore, not purely those intent on making the serious frivolous, but also restage cultural precedents towards revelatory needs. It is a schema set for the playing out of misquotes, as well as for the dynamics by which communication loses itself in the midst of its own imperatives. Fraught with the dread of misfire, the privileged space of dialogue founders as an apparently simple utterance inevitably loses its clarity. Durham Peters writes, 'Communication … is a compensatory ideal whose force depends on [the appearance of] its contrast to failure and breakdown. Miscommunication is the scandal that motivates the very concept of communication in the first place.'[62] For Durham Peters, our dramas of interpersonal desolation are doubly anguished, firstly for the pain they cause, but more so for the revelations that a failed communication may reap for the subject of the enunciation. Pierced not by successful transmissions but by the misfires of language, our efforts at communication inaugurate fertile miscarriages of meaning, a desperate paradox that constitutes a permanent kink in the play of culture. '[The] dream of mental contact [itself] sets up the nightmare of mutual isolation.' Durham Peters adds. 'Longing for shared interiority, the horror of inaccessibility, and impatience with the humble means of language – these are the attributes that "communication" typically instils.'[63] He notes that experiments of the twentieth century – such as Samuel Beckett's novels, or the films of Woody Allen or Ingmar Bergman – have frequently staged the looming horizon of non-communication. Smith enables us to explore the way in which less noble or distinguished representations – and the obscure investments they inspire – may usefully complement and extend our cultural understanding of the fruits of communication gone astray.

As stammerings that take place face-to-face, or the stops, starts and self-losses of writing, the outer limits of communicative possibility mark an absolute

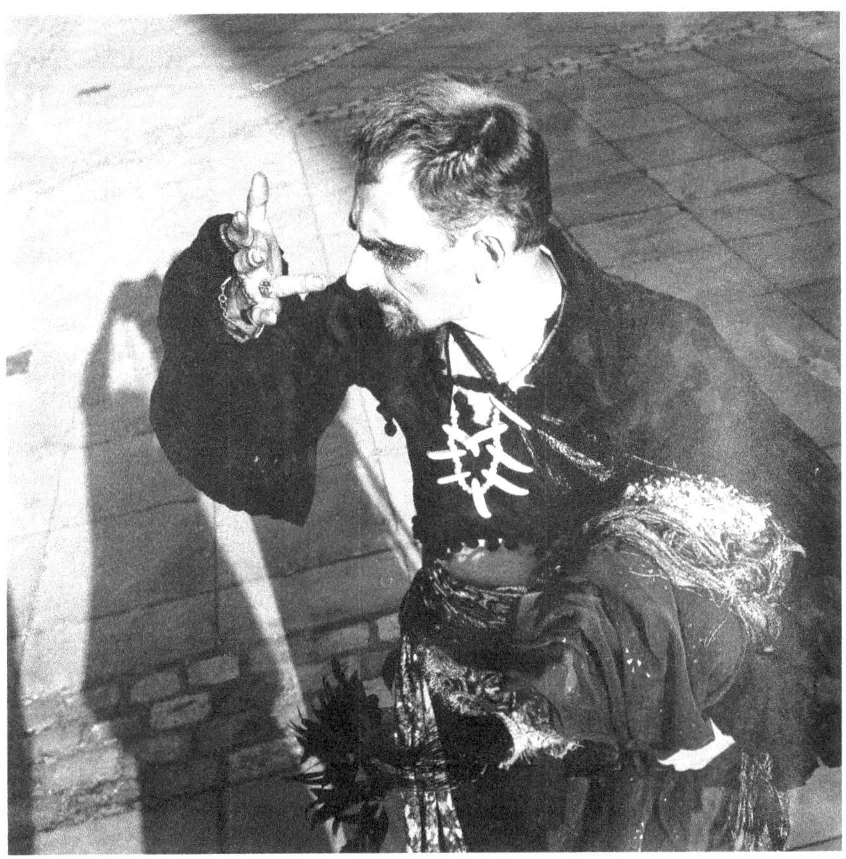

Jack Smith, *Untitled (from 'I Danced with a Penguin')* (c. 1983).   **5.5**

breach in the dream of perfected intelligibility, as well as the full pathos of the demands we put on others in urging them to receive our speech. Durham Peters asserts that the false notion of communication as the reduplication of the self in the other is a project that 'deserves to crash, for such an understanding is in essence a pogrom against the distinctiveness of human beings.'[64] As such, he asserts the violence in ontology: the identification with others as a colonisation that strips the other of her or his individual difference, reducing that other to the normalising prison of the same. Efficacious communication, Durham Peters implies, mimics the ontological venture, provoking the pain of our inability to present one's self-perception, but also our desire to make sense of the bodies of others that we caress with language. Smith revels in such indeterminacy, claiming a radically imperfect body and raising it to the status of ironic saintliness. Rather than demean Montez's performances for their failings, he honours them for their ability to reveal the disasters of a culture.

Communication, therefore, is conditioned by the promiscuity of language – its tendency to stray from its purported responsibilities. A revocable, promiscuous practice – one prone to the promise of faltering – to wield language is to maintain, across all points, the pathos of communication gone awry. Representations of wounds – and the fascinations they hold – augur of an unresolved gap, a break in the functioning of culture, which queer performance mines. The wound, as blockage rather than source, is neither a metaphor for the originary suffering of the homosexual, nor a parable for the stories we might seek to tell ourselves about our own wronged subjectivities. As I imagine it, the wound, here, is not so much a source, buried deep in some imagined core, but a sore, a score in the skin of culture. Exposed in the process of desperate signification, culture's sore points are rehearsed in the fictions that gather – in artificial conjugations – under the slippery sign of a wound that will not heal.

Notes

1 Cited in Ronald Tavel, 'Maria Montez: Anima of an antediluvian world', *Flaming Creature: Jack Smith, His Amazing Life and Times*, ed. Edward Leffingwell, Carole Kismaric and Marvin Heiferman, The Institute for Contemporary Art, P.S.1 Museum (London and New York: Serpent's Tail, 1997), pp. 88–104 (p. 99).

2 Cited in ibid. p. 99.

3 Sophocles, *Philoctetes*, trans. R. G. Ussher (Warminster: Aris & Phillips, 1990), p. 103.

4 Dick Hebdige, *Subculture: The Meaning of Style* (London and New York: Routledge, 1979), pp. 19–20.

5 Cited in Uzi Parnes, 'Pop performance: Four Seminal Influences: The work of Jack Smith, Tom Murrin – the Alien Comic, Ethyl Eichelberger, and the Split Britches Company', unpublished PhD thesis, New York University, 1988, p. 112.

6 John Durham Peters, *Speaking into the Air: A History of the Idea of Communication* (Chicago and London: University of Chicago Press, 1999), pp. 30–1.

7 Jean-Pierre Aumont, *Sun and Shadow*, trans. Bruce Benderson (New York: W. W. Norton, 1977), p. 126.

8 Ibid. p. 96.

9 Tavel, p. 96.

10 Jean-Pierre Aumont, *Sun and Shadow*, trans. Bruce Benderson (New York: W. W. Norton, 1977), p. 122.

11 Jack Smith, 'Capitalism of Lotusland' (1977), *Wait for Me at the Bottom of the Pool*, pp. 11–12 (p. 11).

12 Yvonne de Carlo with Doug Warren, *Yvonne: An Autobiography* (New York: St. Martin's Press, 1987).

13 Juan A. Suárez, *Bike Boys, Drag Queens and Superstars: Avant-Garde, Mass Culture and Gay Identities in the 1960s Underground Cinema* (Bloomington and Indianapolis: Indiana University Press), p. 34.

14 Ibid. p. 40.

15 Tavel, p. 91.

16 Ondine, 'Letter to an unknown woman namely Jack Smith', *Film Culture* 40 (Spring 1966), p. 21 (p. 21).

17 Jack Smith, 'The perfect filmic appositeness of Maria Montez' (1962), *Wait for Me at the Bottom of the Pool: The Writings of Jack Smith*, ed. J. Hoberman and Edward Leffingwell, New York and London: High Risk Books, 1997, pp. 25–35 (pp. 25–7).

18 Ibid. p. 25.

19 Marvin Carlson, 'Performing the self', *Modern Drama* 39.4, (Winter 1996), pp. 599–608 (pp. 599–600).

20 Carlson, p. 600.

21 Alan Sinfield, '"The moment of submission": Neil Bartlett in conversation', *Modern Drama* 39.1 (Spring 1996): Lesbian/Gay/Queer Drama, pp. 211–21 (p. 219).

22 Smith, 'The perfect filmic appositeness of Maria Montez', p. 27.

23 Ibid. p. 33.

24 David Packman, 'Jack Smith's *Flaming Creatures*: With the tweak of an eyebrow', *Film Culture* 63–4 (1977), p. 51 (p. 51).

25 Jack Smith, 'What's underground about marshmallows?' (1981), *Wait for Me at the Bottom of the Pool*, pp. 137–43 (p. 139).

26 Smith, 'The perfect filmic appositeness of Maria Montez', p. 34.

27 Smith, Jack, 'Belated appreciation of V. S.' (1964), *Wait for Me at the Bottom of the Pool*, pp. 41–4 (p. 42).

28 Quentin Crisp, *The Wit and Wisdom of Quentin Crisp*, ed. Guy Kettelhack (London: Arena, 1986), p. 50.

29 Ibid. p. 75.

30 Peter W. Evans, 'From Maria Montez to Jasmine: Hollywood's oriental odalisques', *'New' Exoticisms: Changing Patterns in the Construction of Otherness*, ed. Isabel Santaolalla (Amsterdam and Atlanta: Rodopi, 2000), pp. 157–65 (p. 159).

31 Michael Moon, 'Flaming closets', *October* 51 (Winter 1989), pp. 19–54 (pp. 30–1).

32 Fabio Cleto, 'Introduction: Queering the camp', *Camp: Queer Aesthetics and the Performing Subject, A Reader*, ed. Cleto (Edinburgh: Edinburgh University Press, 1999), pp. 1–42 (p. 29). Emphasis in original.

33 Charles Ludlam, *Ridiculous Theatre: Scourge of Human Folly: The Writings of Charles Ludlam*, ed. Steven Samuels (New York: Theatre Communications Group, 1992), p. 225.

34 Gore Vidal, *Myra Breckinridge & Myron* (London: Grafton Books, 1989), p. 227.

35 Hoberman and Rosenbaum, p. 20.

36 Caryl Flinn, 'The deaths of camp', *Camp*, pp. 433–57 (pp. 437, 443).

37 Ibid. pp. 452–3.

38 Tavel, p. 92.

39 Charles Higham and Joel Greenberg, *Hollywood in the Forties* (London and New York: Zwemmer & Barnes, 1968), p. 10.

40 Ibid. p. 64.

41 Jonas Mekas, 'Announcing a grand competition', *Village Voice* (24 October, 1963), p. 13.

42 Thanks to Joshua Chambers-Letson for sharing this comparison.

43 Tavel, p. 92.

44 Jack Smith, 'Red orchids' (1964), *Wait for Me at the Bottom of the Pool*, pp. 61–71 (pp. 64–6)

45 Gore Vidal, *Myra Breckinridge & Myron* (London: Grafton Books, 1989), p. 218.

46 Jennifer Doyle, *Sex Objects: Art and the Dialectics of Desire* (Minneapolis and London: University of Minnesota Press, 2006), p. 75.

47 Jack Smith, 'The memoirs of Maria Montez, or wait for me at the bottom of the pool' (1964), *Wait for Me at the Bottom of the Pool*, pp. 37–9 (p. 37).

48 Ibid. p. 38.

49 Smith, 'The memoirs of Maria Montez', p. 39.

50 Andrew Ross, 'The uses of camp', *Camp*, pp. 308–29 (p. 321).

51 Jack Smith and Ken Jacobs, 'Soundtrack of *Blonde Cobra*' (1963), *Wait for Me at the Bottom of the Pool*, pp. 158–61 (p. 157).

52 Doyle, pp. 43–4.

53 Philippe Sollers, *Writing and the Experience of Limits*, trans. Philip Barnard with David Hayman, ed. Hayman (New York: Columbia University Press, 1983) p. 190. Emphasis in original.

54 Kenneth Anger, *Hollywood Babylon* (San Francisco: Straight Arrow Books, 1975), p. 12.

55 Ibid. p. 171.

56 Ibid. p. 231.

57 Ibid. p. 223.

58 Ibid. p. 224.

59 Ibid. p. 227.

60 Susan Sontag, 'Notes on "camp"', *Camp*, pp. 53–65 (p. 59).

61 Smith, 'The perfect filmic appositeness of Maria Montez', p. 33.

62 Durham Peters, p. 6.

63 Ibid. p. 16.

64 Ibid. p. 21.

I can never go back on what I've written. If it was not good, it was true; if it was not artistic, it was sincere; if it was in bad taste, it was on the side of life. (Henry Miller)[1]

The attempt to write oneself into the world poses a terminally conflicted effort. In performance, Jack Smith continually stages the failure to summon some language that would hold his experience. To be sure, Smith's work is dominated by breakdowns, dramatising the point at which communication fails us. In his most celebrated text, 'The perfect filmic appositeness of Maria Montez', Smith acknowledges the importance of that which tends towards failure. 'Juvenile does not equal shameful and trash is the material of creators,' Smith writes, while technical accomplishment gives 'no magic – oh I guess a sort of magic, a magic of sustained efficient operation (like the wonder that the car motor held out so well after a long trip)'.[2]

His prose differs from the words spoken in his performances partly due to the discrepancies between writing as a material practice, and the events of speech and face-to-face behaviour. Susan Stewart argues that writing has specific qualities in this regard: its materiality on the page, its defiance of death as a cultural prophylaxis against disappearance, the potential for anonymity, a heightened capacity for deception as well as definition, and a call for critical commentary.[3] The spoken word, with which Smith is more readily associated, tends to be immaterial, live (though not immediate), eponymous to the extent that the words index a discrete speaker, and prone to divulging its deceptions through an accompanying theatre of the lying body: blushes, tics, or averted eyes.

Smith's written works pose questions about the 'scene' of writing, the scaffold around writing that rarely gets discussed. I pursue this idea with close readings of Smiths' copious texts, with reference to similarly difficult writings by Frank O'Hara, William S. Burroughs and others. By asking questions about how writing is carried out, as a supplement to the meanings it produces, this chapter appeals to a reformulated conception of writing as a labour of wayward

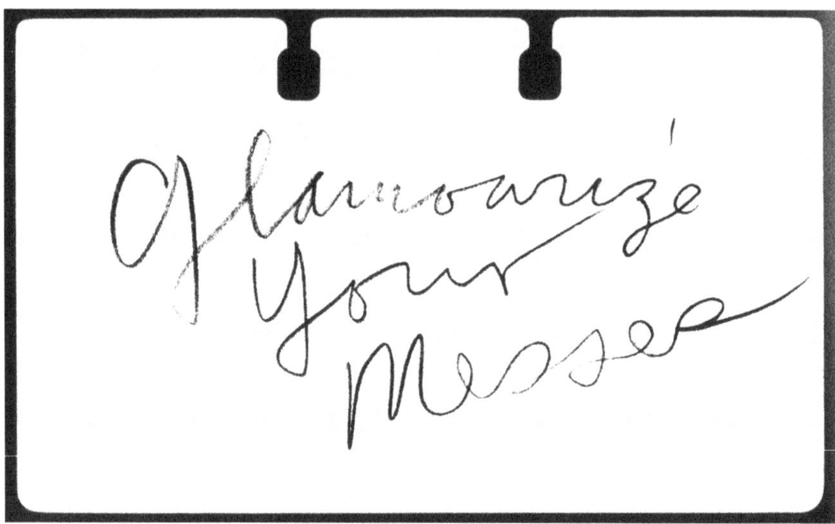

6.1   Jack Smith, *Glamorize Your Messes* (c. 1980s).

performances and ugly feelings. I argue that Smith's apparent fascination with the scene of writing rethinks some of the traditional specificities of the written word, in his prolific yet unacknowledged capacity as a writer.

In an interview published in *Film Culture* in 1967, Smith responded to a question about his writings, stating, 'I didn't get any encouragement, no reception for the writing, so I just stopped.'[4] Despite this early statement of his abandonment of writing for performance, Smith's papers include a multitude of pages lined with evocative statements. He evidently continued to write prodigiously into the late 1980s, even if the majority of his efforts remained unpublished in his lifetime. Some of his earlier texts were taken into performances, to remind him of content and the running order of scenes. These spurs to memory include drafted introductions, quoted lines, rudimentary drawings (of lobsters, clowns and penguins), or the briefest summaries of points he hoped to relay, replete with manic crossing out. Of these scripts or scores, Smith confirms, 'There would be a piece of writing but only *after* the run of the play and [it] typically would never be referred to again. I have an outline of course … but there are long passages of improvisation as the perfection of the story is sought in front of the audience in a very living manner.'[5] As texts that have served their initial function, these provisional sketches, traces or outlines are enigmatic objects. 'Refused as Scarlett O'Hara', reads one, 'Lobster in filling station', another. Gestures towards events larger than their own writing, these notes act as hieroglyphs, or open signs. Dramatic scripts await a further purpose, but many of Smith's texts seem to have relinquished their utility, incapable of serving (for others) the mnemonic triggers they were hoped to have enabled the performer. Regardless, these fragments are evocative, and clearly signal Smith's own fast-held political commitments; one such page begins 'The desire to get rich quickly is also the willingness to make life hell for everyone else for a while so one may retire in style' (see figure 6.2). The script continues with suggestions about how to proceed in the performance, with plenty of room for elaboration and improvisation.

Jack Smith, *Untitled* (c. 1983).   **6.2**

Some performances were more formally scripted. Smith's longer, prose writings are imaginative, difficult variations on what he terms 'fabulous carny gilded memories full of charming arabesques of speech and wise homilies and dignity and beauty'.[6] Between 1962 and 1964, Tony Conrad recorded several sessions of Smith performing, reading and talking with his friends, in the apartment the two artists shared at 56 Ludlow Street (Mario Montez, John Cale and Angus MacLise lived on the floor below). On one of these remarkable documents, Smith reads from 'The great moldy triumph', a text published in a later form in his collected writings. Francis Francine and the filmmaker Ron Rice provoke Smith with quips, commentaries, and laughter throughout. After some discouragement from Francine – 'you've heard it, we've heard it … we've drained that just about as dry as you can drain it' – Smith nevertheless begins to read his 'irreverent ditty'. 'The great moldy triumph. You mean,' he says, and then stops sharply, with a loud, sad sigh. 'Well, I'll read the first paragraph, and then if I feel like going on, I'll try, but maybe I won't.' With newfound vigour, he recommences, 'The roly poly flotilla girls manned the bridge of the gleaming new luxury liner.'[7] The document shows how Smith would riff on his writings in performance. He introduces amusing flourishes, especially in his pronunciation of individual words, and counterintuitive shifts in the pitch and speed of his delivery. Predictably, but wonderfully, the reading falls apart, as Smith bemoans the typographical errors in his script. 'On the lapping Atlantic, tweaked by the moon between nascent continents, continents of nascence, damned typewriter, tides that lap, wash and lap, like a ro – if typists don't understand a word why do they put in a new word?' The words 'tweaked' and 'moon' are performed especially strangely, with a kind of bathos, which leads quickly into his frustration at a typist's apparent failures to transcribe his handwriting, much to the delight of his fellow performers. Regaining confidence in his text, he returns to reading:

> If the world could be considered the inside of a washing machine, with no clothes [*laughter*], no soap, no bleach, no point, awash forever, churned by paddles, in this moooood of frivolity, then the world and everything in it is a mess of moldy laundry, alluringly grinding away like a rusty 1920s washing machine … hypnotising children that stare into them like a bird flying through corridors of ape mopwater... Oh, what can save the tweaky sequinned slipper from sadness?

After a few more lines, and with more comic interjections from Francine and Rice, Smith gives up, sighing deeply, and lamenting the state of his own prose: 'Moldy, moldy, *moldy* writing. Oh.' Tutting loudly, he says, 'Some of this is too purple for words, I can't go on. If you can bring yourself to read it...' Rice valiantly takes over the labour of reading Smith's text, to the sounds of Francine's discomfited companionship.

In a note on the politics of representation, Rice himself wrote in 1961, 'Any scene, no matter what, can evoke more of man to believe and feel [than] a parallelism which contains logic without reality.'[8] Smith's career in writing was seemingly committed to this obscure but poetic transcription of everyday scenes and pedestrian observations, from short scribbles to longer drafts. There are many hundreds of witticisms and aphorisms, such as 'People are evil to cover up some shame,' or 'It's the mixture of stupidity and sadism that makes me particularly repellent to most human beings.' As argued in earlier chapters, Smith was stubborn in his inability to suit the requirements of the market, as a field of production and consumption that sustains criticism and historical narration. This is readily apparent in his performance work and lectures, but passes over into his complex relation to the scene of writing. By engaging in list making, transcription, aphorism, angry rants and infantile storytelling, Smith's relation to the written word is one of strategic redundancy, as a continuation of his persistent revelry in unproductive domains.

As Henry Miller suggests in this chapter's epigraph, in a riposte to a friend's complaint about the declining quality of his later work, texts that disturb the productive imperatives of literature – by being too unpolished, unartistic, or in poor taste – run the risk of failing to register as literary altogether. Culture, it would seem, does not accommodate unproductive artistic labours. As such, Smith's relation to writing might expose and challenge the liberal conception of culture, which seemingly conspires to produce and sustain restrictive definitions of artistic subjectivity and its work. Smith's orientation to labour refuses the productive imperatives of culture, by disrupting the production of discrete, fully readable objects. By engaging with labours of cultural production that trouble easy consumption, reception and theorisation, I argue that Smith's legacies provoke unfamiliar reading practices, by requiring new encounters with cultural texts. How, specifically, might vulgarity, banality, excess or compulsion interrupt conventional definitions of artistic achievement and cultural productivity? In one performance, Smith introduces one of his trademark caesurae, fumbling with his sheaf of papers to half-heartedly lament, 'Uh, oh mother of God, without my glasses, already … Let's see,' amid an endless shuffling of his papers, and pause after interminable pause.[9] Tellingly, Smith delays the production of the stuff of performance, if not that of meaning. By pointing to the troubled relation between the written word and its performance, he stages a loaded slippage between the work of art and incessant interruptions by his body as a site of failure. It seems portentous that this multiple site of production is one derailed by the failing of his sight, not least because it founds the muddling of art and everyday life in a seemingly unachievable act of reading.

Shopping lists and baffled poetry

Many of Smith's texts are short lists, extravagant repetitions that initially seem banal enough. These include shopping lists of items to buy, especially health foods, and moldy items for costumes, such as chiffon, beads, and chandelier drops; many others consist of sums and lists of numbers. There are copious notes of things to do – architectural amendments to his apartment; a reminder to consider 'epidermabrasion' – or suggestions for professional development, including people to phone, and notes on places to go, including locations to film or photograph. 'Wrecked Car/ One on Crosby too?' one list observes, continuing, 'Ruined minaret – BKLYN.' Many pages list titles for new shows: *Sno Flakes of Atlantis*; *Hatchetwoman of Atlantis*. On other pages, Smith lists his many pseudonyms: Sinbad Glick, Mavis Davis, Ronald de Carlo, Sharkbait Starflesh, Donald Flamingo.

His writings are scrawled on piles of Rolodex filing cards, torn scraps of paper, flyers for his and friends' performances and screenings, crushed cigarette packs, used envelopes, wrapping paper, receipts, paper bags, or on the backs of homemade actor cards which read 'Jack Smith – Erotic Theatrical Genius!' One filing card reads:

> eye clinic
> rent check
> roach paste
> SEX clinic
> 80 univ –
> tonite![10]

On another loose page in his files, Smith modifies the apparently banal content of his practice of listing to introduce his famous eccentricity. Smith lists the areas of creative practice he (sometimes spuriously) sees himself as being the originator of:

> INVENTIONS
> Spiritual photography
> Glitter makeup
> Theatrical slideshows
> M.M. [Maria Montez] Religion
> Dropped spider

Covered in his unique scrawl, Smith's lists are written in ballpoint, felt pen, crayon or coloured pencil. Some pages are torn, burnt, or stained with coffee, and all are creased and folded. They range from quotidian reminders – a sexual health check-up – to wistful ideas for development, such as 'smudge proof death mask cosmetics'. Other lists include more florid prose. On the back of a printed advertisement, he writes: 'Say something eager and enthusiastically glamorous about gold stencilling corny bunks as insight while the men are sleeping to save time.' The esoteric imperative is followed by a stranded image of squalid destitution, borne on a solitary phrase: 'Dead bugs.'

In Smith's practice, the dedicatedly unromantic labour of listing often segues into a decisively compulsive, expressive relation to the scene of writing. While he approaches banality in his obsessive compiling and filing of lists, these sit in stark contrast to his vehement onslaughts against friends and foes in the more polemical writings discussed in chapter two. Written on the back of a leaf of General Electric letterhead is a script of sorts. It reads:

> Her Story
> Contract to contract
> Accept humility award on celebrity beanbag
> I don't care what I may seem to your magazine sensibilities!!
> The theatre is the BATTLEGROUND OF PASSIONS
> Where there were artists there is now – destruction.
> That's why there are now parking lots where there were theatres
> The desire for security causes humans to build ugly rooms for himself
> Playwrighting is a craft – I'M NOT AN ARTIST!
> ~~Victims~~
> Prisoners of photography?
> Lets not talk about me.

Each successive line, each seemingly fragmented thought or obligation, reads more ardent than the next. Read as ciphers for the obsessively reiterated concerns in his personal and professional life, the list sums up his suspicions about the way aesthetic and other modes of conformity may compromise artistic integrity. This is denoted by the derisory notion of 'magazine sensibilities', which he saw his early photography suffer under, and his deeply conflicted relation to financial security and emotional safety. Moreover, the list presents Smith's struggle over the interstitial location of his own practice, between contemporary and historical art and theatre, and his reading of canonical theatre as a space that elicits major emotions over and above the minor affects rehearsed in the list itself. Theatre and the writing of plays are celebrated as higher arts, while he distances himself from the conflicted, perhaps corrupted space of contemporary art. The crossing out of 'Victims' may signify a flight from the lure of martyrdom, an ironic distancing that is repeated in his parting refusal – 'Lets not talk about me'.

Herman Melville's *Bartleby* (1893) is a curious tale that brings together many of the ideas I have so far been exploring, and helps set up the key problems in Smith's approach to the scene of writing. In the novella, Bartleby is a 'scrivener' employed to transcribe legal texts. He writes extensively, and does so diligently when instructed to, but only until that time that he deems, in a famous non sequitur, that he 'would prefer not to'. Bartleby demonstrates a measured understanding of what is expected of him, and, moreover, of what is at stake in his obstinately passive refusal. The scrivener's pose can be borrowed as an allegory for the position of the marginal artist – as an agent committed to an inflexible, obscure and seemingly illegible task – to venture the curious implications of such a commitment. Both are marked by their devotion to a self-defined duty, a 'mulish vagary' that is also a taking leave from a specifically social participation.[11] Bartleby is introduced as a man whose mildness screens a fervent commitment to the scene of writing, described in the rhetoric of a distinctly bodily compulsion: 'As if long famishing for something to copy, [Bartleby] seemed to gorge himself on my documents. There was no pause for digestion.'[12] Driven by an absurdly imagined fervour for his task, Bartleby's corporeal investment in the scene of writing contradicts his obstinate refusal later in the novella; it also compares with the ardent manner in which the lawyer-narrator's second clerk wrestles with the obdurate body of his desk, as if fighting the scene of writing.

For Sianne Ngai, 'Bartleby's powerful powerlessness can also be thought of as exemplified by literature or art itself, as a relatively autonomous zone, a more or less cordoned-off zone in an increasingly specialized and differentiated society.'[13] By creating an intransigent and unsympathetic character, Melville triggers Ngai's study of affective gaps and emotional illegibilities – a preponderance of 'ugly feelings' – within the contested play of culture. Moreover, Bartleby's ambivalent commitment allows for the tactical confusion – in my thinking around Smith work – of scenes of writing and sites of action, under the sign of labours that test the limits of artistic agency and social participation. For Smith, the refusal of a certain kind of productivity is tied up with his opting out of a specifically capitalist mode of production, signalled in his description of a 'country [fallen] on its knees before the tin promise of the assembly line and the historically related concept of unlimited profit.'[14]

Bartleby and other wilfully impoverished agents are caught between a position of inactive responsibility to the task at hand, and the frustrated attempts of beaurocratic culture to interpret that orientation and extract productive labours from it. 'I would prefer not to,' Bartleby says to his employer. 'You *will* not?' 'I *prefer* not.'[15] Bartleby's decision is politely unproductive, a stubborn yet obscure defiance, seemingly perpendicular to his otherwise fervent commitment to writing. This contradiction sets the scene for reading Smith's idiosyncratic practice as a writer, as akin to what Ngai reads as a 'self-conscious abdication of writing as a mode of self-expression' in contemporary experimental fiction.[16] Her account is useful for approaching the condition of artists' writings in general, especially those modes where a practitioner prefers not to engage in polemical, critical, or other interventionist forms. Another prolific artist-writer, Keith Haring notes, 'I should be open to everything …

I am merely gathering information'.[17] Akin to Bartleby, various artists demur from the explicit refusals of anarchy for quieter, more solitary rebellions, like those facilitated by writing.

In comparison to his polemical essays, Smith's transcriptions can seem impassive or banal. However, his excessive listing of events, thoughts and locations can also give way to a compellingly poetic architecture of signs and phrases. Written on the back of an advertisement for a Gregory Markopoulos retrospective at the Film-Makers' Cinematheque, one list threatens to cohere into a stark poem of listed lines:

> Disturbed Icing!
> Gypsy Petulance
> Song of the Nihilistic Regicides in Valencia Production Number
> [Lose] your temper or not
> As you see fit
> But gypsy glances smoulder most
> When gypsy lips are pouting. Pouting
> For there is Mystery
> In Gypsy Petulance.
> And gypsy danger
> In tinselled death!
> Painted lips pout round
> The chattering teeth
> Like phantom castanets
> Of a laughing s[k]ull
> That laughs –
> At gypsy death!

Curiously meaningful, pseudo-psychedelic phrasings such as 'The chattering teeth/ like phantom castanets' echo the 'reality sandwich' method of poetic juxtaposition encouraged by Smith's sometime friend and supporter, Allen Ginsberg. Ginsberg's Beat litanies were derived from the word salads of the Dadaists in collision with a hallucinogenic unmooring from conversational language. The poet Ian Hamilton jokes that, immersed in Ginsberg's writings, any list takes on the flavour of his Beat hipster prophesying. On the Index of Proper Names in Ginsberg's *Collected Poems* (1984), he writes, 'if exclamation marks were added [the list] might easily have passed muster as a Ginsberg poem: "Apollo! Arafat! Ardinarishvara! Arthat! Artaud!", and so on,' humor-ously invoking the exclamatory fervour of Ginsberg's mock-prophetic poetry.[18]

Similarly, absorbed in the copious arrangements of listed thoughts and lines in Smith's archive of papers, reading his incursions into baffled poetry infects one's encounters with other, seemingly banal or utilitarian lists, which begin to inadvertently court the status of poetic endeavour.

> Vacant Chambers of the Brain
> Roach Revulsion
> A Lobster Sunset Christmas pageant
> Kusama as Crab Ogress
> John as Clown Frog
> Gas Stations of the Cross – Kusama Easter Pageant
> Contact Gordon Brow ask –
> Mattachine Society

Such a list lures us to confer meaning upon his explicit references. How do Smith's terse recollections relate to the Mattachine Society, the homophile organisation that laid the groundwork for the gay liberation movement of the 1960s? What is the relevance of fellow artists Yayoi Kusama and John Vaccaro? He mentions the 'crab ogress' character in a letter about his unfinished film *Sinbad in the Rented World*, which he worked on from 1978, and Smith dressed Vaccaro as a frog in rushes for *Normal Love* in 1963. Is this information useful? What does it tell us about this list? How do these images or memories conspire to produce a legible poetic architecture? Who is Gordon Brow, and what did Smith ask him? The reference to Kusama is evocative, not least because it suggests a loose link between his own compulsive writing and Kusama's obsessive painting practice. Since the early 1960s, the Japanese artist has covered bodies, soft sculptures and found objects in polka dots, similarly filling vast canvases with painted marks to produce 'infinity nets'. Kusama creates visual fields that are immersive in their grandeur and overwhelming in the professional compulsions that they gesture to. Kusama's commitment to artistic labour has produced an expansive oeuvre that allows for complex engagement, despite or because of the staggering uniformity of her endeavour over half a century of artistic production.

Spending six weeks immersed in Smith's papers in 2005, I had a profound feeling of being overwhelmed by the magnitude of his lists and jottings, and the directions, pathways and dead-ends their contents pointed to. My immersion in these documents gave rise to counterintuitive realisations about his career, and about the labour of the marginal artist more generally, including the peculiar affective charge of Smith's devotion to the practice of listmaking. On a loose, torn sheet of paper, held in his estate, Smith lists the things he achieved in life.

> <u>What you HAVE ach.</u>
> THANK GOD
> 1. A glorious apt.
> 2. A life of exp. and achiev. and learning in ARTS. Awareness of crooks and dangers
> 3. A chance to write a book

4. Correct org. of papers
5. Learned the bus…
6. Chance for
    HAIR
    GYM
    TEETH
7. Ability to write plays and SOME FILMS

The list is amusingly sincere, and tinged with something like pathos. Emotional or experiential naivety (his pride at having learned the New York bus routes) is twinned with the rehearsal of familiar bugbears from his daily life: his fixations on dental health, the joy his unusual living arrangements allowed him, and his assumption of misdeeds on the parts of others. His second and third points suggest a rarely expressed, private pride in his capacities and achievements as an artist, and indeed as a writer. The fourth 'achievement' is bitterly ironic, considering the disastrous legal repercussions of his refusal to prepare a legally binding last will and testament, and the tortured attempts of Penny Arcade and J. Hoberman to organise his papers, works and personal effects. He continues by listing the prospects remaining to be fulfilled in his career:

<u>Next stage of life</u>
Needs that weren't apparent
Money for expanding. Money – teeth – hair – gym
Provide for old age
Need to travel – see where to retire
Money to stay same – rising prices
Settle papers

As the poet Randall Jarrell wrote, in 1953, of Walt Whitman's deceptively simple magic, 'It is only a list – but what a list!'[19] Smith's list would be merely quotidian, but for the fact that his artistic practice, across thirty years, persistently circled its concerns. Throughout his work, he compulsively tracked the things he had achieved in the face of adversity, and his resentment of hindrances to his comfort, lambasting the pervasive 'crooks and dangers', from Uncle Roachcrust to landlordism, to the emergent threats posed by emerging artists and their work, the hateful 'crazy baby poopoo who lays the golden egg'.[20] Jarrell describes Whitman's method of streaming through lines of images and thoughts as the desire to 'manage' a catalogue of emotional experiences. Such an attempt seemingly strains for beaurocratic sense in the ordering of a life, while belying the urgency with which desire is pressed by the objects one's pen rests upon. When written as a list of observations, Jarrell writes, poetry approaches the disorder of the world, which it manages by 'likeness and opposition and continuation and climax and anticlimax'. Mimicking Whitman's breathless, awe-struck composition of lists, he poses an insistent 'and' between itinerant listed impressions. Consecutive observations metamorphose into an ambiguous, overriding sensibility, of conflict and ardour, desire and resistance.

In Smith's lists, an implicit conjunction – a ghostly 'and' or 'but' – similarly reflects a sensation that perhaps evades full legibility in the attentive reader, namely longing and mourning and an almost childlike persistence. If longing registers the things that have yet to materialise in the field of possibility, mourning involves a comparison between the consolations of the reality principle and the aspects of life given up to loss. Longing entails a listing of empty places that the desiring subject yearns to fill, while mourning is a substantially different project, an embattled calculus of achievement and death. If longing represses achievement, mourning involves a spatial measuring up of differences. The latter is an image Mignon Nixon deploys to read the bodily investments involved in constructing stacked sculpture. 'The work of mourning,' Nixon argues, is 'an obsessive kind of listing … The mourner's task is to compile these two inventories and to work through them, sifting and sorting, removing and restoring – until even the energy necessary to mourn is dissipated'.[21]

Smith's list of achievements can therefore be read across these two definitions of longing and mourning. Some of his lists are statements of intent, an attempt to manage mourning by setting up a programme for his life's completion, as a compromise between the 'need to travel' and the desire 'to stay the

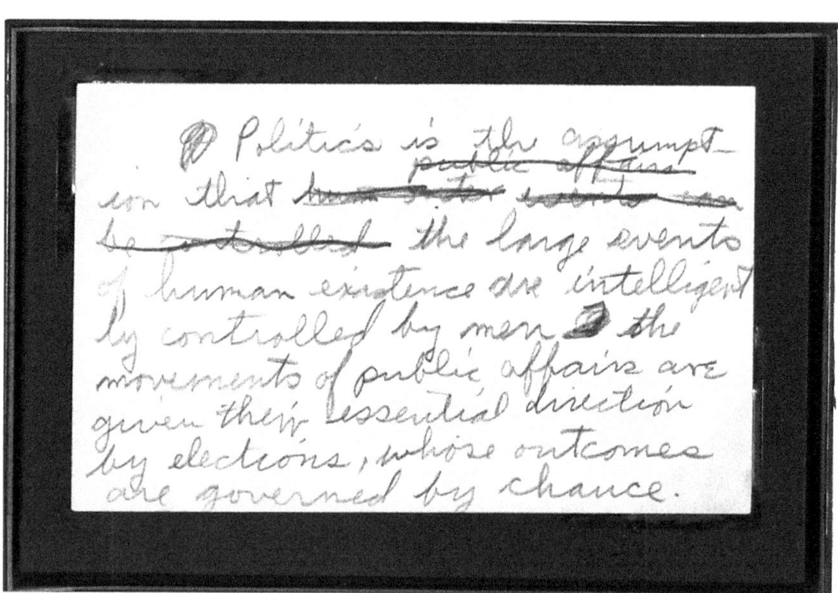

6.3   Jack Smith, *Untitled (Thoughts/Sayings)* (no date).

same'. His lists also compensate for the disasters of a life – the dead letters, tin promises and squandered opportunities catalogued in Smith's performances, polemics and lectures. Therefore, like Bartleby, Smith juggles productive and unproductive labours in his writing practice. On the one hand, Smith's work defies conventions of social participation. As a project pursued in spite of his audience, and with little or no encouragement from commercial gallery circuits, Smith's practices – across performance and writing – inhabit a curious space between artistic endeavour, therapeutic pursuit, and domestic hobbyhorse. His words, lists and stories are not trained towards a need to communicate clearly. On the other hand, Smith invests in strategies bearing a certain psychic weight, as activities trained upon assessing his experiences and achievements, towards making provisions for change.

A sense of the moment

The attempt to theorise Smith's compulsions under the sign of writing contradicts a prevailing attitude towards his filmmaking. Specifically, it sits in tension with the authoritative, anti-literary reading given by Jonas Mekas, the champion of underground cinema:

> I have often been asked to explain … what is there in the meaningless, stupid, absurd movies of … Jack Smith? Our thinking is still so literary. We have no immediate sense of the image, what's happening in it. We are immune to the … non-verbal intelligence of the sensed moving image and which cannot be translated into words or ideas or concepts … Movies, this anti-verbal art, came just in time to save our irrational, nonconceptual, immediate sensing.[22]

A 'literary' study of Smith's work might run the methodological risk of an overly cerebral approach to his practice as an artist, obscuring his commitment to exploring non-verbal, visual phenomena. However, Smith's investment in writing enables some unfamiliar perspectives on his career as an artist, and provokes wider thoughts about the diversity, hybridity, and cultural politics of artistic practice after 1960. Therefore, against Mekas's convincing counsel against purely literary models, I look to some relations between Smith's practice and developments in poetry in the 1960s. Specifically, Frank O'Hara's work may be useful in interrogating Smith's prose work. A poet associated with the New York School, O'Hara's work tested the possibilities raised by the transcription of quotidian experience, posing writing as crucially tied to developments in visual culture. Despite their social differences, Smith and O'Hara must have at least been acquaintances, as Smith attended O'Hara's funeral. As his coffin was lowered into the ground, O'Hara's biographer notes, 'Allen Ginsberg and Peter Orlovsky intoned Indian sutras, while Jack Smith … snapped photographs.'[23]

Perceiving daily occurrences as valid for aesthetic consideration, O'Hara's poems had a profound influence on American poetry as well as visual culture. A critic for *Art News*, author of a monograph on Jackson Pollock, and curator at the Museum of Modern Art (from 1955 until his accidental death in 1966), O'Hara was close friends with many of the leading painters of his time, including Larry Rivers and Jasper Johns. His relation to abstract expressionism and new painting is critically well documented, and is also self-evident in his poems. Marjorie Perloff has analysed the mutual examples set by O'Hara and his collaborators and peers in the visual arts, as an exchange facilitated by the way his 'heterogeneous images and syntactic dislocations "imitate" the process of painting itself'.[24] Another critic elaborates on the relations between poetry and painting in O'Hara's practice, writing that his 'poetic sense of the moment' begs comparison with the traces of 'immediacy' in Pollock's drip-paintings.[25] Such an analogy usefully confuses the lines of a poem with those of a painting, by imagining written and painted lines as maintaining unstable relations between the mnemonic and the indexical, or between the happenstance collision of colours and the random conjugations of words.

The performance critic C. Carr writes, 'What interested [Smith] was that state of mind one enters while creating … If his ideas sound crazy, he actually had a consistent world-view, and his shows, for all their exoticism, came from his daily obsessions.'[26] Similarly, John Ashbery describes O'Hara's method as guided by his 'concept of the poem as the chronicle of the creative act that produces it'.[27] As discussed in chapter one, Smith considered boredom to be a central affect in the production of art, as a sensibility that the artist must face up to in her or his commitment to making art. O'Hara demonstrates a similar attraction to activities that appear boring, fruitless, or run of the mill, most clearly in the many list poems that he wrote during the 1950s and 1960s – his 'I do this I do that' poems.[28] These involved the pursuit of a carefully mediated instantaneous quality. For O'Hara, they were invested in reflecting 'Beauty,/ description, finality, love, but never merely life'.[29] He stages a mannered fascination with daily experience as a catalogue of possibilities whose expansiveness requires a space much larger than 'mere' life, despite having issued from it.

In this spirit, an erotic reverie on his lover Vincent Warren sleeping 'like a temple to no god', is interspersed with seemingly irrelevant details, such as the fact that 'he is waiting for his sofa/ to arrive from Toronto'.[30] In a contemporary study, Paul Carroll notes that some critics dismissed O'Hara's poems as 'insipid prose' – prosaic, even claustrophobic, as a result of his autobiographical 'self-indulgence'.[31] In contrast, Carroll heralds them as fine examples of what he terms 'impure poetry'. For Carroll, O'Hara does not need to justify the inclusion of banal details. They are not asked to contribute to any organic whole; they are simply there, in the world and in the poem. In *The Day Lady Died*

(1959), O'Hara notes in his daily meandering that 'it is 1959 and I go get a shoeshine/ because I will get off the 4:19 in Easthampton/ at 7:15 and then go straight to dinner'.[32] These details will not recur in the poem as tropes that ensure organic balance. Instead, his observations ignore the pretence of poetic 'purity', in favour of a diaristic recording of the facts of a journey to dinner, at the end of a day made less daily by the fact of Billie Holiday's death.

Ashbery writes that O'Hara's quotidian fascination was not a symptom of 'self-absorption' but, rather, 'he talks about himself because it is he who happens to be writing the poem'.[33] If minor experience, by definition, slips from the epistemological frame of history, O'Hara's poetry counters this eventuality by producing a minor inventory of sensations – seemingly arbitrary observations in daily life, such as sharing a Coke with a lover, or looking at things in the street on the way to work. In Smith's outlook, this strategy is twisted by his disposition towards the less pleasurable aspects of daily life, and their unfortunate effects on the people who inhabit it. This tendency colours his worldview and, hence, his transcriptions and catalogues of experience. Put plainly, if O'Hara reproduces his day's inconsequential facts, in what Gavin Butt has described as only 'vaguely antiestablishment' work,[34] Smith proffers his own existential disasters, in a more clearly dissident mode of address. In favour of a generalised outrage, Smith's writing abstains from the pleasure that O'Hara's writing often acknowledges. Introducing one of his own performances, *Swan Lake: Song of Horror*, Smith therefore announces it to be 'an exposition of how people eagerly and with tragic consequences … offer up the wreckage of their own lives to enrich the lives of the audience, people they do not know yet who nevertheless are always watching'. And this queer breed, Smith adds, 'do not know what [or, rather, whom] they are wiping their feet on,' inhibiting any pleasure other than that of identification with the artist's performance of mawkish dread or mannered self-pity.

'Does the text have human form,' asks Roland Barthes; 'is it a figure, an anagram of the body? Yes, but of our erotic body.'[35] As if to court these questions, Smith's longer texts depart from the mundane quality of his lists, venturing into a more explicitly poetic endeavour. He writes, 'Your pockets bristle with knives for every purpose. You do not express regret because you feel none … You seethe with hostility in your lover's arms. I was your lover.'[36] Performing a slippage between emotional and bodily pain, the text that cuts the reader with its vitriol assumes a violent edge that lacerates its own form, shattering the love letter within which it assumes a cutting position. One violent anecdote describes Smith shattering a mirror over the head of his long-suffering lover in the 1960s, the painter Stanley Alboum, to whom the quoted note was directed – 'and that was the end of their affair'.[37] In the vibration between the writing of the letter and the performance that wrenches the quotidian from itself, Smith's dissident orientation to the world rehearses a thought that subtends my argument, here, confusing the text and the body, to tortures the scene of writing. These effects necessarily trouble the pleasures of reading.

Similarly, in an unpublished text, written on a page torn from notebook, with incongruous hearts drawn across the bottom, Smith describes a gruesome scene of torture:

> The turtle grovels among freaks as lobster kicks him (this scene starts after turtle dances to save his sanity) then the Nude Nubians dance with him then (in a procession thru a Excavation Pit?) is taken to Freak Torturing pit. Freaks in white cringe behind [the] scene as the turtle is martyred by being rocked [by] the torture wedgies of lobster (or boots of butterfly) [and] is finally crushed by mandibles of lobster and squeezed – with blood dripping down.

Ostensibly a sketch for a film, the set-up is wrought with violent imaginings, in which a catalogue of tortures in meted out upon the devastated body of the martyr. The ubiquitous lobster is cast in the role of the torturer – spineless, monstrous, cannibalistic – while the persecuted figure of the artist is taken up by the timid, graceful, endangered turtle. The turtle is a variation on Smith's more frequent celebration of the hardy penguin. Smith's sentences engulf themselves, with parentheses undoubled and phrases left to hang loose in failed meaningfulness. The other side of the page continues his nightmare scene:

> Then as the turtle is being martyred he prays and invokes the Madre and she appears to aid him. Death however blasts him with a rifle – killing him. The Madre shrugs her shoulders and says that there is nothing she can do about death. Turtle with dying gasps argues theology with Virgin. Asks what was point of his life – the meaning of that entire section of film.

In this potent last sentence, his life and the film are levelled into proximity, setting up a hinge between the body that lives and the text that it writes. The two, parasitic, inhabit each other's ways of being, so that meaning is simultaneously produced and devastated. Barthes writes that the 'text of bliss' (of jouissance) is that which 'imposes a state of loss, a text that … brings to a crisis [the reader's] relation to language'.[38] Foreclosing the possibility of its own access to culture, the text of bliss – whose gratuitousness mimics, in its jouissance, the gratuitousness of death – falls far of the threshold at which its might have attained pleasure. Its labour is bound instead by a limit, which reads like a break. 'Turtle is dragged by death screaming through the IRON door through which there is no return. The door slams [with a] CLANG.'

Prose ruined for normal love

In chapter 3, I argued that in film works such as *Flaming Creatures* (1962–63), sexual disgust gestures to dissident confusions of authority, redemptive potential, meaning, and power. Smith was also a keen writer of short, vivid pornographic tales. Infantile, vapid, funny and perhaps nauseating, these stories were published in journals, or riffed on during performances. One of these erotic stories is especially interesting. Originally titled 'God's Body', it was published as 'Normal Love' in Diane di Prima and LeRoi Jones' literary journal, *The Floating Bear*. This was a mimeographed publication produced between 1961 and 1969, which had come to national prominence when its editors were the subjects of an FBI investigation in 1961, concluding in their arrest and indictment for distributing an obscene publication through the postal service. Smith's story in the journal narrates a playful and imaginative 'ordeal', featuring shoe fetishism, masturbation, mutilation, rape, bestiality and murder among its catalogue of sexual exploits. It culminates in a triumphantly blasphemous orgy in heaven, in which 'Saints and cupids dicked each other with their wands [and] angels threw their legs open and the skies dripped come.'[39] God is imagined as lording over the flaming saturnalia. Seated upon a zirconium and rhinestone throne to watch the orgiastic proceedings, He rises to 'overstimulate' the 'freaks', precipitating an expansive 'gang fuck' in paradise.

As in much of his prose, Smith's language is quickly paced, opulently phrased, and funny. He has an eye for camp details, including a description of wearing a 'floor length black leather jacket and needle-heeled opera hip boots made of wildebeest leather with … tufted tops', while piggybacking a gaggle of overstimulated 'pinheads'. Smith's protagonist is a 'tumescent' buccaneer-cum-marauding rapist, riding roughshod and '[h]erding the freaks across the fields'. Sufficiently stimulated by his charges, the scene switches inexplicably to a fantasy of the lover 'linger[ing] over his toilette', in narcissistic rapture with his own reflection in a mirror. Unleashing his prodigious 'three foot long 9 inch thick cock', he penetrates the tufted tops of his boots, and then, literalising and exceeding the metaphor of narcissism, shatters and rapes his own reflection: 'I smashed through the mirror and whirled about and stuffed my cock into the jagged hole and fucked and fucked.' Soon again 'concupiscent' after his traumatic act of self-love, he splays a 'pretty young marshmallow cretin' on the field, entices a horse to mount her, and 'charged my horse's asshole … transfixing him in mid-air as he was transfixing the cretin girl', who is subsequently 'ruined for normal love' by the flaming scene. The spectacle of man-on-beast-on-girl eroticism soon inflames the 'freaks' who have congregated to admire the scene, and the landscape explodes into a seething orgy: 'Soon the whole hillside was one gigantic seething, cretin, mongolian and pinhead orgy' he adds, producing a 'churning carnival of freaky sex.'[40]

I am struck by the vulgar brilliance of the story's erotic prose, and by Smith apparent abandonment of the pornographic duty to arouse his reader. Reed Woodhouse describes a counterintuitive 'saving streak' in much post-war gay writing, which embraces vulgarity as a tactically low quality. Vulgar writing, Woodhouse argues, 'will always make it vulnerable to high-minded dismay', therefore sequestering itself to the safety and comfort of a marginal, invested readership.[41] Smith thus disregards the ambitions of properly 'pornographic' writing, revelling instead in the peculiarly marginalising promise of vulgar indulgence. When I first read Smith's erotic fictions, I ignored them as juvenilia, or amateurish play. However, his vulgarity now strikes me as a strategic investment, which relates to his attraction to weeding out the uncommitted members of his audiences in performance. The poet Rene Ricard writes of Smith's refusal of audience satisfaction,

> When the audience represents a one-to-one confrontation at the crossroad of life and art, style and substance are reduced to less than a vapor. So Jack would win this battle (and preclude any theft) by reducing his art to a minimal gesture, winding up chopping onions in front of a paying audience … so that the lousy parasitic audience would have nothing to take home and no ideas would be stolen.[42]

It is tempting to read Smith's refusal of pornographic pleasure as an extension of this devastation of consumer satisfaction in performance. By forging the pornographic from the realm of erotic prose, and by courting vulgarity, Smith confirmed his investment in the peculiar promise of the marginal artist. As a producer of an aesthetic sensibility reserved for a committed audience, 'Jack would – as he liked to say – "distill" the audience down to its most appreciative essence', Penny Arcade recalls.[43] As such, across his performances and writings, Smith cultivated the dedicated few who could maintain their allegiance to his unique, exotic, paranoid charms.

Paranoia, or having all the facts

'Smith's art gives me an impression of rough chunks of something huge that is looming in front of [him]', Mekas writes. These 'sharp and often painful chunks' evoke a sense of looming danger, which augurs of a paranoid apperception in Smith's orientation to the world.[44] This sense figures suggestively in Mekas's and others' understanding of Smith's creative practice. Similarly, Richard Foreman writes of Smith's 'ability to dredge up from the mind what the social beast has not found useful in its struggles to suppress the real evolution of consciousness and spirit'.[45] Foreman locates this ability between Smith's extreme slowness, and his courting of disaster in the space of performance. This dredging is apparent in the detonations of social space that Smith stages, and in the remainders of this process that linger in the muddles of cultural and architectural detritus that he lovingly cultivated in his loft performance spaces.

Other architectural innovations similarly demonstrated Smith's uneasy relation to the world, and to the agents of threat and danger with which he imagined it to be peopled. Smith's lists correlate with a practice of hate writing that a wall in his apartment assisted him in, documented in *Jack's Place* (1990), a posthumous video tour of his living spaces by M. M. Serra. John Vaccaro remembers, 'I remember his last address was on First Avenue … I went there once. And of course he had his "hate wall", all these things on the wall that he hated. I was on it. Jonas Mekas was on it.'[46] (The latter reads 'Mekas will kill art. I survived Mekas'.) Hate-oriented writing can be read as a putatively destructive process of creative worldmaking, a paradoxical act that may include paranoia as a constituent style. Driven by hysterical claims of persecution, and displays of personal and political outrage, his poison pen pursued Mekas – 'less a guru than a praying mantis' – as the personification of establishment exploitation, despite his laborious efforts to create an aesthetic context for Smith's unprecedented cultural activity.[47] Subsidiary to this key hatred was his heated censure of other former friends or supporters, including: Susan Sontag, for her laudatory proclamations on *Flaming Creatures* in the *Nation* in 1964, blamed for the enduring symbolic contamination endured by his landmark work; 'a crust like Warhol', for his perceived weakness in opposition to 'the Lobster'; Ginsberg, whom Smith referred to as, among other things, a 'walking career' in resentment for being such a ruthless (and successful) self-promoter;[48] and Vaccaro, for not revealing to him his source of precious coloured glitter.

Indeed, his antipathy towards others became so all-inclusive that he resorted to performing with stuffed animals in place of collaborators – his favourite co-star towards the end of his career was a sequinned toy, Yolanda La Pinguina, 'the world's most notorious penguin'.[49] Flightless and remote, penguins perhaps represent non-transcendence. Famously communitarian, the penguin struggles against Antarctic adversity, and is notable for its animal commitment to the arduous romance of monogamy. Immortalised in several photographs in Genoa in 1981, and performances including *I Danced with a Penguin* (Hamburg, 1983), Yolanda was nevertheless martyred to Smith's ambivalent cause, in an intermittent performance in New York entitled *Death of a Penguin* (1985–87). Ngai writes that 'ugly feelings' such as paranoia are frequently cultivated in experimental practices – especially writing – for the way that such sentiments enable alternative approaches to critical productivity. Seemingly dystopian and opposed to the production of pleasure, paranoia may resist a double imperative of capitalism: its promotion of high emotions over illegible or troubling expressions, and, secondly, the perverse integration of disenchantment and alienation as generic style of consumption.[50] Smith's paranoia is therefore not merely a personal quirk that erupts into his writings and shapes his performances; it is also a strategic style that ties him to critical and practical developments in the 1960s.

Of his paranoia, Edward Leffingwell writes, 'Smith was no fool. He believed that an unholy team of manufacturers, schools, government and churches had allied to consolidate power and authority none of them could maintain alone.'[51] As such, he would often transfer the blame of social ills onto specific people – Mekas, Warhol, Ginsberg, Yvonne de Carlo – or invented personae, such as the conniving, exploitative figure of the Lobster. In a characteristically paranoid rant, Smith rages that after the *Flaming Creatures* debacle, 'I was being betrayed on an average of twice a week to [Mekas]. It was like being boiled alive. People would turn me in because Uncle Fishook wanted to get me and everybody knew that.'[52] A scribbled reminder in Smith's archive similarly augurs of his paranoid orientation: 'Eliminate federal govt. before we become a nation of pickpockets.' The note troubles the reader with its implicit humour – he requires himself to write it down and file the thought, as if he might forget a concern of such grandeur. Smith saw conformity as a symptom of cowing to the pressures of a widespread conspiracy, a system of coercion he identified across the art, performance and film establishments, in mainstream entertainment, and in government policy. This orientation certainly alienated his peers, and may have held back his professional development, but it also enabled a striking political utility in Smith's practice, for it questioned conventions of spectatorship and engagement, and redrew the traditional relations between art and the everyday.

Smith's hatred of Mekas was not merely paranoid in the pathological sense, but symptomatic of what he saw as an ominous culmination of attacks and abuses. While writings about Smith's life and work often contain perplexed references to Smith's fabled hatred of Mekas, unpublished papers held by his estate include a note written by Smith, listing the reasons why he held him in such contempt. Smith's list gives a comprehensive sketch of the motivating circumstances that led him to his vehement dislike: annoyance at the apparent non-payment of fees for the publication of his manuscripts in *Film Culture*; the purchase of *Blonde Cobra* by Mekas, and what Smith saw to be its unfair attribution of authorship to Ken Jacobs and Bob Fleischner; private screenings of *Flaming Creatures*, for Jean-Luc Godard, Agnes Varda and Roman Polanski, among others, during Mekas's European tour in 1964, given without Smith's permission; the Supreme Court case against *Flaming Creatures*, 'provoked deliberately by Mekas', and its concomitant effects on Smith's career; and Mekas's sale of a print of *Flaming Creatures* to 'an institution in Europe'. His list of antipathies culminates in a classic indictment, of the kind that characterised the public rants that dominated his live performances from 1965 until his death in 1989. Of Mekas's programming and archival practice, Smith writes, 'He [would give] the filmmaker a 2 night screening, [while] overnight he copies the film. He travels around showing the films and selling them in ways the filmmakers can never find out about. He sucks the film, the life and the travels out of the filmmakers'.

In his list, Smith is direct and clear about his reasons for distrusting Mekas. His second qualm can be clarified with reference to a correction published in *October* by Jacobs. Fleischner filmed *Blonde Cobra*, and Smith had the starring role as performer; after a series of quarrels, Fleischner felt unable to cope with Smith's behaviour and withdrew from the project, handing the footage over to Jacobs for completion.[53] Smith's complaints about the screenings in Knokke-le-Zoute, and the Supreme Court case, are more complicated. In an interview in *Semiotext(e)*, Smith explains that Mekas 'wanted to have something in the courts at the time. It was another way by which he could be made to look like a saint, to be in the position of defending something when really he was kicking it to death'.[54] The final complaint, signalled by his persistent return to the motif of thievery, concerns the lost original of *Flaming Creatures*. This situation is especially convoluted, owing to some secrecy around the specific terms by which the print went missing.[55]

Nevertheless, a question arises about whether or not Smith's paranoia is oddly complicit with paranoia as a conservative affect. To a certain extent it may well be. Sexual difference has insistently conjured a sense of paranoia in normative society, perhaps due to the tendency of queers to inhabit ambivalent positions within the heterosexual imaginary: as race apart, yet enemy within. Such suspicions were vehemently attested to in paranoid journalism contemporary to Smith's first ventures into creative labour. In the wake of Senator Joseph McCarthy's witch hunts in the 1950s, journalists argued that 'members of one conspiracy are apt to join another conspiracy' – a justification for the ousting of 119 suspected homosexuals from the US State Department in 1960, as men in danger of being conscripted into Communism. 'This is one reason why so many homosexuals from being enemies of society in general, become enemies of capitalism in general,' wrote one fantasist.[56] This conservative paranoia was heightened in the 1980s, at the end of Smith's lifetime, when AIDS re-energised the Far Right's homophobia. As Jerry Falwell reminded America, 'homosexuals do not reproduce! They recruit! And, many of them are out after my children and your children'.[57] However, Smith's paranoid orientation can perhaps be thought as a curiously creative remodelling of the network of social and cultural relations that one intuits being embedded within.

Against the normative account of paranoia as an apparently pathological fear of alterity, William S. Burroughs famously redefined paranoia as 'having all the facts'.[58] Burroughs and Smith were friends in the early 1960s, as documented in a photograph of them both having dinner with Warhol, in

Mary Jordan's documentary *Jack Smith and the Destruction of Atlantis* (2006). In his writings, Burroughs flirts with the conservative terror of difference, but implies that a dissident orientation might appropriate this fear and convert it into a positive celebration of radical heterogeneity. With this new conception, Burroughs urged his readers to question authority and conventional understandings of the body and its pleasures, at the expense of a merely comfortable disposition towards moral and mental stability. To facilitate this insight, Burroughs and his colleague Brion Gysin pioneered the 'cut-up', a technique that Smith's sequential forms resemble. The cut-up involves physically cutting apart found or written texts, and pasting them together to create new perspectives, unburdened from the weight of an individual consciousness. The process and its results refuse cultural standards of legibility, ensuring that the authoritative attempt to decode the works – to read against illogicality – is met with frustration. The process provoked developments in postmodern creative writing, scuppering the desire of conventional literary criticism to assume a relation between intentions of a unified author-subject, and the discrete truth of written texts. Similarly, the cut-up scuppers the formalist ideal of a text as self-sufficient totality, readable without recourse to material conditions of production and reception. Burroughs proposed that the cut-up process functioned as a transliteration of daily perception, reinforcing the suitability of a paranoid disposition to the way in which we encounter the world around us. 'Some time ago,' he writes, 'a young man came to see me and said he was going mad. Street signs, overheard conversations, radio broadcasts, seemed to refer to him in some way. I told him "Of course they refer to you. *You* see and hear them".'[59] This is a specifically paranoid account of meaning-production. While we do perceive the world around us as a cut-up – a stream of perceptions cut by random and contradictory signs – only the paranoiac confers meaning upon arbitrary connections. Burroughs celebrates paranoia as an orientation towards the future of writing, because it creates unfamiliar, disconcerting texts that break with the tradition of narrative fiction.

Ngai convincingly describes paranoia as a distinctively masculine order of perception and meaning production. Moreover, the gendered cultural narratives that deploy it – conspiracy theories, pulp literature, film noir, TV crime thrillers – are ordered around a specifically 'theoretical' understanding of the dissemination of information and the production of meaning. In these narratives, the knowledge-seeking protagonist will always attempt to translate networks of signs and pursue hierarchies of power, each an allegory for the potentially infinite network of relations that constitutes, conditions and maintains the social order. Smith's orientation is categorically paranoid, as a programme of reading putatively random signs as markers of a meaningful system of relations, which are then traced to a necessarily elusive or imagined master signifier – Uncle Roachcrust, the Lobster, art schools, or landlordism.

'The disposition to theorize', Ngai states, 'finds itself aligned with paranoia, defined here not as a mental illness but as a species of fear based on the dysphoric apprehension of a holistic and all-compassing system,' where critical thought threatens to become a paranoid economy.[60]

For Ngai, moreover, the sublation of art and life in transcription-oriented writing – such as, perhaps, that of Smith's list-making – 'calls attention to the kind of articulating logic central to paranoid knowledge, which insists that there must be a link … between situations and events,' in the relentless accounting for arbitrary events whose very aggregation suggests 'the desire and effort to think "a system"'.[61] Critical theory has clearly nurtured this type of project, from Michel Foucault's analysis of networks of power in the structure of prisons, schools, hospitals and other disciplinary institutions, to Jacques Lacan's account of the all-seeing function of the symbolic, which sustains and conditions the unconscious, as a structure that pre-exists the subject. After Lacan and Foucault, critical thought therefore flirts with the status of a paranoid economy. The disposition to theorise aligns itself with paranoia, as an unnerving apprehension of an all-compassing system. Smith's lists, lectures and polemics reflect the logic of paranoid knowledge, which insists that there must be a link between situations and malign agency. The effects of meaning-production involved in paranoid reading therefore reflect the theoretical disposition of postmodern creative writing and poststructuralist thought. This reading usefully relates Smith's work to contemporary literary experiments such as Burroughs' cut-ups. The comparison between Burroughs and Smith also contextualises the latter's innovations in terms of postmodernism as an emergent discourse.

Compulsion

In 1960, Burroughs' friend Alexander Trocchi analysed his own writing as driven by the 'anguish of this compulsion to record'. 'Everything I have written is a kind of inventorizing', he wrote, 'I don't expect ever to be able to do much more, and the inventories will always be unfinished.'[62] Similarly, Smith's obsessive cataloguing of a whole host of schemes, observations, gripes and protestations – across his practice – seems to inventory his experience. I read this as a specifically authorial compulsion. In a moment of poetic lucidity, Smith writes, 'We are all of us a bubble that makes transatlantic random voyages … [There] are those who see the bubble and the pink and green sparkles remain on their eyes. These are they who see brooches in snowflakes … and catalogue the tiny points of light.'[63] He was touched by an imperative to order the objects and elements of lived experience, the horizon of encounters spanning from the stupid to the sublime: from the minutiae of life lived in a minor key, to the grand upheavals of full-scale tragedy. Smith's list-writing, his paranoid worldmaking, his publicly rehearsed hatred of friends and enemies, his hysterical identification with Maria Montez, and violent demonising of her studio replacement, Yvonne de Carlo – each confirm a need on his part to record these seemingly random, painful or insignificant situations. Moreover, they confirm a compulsion to document his affective responses to those fragments, in the practice of performance, as a function of the scene of writing.

Unlike the urge to perform, the urge to write is the compulsion to keep things that are predisposed to disappear. To write – *to catalogue the tiny points of light* – is a position of incline towards the thing we see leaving us. The consolations of those lingering sparkles are clung to in wishful acts of compensation for the threat of forgetting, or of being forgotten. 'All of us have lives, waste time,' Smith continues, '[and] die depending on our health more than what we think about. Sadly, bubbles burst. But the Socratic part of bubbles stays on and a ravaged bubble is a beautiful thing.'[64] This authorial compulsion stages a need on the part of the writer-performer both to mourn the loss of little things, as well as to prepare a body that might survive the writer's death. If the compulsion to write soothes the discomfort inflicted by the word, the struggle of the writing produces a new kind of difficulty. 'In olden days they wrote on stone', wrote Irving Rosenthal, an early friend of Smith's. 'We write on paper in stone prose, for the love to last.'[65]

Like much of performance since the 1960s, Smith's work suggests ways of rethinking art's histories by blurring the distinctions between verbal and visual art. The confusion of formal hierarchies between the word and the image has political implications. As Craig Owens has argued, the denial of external, non-essential reference is a central strategy of formalism, as 'one symptom of a modernist aesthetic, specifically, of its desire to confine the artist within the sharply delineated boundaries of a single aesthetic discipline. This desire is sanctioned by an unquestioned belief in the absolute *difference* of verbal and visual art,' and I argue that this desire is usefully troubled by artists such as Jack Smith.[66] Debunking the myth that such a hierarchy signals a trans-historical antagonism between art and theatre, Owens describes the synthetic, discursive process that distinguished the 'verbal' arts, including poetry and the theatre, from the 'visual' arts, such as painting and sculpture. The former were located along a dynamic axis of temporal succession, and the latter along a separate, static axis of spatial simultaneity. As a result, the visual arts were reconstructed as *distinct* from discourse, which unfolds in time, except in the form of critical or complementary texts that, exterior or anterior to the work, might supplement it. These distinctions were made in order to establish hierarchies of the relative merits of the segregated arts, and therefore operated in terms of a disciplinary practice. The process was upheld by the discursive practice of criticism that set itself up to regulate the value of artistic production, and police the boundaries within which it was confined. For formalism,

> The linguistic origins ... *had* to remain unconscious; were the subordination of all the arts to language exposed, the visual arts would effectively be denied a proper territory, and the thesis that the arts are rigorously isolable and definable would be challenged. Thus repressed, language became an invisible reserve which constituted ... modernism's unconscious.

With the rise of artist writing in the 1960s, among performance makers – but also sculptors such as Robert Smithson, Carl Andre and Donald Judd – critics reassessed and sometimes reinforced the compromised distinction between the verbal and the visual. For those critics who hoped to restrict the potential for art to bleed across disciplines, 'the eruption of language into the aesthetic field in the 1960s would occur with all the force of the return of the repressed'.[67] Smith's recalcitrant spirit can be understood as a potent contribution to this disruptive potential of art in the 1960s and after.

The reorientation of different registers of artistic practice as an interruption of – and flaw within – historical narration poses useful problems for critical thinking. Artists' writings pose such an interruption. Inhabiting unfamiliar, unnerving spaces between creative practice and everyday life, they also augur of a dereliction of the boundary between the actuality of catastrophe and the belated encounters conditioned by artistic labour. 'I could spend the rest of my life demolishing very happily', Smith once remarked. 'You couldn't, but it has just been my lot to clean out the toilets ... Nobody wants to open a can of worms, but that's the thing that has been handed for me to do.'[68] As a writer, no less than as a performer or filmmaker, Smith collapsed extremes of experience into the stuff of artistic labour, as part and parcel of his total commitment to glorious catastrophe. His written works, across lists, poetry, erotic prose and paranoid fantasies often hint at equivalences between the failings of bodies and the openings in texts. Inhabiting unfamiliar spaces between creative practice and everyday life, his writings confuse the boundary between the catastrophes of failure, crisis, death – and the difficulties conditioned by scenes of reading, and of writing.

Notes

1. Cited in Erica Jong, *The Devil at Large: On Henry Miller* (New York: Random House, 1993), p. 173.
2. Jack Smith, 'The perfect filmic appositeness of Maria Montez' (1963), *Wait for Me at the Bottom of the Pool: The Writings of Jack Smith*, ed. J. Hoberman and Edward Leffingwell (New York and London: High Risk Books, 1997), pp. 25–35 (p. 26).
3. Susan Stewart, *Crimes of Writing: Problems in the Containment of Representation* (Oxford and New York: Oxford University Press, 1991), p. 18.
4. Gerard Malanga, 'Interview with Jack Smith', *Film Culture* 45 (Summer 1967), pp. 12–16 (p. 15).

5 Smith cited in Edward Leffingwell, 'Jack Smith: The only normal man in Baghdad', *Flaming Creature: Jack Smith, His Amazing Life and Times*, ed. Edward Leffingwell, Carole Kismaric and Marvin Heiferman, The Institute for Contemporary Art, P.S.1 Museum (London and New York: Serpent's Tail, 1997), pp. 68–87 (p. 84). Emphasis in original.

6 Jack Smith, 'Red orchids' (1964), *Wait for Me at the Bottom of the Pool*, pp. 61–71 (p. 69).

7 Jack Smith, *Les Evening Gowns Damnees* and *Silent Shadows on Cinemaroc Island*, Audio CDs, New York: Tony Conrad's Audio ArtKive/Table of the Elements, 1997.

8 Ron Rice, 'An ode to the eye: Note to Jonas Mekas', *Film Culture* 70.1 (1983), p. 158.

9 Jack Smith, 'What's underground about marshmallows? (1981), *Wait for Me at the Bottom of the Pool*, pp. 137–43 (p. 141).

10 Jack Smith, unpublished note, date unknown, the Estate of Jack Smith, Gladstone Gallery, New York. Subsequent quotations are from papers in his Estate.

11 Herman Melville, 'Bartleby', *Bartleby and Benito Cereno* (New York: Dover Publications, 1990), p. 13.

12 Ibid. p. 9.

13 Sianne Ngai, *Ugly Feelings* (Cambridge and London: Harvard University Press, 2005), p. 2.

14 Jack Smith, 'Taboo of Jingola' (1972), *Wait for Me at the Bottom of the Pool*, pp. 102–5 (p. 102).

15 Melville, p. 14. Emphasis in original.

16 Ngai, p. 325.

17 Keith Haring, *Journals* (New York: Viking, 1996), p. 42.

18 Ian Hamilton, *Against Oblivion: Some Lives of the Twentieth Century Poets* (London and New York: Penguin, 2002), p. 263.

19 Randall Jarrell, *Poetry and the Age* (London: Faber and Faber, 1996), p. 105.

20 Jack Smith, 'Remarks on art & the theater', *Historical Treasures* ed. Ira Cohen (Madras and New York: Hanuman Books, 1990), pp. 111–36 (p. 127).

21 Mignon Nixon, *Fantastic Reality: Louise Bourgeois and a Story of Modern Art* (Cambridge and London: MIT Press, 2005), p. 147.

22 Jonas Mekas, *Movie Journal: The Rise of the New American Cinema 1959–1971* (New York: Macmillan, 1972), pp. 78–9.

23 Brad Gooch, *City Poet: The Life and Times of Frank O'Hara* (New York: HarperCollins, 1994), p. 10.

24 Marjorie Perloff, *Frank O'Hara: Poet Among Painters* (Chicago and London: University of Chicago Press, 1998), p. 79.

25 Anthony Libby cited in Alice C. Parker, *The Exploration of the Secret Smile: The Language of Art and Homosexuality in Frank O'Hara's Poetry* (New York and Bern: Peter Lang, 1989), p. 4.

26 C. Carr, 'Magnificent obsessions: The art and artifacts of the world according to Jack Smith', *Village Voice* (2 December 1997), p. 39 (p. 39).

27 John Ashbery, 'Introduction', *The Collected Poems of Frank O'Hara*, ed. Donald Allen (Berkeley, Los Angeles and London: University of California Press, 1995), pp. viii–ix.

28 Frank O'Hara, 'Getting up ahead of someone (sun)' (1959), *Collected Poems*, p. 341.

29 Frank O'Hara, 'Dialogues' (1956), *Collected Poems*, p. 241.

30 Frank O'Hara, 'Saint' (1959), *Collected Poems*, p. 332.

31 Paul Carroll, *The Poem in Its Skin* (Chicago and New York: Follett, 1968), p. 159.

32 Frank O'Hara, 'The day Lady died', *Collected Poems*, p. 325.

33 Ashbery, pp. x–xi.

34 Gavin Butt, *Between You and Me: Queer Disclosures in the New York Art World, 1948–1963* (Durham and London: Duke University Press, 2005), p. 96.

35 Roland Barthes, *The Pleasure of the Text*, trans. Richard Miller (Oxford: Basil Blackwell, 1990), p. 17.

36 Jack Smith, 'I knew he would never come to me' (1962–63), *Wait for Me at the Bottom of the Pool*, p. 59.

37 Joan Adler, 'On location' in Stephen Dwoskin, *Film Is … The International Free Cinema* (London: Peter Owen, 1975), p. 21.

38 Barthes, *The Pleasure of the Text*, p. 14.

39 Jack Smith, 'Normal love' (1963), *Wait for Me at the Bottom of the Pool*, pp. 51–2 (pp. 51–2).

40 Ibid.

41 Reed Woodhouse, *Unlimited Embrace: A Canon of Gay Fiction, 1945–1995* (Amherst: University of Massachusetts Press, 1998), p. 50.

42 Rene Ricard, '"No dice", Jack by popular demand: Jack Smith in retrospect', *Artforum* 36 (October 1997), p. 115.

43 Penny Arcade, unpublished interview with the author, New York (18 May 2005).

44 Mekas, pp. 96–7.

45 Richard Foreman, 'During the second half of the sixties', *Flaming Creature*, pp. 25–7 (p. 27).

46 John Vaccaro, unpublished interview with the author, New York (5 June 2005).

47 Smith, 'Taboo of Jingola', p. 104.

48 Jack Smith in Sylvère Lotringer, 'Uncle Fishook and the sacred baby poo poo of art' (Interview with Jack Smith, 1978), *Wait for Me at the Bottom of the Pool*, pp. 107–21 (pp. 109, 119).

49 Jack Smith, 'Penguin panic in the rented desert' (1981), *Wait for Me at the Bottom of the Pool*, pp. 123–35 (p. 135).

50 Ngai, pp. 3–4.

51 Leffingwell, p. 70.

52 Smith in Lotringer, p. 110.

53 Ken Jacobs, 'Correction: Flaming closets', *October* 55, (Winter, 1990), p. 144 (p. 144).

54 Smith in Lotringer, p. 107.

55 David Curtis, of the London Filmmakers Co-Op, received the original in 1964, from the film historian P. Adams Sitney. While screening the film in Europe, he was asked by Mekas to give the print to gallerist Ileana Sonnabend in New York, for her to raise funds for the production of Smith's follow-up venture, *Normal Love*. The print was given to Nancy Thomas at the BBC, who could transport the reel through channels that would avoid its being impounded by US Customs. Thomas reneged on the offer after receiving the reel, and stored it for three years.

It was then passed to Curtis, and in 1968, the original was returned to Sitney. In the mid-1970s, Jerry Tartaglia retrieved the print, and passed it back to Smith, enduring the latter's ire under suspicion of involvement in the affair. See P. Adams Sitney, unpublished letter to Jonas Mekas (30 May 1968). Estate of Jack Smith.

56 Cited in Paul Hallam, *The Book of Sodom* (London and New York: Verso, 1993), p. 29.

57 Cited in Neil Miller, *Out of the Past: Gay and Lesbian History from 1869 to the Present* (London: Vintage, 1995), p. 409.

58 Edmund White, 'The inner Burroughs', *Burroughs Live: The Collected Interviews of William S. Burroughs, 1960–1997*, ed. Sylvère Lotringer (New York: Semiotext(e), 2001), p. 476.

59 William S. Burroughs, *The Adding Machine: Selected Essays* (New York: Seaver Books, 1986), p. 54. Emphasis in original.

60 Ngai, pp. 300, 317.

61 Ibid. p. 330.

62 Alexander Trocchi, *Cain's Book* (New York: Grove Press, 1992), pp. 113, 232–3.

63 Smith, 'Red orchids', p. 68.

64 Ibid. p. 69.

65 J. Sheeper [Irving Rosenthal], 'Style', *Gnaoua* 1 (Spring 1964), pp. 43–5 (p. 45).

66 Craig Owens, 'Earthwords' (1979), *Beyond Recognition: Representation, Power, and Culture*, ed. Scott Bryson *et al.* (Berkeley, Los Angeles and London: University of California Press, 1992), pp. 44–5.

67 Ibid. p. 45.

68 Lotringer, p. 121.

The times are the times they are, spectacularly bad times comparable only to the last days of Rome, Pompeii, or Atlantis … [where we are] made to feel like cockroaches deserting a sinking continent … and where our schools are busily erasing the history of the recent past. (Jack Smith)[1]

In the year of Jack Smith's death, Nan Goldin wrote, 'I feel my own recovery from addiction, and that of many of my friends, is directly related to AIDS. With … a fatal illness in our midst, the glorification of self-destruction wore thin. We were no longer playing with death – it was real and among us, and not all that glamorous.' Goldin resolves that, as artists working on the radical fringes of commercial art, and as individuals touched by the brutal fact of disease and death, the disastrous losses of the 1980s had forced a confrontation with 'the legacy of our past without contrition, regret, or revision, but with a new belief in the possibility of future'.[2] If the 1980s were the context for a re-emergence of sorts for Smith, it was also, undoubtedly, a turbulent decade. The political landscape of the US underwent a stark tilt to the right, and the role of the arts was powerfully contested during the ill-famed Culture Wars. In the midst of government inaction, AIDS claimed the lives of hundreds of thousands of people in the US alone, including countless important artists such as Smith, Paul Thek, Peter Hujar, Keith Haring, Klaus Nomi, Hibiscus, Jobriath, John Sex, Tseng Kwong Chi and Cookie Mueller. Goldin reminds us, however, that art hints at the ways we can assuage the memory of disaster, even if in meagre, partial and provisional ways.

Twenty years after the publication of Goldin's text, the possibility of a 'future' has been afforded a loaded critical currency, especially in the aftermath of Lee Edelman's forceful polemic, *No Future: Queer Theory and the Death Drive*. His argument entails refusals of 'the figural child' and 'the political', and, furthermore, of 'communal relations', 'positive social value' and 'social viability', each an ideological marker for what he terms 'the logic of reproductive futurism'. In Edelman's formulation, this idea stands for a punitive system that abandons, into jouissance, the non-reproductive body of the queer, as a force of undoing whose obstinacy forecloses full and binding subjectivity.[3] Seemingly exempt from Goldin's hope, and sequestered to an uninhabitable destitution, queer sexualities – for Edelman – must neither avoid nor recuperate loss, but, rather, embrace the death drive as the force of undoing that 'refuses identity or the absolute privilege of any goal'.[4] *No Future* has received trenchant critiques, not least for the political impasse it seems to confirm in lesbian and gay scholarship. Judith Halberstam, for example, upholds the definition of queer practice as that which 'works against the grain of the true, the good, and the right', but urges, against Edelman, for a praxis 'that nonetheless refuses to make a new orthodoxy out of negativity'.[5] Convincingly, Edelman stresses 'the fact that nothing could be more orthodox than this warning against a new orthodoxy', signalling the conservative anxieties that perhaps condition Halberstam's wishful negation.[6] There may seem to be an apparent contradiction between the conservatism of 'negation' and the implied progressiveness of 'negativity'. Nevertheless, in Sigmund Freud's definition, negation is an explicitly conservative strategy: he writes, 'To deny something in one's judgment is the same thing as to say: "That is something I would rather repress". A negative judgement is the intellectual substitute for repression; the "No" in which it is expressed is the hallmark of repression.'[7] As Edelman argues, 'critical negativity, lacking a self-identity, can never become an orthodoxy. To the contrary, the resistance to the straw man of an orthodox negativity constitutes the final ruse of "the good," the final defence against the risk of "epistemological self-destruction." Why not endorse "epistemological self-destruction" for all?' he asks. 'Why not accept that queerness, taken seriously, demands nothing less?'[8]

As a means of navigating between Edelman's critical negativity and Halberstam's negation, Smith's practice is examined here in order to pose a counterpoint to this forceful opposition. Indeed, for José Esteban Muñoz, 'Smith is the progenitor of queer utopian aesthetics', 'the exemplary figure of the queer utopian artist and thinker who seeks solitariness yet calls for a queer collectivity'.[9] In *Cruising Utopia*, Muñoz's study of visionary tendencies in recent art, Smith is an origin of sorts for a wide range of utopian potentialities that performance continues to herald. Muñoz's project entails thinking the future of queerness by way of a hopefully enigmatic faith in the 'not-yet', especially when futurity is figurally tied to 'heterosexual temporality', a straightened conception of time conditioned by political investments in childbearing. He supports Edelman's thesis, yet argues that the critique of reproductive futurity should not prevent the utopian ambition to unpick the binds that tie futurity to political conservatism. 'Heteronormative culture', he writes, 'makes queers think that both the past and future do not belong to them. All we are allowed to imagine is barely surviving the present.'[10] By unmooring the future of queerness from reactionary politics, Muñoz argues, artists such as Smith uphold the work of 'the utopian performative', often through performance.

However, Smith is a difficult standard-bearer for utopia as 'a time and place that is not yet here'.[11] Debunking the 'not yet' in favour of a 'has-been' – with all the degraded implications this term implies – Smith's utopia is allegorised through the myth of Atlantis, as a vanquished plenitude that has been and gone. This belief system does not foreclose paradisiacal futures. He certainly doesn't look too lightly upon wishful thinking. As suggested in this chapter's epigraph, Smith's Atlanteanism is pessimistic, but also painfully prescient, if only for the fact that he certainly did not live to see utopian regeneration manifested in his lifetime, dying as he did in a time of political, epidemiological, and cultural catastrophe – a triad of misfortunes that can be condensed into the three disastrous (and co-implicated) signifiers of Ronald Reagan, AIDS, and Culture Wars. This chapter draws together some thoughts on Smith's practice by sketching what might be called his peculiarly apocalyptic utopianism. Put simply, his fostering of the future is an ambivalent gesture, nurtured without any concern for its material realisation, and problematically modelled upon a fascination with the figure of apocalypse.

While Muñoz mines the Marxist writings of Ernst Bloch, I see Louis Marin's writings as a similarly potent means of defining the volatile potentiality of utopian practices. For Marin, 'utopic discourse' is defined explicitly as the space between contradictory terms. The 'aesthetic' utopia, for Marin, produces incongruous spaces, or 'semiological play', within the totality of discourse. Such 'play' derives from utopia's condition as a strategic forgetting of place, registered in the Greek origin, '*ou-topos*', or no-place.[12] "How can pure contradiction be thought unless by fiction?" Marin asks. Despite a threatening perspectival magnitude, current totalities nevertheless retain minute fissures, which may be glimpsed by focusing on the possibility of contradiction as 'an antagonism of forces', a 'fantasy of the limit' rendered as struggle and conflict.[13] Modelled on the hopelessly discredited fable of Atlantis, collaged with his critical re-imaginings of the 'exotic' landscapes of Technicolor capers of the 1940s, Smith's utopian gesture might rethink the status of hope itself, by paradoxically focusing on the fissures that emerge from vividly imaginative contradictions. Smith's lingering in the troubled category of the exotic allows for the articulation of a perverse variation on hopefulness based nevertheless on a grim recognition of unavoidable suffering: his is a troubled 'collectivity' structured by an investment in apocalypse. It should be noted that a critical investment in crisis has been taken to task, especially in Alan Read's recent polemic against the 'naturalising' of conflict in the study of performance.[14] Nevertheless, with an admitted bent towards a kind of pragmatism, I assume that a negation of conflict is a dubious (if convenient) critical privilege in a time of escalating political, economic and ecological crises.

The following letter, held in Smith's papers at the Plaster Foundation, brings together his investments in camp exotica, the myth of Atlantis, and a vexed negotiation of both looming (or overcome) apocalypse and predestined futures. It is also a reminder of his irascible tenacity – a characteristically eccentric entreaty to those who seemingly held sway over his personal, creative and professional development.

> Dear Program Director,
>
> Since I have begun to emerge from the mists of the twin evils of nymphomania and procrastination [I have] been able to become a little more interested in my stage work which has not been as known as my film work. Though I *have* been labouring in the cornfields, so to speak, for a while now, I have a play that I am preparing to place in a theatre on a long-run basis.
>
> It started as a cabaret performance entitled *Clash of the Brassiere Goddesses* at the Pyramid Cabaret on April 28 of 1984. It was a script for 4 actors including the star, Sinbad Rodriguez, and featured slides, records, mime, dance, sound effects, etc. so that it really was a mixed media spectacle, being set upon an Amazon pirate ship in Outer Space in the spray aluminum future, after the final 'hollow-crust' of Atlantis … It was well-received, or at least nobody said anything to me, so I know it must have been quite good and frankly I think the theatre is already overdue for a gorgeous pirate production with weird comedy and mad images, which it definitely, in my opinion, was.
>
> I may be reached at tel. 254–7911 and would be delighted to discuss this and grovel as interestingly as possible with you over this production, which is now titled *The Decline of Jingola*, at which time I will be,
>
> Exotically yours,
>
> Jack Smith[15]

Despite repeated setbacks, financial destitution, domestic squalor, and his rapidly failing health, Smith persisted in his attempts to find performance spaces that would foster his ailing practice. In the 1980s, Smith's career as a performer underwent a revival of sorts. Invited to participate in festivals and art school residencies, he also presented pieces in the new performance spaces that blossomed on New York's downtown scene. The rise of club performance spaces provided Smith with a new context for his work. Late performances included *Penguin Rustling Out by the Old Archives: A Boiled Lobster Color Slide Show* (1983) with his doomed penguin sidekick, Yolanda La Pinguina, at Club 57; *Impacted Croissants of Outer Space: Unexotic Aftermath of Nuclear Hollow-Crust* (1983) and *Clash of the Brassiere Goddesses* (1984) with Ronald Tavel at the Pyramid Club; and *3 Oily Tuesdays with Jack Smith* (1987) at Limbo Café. In his interminable attempts to 'emerge from the mists' of both his excessive investment in artistic production ('nymphomania') and his self-destructive tendencies ('procrastination') Smith's letter sustains his own creative vision of tropical excess – in spite of his 'labouring in the cornfields', that is, his forgetting by the establishment. At the nadir of his powers in the late 1980s, after his short-lived return to public visibility, Smith would recount his pleasure at finding a fresh medium through which to reach new audiences. From his sickbed, he could be heard 'addressing the nation' on the QVC television shopping channel, during late night telephone calls; finding a new metier, Smith would lend his captive audience gems of esoteric counsel, such as 'the world needs to know that it is time to mix silver and gold'.[16]

In his letter, his imagery is a similarly 'moldy' mishmash of Amazonian, dime store Space Age, and ('after the final "hollow-crust" [holocaust] of Atlantis') post-apocalyptic motifs. His newfound taste for sci-fi textures taps into the contingent emergence of a tinfoil and Day-Glo retro-futuristic aesthetic. In the late 1970s and early 1980s, artists of the New Wave art scene of downtown New York – most prominently Klaus Nomi and Kenny Scharf – used domestic means of production to figure the excitement and peril of standing at the precipice of a technologically advanced future, a decade after NASA colonised the moon. These figurations filter into Smith's fascination with camp 1940s exotica, ancient Egyptian, Baroque and Polynesian imagery – each cobbled together in their most brilliantly hackneyed forms. A foundational study of such tendencies in oppositional cultural practice, Theodore Roszak's *Making of a Counter Culture* (1968) is a useful apparatus for exploring the 'exotic' as a sign of oppositional politics in the 1960s, as the decade in which Smith's performance practice took shape. Roszak notes the emergence in the period of a range of esoteric interests, led by the hallucinogenic mysticisms of Allen Ginsberg and Timothy Leary, and interpretations of Zen Buddhism by Alan Watts and John Cage. For Roszak, youth cultures took up these challenges as a means to counteract the increasing instrumentalisation of 'technocratic society' and its 'commercializing and trivializing tactics', prompted by the deepening crisis in Vietnam, and a perceived Soviet threat of thermonuclear apocalypse.[17] The popular culture of the 1960s opposed these disastrous tensions, Roszak maintains, through a proliferation of 'exotic clutter', which signalled 'a powerful and important force at work in this wholesale willingness to scrap [official] culture's entrenched prejudice against myth … and ritual'.[18] Interestingly, Roszak ties this 'penchant for the occult, the magic, and for exotic ritual' to a specifically nihilistic imperative that set the counterculture of the 1960s apart from the youthful revolts of previous generations, in its perverse identification with the threat of total annihilation: 'The cry is not for revolution,' Roszak writes, 'but for an apocalypse: a descent into divine fire.'[19]

Rehearsals for the destruction of Atlantis

The redirecting of pressing anxieties into outlandish imagery was inaugurated in Smith's first major performance, *Rehearsal for the Destruction of Atlantis: A Dream Weapon Ritual*, (1965), starring underground legends Mario Montez,

Tosh Carillo, John Vaccaro, Tally Brown and others. The performance was devised in response to his arrest, in August 1965, during a protest at the ballroom of the Old Broadway Central Hotel, retrospectively described as 'the night of the Lobster-moon charade of the Narco goon squad'.[20] The protest, 'Grass Busts of the Brassiere World' was co-organised by Smith as a benefit in support of Jack Martin, a jazz musician, and his friend Dale Wilbourn, who were both facing imprisonment in an entrapment case. Arrested for possession of an illegal substance, Martin had been unlawfully pressured to provide information that would enable the police to arrest and convict Allen Ginsberg on narcotics charges. According to the historian Barry Miles, the Supervisor of the New York Bureau of Narcotics threatened Martin with an increase in his bail, from five to ten thousand dollars, should he refuse to co-operate.[21] Smith arranged for Martin to speak at the event, and called for an investigation into police bargaining procedures. Undercover agents infiltrated the event and a small riot erupted, during which Smith, Piero Heliczer and Irene Nolan were arrested by '3 or 4 men of remarkably low aspect, sweating and panting clad in Hawaiian sport shirts'. Charged with assault and resisting arrest, Smith became drawn into 'a protracted struggle to remain out of jail – wasteful of money and disruptive of work'.[22] Moreover, Smith had his leg broken in a scuffle with police, and reportedly was 'brutally beaten' in custody.[23] As Ginsberg wrote in defence of Smith, 'We are assailed on every side by rancor and hostility multiplied billionfold [and] megaphoned into our senses … [until] the populace has lost control with its own meaty Self. We are not born for this, and we will destroy ourselves if it continues.'[24] Smith and Heliczer were convicted in April 1966 and received suspended sentences (Nolan was acquitted). Nevertheless, the episode became the raw material for Smith's *Rehearsal for the Destruction of Atlantis*. Here and elsewhere, Smith consistently recycled personal experiences, using performance to piece together 'the unglued surfaces of life for passers by to pick their way through'.[25] The performance was staged at the Film-Makers' Cinematheque on two consecutive nights in November 1965, three months after his arrest, alongside live works by Claes Oldenburg, Robert Rauschenberg, Nam June Paik and others. Vaccaro vividly described the performance:

> I played the lobster. We had spent a year with Tosh Carillo making the costume... I had studied the way lobsters move, how they go backwards … I entered and Jack had these two fat women who were joined together like Siamese twins. They were North and South Atlantis, actually North and South Vietnam, and I had to come in with a buzz-saw and cut them apart. Now my loft at that time was right up the street from there, so I figured I had to make something, so I made tons of red Jell-O, and there were all these people in the audience, including the photographer Weegee, and when I sawed the twins in half, I picked up all this Jell-O and threw it out into the audience.[26]

The lure of the 'exotic' – rooted in Smith's enthusiasm for the déclassé myth of Atlantis as a fantasy civilisation in 'decline' – might also be read as a vehicle for his ambivalent gestures towards a better space and time, the impossible dream of an altogether more wishful locality before or after The Fall.

The aftermaths of Jack Smith

Smith's utopic confusion of opposites has had a powerful influence over other artists. From 1990 to 1993, Ron Vawter famously staged sections of Jack Smith's performance *What's Underground About Marshmallows?* (1981) alongside an imagined after-dinner speech by Senator McCarthy's closeted lawyer, Roy Cohn, written by Gary Indiana. In the resulting piece, *Roy Cohn/Jack Smith*, Vawter framed a collision between two radically divergent personalities, bound by conspicuous equivalences. As Vawter would state in his introductory remarks to the performance,

> I am a person living with AIDS, and … I've taken only particular aspects of [Cohn's and Smith's] personalities and balanced one against the other for my own theatrical motives. This is not documentary, but rather a subjective reaction, a response, to the lives of two very different white male homosexuals who had two powerful things in common: a virus, and a society which sought to repress their sexuality.[27]

Roy Cohn/Jack Smith is an iconic piece of queer performance, which powerfully collides two divergent approaches to a mutual challenge, namely Cohn's compensatory scapegoating of other homosexuals, and Smith's dissident embrace of difference, marginality, and disaster.

In a very different vein, Ken Jacobs' *Star Spangled to Death* is a five-hour homage to Smith. The film collages eclectic found footage with reels documenting performances by Smith and friends, between 1957 and 1959. Newsreels, minstrel shows, cartoons, and public information broadcasts of the post-war era are edited together with performed interpretations and invocations by Smith and his superstars. Completed in 2003, Jacobs' film forges collisions into a political narrative of sorts that – despite its nihilism – critiques state terrorism and the suppression of the activist spirit. '*Living*, unlike *life*,' Jacobs' prologue tells us, 'is not an abstraction born of the mind. It includes, rather than opposes, dying. Any pinhead can be "for life", which sidesteps the inherent evil of lives-interrupting-lives. (Most of us recognize evil only when it's ourselves being eaten) … The Spirit Not Of Life But Of Living celebrates actuality.' Like Smith, Jacobs revels in and unveils the contradictions of political and popular culture, staging a melancholic disposition that places their legacies at odds with affirmative critical agendas. Each artist digs up less palatable tendencies, beyond those that have been afforded a place within the dominant narratives of the period: 'There were,' he notes, 'other memories too.' The diverse narratives that Jacobs quotes and critiques range from economic regeneration propaganda to Elizabeth Taylor's marital scandals.

However, this reinvention of past histories passes over into his filmic appropriation and reinvention of the political persona of his key collaborator, Jack Smith, towards hopeful political ends that mirror the sentiments posed by Goldin, above. In *Star Spangled to Death*'s final segment, Jacobs films a group of young protesters at a 'Drop Bush Not Bombs' demonstration against the US-led war on Iraq, whose collective insurgence he defines as a posthumous manifestation of 'The Spirit Of Jack'. Here, The Spirit Not Of Life But Of Living, whose role Smith is cast in, is incarnated retrospectively as a spirit in revolt against the standards and inequalities encouraged by George W. Bush's administration. By summoning 'The Spirit Of Jack' in the final moments of the film, Jacobs claims Smith for a manifest political purpose. In a period of overt social political and economic crisis, Jacobs celebrates Smith's oblique political horror, recognising it retrospectively as a valid position of creative resistance, available for deployment against an identifiable enemy.

From under the layers of mystification, absurdity and madness, Smith's statements in the film carry a force of ambivalent opposition. 'Peekaboo,' he insistently squeals. 'Peekaboo!' Anticipating his playful yet disconcerting performances in Jacobs' later film, *Little Stabs at Happiness* (1960), Smith's utterances testify to a refusal to accept the terms upon which conventional, acquiescent standards of life are predicated. Near the end of the second hour of *Star Spangled to Death*, there is an appropriated instructional segment for youngsters about 'conscience', and a long statement by a pre-Watergate Richard Nixon publicly avowing his honesty, sincerity and political integrity. Smith responds to these stolen gems by performing a self-consciously conscience-free dance of destruction, disregarding the narrator's pinched encouragements that 'obedience to that voice [of conscience] brings spiritual peace'. These 'dances' take the form of impromptu street interventions, referred to by Jacobs, in the film, as a kind of 'extemporaneous street-theater [that] Jack and I fooled with'. In another long section of found footage, a baby Rhesus monkey in a psychology lab sets one of the central performance tropes in the piece. The footage documents the disturbing 'Goon Park' experiments by Harry Harlow, who used monkeys to test his theories of love, affection and neglect in the 1950s and 1960s. In genuine educational material, distressed monkeys are manipulated and tortured to test the source and function of love, by perverse and paternal scientists. Elsewhere, black-and-white minstrel child-angels Gabriel and Peter tap-dance, surrounded by giant swaying watermelon slices that group to make a whole fruit, while hula-dancing girls perform further demoralising variations on colonialist patriarchal titillation. The appropriated, profoundly racist dance sections are inter-cut with Jacobs' own footage of a man in blackface wearing a hat of light bulbs. Again Smith retorts with a brief dance, one labelled with the wishful yet knowingly misguided epithet: 'Jack frees the slaves'.

Jacobs' practice had clear influences on Smith's work, most notably the combination of original performances and found footage in *No President* (1969). Here, in a twist of sorts on the avant-garde project of denaturalising the familiar, Smith presents the mundane in its overwhelmed relation to the extravagance and excess of creatures in their superstar celluloid turns. In *No President*, this relation is put to work to expose the limitations of liberal politics, with characteristically off-centre and indeterminate results. Smith collages footage of a hospitalised baby-fetishist being teased by a hag in horror-drag, with a televised campaign speech of 1940 by the failed presidential candidate Wendell Willkie. Similarly, clips of a courting debutante singing muted ditties of happy love and vanilla sex are bridged with scenes of a floppy dick soaking in a martini. The audio track is played out of synch, or slowed down to give a languid, slightly monstrous tonality to the work.

The narrative underlying the filmed performances of *Star Spangled to Death* is the attempts by Jerry Sims to find happiness, foiled by a character called Evil Bill, with Smith in a kind of wise fool's role as the aforementioned Spirit. Evil Bill steals Jerry's dolls, figures of compulsive consolation that parallel the wire-mother in the Rhesus monkey experiments shown periodically throughout the film. Smith appears, and the on-screen titling states that 'The Spirit Not Of Life But Of Living looks on, concerned that Bill may be moved by Jerry's appeal, and that Jerry will be unlawfully happy again, disrupting cosmic integrity'. The notion that happiness could itself be unlawful, in the sense that it contravenes a rule determining the social order, relates closely to the overriding conception of or attitude towards sexuality, pleasure and desire charted throughout Smith's work, in the curious hinterland between hope and despair that his enterprises inevitably limn. *Star Spangled to Death* is a film that is suspicious of affirmation, in its engagement with obstacles to happiness, pleasure, fulfilment or love; Sims' character is a 'hopeless pariah' yearning to recapture lost dolls, cats and dreams, only to be constantly dissuaded by Smith's Spirit Not Of Life But Of Living, who tells him, in every way he can, that the task is probably not worth its effort. Nevertheless, echoing Goldin's call to face up to crisis 'without contrition', the closing lines of Jacob's film tell us: 'There is plenty of reason to despair. We can't despair. Despair is collaboration with the enemy'. While the sentiments roughly delineated by Smith might appear to be a renunciation of hope, Jacobs deploys Smith's work as a utilisable exploration of political and psychic subject positions, ones that perhaps offer us explicit sites from which to reassess possibilities for the use of pleasure, as well as the place of suffering.

Rethinking the 'exotic'

In Smith's work, as gestured to in Jacobs' monument, curious negotiations of hope and despair are frequently articulated in proximity to both high camp exotica and discomfortingly ambivalent appropriations of potentially racist imagery. Smith's later performances, film rushes and photo sessions, for example, reproduce an almost naturalised vision of ancient Egypt, one inherited from the 'cult of Egyptomania' incited by the Napoleonic occupation of Egypt in the early nineteenth century, and the ensuing touristic 'epiphany' of 'the Orient', in which the French and British bourgeoisie 'reconfigured the aristocratic Grand Tour ... and extended it to the east'.[28] Howard Carter's excavation of the tomb of Tutankhamen in 1922 revivified the European taste for Egyptianate references, especially in its translation into Art Deco design. This spur to imitation was again inspired some forty years later, in the wake of Elizabeth Taylor's performance in Joseph L. Mankiewicz's lavish sword and sandal epic, *Cleopatra* (1963). Smith's estate contains many design books, including Art Deco publications, and one can imagine that *Cleopatra* would have been a suitably pleasurable confection for Smith, considering its visual excess, lengthy duration and critical and commercial failure.

While performing a version of what Tavia Nyong'o describes as 'racial kitsch', Smith's oppositional practice is marked in its volatile distances – through strategies of appropriation – from a straightforwardly malign reproduction of racist tendencies. Nyong'o shows that performance and other solicitations of racial kitsch can usefully stage the subject's ambivalent refusal of the racist object's abusive power. In Smith's taste for Montez vehicles and other instances of cheesecake Orientalia, he seems to question the implications of such modes of representation. Through 'the pleasure of mastering the urge to laugh with the joke,' Nyong'o writes, 'we reassert our dignity and attain distance from the pleasure that the stereotype urges upon us'.[29] In a Super 8 film rush from 1977, screened in live film performances, Smith descends the marble stairs of the National Gallery of Art in Washington D. C., leaving its *Treasures of Tutankhamen* exhibition. He strikes a dramatic Egyptianate pose, and sits on a bench with an expression of feigned shame. In acts of ritualised penance, he hides golden foil-wrapped Easter eggs in pipes, flowerbeds and between the buttocks of a bronze sculpture. In a further rush, he proceeds to the fountain of the Arlington National Cemetery, floats eggs of many colours across the memorial pond and pours an efflorescence of egg-dye into the water.

As suggested by the relation between his 'exotic' pleasures and apologetic rituals, Smith stages racist tendencies in a critical manner, exploring the system of signs that Euro-American producers and consumers of culture have normalised. As such, Smith intervenes in the mandate to reproduce difference as a manageable and containable 'surrogate'. For Edward Said, these productions

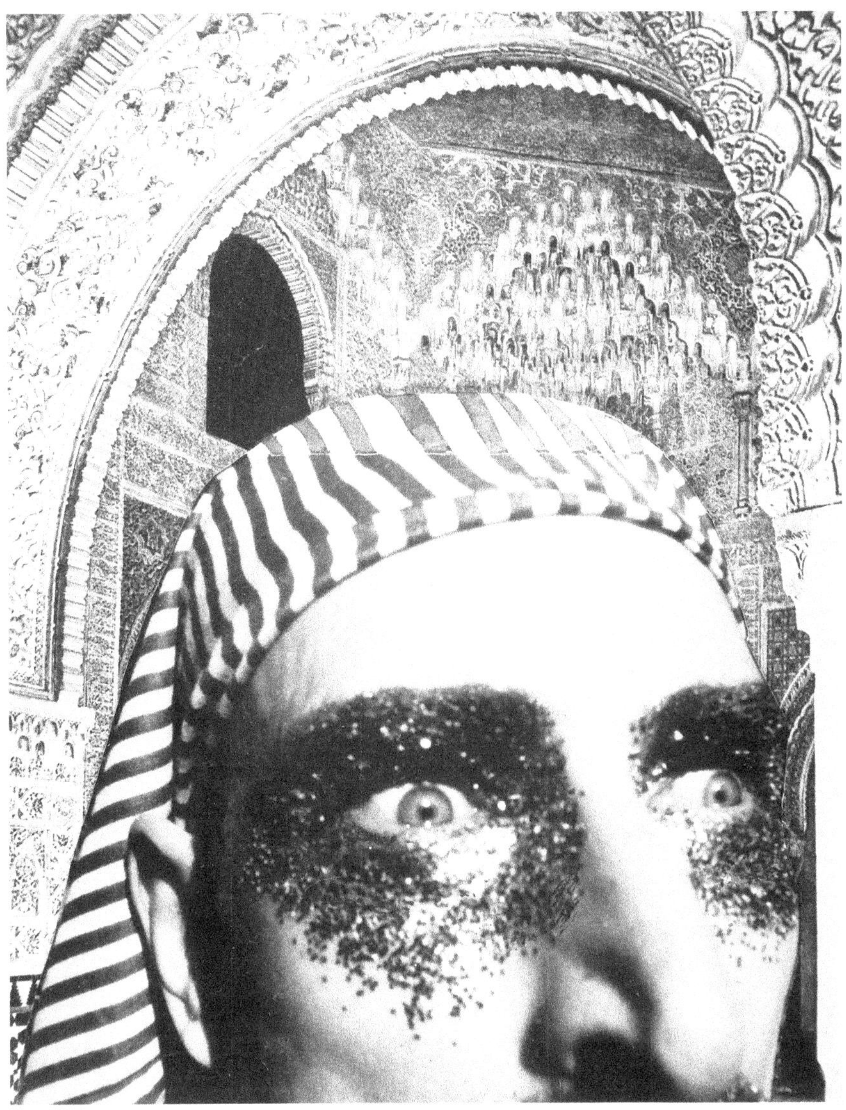

Jack Smith, *Untitled* (c. 1973).   **7.1**

of surrogacy are defensive mechanisms, sets of representations that aim to
recreate the 'underground self' as a body of otherwise restricted pleasures that
can be more successfully policed and mastered by the (Occidental) subject.[30]
In popular Western caricatures of Egypt, a set of colonial imperatives can
be read as masquerading as an interest in antiquity; however, Smith's love of
Egyptiana and his inhabiting of a glamorous quasi-Nefertiti in performances

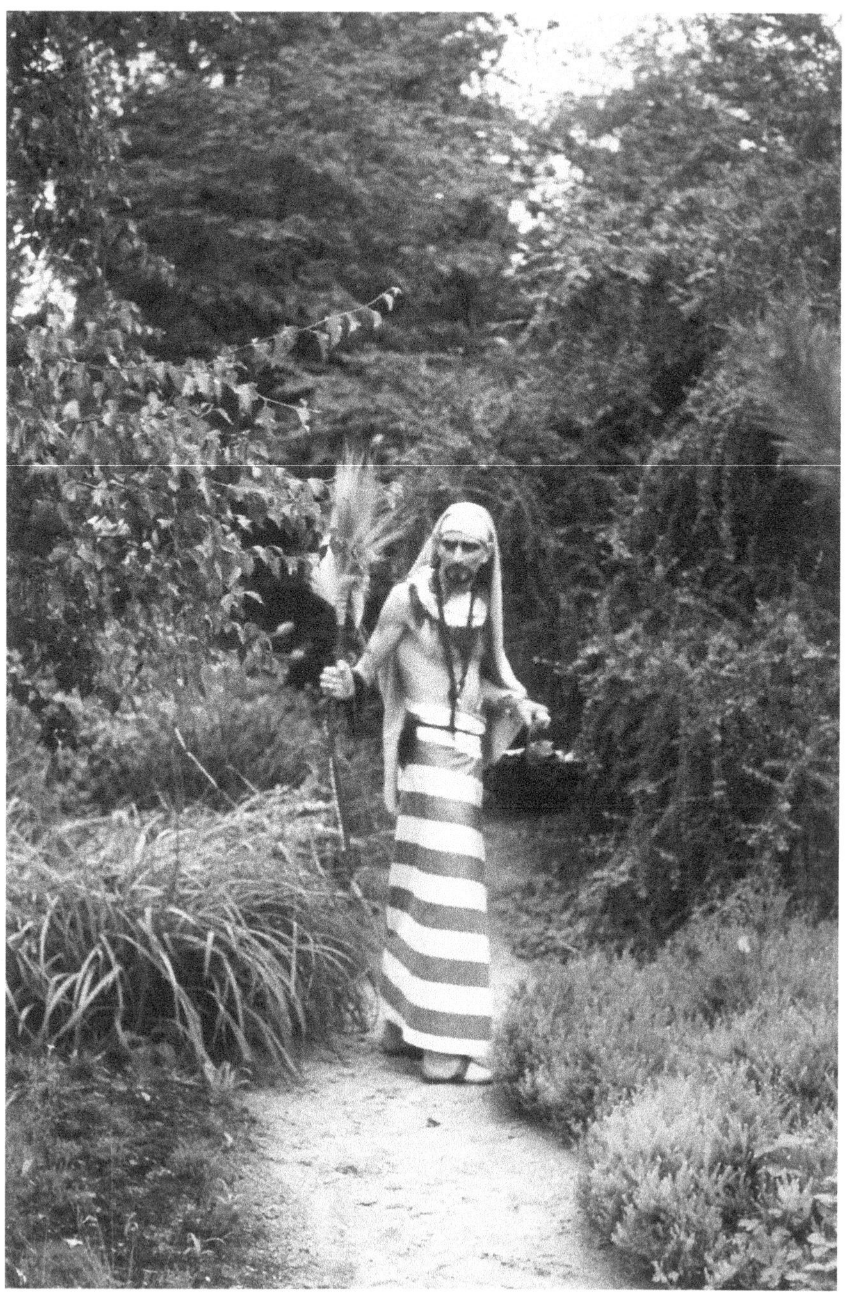

7.2   Jack Smith, *Moses* (1974).

in the 1970s and 1980s read too strongly as pastiche to function as a straight-forwardly racist economy of representation. Smith's portrayals are marked by their performed distance from the 'cultural profanity' of minstrelsy – the painful colonial pantomiming of racial and cultural difference.[31] Moreover, his distance is also a performance away from scholarly Orientalism, the (curiously minstrel-like) touristic practice of 'proving the validity of … musty "truths" by applying them … to uncomprehending, hence degenerate natives'.[32]

In one series of photographs, used in a slide performance entitled *Moses* (1974), Smith performs a highly artificial characterisation of a mock-biblical figure (see figure 7.2). His garb clearly references caricatures of Egyptian dress, while being a 'look' that is distinctly his own. In the images, by German experimental filmmaker Wilhelm Hein, Smith poses beside a large pond or among trees in a park in Cologne. He brandishes a totem made from palm fronds, or takes up exotic positions among the reeds, wearing copious amounts of jewellery, a blue-and-white headdress, and a rudimentary striped green tunic. According to Hein, the headdress was fashioned from a wall covering Smith stole from an exhibition by Daniel Buren (as noted in chapter two, Smith and Buren were both participating in the exhibition *Projekt '74* in Cologne at the time).[33] His beard has been accentuated with brown paint, and smudges of Blue Nile glitter adorn his eyes. In one shot, he holds a wrapped bundle in his arms, and approaches a basket nestled in the reeds, emoting an expression of cringing tragedy on his sparkling, painted face.

Smith's Egyptophilic tendencies apparently take shape in the early 1970s, after having abandoned filmmaking for live performance, expanded cinema and performance-for-camera. However, the recurrence of this motif in his performances perhaps signals the persistence of a specifically cinematic desire. As Antonia Lant argues, an intersection may be at work 'between Egyptianate material and prefilmic and filmic culture [at] both a physical and conceptual [level]'. Lant notes a series of striking parallels or unresolved tensions: a perception of 'cinema as a necropolis', its projections seemingly issuing a warning to spectators; an understanding of cinema as a form that speaks through a pictorial language, 'as hieroglyphics revealed by light'; a relation between the chemical process of mummification and that of film development and printing, both being efforts at saving or documenting dead matter; and 'an alliance between modern sexuality, particularly female screen sexuality [typified in the figure of the "vamp"], and myths surrounding the sphinx and its silent unreadability'.[34]

However, if Smith's attraction to performing 'Egyptomania' reveals the remnants of his significant investments in both early (trash) cinema and the practices of filmmaking, it might also be read as a ransacking of specifically theatrical conventions in order to deploy a politics of performance. For Said, the discursive field of Orientalism is the scene across which its participants act out the construction and normalisation of 'imaginative geographies'. In the fictional binaries of 'us' and 'them' set up in such geographies, the distinctions are 'arbitrary', for the 'Oriental' other is not required to acknowledge the difference.[35] Nevertheless, it sustains a set of techniques that reinvent the local as the familiar, and its 'beyond' as the exotic, frightening, uncivilised and, by extension, queer. Describing the terrains formulated by such imaginative flights as a field of discourse, Said reminds the reader, '[a] field is often an enclosed space,' conjuring the analogy not only of a prison, but a theatre. He continues, 'The idea of representation is a theatrical one: the Orient is the stage on which the whole East is confined,' and rehearsed in the fields of play of Occidental subject formation. Said develops his implicit analogy between Orientalism and theatre, stating, 'An Orientalist is but the particular specialist in knowledge for which Europe at large is responsible, in the way that an audience is historically and culturally responsible for (and responsive to) dramas technically put together by the dramatist.'[36] The European subject is cast as the analogue to the position of audience, in mutual relations to an author/scholar, such that the processes by which racial and ethnic stereotypes take form in the cultural imaginary clearly amount, for Said, to forms of theatrical staging.

Smith exploits the apparent theatricality of Orientalist ideology, invoking a metatheatrical mode to critique its processes. As such, he burlesques Orientalist cultural orthopraxis in a parodic, comic-theatrical space of performance. Burlesque is defined as a properly Victorian practice of theatrical 'travesty', a comical 're-dressing' of source material towards oppositional ends. For Richard Schoch, this process involves browbeating assumptions of cultural licence and social power with the weapon of 'theatrical vulgarity'.[37] In its elevation of daily occurrence into situations of classic dignity, and dressing up subjects or events of 'great pith and moment' in 'the costume and dialect of vulgar life',[38] burlesque clearly anticipates the cultural techniques of camp, each a historically contingent form of critical diagnosis that aims to expose and undermine cultural authority through methods of constructive ridicule. A co-conspirator with Smith (and Vaccaro) in the Theatre of the Ridiculous, Charles Ludlam confirms the political character of their mutual camp strategising: 'We did everything in a defiant way – radically wrong, you might say ... We upheld the idea of the Ridiculous and of ridicule as a weapon in defiance of theatrical pretension and class distinction disguised as aesthetic criteria or pseudo-standards of professionalism.'[39]

Across his various performances for camera, moreover, by burlesquing Orientalism, Smith cites its vocabulary as camp, foregrounding the fact that, as Said argues, its visible tropes are 'to the actual Orient ... as stylized costumes are to characters in a play'.[40] In other words, correspondences should not be sought between the language of Orientalism and 'the Orient' itself, because the vocabulary of images are effects of a schema of representation whose proper frame of relevance – its stage of occurrence – is the Occidental subject. As such, the 'Oriental' is always an 'impostor': estranged for being an object whose difference to the subject is repeatedly affirmed, yet paradoxically familiar for being an intimate construction. The twinned difference and familiarity of the impostor are each a function of the same 'theatrical' fantasies through which foreignness itself is formulated and maintained. Smith rehearses this impostor status as a pose, revealing the thorough fraudulence of the cinematic or literary other, while also demeaning the myth of a coherent cultural identity set apart from the compulsion to represent our fantasies of that other. This strategy conditions his later performances, but was first developed in his early photographic practice.

Exotic photography

Smith's early photography usefully demonstrates this emphasis on setting up irreconcilable tensions. Smith was a prolific yet relatively unsung photographer, and his archives include over a thousand black-and-white and colour negatives. The exhibitions and publications that have been produced since his death include a number of these evocative photographs by Smith. These documents demonstrate the diversity of his practice, beyond his more widely known film works. His photographic productivity peaked around 1960–61, and surviving photos show friends and acquaintances in extravagant harem poses, amongst the bric-a-brac Orientalia of his Ludlow Street apartment.

In one such image, published in *The Beautiful Book* (1962), a fleshy body is draped over the bottom of the frame like a plaintive corpse. His head lolls in an exhausted diagonal, as a woman engages the onlooker in a steely gaze while resting a graceful arm on the masked man's lifeless form (see figure 7.3). A kohl-eyed friend poses behind a polka-dotted gauze. The three figures fall together as enigmatic remnants of a ritual we have missed. Intended as a spread for *Film Culture*, Smith published a selection of 19 photographs as *The Beautiful Book* (1962). A limited edition of 200 copies were assembled by hand and printed by The Dead Language Press, under the auspices of poet and filmmaker Piero Heliczer. The books contain small black-and-white contact prints mounted on yellow card adorned with Magic Marker additions by Smith, and a Surrealist screen print on its cover by his muse at the time, Marian Zazeela.[41] The photographs are mostly orientalist tableaux, featuring Zazeela, Joel Markman, Francis Francine, Mario Montez, Irving Rosenthal, Smith himself, and others, shot in the Ludlow Street apartment Smith shared with Tony Conrad. Zazeela vividly remembers the alchemical hilarity and rococo lushness of the shoots: "'Project ecstasy!' he would entreat us, and ecstasy would flow from our pores into the chiaroscuro of his lens.'[42] Sold for $4 a copy, the book has been heralded by A. A. Bronson as a crucial

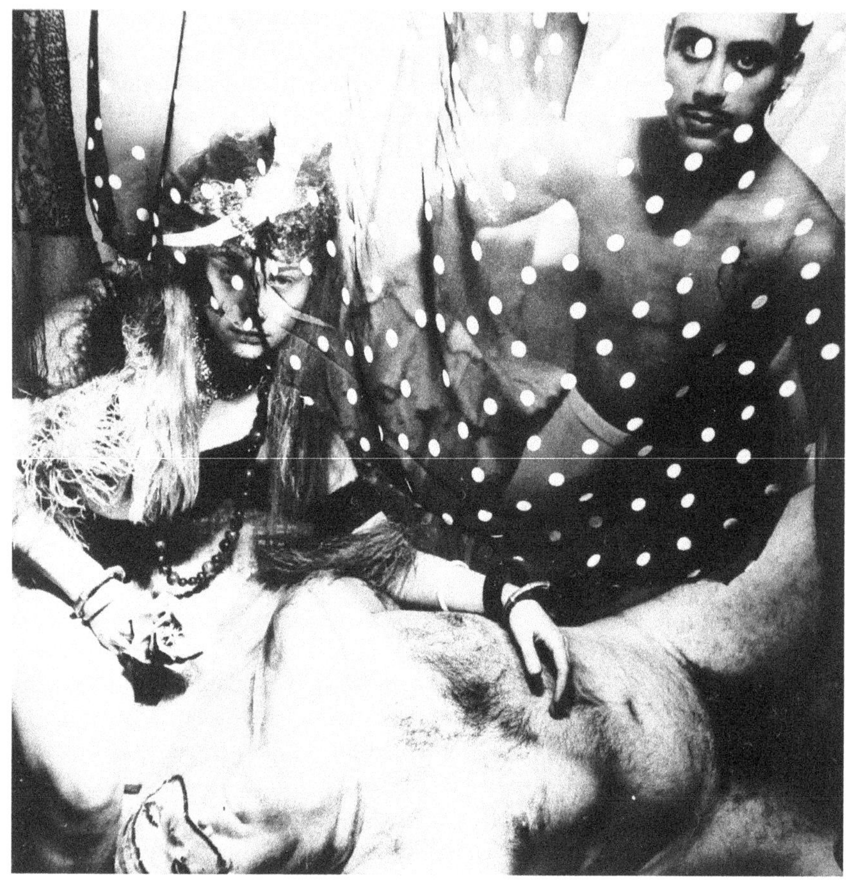

7.3   Jack Smith, *Untitled* (c. 1958–62).

forerunner to Xerox fanzine culture, which thrived in the post-punk, queer DIY underground of the 1980s.[43] Most of the images date from the winter of 1961, with some exceptions including the signature photograph of Smith taken by Jacobs on the steps of the Brooklyn Bridge around 1959. The high-contrast, sometimes over-exposed photographs were printed and the books assembled over a period of months in the spring and early summer of 1962, before Smith commenced filming *Flaming Creatures*.[44]

The styling of the early photographs is ostensibly cribbed from the dated movies he filled his nights watching. The exotic motifs and muted, smoky colorations of these photographs recall silent movies of the 1920s set in far-off lands of allure and danger, most notably a mythical 'Bagdad' – sources of a fascination that would become a key theme of Smith's outlandish, idiosyncratic lexicon. Here and elsewhere, Smith performs his own volatile white

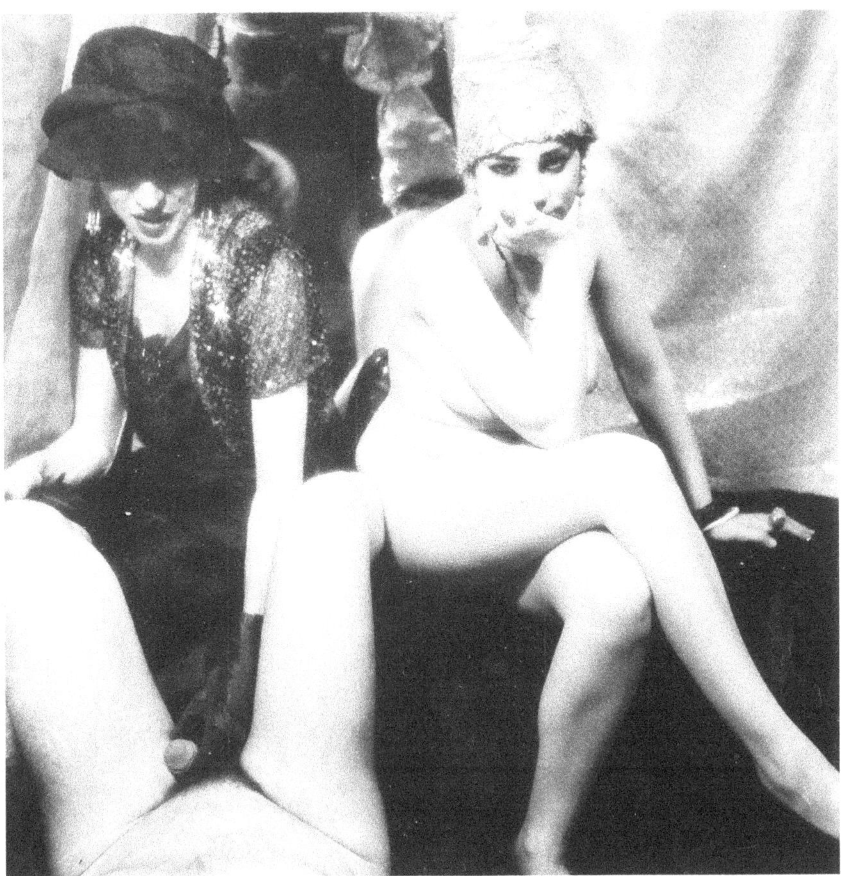

Jack Smith, *Untitled* (c. 1958–62).   **7.4**

masculinity, and a heavily pastiched non-white otherness, as equally, radically artificial; moreover, the coherence of either is powerfully undermined by the excessive vocabulary of imagined identities he cites. In one image, Smith divides the visual depth with a black gossamer drape (see figure 7.6). In the foreground, Joel Markman holds a plastic doll in one hand and a paper flower lantern in the other, as if to sniff it. Three corners of the frame are cluttered with debris – crinkled brown paper, netting and fabric. In the upper right corner, an ambiguously gendered figure poses in a white bridal veil. The figure's face and body have been darkened, accentuating her or his metallic eyes and lips. She or he is not simply an instance of blackface. Rather, the string of lanterns creates a configuration of lights and darks throughout the image, and the figure's face accentuates Smith's careful distribution of chiaro-scuro through make-up and costume. Markman wrote of the photo shoot that produced this and other images, confirming Smith's interests in Orientalist imagery, tying this to a queer literary investment in exoticism. He writes of their 'general dreams of Gide, Genet, Oscar Wilde and Maria Montez' lotus blossoms,' and his work's relation to 'phonecian alphabets and the mysteries of sphinx and pyramid [and] the stark reality of the voluptuary: a gaudy Moroccan brothel, an Egyptian slum buried and recreated annually for the last five thousand years'. For Markman, this combination produces a 'farce of cosmic misproportion', playing on Smith's photographic grandeur and his work's inevitable straying into confusion, tension and semiological play.[45] As such, Smith's photographs move beyond the coding by which the exotic is equated with or unilaterally reduced to a colonial imperative. Pursuing the tropes introduced in Smith's letter, further historical and cultural implications of the term may be sought, culminating especially in the apocalyptic tone in

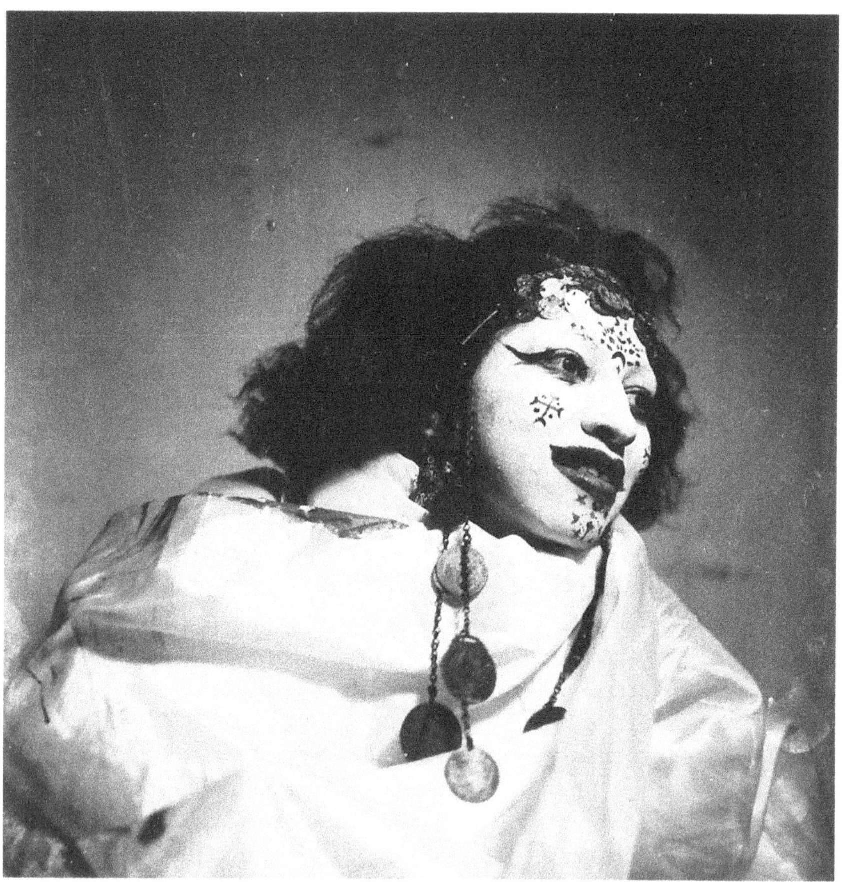

7.5   Jack Smith, *Untitled* (c. 1958–62).

which he attends to the myth of Atlantis, gestured to in Smith's 'weird comedy and mad images' staged under the quasi-mystical sign of 'decline'.

The lost continent of Atlantis

Our time, Smith noted in 1972, is 'The Age of the Lobster … an astrological development out of *Scorpio Rising* in the Age of Aquarius'; as such, America is reinvented as 'the reincarnation of the lost continent of Atlantis.'[46] The key historian of the lost continent was Ignatius Donnelly, whose *Atlantis: The Antediluvian World* (1882) was perhaps the most influential pseudo-scientific work of the late nineteenth century.[47] Since Plato, Atlantis had been imagined as a ancient world of purest beauty, a plenitude of human goodness before The Fall. For Donnelly, it was 'the true Antediluvian world; the Garden of

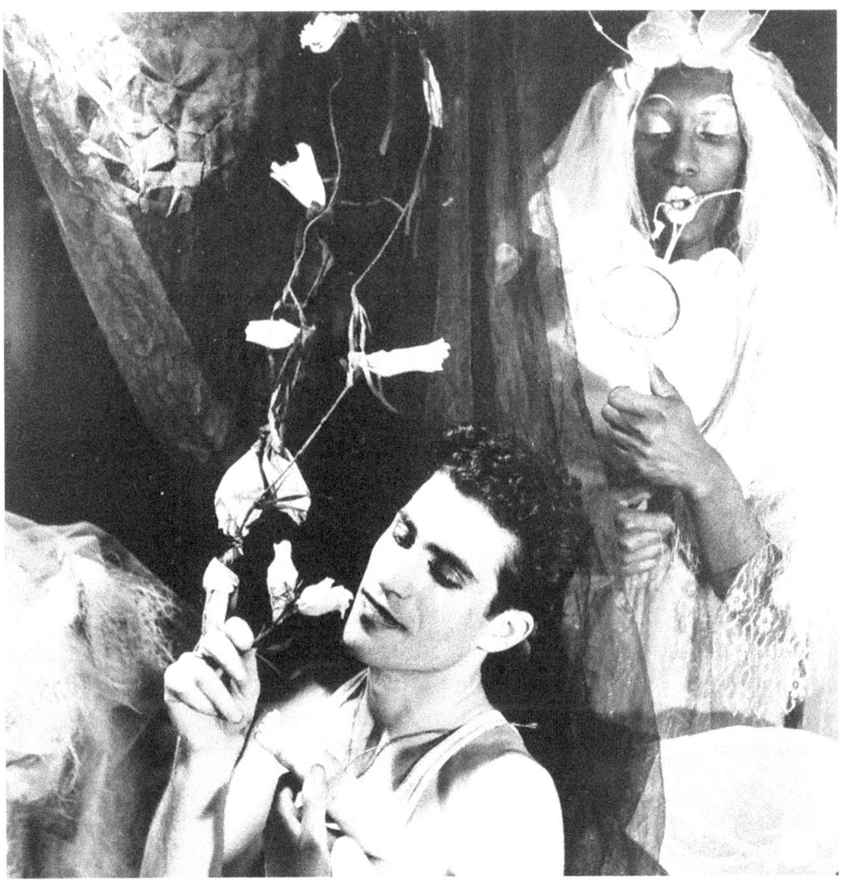

Jack Smith, *Untitled* (c. 1958–62).   **7.6**

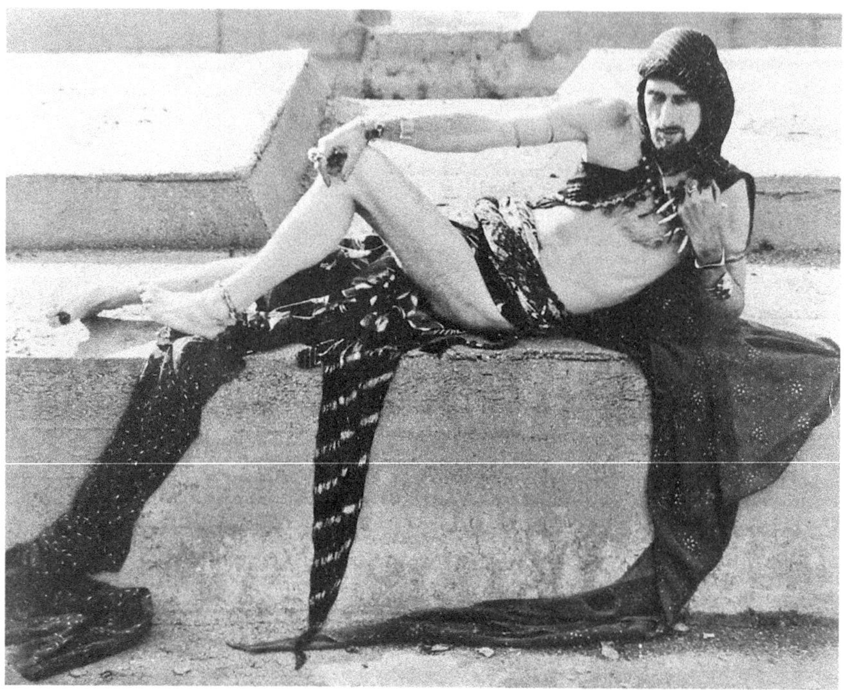

7.7   Jack Smith, *Untitled* (c. 1982).

Eden; the Gardens of the Hesperides; the Elysian Fields … representing a universal memory of a great land, where early mankind dwelt for ages in peace and harmony'.[48] Donnelly's account misreads Plato's philosophical myth of Atlantis – in the *Timaeus* – as a historical reality, and argues for the exact geographical location of the sunken civilisation ('opposite the mouth of the Mediterranean Sea') and the reasons for the terminal deluge that eradicated it. He attributes this loss to a catastrophic event of continental subsidence around 9000 BC, quixotically invested with a causality based on the corruption of the inhabitants of Atlantis. Similarly, noted Atlantis mythologisers such as Helena Blavatsky and Rudolf Steiner believed current civilisations to be subsequent forms of corporeality derived from Atlantis. For Steiner, man began as a completely 'etherealized' being, who has become more 'solid' with each step in his evolution – a material concretion apparently exponential to the developing corruption of the world each 'root race' inhabits. Across Donnelly, Blavatsky and Steiner, the Atlanteans' 'use of their destructive forces led to the catastrophe … that caused the disappearance of Atlantis beneath the waves'.[49] While it was the annexation of the lost continent by occultists that caused the myth to fall into disrepute, it is this arcane, tendentious quality that attracted and sustained Smith's perverse devotion.

Readers have no doubt jeered at Donnelly's sincere but weird science – laughing at his *Atlantis*, as well as later works including *The Great Cryptogram* (1887), which used 'mathematical' tabulations to extract hidden messages from the plays of Shakespeare, Marlowe, and Jonson, as well as Cervantes' *Don Quixote*, in order to prove that each had been written by Francis Bacon.[50] However, Smith embraced the legacy of Donnelly's debunked mythology as an esoteric counterpoint to his own grim imaginings of an inescapable present. For Smith, Atlantis figures in his writings, and most notably in his titles, as an ambivalent construct, a metaphor for both the destitution of contemporary culture and the utopian possibility of a nebulous temporality – a thwarted time before or beyond corruption. Donnelly's precarious myth accounts for this ambivalence: Atlantis is a vision of beauty, but one whose glory is ominously predetermined by its impending fall towards dereliction and failure. As utopia, it is shadowed, that is, by its violent flowering into loss. As Smith wrote, 'Happiness destroyed Atlantis / Anarchy in Lobsterland! Atlantis needs Anarchy … truth forever teetering breathlessly.'[51] The subsequent appropriations of Smith's quasi-mystical, apocalyptic ideals, by Jacobs, Vawter and others, are therefore noteworthy. Smith's example seems apposite for cultural redeployment in other times of ethically dubious circumstances on the political world stage.

For Richard Dellamora, a key voice in recent thinking around apocalypse, contemporary cultural practice and critical theory do not imagine the future as plenitude that opens onto utopia but, rather, as serial finitude: 'progress as a single, ongoing catastrophe' made up of scenarios of destitution or disaster.[52] In his writing on William S. Burroughs, David Cronenberg and others, Dellamora is careful not to romanticise apocalypse, suggesting instead Walter Benjamin's account of history, 'one single catastrophe which keeps piling wreckage upon wreckage', which the allegorical 'angel of history' surveys while being thrust into the future by the storm called 'progress'.[53] Nevertheless, critical theory also acknowledges the radical violence of apocalypse and the political strategies in whose purposes apocalyptic overtures are deployed in cultural practice. As Andrew Hewitt argues, the Holocaust – as 'the privileged modality of the apocalypse' – troubles the mode of thinking (and is, of course, referenced obliquely in Smith's letter). The historical telos of fascism is constituted by eugenic and genocidal imperatives, and therefore by 'a dialectical narrative that fantasizes a cultural rebirth beyond the apocalyptic end of European fascism'.[54] For Dellamora, nevertheless, a careful negotiation of apocalypse offers a means for reorienting the historical development of sexual identities and cultures as constituted not only by rupture, but also by catastrophe. Focusing on specific events in lesbian, gay and transgender history, from the local trauma engendered by the trial of Oscar Wilde, to the global disaster of AIDS, Dellamora posits a sexual politics of apocalypse 'in the sense of opening new possibilities of meaning by unsettling the norms of representation,' reiterating Marin's notion of utopic discourse as semiological play.[55] Dellamora emphasises the prevalence of tropes in recent cultural practice that he deems apocalyptic in tone, including narratives of menace, conspiracy theories, the projection of an enemy within, hallucinatory episodes, and (often unflattering) representations of homosexuality. William S. Burroughs's novels of the 1950s and 1960s are Dellamora's apocalyptic ur-texts, though his standard may be extended to contemporary practices such as Smith's, with its persistence of triumphant failure, mystic horror and erotic destitution. For Dellamora, apocalyptic tone often takes shape in relation to 'the familiar narrative of an artist who sacrifices life … to art and whose art becomes his life,' a description that neatly summarises not only Burroughs' blurring of categories, but also the sentiments at work in Smith's performances, films, and idiosyncratic writings, including his letter.[56]

On New York's Lower East Side, Smith was not alone in his apocalyptic, faux-Pharaohonic aspirations. From 1961, Sun Ra and his Galactic Research Arkestra were key fixtures. Having experienced his first 'transmolecularization' in 1936, Ra created a persona salvaged from 1930s Buck Rogers and Flash Gordon comics, in collision with Smith-esque Egyptiana, and began lecturing musicians about space travel, electronic sound and occult ritual from 1944. Ra maintained that people of colour had been sent down from a more advanced Solar System, and could develop electronic music as an intergalactic medium for communicating with the Mother Race. As Ken Hollings notes, 'Claiming its descent from the stars and the fertile prima material of the Nile Delta, Sun Ra's cosmo-drama has been up and running ever since,' continued by his Arkestra since his death in 1993.[57] With his Funkadelic protégé, George Clinton, Ra 'combined mad movie science and myth … into a dancefloor cosmology that made an open display of its secret codes and esoteric rites: an encrypted Black Mass acted out in plain sight for the Television Age.'[58] His feature film, *Space is the Place* (1974), gives an official account of Ra's mythology as radical outsider identification – Outer Space as outsider space, perhaps – specifying his intergalactic esoterica as a highly original rethinking of Blaxploitation politics. Like Ra's contemporaneous vision of an escape into space, Smith saw Atlantis – its Elysian purity as well as its haunting by corruption – in his squalid surroundings, seeking glimpses of the lost paradise in Maria Montez movies, Hollywood lore, and the underground cinema and performance scenes in which he was a key player. Each of these domains is imaginatively recreated as the unreachable vision of a golden past, a half-remembered plenitude that has been squandered. Smith's fostering of the myth of Atlantis is a clever ploy – his whole career had, after all, been a 'rehearsal' for its destruction. The distinct unreality of the lost continent does not provide solace from his fears but, rather, hardens the difficulty of his surroundings, quickening his torment with melodrama. His rehearsals for the destruction of Atlantis provided a pseudo-historical space into which he might have imaginatively escaped – if it weren't that, in the same gesture, its profound spuriousness revokes the very possibility that his utopian vision might evoke.

For Roszak, writing in general terms, this illogicality is not a problem but, rather, emblematic of the countercultural moment of the 1960s. He writes, 'it is nothing new that there should exist anti-rationalist elements' in the rarefied registers of cultural practice. 'What *is* new,' however, 'is that a radical rejection of science and technological values [in favour of, say, pseudo-science or science-fiction] should appear so close to the center of our society' – that is, perhaps, in performance and visual culture – 'rather than at the negligible margins.'[59] The mass popularity of anti-rationalist imperatives are emphasised in Roszak's reading, explaining the conditions of emergence for esoteric sentiments across Smith and Ra's exotic rituals and apocalyptic fictions.

Performance research and joke-work

Couched in his peculiar idiom, Smith's observations toe a clearly absurdist line, luring his audience with the possibility of disregarding his practice for the harlequin ramblings of a joker. Nevertheless, the logic of the joke may present a method of thinking the complex interrelation of danger, hope and laughter, in his vision of Atlantis and beyond. In *Jokes and Their Relation to the Unconscious*, Freud comments on the cultural tendency for laughter to turn nasty, in his reading of the joke's labour in asserting power relations among collectives:

> Brutal hostility, forbidden by law, has been replaced by verbal invective … which aims at enlisting the third person against our enemy. By making our enemy small, inferior, despicable or comic, we achieve in a roundabout way the enjoyment of overcoming him – to which the third person, who has made no efforts, bears witness by [her or] his laughter.[60]

Smith sought the benefits of laughing at his own seemingly intolerable situation, cultivating a feral sort of joke, a serious laughter that flirts with the painful knowledge sustained in one's own investment in actual crisis. Bearing in mind the joke's tendency towards hostility, and the invitation to humiliation involved in laughing at oneself, the project of the joke is, perhaps, that of a stranger politics, a fraught and uneven commonality that sanctions a volatile relation between subjects: not purely oppositional – me and you, us and them – but, rather, more implicated.[61] It is a process that is at once more readily jovial and hopeful, but also dangerously proximate to hatred and abuse, as per Freud's definition of the joke and its anxious relational province. In short, Smith gestures towards a slippery conjugality, and a fraught schema for the production of meaning and affect, by unsettling norms of representation and reception through 'joke-work'. Smith's difficult investments in the labour of joking further demonstrate his commitment to utopic strategies that stage binaries by uncoupling them, instituting confusion into their structure.

In conclusion, I point to the relation between Smith's immersions in awkward and ambivalent spaces, and the possibility of an erotic invigoration of scholarly endeavour. As gestured to by lingering in unfamiliar or contradictory spaces – the locus of the hoax, the joke, of laughter and of hope – perhaps a stranger, more 'exotic' politics of engagement might be summoned: a more honest, and perhaps riskier encounter with the body, with performance, and the traces of each. For William Haver, 'queer research' is characterised by the process of rendering intellectual life uncanny. Queer research 'does not make the world familiar or comfortable, for the student or reader, but [rather] defamiliarises, or makes strange, queer or even cruel what we had thought to be a world'.[62]

In a consideration of the constitutive elements of a life, Haver defines as 'pornographic' all that which 'conceptuality and its attendant subjectivities can only imagine as their inessential surplus'.[63] The pornographic life encompasses all that is sequestered beyond the socially and culturally acceptable yet nevertheless summons the register of difficult laughter. As such, the pornographic resembles the spatiality of the exotic, as that which etymologically (deriving from the Greek, '*exo*') is a sign for anything that finds itself on the 'outside'. Pursuing Haver's provocation, and in concert with Roszak's understanding of the primacy of 'ritual excess' and 'exotic clutter' for the countercultures of the 1960s, a figuring of the exotic in pornographic proximity to apocalyptic tone may pose a modality of intellectual and creative estrangement that is predicated upon an investment in difference, failure, irrationality and rupture. Haver defines the strategy of intellectual estrangement in spatial terms, as both the 'outside' of culture, as well as the 'interstitial', the apparently negligible in-betweens of official spaces, epistemologies or cultures.[64] The private territory of authorship, of personal space, of the image and the very body of the other – these are all challenged and threatened with invasion and estrangement in Smith's apocalyptic project. Anticipating Edelman, Haver reveals the possibilities at stake in ambivalent positions and volatile positions, gesturing to those provoked by Smith, in his persistent reinventions of the body, and its desires, as paranoid, chaotic, ridiculous and destitute.

Of their mutually 'Ridiculous' predilection towards Maria Montez-inspired performance pranks, and this desire's rootedness in the need to act out against difficult memories of a specifically provincial solitude, John Vaccaro recalls, 'Jack and I were both from Ohio. We grew up watching the movies that I still love, and we carried on our lives as if we were living in the days of *The Arabian Nights*. I remember times when we didn't even go up the stairs to his loft, we climbed up the fire escape; that was it, we were scaling the walls of Bagdad.'[65] Others have similarly approached Smith's way of working in escapist, seemingly utopian terms. 'I remember,' Kathy Acker writes in 1990, 'Jack Smith telling me that what he most wanted to do was to build a huge dome somewhere in North Africa. Whoever entered this dome would tell Jack his or her dreams and instantaneously Jack would make a movie of this dream … Movies would be shown twenty-four hours a day.'[66]

Vaccaro and Acker emphasise the impossibility that haunts Smith's fantasies of transcendence, and their tendency towards a troubling Orientalism. Accounts of his performances attest to this twinning of disaster and possibility. Of Smith's queerly productive immersion in failure and crisis in performance, Richard Foreman writes,

> Before you could even think a glimmer of 'Oh no, this is awful,' Jack would beat you to the punch … And in his nasal, cracked voice, he'd start complaining and changing the costume of one of his co-actors as a piece of scenery fell over; he'd stop to visibly struggle with that inside his head, but everything would be so slow and deliberate and 'tasted' by his aesthetic consciousness that [at] every moment the stage began to glow with total potential.[67]

Shadowed by his compulsive imaginings of uncanny spaces, from the wrecked ceiling of The Plaster Foundation of Atlantis to the fabled 'hate wall' in his apartment, Smith's peculiar utopia is repeatedly compromised by danger, failure, and persecution anxieties, so as to maintain a kind of harsh realism throughout his flights of Technicolor fancy. Imbuing the home with disaster and desire, utopia is kept just in sight, but out of reach for the subject. Smith's lofts were famously dishevelled. He had transformed them into ragged performances spaces, infamously by wrecking the middle ceiling of the double-storey Plaster Foundation, to leave a pile of cement, plaster and twisted girders that had fallen through to the floor. Lovingly cared for by Smith, this pile of debris became the base for his scenographic invention, which Smith tended laboriously in the course of his performances. Smith lived and worked among the mountain of rubble, and decorated it with an accretion of junk, salvaged from the streets, alleyways and rubbish dumps of New York. During performances, Smith would encourage contemplation of his set by making adjustments to its distribution of fairy lights, rearranging the shrivelled Christmas trees or road-signs that adorned it, as prologues, impromptu intermissions or moments of respite in his arduous midnight performances. In Smith's domestic performances, the nostalgic associations that lived spaces may garner are pitted against the threatening or subversive oppositional structures that often encroach upon them. The set of processes by which architectures become strange are deployed as a neat proxy for the ways in which they approximate other social and cultural tendencies towards estrangement.

As a research practice, the act of rendering a space, archive or history uncanny echoes Acker's recollection – in which Smith redesigns the home as the dream of an impossible space – unsettling the inevitability of the home as a site of happiness and shelter. Against purely affirmative poetics, the ravaged domestic may be read as a cipher for the exotic, as a space that invites an experience of itself as always already estranged – hence as a category thought away from, or at a tangent to, the exotic's currency as a symptom of purely colonialising imperatives. Indeed, it is the volatile relationship between the glimmer of hope and the looming promise of disaster that provides a rich – if architecturally unsound – space for the deliberation of new modes of artistic and, finally, scholarly practices. 'Take off your blindfolds,' Smith urges us, with a seduction that harbours a hint of warning; 'now you are in Atlantis!'[68] The conceit of imagining the practices of performance and visual culture as rehearsals for the destruction of Atlantis is Smith's apposite political gesture. In his recalcitrant threats, he reminds us that the shaky yet singular space of culture offers an ersatz paradise, prone to fantasy, pleasure and desire, while also, in the same gesture, invoking a presentiment of something catastrophic.

In the essay that remembers Smith's impossible dream, Acker concludes that in order to write with political effect, 'it is imperative to return to the body … [insofar as] language relates to and occurs in the whole body.'[69] Such languages of the body are those of flux, wonder, laughter and rage, techniques of serious play that constitutes insufficient, contradictory and forgetful

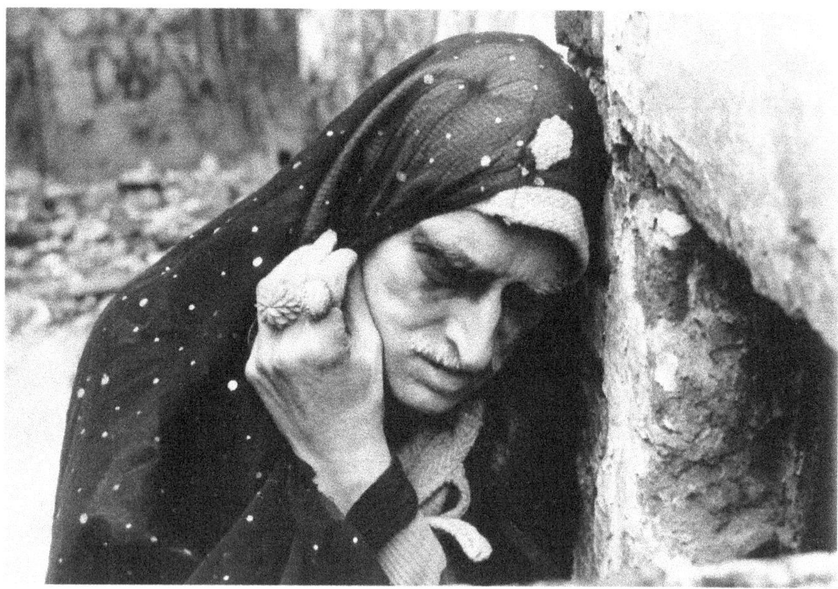

7.8   Ari Roussimoff, *Shadows in the City* (1990).

structures for thinking. 'Let these be the language of art criticism,' Acker's polemic concludes: 'to scream, to forget, to do anything except reduce radical difference, through representation, to identities, singularity, calculable and controllable.'[70] Similarly, Edelman emphasises the political promise of queerness as that which unbinds the illusory coherence of the subject. Abandoned to jouissance, queer sexualities must embrace the death drive, as the force of undoing that 'refuses identity or the absolute privilege of any goal'.[71] This refusal could be pursued as an exhortation to accept, to endure, and to record the experience of struggle as a bearing witness to one's own confusion, one's own possible destitution in the encounter with the unfamiliar. This gathering of information could foster other types of engagement, other modes for the production of knowledge: be they glorious, catastrophic, affirmative, pornographic, exotic and/or apocalyptic.

Smith's refinement is a ruinous one. He abandons himself to failure, and offers consolations for its inevitability in the spaces between art and the everyday. Such spaces are often sexual, not least because sex is the province of ardour and energy, of intimate exertions, but also of failures, inasmuch as intimacy is frequented by incomprehension, misrecognition, and other meagre humiliations. Smith strays into catastrophe because his work was a persistent attempt to take stock of and attend to the disasters of a life. His films, performances and writings enable oblique perspectives on the minor – the peripheral, marginal or parenthetical spaces occupied by artists who cannot figure in triumphant narratives of art or life. Nevertheless, Smith prevents his audiences from using him to affirm the familiar logics of survival against the odds, the dignity of persistence, or the honour of sticking to one's guns, and other romantic platitudes. By investing himself in a catastrophic decline that troubles the critical promise of recuperation, he revels in the dubious privileges of desperate marginality. In his elegiac travails, Smith honours instead the curious grace that disaster bestows on one's exertions. Finally, this grace is neither the opportunistic, existential romance of the outcast, nor a personification of the modernist celebration of angst as the definitional promise of modernity. Draped in veils of harlot colour, Jack Smith refuses such rational consolations, posing instead among lofty peaks and death-stained marble domes in a rubble-strewn vista modelled on the great dry oceans of the moon. Unequivocal in his assertions of having been a failure – in art, life and love – dignity is devastated, or at least permanently deferred. Alchemised in street-worn magic, the rhinestone misanthrope forages in his Aztec garden, heralding the misery of billboard deities. In his hour of doubt, Smith smiles a smile of crystalline defeat, evoking a joy so slow its milk turns sour on culture's doorstep.

The details are missing. Life is somewhere else. Faith wavers and idols gleam with tempting splendour.

Notes

1 Jack Smith, 'Ammonia pits of Atlantis: Evil in the art world, or Walter versus the giant knick-knacks' (1966), *Wait for Me at the Bottom of the Pool: The Writings of Jack Smith*, ed. J. Hoberman and Edward Leffingwell (New York and London: High Risk Books, 1997), pp. 97–101 (p. 97).

2 Nan Goldin, *Witnesses: Against Our Vanishing* (New York: Artists Space, 1989), p. 4.

3 Lee Edelman, *No Future: Queer Theory and the Death Drive* (Durham and London: Duke University Press, 2004), pp. 2–17.

4 Edelman, *No Future*, p. 23.

5 Halberstam in Lee Edelman, Carolyn Dinshaw *et al.*, 'Theorizing queer temporalities: A roundtable discussion', *GLQ* 13.2–3 (2007), pp. 177–195 (p. 194).

6 Edelman in ibid. p. 195.

7 Sigmund Freud, 'Negation', *General Psychological Theory*, trans. Joan Riviere (New York: Collier, 1963), p. 214.

8 Edelman in 'Theorizing queer temporalities', p. 195.

9 José Esteban Muñoz, *Cruising Utopia: The Then and There of Queer Futurity* (New York and London: New York University Press, 2009), pp. 169–70.

10 Ibid. p. 112.

11 Ibid. p. 99.

12 Louis Marin, *Utopics: The Semiological Play of Textual Spaces*, trans. Robert A. Vollrath (Atlantic Highlands: Humanities Press International, 1990), pp. xiv–xviii.

13 Marin, p. xxii.

14 Alan Read, *Theatre, Intimacy & Engagement: The Last Human Venue* (Basingtoke: Palgrave Macmillan, 2008), pp. 58–63.

15 Jack Smith, typed letter with handwritten amendments (1984). Estate of Jack Smith, Gladstone Gallery, New York. Emphasis in original.

16 Thanks to Penny Arcade for sharing this memory with me in Berlin in March 2009.

17 Theodore Roszak, *Making of a Counter Culture: Reflections on the Technocratic Society and its Youthful Opposition* (London: Faber and Faber, 1970), p. 72.

18 Ibid. p. 145.

19 Ibid. pp. 125–6.

20 Jack Smith, 'Lobotomy in Lobsterland' (1965), *Wait for Me at the Bottom of the Pool*, pp. 81–8 (p. 83). Smith participated in other activist events.

21 Barry Miles, *Ginsberg: A Biography* (New York and London: Simon and Schuster, 1989), p. 389.

22 Smith, 'Lobotomy in Lobsterland', p. 84.

23 Miles, p. 390.

24 Cited in Leffingwell's editorial notes on 'Lobotomy in Lobsterland', p. 88.

25 Smith, 'Lobotomy in Lobsterland', p. 85.

26 John Vaccaro, unpublished interview with the author, New York (5 June 2005).

27 Ron Vawter, 'Roy Cohn/Jack Smith', *O Solo Homo: The New Queer Performance*, ed. Holly Hughes and David Román (New York: Grove Press, 1998), pp. 456–76 (p. 457).

28 Derek Gregory, 'Emperors of the gaze: Photographic practices and productions of space in Egypt 1939–1914', *Picturing Place: Photography and the Geographical Imagination*, ed. by Joan M. Schwartz and James R. Ryan (London and New York: I.B. Tauris, 2003), pp. 195–225 (pp. 199, 223).

29 Tavia Nyong'o, 'Racial kitsch and black performance', *Yale Journal of Criticism* 15.2 (2002), pp. 371–91 (p. 385).

30 Edward Said, *Orientalism* (London and New York: Penguin, 2003), p. 6.

31 Nyong'o, p. 385.

32 Said, p. 52.

33 Thanks to Hein for sharing this memory in Berlin, March 2009.

34 Antonia Lant, 'The curse of the pharaoh, or how cinema contracted Egyptomania', *October* 59 (Winter, 1992), pp. 86–112 (pp. 89–90).

35 Said, p. 54.

36 Said, p. 63.

37 Richard W. Schoch, *Victorian Theatrical Burlesques* (Burlington: Ashgate, 2003), p. xi.

38 Schoch, p. xii.

39 Charles Ludlam, *Ridiculous Theatre: Scourge of Human Folly: The Writings of Charles Ludlam*, ed. by Steven Samuels (New York: Theatre Communications Group, 1992), pp. 20, 36.

40 Said, p. 71.

41 The preface to a 2001 reprint in the library of the Getty Research Institute states, 'Noting the scarcity of [the first edition] on the rare book market and its absence from many prominent collections … it is likely that considerably fewer than 200 books were actually finished and distributed.' Jack Smith, *The Beautiful Book* (New York: Granary Books, 2001), n.p.

42 Marian Zazeela, '"Maja rising", Jack by popular demand: Jack Smith in retrospect', *Artforum* 36 (October 1997), p. 119.

43 A.A. Bronson, *Queer Zines* (New York: Printed Matter, 2008), p. 7.

44 Other key photographic works published in his lifetime include a series of black and white photographs in *Film Culture* (which had rejected the photos collected in *The Beautiful Book*). See Jack Smith, 'The moldy hell of men and women: A fotographic essay', *Film Culture* 35 (Winter 1964–5), pp. 33–9.

45 Joel L. Markman, 'Letter to *Film Culture*: Some thoughts on Jack Smith', *Film Culture* 31 (Winter 1963–64), p. 21.

46 Smith cited in Carel Rowe, *The Baudelairean Cinema: A Trend within the American Avant-Garde* (Ann Arbor, Michigan: UMI Research Press, 1982), p. 47.

47 The book had been reprinted 22 times by 1890. See E. F. Bleiler, 'Ignatius Donnelly and Atlantis' in Ignatius Donnelly, *Atlantis: The Antediluvian World* (New York: Dover Publications, 1976), pp. v–xx (p. ix).

48 Donnelly, *Atlantis*, pp. 1–2.

49 Colin Wilson, *From Atlantis to the Sphinx* (London: Virgin Books, 1996), pp. 91–2.

50 Bleiler, pp. x–xi.

51 Smith, 'Lobotomy in Lobsterland' (1965), *Wait for Me at the Bottom of the Pool: The Writings of Jack Smith*, ed. J. Hoberman and Edward Leffingwell (New York and London: High Risk Books, 1997), pp. 81–8, (p. 86).

52 Richard Dellamora, 'Introduction', *Postmodern Apocalypse: Theory and Cultural Practice at the End* (Philadelphia: University of Pennsylvania Press, 1995), pp. 1–14 (p. 2).

53 Walter Benjamin, 'Theses on the philosophy of history', *Illuminations*, ed. Hannah Arendt, trans. Harry Zorn (London: Pimlico, 1999), pp. 245–55 (p. 249).

54 Andrew Hewitt, 'Coitus interruptus: Fascism and the deaths of history', *Postmodern Apocalypse*, pp. 19–40 (pp. 18–20).

55 Richard Dellamora, 'Queer apocalypse: Framing William Burroughs', *Postmodern Apocalypse*, pp. 136–67 (p. 161).

56 Ibid. p. 162.

57 Ken Hollings, 'The solar myth approach: the live space ritual: Sun Ra, Stockhausen, P-Funk, Hawkwind', *Undercurrents: The Hidden Wiring of Modern Music*, ed. by Rob Young (London and New York: Continuum, 2002), pp. 99–113 (pp. 101).

58 Hollings, p. 104.

59 Roszak, p. 51. Emphasis in original.

60 Sigmund Freud, *Jokes and their Relation to the Unconscious*, trans. and ed. James Strachey (London: Routledge and Kegan Paul, 1960), pp. 102–3.

61 James English defines 'joke-work' as 'the most social form of dreamwork', a fraught practice at that, for 'the group that laughs is as divided and unstable as the target of laughter … [for] we do not know who the "we" is that is laughing'. See his *Comic Transactions: Literature, Humor, and the Politics of Community in Twentieth-Century Britain* (Ithaca and London: Cornell University Press, 1994), pp. 12–14.

62 William Haver, 'Queer research; or, how to practise invention to the brink of intelligibility', *The Eight Technologies of Otherness*, ed. by Sue Golding (London and New York: Routledge, 1997), pp. 277–92 (p. 291).

63 William Haver, 'Really bad infinities: Queer's honour and the pornographic life', *Parallax* 5.4 (1999), pp. 9–21 (p. 13).

64 Haver, 'Queer research', p. 282.

65 Vaccaro, unpublished interview.

66 Kathy Acker, 'Critical languages', *Bodies of Work: Essays by Kathy Acker* (London: Serpent's Tail, 1997), p. 82.

67 Richard Foreman, '"Awful great", Jack by popular demand: Jack Smith in retrospect', *Artforum* 36 (October 1997), p. 74.

68 Jack Smith, 'Rehearsal for the destruction of Atlantis: A dream weapon ritual' (1965), *Wait for Me at the Bottom of the Pool*, pp. 90–5 (p. 92).

69 Acker, p. 82.

70 Ibid. p. 92.

71 Edelman, *No Future*, p. 23.

Bibliography

Acker, Kathy, *Bodies of Work: Essays by Kathy Acker* (London: Serpent's Tail, 1997).

Ahmed, Sara, *Queer Phenomenology: Orientations, Objects, Others* (Durham and London: Duke University Press, 2006).

Albee, Edward, *Who's Afraid of Virginia Woolf?* (Harmondsworth: Penguin Books, 1965).

Anger, Kenneth, *Hollywood Babylon* (San Francisco: Straight Arrow Books, 1975).

Arcade, Penny, unpublished interview with the author, New York (18 May 2005).

Aumont, Jean-Pierre, *Sun and Shadow*, trans. Bruce Benderson (New York: W. W. Norton, 1977).

Badiou, Alain, *Ethics: An Essay on the Understanding of Evil*, trans. Peter Hallward (London and New York: Verso, 2001).

Badiou, Alain, *Handbook of Inaesthetics*, trans. Alberto Toscano (Stanford: Stanford University Press, 2005).

Bailes, Sara Jane, 'Some slow going: Considering Beckett and Goat Island', *Performance Research* 12.1 (2007), pp. 35–49.

Banes, Sally, *Greenwich Village 1963: Avant-Garde Performance and the Effervescent Body* (Durham and London: Duke University Press, 1993).

Barnes, Clive, 'Review: *Boys in the Band* opens Off Broadway', *New York Times* (15 April 1968), p. 48.

Barrett, Michèle, *Women's Oppression Today: Problems in Marxist Feminist Analysis* (London: Verso, 1980).

Barthes, Roland, *The Pleasure of the Text*, trans. Richard Miller (Oxford: Basil Blackwell, 1990).

Battcock, Gregory, 'The New American Cinema', *Art and Literature: An International Quarterly* 8 (Spring 1966), pp. 95–110.

Baxandall, Lee, 'The theatre of Edward Albee', *Tulane Drama Review* 9.4 (Summer 1965), pp. 19–40.

Benderson, Bruce, *Sex and Isolation and Other Essays* (Madison and London: University of Wisconsin Press, 2007).

Benjamin, Walter, *Illuminations*, ed. Hannah Arendt, trans. Harry Zorn (London: Pimlico, 1999).

Bersani, Leo, *A Future for Astyanax: Character and Desire in Literature* (London: Marion Boyars, 1978).

Bersani, Leo, 'Is the rectum a grave?', *AIDS: Cultural Analysis / Cultural Activism*, ed. Douglas Crimp (Cambridge and London: MIT Press, 1988), pp. 197–222.

Bersani, Leo, *Is the Rectum a Grave? And Other Essays* (Chicago and London: University of Chicago Press, 2010).

Binstein, Michael and Charles Bowden, *Trust Me: Charles Keating and the Missing Billions* (New York: Random House, 1993).

Blake, Nayland, 'The message from Atlantis', *Flaming Creature: Jack Smith, His Amazing Life and Times*, ed. Edward Leffingwell, Carole Kismaric and Marvin Heiferman, Institute for Contemporary Art, P.S. 1 Museum (London and New York: Serpent's Tail, 1997), pp. 168–83.

Bloom, Harold, *The Western Canon: The Books and School of the Ages* (London: Macmillan, 1995).

Bottoms, Stephen J., 'The efficacy/effeminacy braid: Unpicking the performance studies/theatre studies dichotomy', *Theatre Topics* 13.2 (September 2003), pp. 173–87.

Bottoms, Stephen J., *Playing Underground: A Critical History of the 1960s Off-Off-Broadway Movement* (Ann Arbor: University of Michigan Press, 2004).

Bourdieu, Pierre, *On Television*, trans. Priscilla Parkhurst Ferguson (New York: The New Press, 1996).

Brakhage, Stan, *Film at Wit's End: Essays on American Independent Filmmakers* (Edinburgh: Polygon, 1989).

Brantley, Ben, 'Review: As the boys return, the party isn't over', *New York Times* (21 June 1996).

Braunstein, Nestor, 'Desire and jouissance in the teachings of Lacan', *The Cambridge Companion to Lacan*, ed. Jean-Michel Rabaté (Cambridge: Cambridge University Press, 2003) pp. 102–15.

Brecht, Stefan, *Queer Theatre* (Frankfurt am Main: Suhrkamp Verlag, 1978).

Bronson, A. A., *Queer Zines* (New York: Printed Matter, 2008).

Brooks, David, 'Free association interview with Jack Smith – April 23rd, 1964', *Film Culture* 77 (1992–93), pp. 24–33.

Burroughs, William S. *The Adding Machine: Selected Essays* (New York: Seaver Books, 1986).

Butt, Gavin, *Between You and Me: Queer Disclosures in the New York Art World, 1948–1963* (Durham and London: Duke University Press, 2005).

Cameron, Dan, ed., *East Village USA* (New York: New Museum of Contemporary Art, 2005).

Carlson, Marvin, 'Performing the self', *Modern Drama* 39.4 (1996), pp. 599–608.

Carr, C., *On Edge: Performance at the End of the Twentieth Century* (Middletown: Wesleyan University Press, 1993).

Carr, C., 'Magnificent obsessions: The art and artifacts of the world according to Jack Smith', *Village Voice* (2 December 1997), p. 39.

Carroll, Paul, *The Poem in Its Skin* (Chicago and New York: Follett, 1968).

Chauncey, George, *Gay New York: The Making of a Gay Male World, 1980–1940* (London: Flamingo, 1994).

Cleto, Fabio, ed., *Camp: Queer Aesthetics and the Performing Subject, A Reader* (Edinburgh: Edinburgh University Press, 1999).

Corso, Gregory, *The Happy Birthday of Death* (New York: New Directions, 1960).

Crimp, Douglas, 'Getting the Warhol we deserve', *Social Text* 59 (Summer 1999), pp. 49–66.

Crisp, Quentin, *The Wit and Wisdom of Quentin Crisp*, ed. Guy Kettelhack (London: Arena, 1986).

Crow, Thomas, *Modern Art in the Common Culture* (New Haven and London: Yale University Press, 1996).

Crow, Thomas, *The Rise of the Sixties: American Art in the Era of Dissent 1955–69* (London: Everyman, 1996).

Crowley, Mart, *The Boys in the Band* (Harmondsworth: Penguin Plays, 1968).

D'Emilio, John, *Sexual Politics, Sexual Communities: The Making of a Homosexual Minority in the United States, 1940–1970* (Chicago and London: Chicago University Press, 1983).

De Carlo, Yvonne with Doug Warren, *Yvonne: An Autobiography* (New York: St. Martin's Press, 1987).

De Lauretis, Teresa, *Figures of Resistance: Essays in Feminist Theory*, ed. Patricia White (Urbana and Chicago: University of Illinois Press, 2007).

Dellamora, Richard, ed., *Postmodern Apocalypse: Theory and Cultural Practice at the End* (Philadelphia: University of Pennsylvania Press, 1995).

Diski, Jenny, *The Sixties* (London: Profile Books, 2009).

Donnelly, Ignatius, *Atlantis: The Antediluvian World* (New York: Dover Publications, 1976).

Doyle, Jennifer, 'Queer wallpaper', *A Companion to Contemporary Art since 1945*, ed. Amelia Jones (Malden and Oxford: Blackwell, 2006), pp. 343–55.

Doyle, Jennifer, *Sex Objects: Art and the Dialectics of Desire* (Minneapolis and London: University of Minnesota Press, 2006).

Durham Peters, John, *Speaking into the Air: A History of the Idea of Communication* (Chicago and London: University of Chicago Press, 1999).

Dwoskin, Stephen, *Film Is … The International Free Cinema* (London: Peter Owen, 1975).

Echols, Alice, *Shaky Ground: The Sixties and Its Aftershocks* (New York: Columbia University Press, 2002).

Edelman, Lee, *No Future: Queer Theory and the Death Drive* (Durham and London: Duke University Press, 2004).

Edelman, Lee, Carolyn Dinsham *et al.*, 'Theorizing queer temporalities: A roundtable discussion', *GLQ* 13.2–3 (2007), pp. 177–95.

Ehrenstein, David, *Film: The Front Line, 1984* (Denver: Arden Press, 1984).

Eng, David L. with Judith Halberstam and José Esteban Muñoz, 'What's Queer about Queer Studies Now?', *Social Text* 84–5, 23.3–4 (2005), pp. 1–17.

English, James F., *Comic Transactions: Literature, Humor, and the Politics of Community in Twentieth-Century Britain* (Ithaca and London: Cornell University Press, 1994).

Evans, Peter W., 'From Maria Montez to Jasmine: Hollywood's Oriental Odalisques', *'New' Exoticisms: Changing Patterns in the Construction of Otherness*, ed. Isabel Santaolalla (Amsterdam and Atlanta: Rodopi, 2000), pp. 157–65.

Flinn, Caryl, 'The deaths of camp', *Camp: Queer Aesthetics and the Performing Subject, A Reader*, ed. Cleto (Edinburgh: Edinburgh University Press, 2002).

Foreman, Richard, '"Awful great": Jack by popular demand: Jack Smith in retrospect', *Artforum* 36 (October 1997), p. 40.

Foucault, Michel, *Language, Counter-Memory, Practice: Selected Essays and Interviews,* ed. Donald F. Bouchard (Ithaca: Cornell University Press, 1977).

Foucault, Michel, *Foucault Live: Collected Interviews, 1961–1984*, ed. Sylvère Lotringer, trans. Lysa Hochroth and John Johnston (New York: Semiotext(e), 1996).

Frascina, Francis, *Art, Politics and Dissent: Aspects of the Art Left in Sixties America* (Manchester and New York: Manchester University Press, 1999).

Freud, Sigmund, *Jokes and Their Relation to the Unconscious*, trans. and ed. James Strachey (1905 rpt, London: Routledge and Kegan Paul, 1960).

Freud, Sigmund, *General Psychological Theory*, trans. Joan Riviere (New York: Collier, 1963).

Freud, Sigmund, *On Metaphysics*, ed. James Strachey (London and New York: Penguin Books, 1991).

Fried, Michael, *Art and Objecthood: Essays and Reviews* (Chicago and London: University of Chicago Press, 1998).

Gallagher, Catherine and Stephen Greenblatt, *Practicing New Historicism* (Chicago and London: University of Chicago Press, 2000).

Gates, Jr, Henry Louis, *Loose Canons: Notes on the Culture Wars* (New York and Oxford: Oxford University Press, 1992).

Genet, Jean, *Our Lady of the Flowers*, trans. Bernard Frechtman (New York: Grove Press, 1963).

Goldin, Nan, *Witnesses: Against Our Vanishing* (New York: Artists Space, 1989).

Golding, Sue, 'Pariah Bodies', *Sexy Bodies: The Strange Carnalities of Feminism*, ed. Elizabeth Grosz and Elspeth Probyn (London and New York: Routledge, 1995), pp. 172–80.

Goldman, Albert, *Freakshow* (New York: Atheneum, 1971).

Goldsmith, Kenneth, ed., *I'll Be Your Mirror: The Selected Andy Warhol Interviews, 1962–1987* (New York: Carol & Graf, 2004).

Gooch, Brad, *City Poet: The Life and Times of Frank O'Hara* (New York: HarperCollins, 1994).

Gregory, Derek, 'Emperors of the gaze: Photographic practices and productions of space in Egypt 1939–1914', *Picturing Place: Photography and the Geographical Imagination*, ed. Joan M. Schwartz and James R. Ryan (London and New York: I.B. Tauris, 2003), pp. 195–225.

Guillory, John, *Cultural Capital: The Problem of Literary Canon Formation* (Chicago and London: University of Chicago Press, 1993).

Hallam, Paul, *The Book of Sodom* (London and New York: Verso, 1993).

Hamilton, Ian, *Against Oblivion: Some Lives of the Twentieth Century Poets* (London and New York: Penguin, 2002).

Hamilton, Marybeth, 'Sexual politics and African-American music: Or, placing Little Richard in history', *History Workshop Journal* 46 (Autumn 1998), pp. 161–76.

Haring, Keith, *Journals* (New York: Viking, 1996).

Harvie, Jen, *Staging the UK* (Manchester and New York: Manchester University Press, 2005).

Haskell, Barbara, *Blam! The Explosion of Pop, Minimalism, and Performance 1958–1964* (New York: Whitney Museum of Art, 1984).

Haver, William, *The Body of this Death: Historicity and Sociality in the Time of AIDS* (Stanford: Stanford University Press, 1996).

Haver, William, 'Queer research; or, how to practise invention to the brink of intelligibility', *The Eight Technologies of Otherness*, ed. Sue Golding (London and New York: Routledge, 1997), pp. 277–92.

Haver, William, 'Really bad infinities: Queer's honour and the pornographic life', *Parallax* 5.4 (1999), pp. 9–21.

Hebdige, Dick, *Subculture: The Meaning of Style* (London and New York: Routledge, 1979).

Helms, Senator Jesse (R-NC), 'Amendment No. 2396 to the Excepted Committee Amendment', *Congressional Record* 81:7 (25 July 1994).

Higham, Charles and Joel Greenberg, *Hollywood in the Forties* (London and New York: Zwemmer & Barnes, 1968).

Hoberman, J., 'The theatre of Jack Smith', *The Drama Review* 23.1 (March 1979): Autoperformance, pp. 3–12.

Hoberman, J., 'Obituary: Jack Smith, 1932–89', *Village Voice* (3 October 1989), p. 74.

Hoberman, J., 'Treasures of the mummy's tomb: The lost films of Jack Smith', *Film Comment* (November–December 1997), pp. 42–5.

Hoberman, J., *On Jack Smith's Flaming Creatures and Other Secret-Flix of Cinemaroc* (New York: Granary Books, 2001).

Hoberman, J. and Jonathan Rosenbaum, *Midnight Movies* (New York and London: Harper & Row, 1983).

Hollings, Ken, 'The solar myth approach: The live space ritual: Sun Ra, Stockhausen, P-Funk, Hawkwind', *Undercurrents: The Hidden Wiring of Modern Music*, ed. Rob Young (London and New York: Continuum, 2002), pp. 99–113.

Hopkins, David, *After Modern Art, 1945–2000* (Oxford and New York: Oxford University Press, 2000).

Indiana, Gary '"Insistent director", Jack by popular demand: Jack Smith in retrospect', *Artforum* 36 (October 1997), pp. 67, 115.

Jackson, Shannon, 'Performing show and tell: Disciplines of visual culture and performance studies', *Journal of Visual Culture* 4.2 (2005), pp. 163–77.

Jacobs, Ken, 'Correction: Flaming closets', *October* 55, (Winter, 1990), p. 144.

Jameson, Fredric, *Postmodernism, or The Cultural Logic of Late Capitalism* (London and New York: Verso, 1991).

Jarman, Derek, *At Your Own Risk: A Saint's Testament* (New York: Overlook Press, 1993).

Jarrell, Randall, *Poetry and the Age* (London: Faber and Faber, 1996).

Jerome, Judith, 'Creating the world to be created: Karen Finley and Jack Smith', *Women and Performance: A Journal of Feminist Theory* 10.1–2 (1999), pp. 135–54.

Jones, Amelia, *Body Art / Performing the Subject* (Minneapolis and London: University of Minnesota Press, 1998).

Jong, Erica, *The Devil at Large: On Henry Miller* (New York: Random House, 1993).

Joseph, Branden W., *Beyond the Dream Syndicate: Tony Conrad and the Arts after John Cage (A 'Minor' History)*, (New York: Zone Books, 2008).

'Justice Fortas and a Matter of National Concern', *Congressional Record* 90:2 (4 September 1968), pp. H25550–606.

Kaplan, Donald M., 'Homosexuality and American theatre', *Tulane Drama Review* 9.3 (1965), pp. 25–55.

Kaprow, Allan, *Essays on the Blurring of Art and Life*, ed. Jeff Kelley (Berkeley: University of California Press, 1993).

Katz, Jonathan D. and David C. Ward, *Hide/Seek: Difference and Desire in American Portraiture* (Washington: Smithsonian Books, 2010).

Kaufman, David, *Ridiculous! The Theatrical Life and Times of Charles Ludlam* (New York: Applause, 2002).

Krauss, Rosalind E., 'Two moments from the post-medium condition', *October* 116 (Spring 2006), pp. 55–62.

Kuspit, Donald, *The Cult of the Avant-Garde Artist* (Cambridge and London: Cambridge University Press, 1993).

Lacan, Jacques, *The Four Fundamental Concepts of Psycho-Analysis: The Seminar of Jacques Lacan, Book XI*, ed. Jacques-Alain Miller, trans. Alan Sheridan (Harmondsworth and New York: Penguin, 1979).

Lacan, Jacques, *The Ethics of Psychoanalysis, 1959–1960: The Seminar of Jacques Lacan, Book VII*, ed. Jacques-Alain Miller, Book VII, trans. Dennis Porter (London and New York: Routledge, 1992).

Lant, Antonia, 'The curse of the pharaoh, or how cinema contracted Egyptomania', *October* 59 (Winter 1992), pp. 86–112.

Last, Martin, 'Flim-flam man: An open letter about Jonas Mekas', *Village Voice* (30 November 1967), p. 4.

Leffingwell, Edward, Carole Kismaric and Marvin Heiferman, eds, *Flaming Creature: Jack Smith, His Amazing Life and Times*, Institute for Contemporary Art, P.S.1 Museum (London and New York: Serpent's Tail, 1997).

Leffingwell, Edward, 'Jack Smith: The only normal man in Baghdad', *Flaming Creature: Jack Smith, His Amazing Life and Times*, ed, Leffingwell, Edward, Carole Kismaric and Marvin Heiferman, Institute for Contemporary Art, P.S.1 Museum (London and New York: Serpent's Tail, 1997), pp. 68–87.

Lotringer, Sylvère, ed., *Burroughs Live: The Collected Interviews of William S. Burroughs, 1960–1997* (New York: Semiotext(e), 2001).

Loy, Mina, *The Lost Lunar Baedeker* (Manchester: Carcanet, 1982).

Ludlam, Charles, *Ridiculous Theatre: Scourge of Human Folly: The Writings of Charles Ludlam*, ed. Steven Samuels (New York: Theatre Communications Group, 1992).

Mailer, Norman, *The Time of Our Time* (London: Little, Brown and Company, 1998).

Malanga, Gerard, 'Interview with Jack Smith', *Film Culture* 45 (Summer 1967), pp. 12–16.

Marin, Louis, *Utopics: The Semiological Play of Textual Spaces*, trans. Robert A. Vollrath (Atlantic Highlands: Humanities Press International, 1990).

Marinetti, F. T., *Marinetti: Selected Writings*, ed. R. W. Flint (New York: Farrar, Straus & Giroux, 1971).

Markman, Joel L., 'Letter to *Film Culture*: Some thoughts on Jack Smith', *Film Culture* 31 (Winter 1963–64), p. 21.

Marx, Karl, *Selected Writings*, ed. David McLellan (Oxford: Oxford University Press, 1977).

Mekas, Jonas, 'Announcing a grand competition', *Village Voice* (24 October 1963), p. 13.

Mekas, Jonas, *Movie Journal: The Rise of the New American Cinema 1959–1971* (New York: Macmillan, 1972).

Mekas, Jonas, unpublished interview with the author, New York (8 September 2011).

Melville, Herman, *Bartleby and Benito Cereno* (New York: Dover Publications, 1990).

Menninghaus, Winfried, *Disgust: Theory and History of a Strong Sensation*, trans. Howard Eiland and Joel Golb (Albany: State University of New York, 2003).

Meyer, Richard, *Outlaw Representation: Censorship and Homosexuality in Twentieth-Century Art* (Boston: Beacon Books, 2002).

Miles, Barry, *Ginsberg: A Biography* (New York and London: Simon and Schuster, 1989).

Miller, D. A., 'Sontag's urbanity', *The Gay and Lesbian Studies Reader*, ed. Henry Abelove, Michèle Aina Barale and David M. Halperin (New York and London: Routledge, 1993), pp. 212–20.

Miller, Henry, *Tropic of Cancer* (London: John Calder, 1963).

Miller, Neil, *Out of the Past: Gay and Lesbian History from 1869 to the Present* (London: Vintage, 1995).

Millett, Kate, *Sexual Politics* (London: Virago, 1977).

Monette, Paul, *Last Watch of the Night: Essays too Personal and Otherwise* (San Diego: Harcourt Brace & Company, 1994).

Moon, Michael, 'Flaming closets', *October* 51 (Winter 1989), pp. 19–54.

Mueller, Cookie, *Walking Through Clear Water in a Pool Painted Black* (New York: Semiotext(e), 1990).

Muñoz, José Esteban, *Cruising Utopia: The Then and There of Queer Futurity* (New York and London: New York University Press, 2009).

Newton, Esther, *Mother Camp: Female Impersonators in America* (Chicago and London: University of Chicago, 1979).

Ngai, Sianne, *Ugly Feelings* (Cambridge and London: Harvard University Press, 2005).

Nietzsche, Friedrich, *Ecce Homo*, trans. Anthony M. Ludovici (Mineola: Dover Publications, 2004).

Nixon, Mignon, *Fantastic Reality: Louise Bourgeois and a Story of Modern Art* (Cambridge and London: MIT Press, 2005).

Nochlin, Linda, *Women, Art, and Power and Other Essays* (London: Thames & Hudson, 1989).

Nyong'o, Tavia, 'Racial Kitsch and Black Performance', *Yale Journal of Criticism* 15.2 (2002), pp. 371–91.

O'Hara, Frank, *The Collected Poems of Frank O'Hara*, ed. Donald Allen, Introduction by John Ashbery (Berkeley, Los Angeles and London: University of California Press, 1995).

Ondine, 'Letter to an unknown woman namely Jack Smith', *Film Culture* 40 (Spring 1966), p. 21.

Owens, Craig, *Beyond Recognition: Representation, Power, and Culture*, ed. Scott Bryson, Barbara Kruger, Lynne Tillman and Jane Weinstock (Berkeley, Los Angeles and London: University of California Press, 1992).

Packman, David, 'Jack Smith's *Flaming Creatures*: With the tweak of an eyebrow', *Film Culture* 63–4 (1977), p. 51.

Parker, Alice C., *The Exploration of the Secret Smile: The Language of Art and Homosexuality in Frank O'Hara's Poetry* (New York and Bern: Peter Lang, 1989).

Parnes, Uzi, 'Pop performance: Four seminal influences: The work of Jack Smith, Tom Murrin – the Alien Comic, Ethyl Eichelberger, and the Split Britches Company', unpublished PhD thesis, New York University, 1988.

Perloff, Marjorie, *Frank O'Hara: Poet Among Painters* (Chicago and London: University of Chicago Press, 1998).

Phelan, Peggy, *Unmarked: The Politics of Performance* (London and New York: Routledge, 1994).

Phillips, Adam, *On Kissing, Tickling and Being Bored: Psychoanalytic Essays on the Unexamined Life* (London and Boston: Faber and Faber, 1993).

Pollock, Griselda, *Differencing the Canon: Feminist Desire and the Writing of Art's Histories* (London and New York: Routledge, 1999).

Pooter, 'Review', *The Times* (1 June 1968), p. 21.

Rabkin, Gerald, 'Bizarre survivor: Review of *The Secret of Rented Island*, Collation Center', *Soho Weekly News* (11 November 1976), p. 28.

Rancière, Jacques, *The Emancipated Spectator* (London and New York: Verso, 2009).

Rarick, Representative John R. (LA), 'Abe Fortas opposed by Citizens for Decent Literature', *Congressional Record* 90:2 (22 July 1968), pp. E22717–20.

Read, Alan, *Theatre, Intimacy & Engagement: The Last Human Venue* (Basingtoke: Palgrave Macmillan, 2008).

Rechy, John, *City of Night* (London: Granada Publishing, 1964).

Renan, Sheldon, *The Underground Film: An Introduction to Its Development in America* (London: Studio Vista, 1968).

Ricard, Rene, '"No dice", Jack by popular demand: Jack Smith in retrospect', *Artform* 36 (October 1997), pp. 68, 115.

Ricco, John Paul, *The Logic of the Lure* (Chicago and London: University of Chicago Press, 2002).

Rice, Ron, 'An ode to the eye: Note to Jonas Mekas', *Film Culture* 70.1 (1983), p. 158.

Ridout, Nicholas, *Stage Fright, Animals, and Other Theatrical Problems* (Cambridge and New York: Cambridge University Press, 2006).

Rifkin, Adrian, *Ingres, Then and Now* (London and New York: Routledge, 2000).

Rinder, Lawrence, 'Anywhere out of the world: The philosophy of Jack Smith', *Flaming Creature: Jack Smith, His Amazing Life and Times*, ed, Leffingwell, Edward, Carole Kismaric and Marvin Heiferman, Institute for Contemporary Art, P.S.1 Museum (London and New York: Serpent's Tail, 1997), pp. 139–51.

Rodgers, Gaby, 'Casting by candlelight', *Soho Weekly News* (4 November 1976), p. 29.

Rosenberg, Harold, *The Anxious Object* (Chicago and London: University of Chicago Press, 1966).

Roszak, Theodore, *Making of a Counter Culture: Reflections on the Technocratic Society and Its Youthful Opposition* (London: Faber and Faber, 1970).

Rowe, Carel, *The Baudelairean Cinema: A Trend within the American Avant-Garde* (Ann Arbor, Michigan: UMI Research Press, 1982).

Rugoff, Ralph, 'Mr. McCarthy's neighbourhood', *Paul McCarthy* (London: Phaidon, 1996).

Said, Edward, *Orientalism* (London and New York: Penguin, 2003).

Sandler, Irving, *American Art of the 1960s* (New York: Harper & Row, 1988).

Schoch, Richard W., *Victorian Theatrical Burlesques* (Burlington: Ashgate, 2003).

Sheeper, J., 'Style', *Gnaoua* 1 (Spring 1964), pp. 43–5.

Shewey, Don, 'The flame goes out', *Soho Weekly News* (18 June 1980), p. 59.

Siegel, Marc, 'Documentary that dare/not speak its name: Jack Smith's *Flaming*

Creatures', *Between the Sheets, in the Streets: Queer, Lesbian, Gay Documentary*, ed. Chris Holmlund and Cynthia Fuchs (Minneapolis and London: University of Minnesota Press, 1997), pp. 91–106.

Sinfield, Alan, '"The moment of submission": Neil Bartlett in conversation', *Modern Drama* 39.1 (1996): Lesbian/Gay/Queer Drama, pp. 211–21.

Sinfield, Alan, *Out on Stage: Lesbian and Gay Theatre in the Twentieth Century* (New Haven and London: Yale University Press, 1999).

Sinfield, Alan, *Cultural Politics: Queer Readings* (London and New York: Routledge, 2005).

Sitney, P. Adams, *Visionary Film: The American Avant-Garde, 1943–2000*, Third edition (Oxford: Oxford University Press, 2002).

Smith, Jack, 'The moldy hell of men and women: A fotographic essay', *Film Culture* 35 (Winter 1964–65), pp. 33–9.

Smith, Jack, '*Pink Flamingos* formulas in focus', *Village Voice* (19 July 1973), p. 69.

Smith, Jack, 'Fear ritual of shark museum', *Avalanche* (December 1974), pp. 26–7.

Smith, Jack, *Historical Treasures*, ed. Ira Cohen (Madras and New York: Hanuman Books, 1990).

Smith, Jack, 'Notes for the Ford Foundation Application: Program in Humanities and the Arts', *Film Culture* 77 (1992–93), pp. 24–6.

Smith, Jack, 'Historical treasures: Remarks on art & the theater', *In a Different Light: Visual Culture, Sexual Identity, Queer Practice*, ed. Nayland Blake, Lawrence Rinder and Amy Scholder (San Francisco: City Lights Books, 1995), pp. 287–93.

Smith, Jack, *Wait for Me at the Bottom of the Pool: The Writings of Jack Smith*, ed. J. Hoberman and Edward Leffingwell (New York and London: High Risk Books, 1997).

Smith, Jack, *The Beautiful Book* (New York: Granary Books, 2001).

Smith, Jack, *Drawings, Photographs and Ephemera from the Collection of Maria Antoinette and Edwin Ruda* (New York: Mitchell Algus Gallery, 2003).

Sollers, Philippe, *Writing and the Experience of Limits*, trans. Philip Barnard with David Hayman, ed. Hayman (New York: Columbia University Press, 1983).

Sontag, Susan, *Against Interpretation and Other Essays* (New York: Farrar, Straus & Giroux, 1967).

Sontag, Susan, *AIDS and Its Metaphors* (London: Penguin, 1988).

Sontag, Susan, 'Notes on "camp"', *Camp: Queer Aesthetics and the Performing Subject, A Reader*, ed. Cleto (Edinburgh: Edinburgh University Press, 1999), pp. 53–65.

Sophocles, *Philoctetes*, trans. R. G. Ussher (Warminster: Aris & Phillips, 1990).

Stewart, Susan, *Crimes of Writing: Problems in the Containment of Representation* (Oxford and New York: Oxford University Press, 1991).

Stoller, James, '16mm', *Village Voice* (7 December 1967), p. 37.

Strub, Whitney, 'Perversion for profit: Citizens for decent literature and the arousal of an antiporn public in the 1960s', *Journal of the History of Sexuality* 15.2 (2006), pp. 258–91.

Suárez, Juan A., *Bike Boys, Drag Queens and Superstars: Avant-Garde, Mass Culture and Gay Identities in the 1960s Underground Cinema* (Bloomington and Indianapolis: Indiana University Press).

'Supreme Court of the United States', *Congressional Record* 90-2 (27 September 1968), pp. S25857–600.

'Supreme Court of the United States', *Congressional Record* 90–2 (30 September 1968), pp. S28759–89.

Tartaglia, Jerry, 'The perfect queer appositeness of Jack Smith', *Experimental Cinema: The Film Reader*, ed. Wheeler Winston Dixon and Gwendolyn Audrey Foster (London and New York: Routledge, 2002), pp. 163–72.

Tavel, Ronald, 'Maria Montez: Anima of an antediluvian world', *Flaming Creature: Jack Smith, His Amazing Life and Times*, ed, Leffingwell, Edward, Carole Kismaric and Marvin Heiferman, Institute for Contemporary Art, P.S.1 Museum (London and New York: Serpent's Tail, 1997), pp. 88–104.

Thompson, E. P., *The Making of the English Working Class* (Harmondsworth: Pelican Books, 1968).

Thurmond, Senator Strom (R-SC), 'Nomination of Justice Fortas', *Congressional Record* 90:2 (11 September 1968), pp. S31396–7.

Trocchi, Alexander, *Cain's Book* (New York: Grove Press, 1992).

Tyler, Parker, *Underground Film: A Critical History* (London: Penguin, 1971).

Vaccaro, John, Unpublished interview with the author, New York (5 June 2005).

Vawter, Ron, 'Roy Cohn/Jack Smith', *O Solo Homo: The New Queer Performance*, ed. Holly Hughes and David Román (New York: Grove Press, 1998), pp. 456–76.

Vidal, Gore, *Myra Breckinridge & Myron* (London: Grafton Books, 1989).

Vidal, Gore, *The City and the Pillar* (London: Abacus, 1997).

Warhol, Andy with Pat Hackett, *POPism: The Andy Warhol '60s* (New York and London: Harcourt Brace Jovanovich, 1980).

Watson, Steven, *The Birth of the Beat Generation: Visionaries, Rebels, and Hipsters, 1944–1960* (New York: Pantheon Books, 1995).

Wheeler, Daniel, *Art Since Mid-Century: 1945 to the Present* (London: Thames and Hudson, 1991).

Williams, Raymond, *Culture and Society: Coleridge to Orwell* (London: Hogarth Press, 1987).

Wilson, Colin, *From Atlantis to the Sphinx* (London: Virgin Books, 1996).

Wölfflin, Heinrich, *Renaissance and Baroque*, trans. Kathrin Simon (London: Collins, 1984).

Woodhouse, Reed, *Unlimited Embrace: A Canon of Gay Fiction, 1945–1995* (Amherst: University of Massachusetts Press, 1998).

Zazeela, Marian, '"Maja rising", Jack by popular demand: Jack Smith in retrospect', *Artform* 36 (October 1997), pp. 72, 119.

EU authorised representative for GPSR:
Easy Access System Europe, Mustamäe tee 50,
10621 Tallinn, Estonia
gpsr.requests@easproject.com